ORGANIC
CREATIVITY
IN THE CLASSROOM

ORGANIC CREATIVITY

IN THE CLASSROOM

Teaching to Intuition in Academics and the Arts

Edited by Jane Piirto, Ph.D.

COPUBLISHED WITH THE

NATIONAL ASSOCIATION FOR
Gifted Children

PRUFROCK PRESS INC.
WACO, TEXAS

And, therefore, let the immeasurable come.
Let the unknowable touch the buckle of my spine.
—Mary Oliver

Library of Congress catalog information
currently on file with the publisher.

Copyright ©2014, Prufrock Press Inc.

Edited by Lacy Compton

Cover and layout design by Raquel Trevino
Cover art copyright ©2014 by Isabella Taylor, http://www.isabellarosetaylor.com.
    Isabella Rose Taylor is a 12-year-old fine artist and fashion designer from Austin, TX. She is
currently enrolled in college and is a lifetime member of Mensa.

ISBN-13: 978-1-61821-102-6

Printed in the United States of America.

At the time of this book's publication, all facts and figures cited are the most current available. All
telephone numbers, addresses, and websites URLs are accurate and active. All publications, organizations, websites, and other resources exist as described in the book, and all have been verified.
The editor and Prufrock Press Inc. make no warranty or guarantee concerning the information
and materials given out by organizations or content found at websites, and we are not responsible for any changes that occur after this book's publication. If you find an error, please contact
Prufrock Press Inc.

Prufrock Press Inc.
P.O. Box 8813
Waco, TX 76714-8813
Phone: (800) 998-2208
Fax: (800) 240-0333
http://www.prufrock.com

Table of Contents

> Piirto introduces the book and recounts how she tried to reconcile the disconnect between the intuitive artistic process and the prevailing cognitive point of view, which led to the Five Core Attitudes, Seven I's, and General Practices for Creativity.

Part I: Organic Creativity in Academic Domains

> Kettler and Sanguras present a creative pedagogy of literature in a way that places primary emphasis on the creation of ideas and meaning through insight and imagination. The creative pedagogy of literature includes four points of emphasis: disciplined improvisation, focus on imagination, modeling and developing creative dispositions, and problem solving within the context of the literature curriculum.

> Daniels presents ideas to break the rigid structure that occurs in too many math classrooms. Suggestions for enhancing creativity focus on the inclusion of risk-taking, incubation, motivation, imagery, and imagination. The chapter addresses the common misconceptions and pitfalls found in a math classroom that is inherently positioned to think "inside the box," while proposing ways to break out of the norm.

> Peppercorn describes his 6 C's for engaging students in social studies: creativity, competition, comedy, camaraderie, connections, and chinos. Incorporating these elements into activities enables students to: (a) be imaginative, (b) take part in benign competitions, (c) feed off of everyone's use of humor, (d) display teamwork, (e) feel connected with their teacher, (f) try to win chinos (the classroom currency), and (g) connect history to current events and their own lives.

> Taber explains how doing science is inherently a creative process and argues that this needs to be reflected in science education itself. Too often, learners experience studying science as a passive process of being told other people's ideas. The best science teachers are not only creative in their teaching, but also find ways to allow students to experience learning as an imaginative process of knowledge creation.

MacDowell and Michael discuss how students are often at a loss for how to approach the subject of physics. Reaching these students requires a flexible and creative methodology. As soon as the students realize that they can be creative in how they approach the subject, the door to learning starts to open for them. The successful classroom then turns into an organic synthesis with mentor and student both giving and gaining.

Reynolds defines the three creative intelligence capacities in French as (a) the capacity to create using French, (b) the capacity to respond to originality using French, and (c) the capacity to move beyond school into an authentic, original life enriched by Francophone culture. Reynolds explains how to enhance student creativity through a technique called "feeding back." Feeding back includes a radical receptivity to the originality of another person.

Part II: Organic Creativity in the Arts

Oreck recounts his lifelong investigation into the nature of creativity and artistry. Calling on his experiences as a dancer/choreographer and teacher and his research into the identification of talent in young people, he grapples with the questions of what makes certain people extraordinary and whether some of those qualities can be taught.

To make space for students' creativity, teachers sometimes need to get out of the way even when students request more help. Nicoll examines students' dance-making processes, in a range of settings, and recognizes that making space for students' intuition and creativity can be one of the most challenging—and essential—tasks undertaken by any teacher.

Dubin discusses the cultivation of a classroom atmosphere conducive to risk-taking and how the study of improvisation and exposure to classical texts—particularly Shakespeare—can facilitate exploration of intuition, instinct, and imagination.

Davis becomes his childhood hero, Doctor Who, who taught him to use compassion, intuition, and improvisation inside the classroom. As a teaching artist in New York City, he aims to unlock the confidence his students will need to be their own free thinking, artistic selves, unafraid of making mistakes even though the systems that surround them are actively discouraging experimentation and plurality of ideas.

Stephenson shares her personal insights and inspires readers to take a leap into the uncharted waters of musical self-expression. She includes tips and strategies for songwriting, improvising music with others, integrating music into language arts and other lessons, and finding one's personal musical voice, regardless of self-perceptions of talent or training

McKenzie recalls her experience as a music teacher in the ArtsConnection program. She discusses music talent and the intuitive recognition of it from the point of view of children as well as their teachers.

Tolan indicates that what can be called "intuition" is a critical ingredient in creativity—what she prefers to call the "magic of writing." Tolan believes that the craft necessary to good writing can be learned, but the magic needs only to be awakened, courted, honored, and listened to.

Part III: Organic Creativity in the Teacher, the Classroom, and the School

Chapter 18: Visceral Creativity: Organic Creativity
in Teaching Arts/Dance Education 253
by Celeste Snowber

Snowber explores the reclaiming of the body as a place to nourish creativity as
a way of life. She connects dance and movement as an experiential way of learning
through sensuous knowledge and focuses on four principles, including play, passion,
physicality, and practice.

Chapter 19: The Mirror: Creativity as Seeing
and Being Seen: Autoethnography of a Teacher.........................267
by Jennifer L. Groman

Groman writes an autoethnographical integration of her own personal and professional creative work as a singer, songwriter, and explorer of creativity as it is used
to frame and develop her teaching practice. Her chapter includes prose, lyrics, poetry,
and visual art to show the construction of and shifting in her professional philosophy
of teaching.

Chapter 20: The Missing Link: Teaching the
Creative Problem Solving Process...285
by Cyndi Burnett

Burnett explores the relationship between deliberate Creative Problem Solving
models and the working practices of a performing artist. By examining the tensions
and overlaps, she highlights the opportunities for students from many disciplines to
expand their creative repertoire and understand creativity as both a mechanism to
solve problems and a process of self-expression.

Chapter 21: That "Uh-Oh" Feeling: Organic Creativity
in School Counseling...299
by Maria Balotta

Balotta believes that organic creativity in her work results from heeding that
"uh-oh" feeling, the intuitive messages heard from within that facilitate her access to
ideas that already exist in the spiritual, unconscious world. To Balotta, the ideas feel
natural, almost instantaneous, but she is convinced that they come out of a subconscious incubation process in which old experiences and knowledge combine to inspire
on-the-spot decisions that lead to life-altering actions and interactions.

McElfresh describes her journey as a school leader who worked with faculty and staff to promote a culture of organic creativity within two public elementary schools. This narrative provides a description of specific activities designed to promote a creative culture through regular and programmed experiences as well as through experiences that arise organically from the needs of the students and the teachers at any given time.

Playing Candleland

Your kindergarten teacher says that children
need to be yelled at. She calls you
the little walking encyclopedia,
who ends her game of what-is-smaller-than-that
by saying quarks. She tells me you are silent
and withdrawn; write your name small and crooked,
have trouble descending the stairs.
She thinks you should learn to play soccer.

At home you romp with the rabbit, roar
through the yard as Tyrannosaurus Rex,
and begin to choreograph
the Broadway musical version of
"Close Encounters of the Third Kind."
"This is how I am in school," you explain,
hunching your shoulders forward, folding in
your arms so your face falls into shadow.

When the teacher asks what you do best,
you tell her, "Playing Candleland."
She thinks this is a packaged game, the rules
inflexible as her own. She's never seen
you patiently dripping wax, the slow rivers
of color covering matchstick structures.
Humming Mussorgsky, you erode a mountain range
or invent a Venusian landscape of red rock.

Over here life starts, volcanoes rising
out of a sluggish sea. Smiling, you await
the advent of the hadrosaurs.
Bent intently over a flame
in this place of your own shaping,
you have kindled the light in which
I will always see your face. Tell her what fire
creates—a vast and malleable country.

Susan Irene Rae Katz[1]

PREFACE

What Is Organic Creativity?

Jane Piirto

Figure P.1. *Jane Piirto in her office with Claudia Liu, Taiwanese graduate student in the Talent Development Education program.*

In June 2012, I received an intriguing e-mail from one of my publishers, Joel McIntosh, of Prufrock Press. He was wondering whether I might like to edit a book that would speak to

> . . . creativity that emphasizes the intuitive . . . the unconscious—I'm having trouble putting my finger on it—but it's a perspective that captures the spiritual (though, when I use that term, I do not mean supernatural) as a source of creative energy and production.
>
> Frankly, my idea for this is a bit half-baked . . . I just feel that here is a place for talking about creativity in a way that goes beyond conscious process . . . and emphasizes intuition . . .

What McIntosh was referring to is the fact that the world of advice about practical creativity is rife with the 60-year-old terminology of J. P. Guilford, who invented the term *divergent production* in his Structure of Intellect Theory in the 1940s, 1950s, and 1960s. When I responded to indicate interest, he answered:

> Let's face the fact that the enthusiasts of a cognitive/behavioral psychology approach to creativity in schools have created a body of practical tools. I think one reason these tools are popular is that they are easy to grasp and use (whether for assessment or instruction). However, as the articles you sent me so clearly state, there "is little evidence that such training leads to MORE adult creativity." I believe an edited book by you featuring other scholars and practitioners and offering a practical approach to nurturing organic/intuitive creativity in schools would be "just the thing."

What the writers in this volume speak about is much older than the cognitive psychological approach that now makes up much of the writing on creativity in education and psychology, yet their advice is also new—that makes it timeless, I guess. Much of the thought on creativity and activities to enhance creativity focuses on aspects of divergent production—fluency, flexibility, elaboration, originality—on "thinking hats"[2] and strategies for problem solving. Many people have created assessments to measure it (e.g., Torrance Tests of Creative Thinking; Creative Problem Solving process; Williams Creative Assessment Scale; Meeker Structure of Intellect Learning Abilities Test). Many have creative assessments based on divergent production that are fun and omnipresent in the literature, and have been helpful in understanding the cognitive aspect of creativity (e.g., Structure of *Intellect*; italics intended). The aisles of educational conferences for teachers are filled with glossy-covered books with reproducibles that give a lot of activities to help teachers teach creativity. But, for the most part, these books seem not to contain practices that really occur while people are creating.

My Background

I have been an educator since the mid-1960s, when I was getting an M.A. in English literature at Kent State University, where I taught, as a graduate assistant, men who had been in the military and who were older than I—I was 23. In 1965, with a student husband and a baby, I needed a better paying job. I had a teacher's certificate in high school English from Michigan, so I gave up the assistantship and took a job as an English, French, and journalism high school teacher for about $3,000 at a rural high school nearby. It was my first year of my 14 years as a teacher and then administrator in the K–12 systems. We moved back to Michigan after I finished my master's, and I taught at Northern Michigan University as an instructor in the English department until my husband finished his master's degree in regional planning on the G.I. Bill, and we moved to South Dakota for his first professional job. There I picked up a second master's degree in guidance and counseling, while working as a counselor and social studies teacher for a year at a small rural high school and then for a year as a counselor at a high school in the college town of Brookings.

We moved back to Ohio, where I did my Ph.D. in educational leadership, and in 1977, I began my career as an educator of the gifted and talented as one of the first gifted coordinators in Ohio. Then I took a job as a gifted coordinator in Michigan, across the border north of Toledo from 1979 to 1983, when I moved to New York City as the principal of New York City's oldest school for gifted children, Hunter College Elementary School, where I taught my first college creativity course for the Hunter College education department. From there, I moved back to Ohio, where I took a job as a college professor.

But simultaneously—since college and formally, from 1963 when I published my first poems in my college's literary journal, in my inner life, my real life, I was also an artist—a published poet—and later, short story writer and novelist—and I saw the world through an artist's eyes.[3] I worked for a while as a Poet in the Schools in the National Endowment for the Arts "Artist in the Schools" program during the late 1970s and early 1980s. Among my proudest moments were when I won Ohio Arts Council Individual Artist Fellowships in fiction and in poetry, and when my novel won the Carpenter Press First Novel Award.

The Disconnect

When I entered the world of talent development education, I began to take workshops in Creative Problem Solving (CPS), and in other models such as lateral thinking creativity, and I began to be interested in creativity assessment. I became the first advanced trainer for the Structure of Intellect Institute, doing workshops throughout the country when Mary Meeker, its founder, was too booked up. I began to think about my own creative process, for I was also a literary creator, wasn't I, and shouldn't these workshops I was giving and taking help me learn how to be more creative? Here I was giving Guilfordian workshops on fluency, flexibility, and the like, but my own creative life contained little brainstorming, SCAMPERing, generating of alternative solutions, or creative problem solving according to the flow charts I had been given at the many workshops I attended.[4]

In fact, I only knew one person who had really used the CPS process in her real life, and she was a fellow coordinator of programs for the gifted and talented. She and her husband, a teacher, had had some rocky times in their marriage, and they had gone to a restaurant, jotted down the "mess," and brainstormed and criteria-rated solutions. (As far as I know, they are still married, so it must have worked.) My artist friends were more likely to think as painter Leo Gorel said, "The present fashionable psychological talk about the left-brain, right-brain, creative-intellectual concept and the do-it-yourself art books that suggest exercises with either hand to improve your imagination, I think are a joke."[5]

I began to feel a disconnect in my own life and work, as I wrote poems and stories at home at night after my family was asleep, drinking wine and smoking, at the same time as I was conducting creativity training using divergent production activities by day. I decided to explore this disconnect. I began to read interviews and memoirs and biographies about and with creators who described what happened while they create. I still do so; I saw an interview on television recently, of Charlie Musselman, a harmonica player, in which he described how he is when playing music:

> When the spirit of the music takes over it's almost like you're not playing anymore. The spirit is playing you. I call it following the will of the music. When that feeling shows up you just go with it. It's almost like I'm a bystander watching this happen. It's just spontaneous. It's almost mystical.[6]

Seldom in the cognitive activities focusing on divergent production is this type of interiority mentioned. But creators throughout time have described it. My notebooks and files began to fill with quotations and my books with annotations.

As I read and reflected, I found that most adult creators who had had biographies written about them, who had written memoirs, who had been interviewed and researched, talked about their creative process in more organic terms. The creative process has engaged the best thinkers of the world from prehistoric times. Common mythological perspectives on the creative process have viewed it as the visitation of the Muse, a mysterious overtaking of the creator by the primal forces of love, nature, revenge, tragedy, or the like.

Historically, the creative process has been tied with erotic desires, desires for spiritual unity, and with the need for personal expression. The use of substances to enhance the creative process has been prominent in the lives of creative people. Many creative products have resulted from insight, illumination, and unconscious processing. Solitude seems to be a necessary condition during some aspects of the creative process. The creative process can be viewed in the context of a person's life and of the historical milieu, the zeitgeist. Contemporary psychological and religious thought have emphasized that the creative process has universal implications. What is popularly called "right-brain thinking," as well as visualization, metaphors, and imagery, seem to help people in the creative process. The creative process is a concern of scientists as well as those in the humanities. Scientific experimentation has resulted in the demystifying of many popular creative process beliefs. I concluded that the repertoires of school people, who often use only the cognitive in enhancing creativity, should be expanded.

I found much similarity in what I read from people in the various domains. For example, the poet, novelist, and screenwriter Jim Harrison described his creative process in writing poetry:

> A poem seems to condense the normal evolutionary process infinitely. There is the distressed, nonadaptive state; an unconscious moving into the darkness of the problem or irritant; a gradual surfacing, then immediate righting or balancing by metaphor, as if you tipped a buoy over by force then let it snap upwards; the sense of relief, and the casting and recasting the work into its final form. The last stage "calcifies" or kills the problem and you are open to a repetition of the process, though not necessarily willing. Though this is all rather simplified, it is, I think, the essence of the process. There must be the understanding of time lapse though—the "gradual surfacing" may take months, the space between the first sketch and final form an even longer period of time.[7]

What I Did

In the early 1990s, I began to offer an undergraduate interdisciplinary studies course called "Creativity and the Creative Process," and I began to try out some ideas that tapped into this "oceanic consciousness," as Brewster Ghiselin called it.[8] The course became popular with undergraduates majoring in the liberal arts, although not so popular among education majors. When schools asked me to do workshops, and when I spoke at conferences, I began to try my newly derived and idiosyncratic exercises out with the participants. I began to teach a similar syllabus with my graduate students, and to include some of the activities with my doctoral educational leadership students. My students in the graduate course in talent development education, called "Creativity for Teachers of the Talented," also tried them out. I was beginning to operationalize what I had read about in the biographies, memoirs, and interviews.

Many of the creative and productive adults whose creativity I read about seemed to have creative processes that were organic—that is, they created not by writing down criteria or by brainstorming or by consciously putting together opposites, or by mashing up ideas, although the latter, at least, happened. Rather, their process of creating—their work—rose from such prosaic practices as preparedness, self-discipline, and awareness—thus the title of this book. I created themes—distilled into the *Five Core Attitudes* (openness to experience or naïveté, risk-taking, group trust, self-discipline, and tolerance for ambiguity), *Seven I's* (intuition, imagination, imagery, inspiration, insight, incubation, and improvisation), and *General Practices for Creativity* (ritual, exercise, meditation, the decision to live a creative life, a preference for introversion and solitude).[9] All of these practices seem to be used by creators in all domains of creative expertise—although not all by any one creator. What this tells us is that there are many ways to enhance creativity, and an expanded repertoire of understandings about the creative process helps. This is probably why Joel McIntosh thought of me to write to about a different kind of creativity book.

I have assembled a full course of activities that tap into the mysterious, nebulous, dreamy, solitary quietness of the creative process as it has been written about and talked about by adult creators. As a person who is in the education department, one of my tasks is to make practical applications of complex concepts, so that those concepts are able to be taught to students young and old. A typical creativity course or workshop (time permitting) taught by me utilizes exercises in the *Five Core Attitudes*. We do a lot of (a) *group trust* building by cheering each other's creative efforts. The students also try exercises in cultivating (b) *self-discipline* by working daily in creativity Thoughtlogs. We practice (c) *risk-taking*, both personal and in a group. We try to see the world with (d) *naïveté* (or openness, practicing mindfulness); we note a (e) *tolerance for ambiguity*, that there is no one right answer, and we try to become comfortable with that.

We work with the *Seven I's*: (a) *Imagery*, including guided imagery and film script visualizing; (b) *Imagination*, including storytelling; (c) *Intuition*, including the intuition probe, psychic intuition, and dreams; (d) *Insight*, including grasping the gestalt, going for the aha! moment, and Zen sketching; (e) *Inspiration*, including the visitation of the Muse; (f) *Incubation*, including a final individual creativity project; and (g) *Improvisation*, including drumming, acting, joke-telling, and scat singing.

We notice our own general practices for creativity, *rituals* such as solitude, creating ideal conditions, and using background music. We try *meditation*, meditating on beauty, on the dark side, on god. We cultivate all five of our senses and also blend them for a sense of synesthesia. We vigorously *exercise* so endorphins will kick in. We talk about how the creative life is a choice and not an accident. We focus on my notion of the *thorn* of fiery passion as explicated in my Piirto Pyramid of Talent Development. See Figure P.2.

We try to find our domains of passion, that which we can't *not* do. We explore the joys of good conversation and have a salon. We visit a cemetery to meditate on the dark side. We visit a beautiful and silent church with stained glass windows constructed with religious symbolism to meditate on God. We hike in nearby nature parks to meditate on nature. We go to an art museum to meditate on beauty. We attend a live concert, a play, a poetry reading, or a lecture to honor the creativity of talented others. We practice Reynolds' process of feeding back, discussed in Chapter 6 on teaching world languages in this volume. Although these are simulations with the intent of having the students experience what creators have said they do while creating, these simulations seem to have a profound effect, and many students have said in evaluations that this course is their favorite of the sequence of courses in our endorsement. I say that you can't teach how to be creative unless you've experienced the joys and frustrations of the creative process.

The culmination of the course is an individual creativity project. One student in Finland wrote a poem when we visited the art museum, and it became the lyrics for the first song she composed. Other individual creativity projects have included photography exhibits from the nature walk, cycles of sonnets and other poems, quilts (designed without a preexisting pattern), a

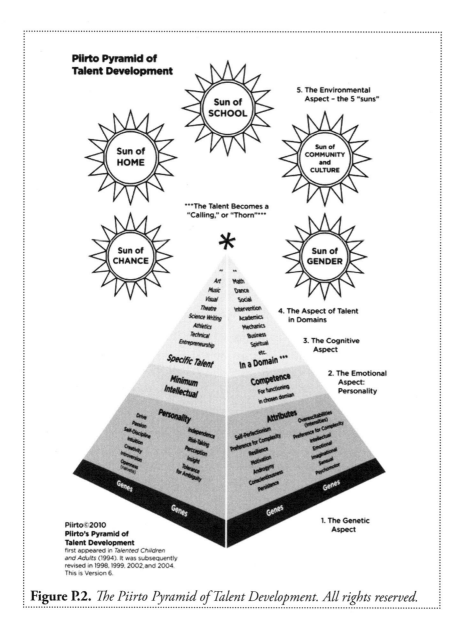

Figure P.2. *The Piirto Pyramid of Talent Development. All rights reserved.*

synchronized swimming routine, an exhibit of original artworks, a reading of an original short story, an original dance, and display and demonstration of a particularly creative Thoughtlog.

In one remarkable individual creativity project, a football player, a defensive back, took all of the game tapes for his entire college career and spliced them together to show himself in the improvisatory acts of dodging, running, and hitting. One teacher designed and built himself a podium from which to teach, in homage to his own middle school teacher, who had inspired him. One art teacher submitted his daily Thoughtlog sketches; one of his paintings is the cover of my 2011 book. We are often so moved at the projects that we weep. At the end of the course, most agree that indeed, creativity can be enhanced through direct teaching.

"But I couldn't do these with my own students, my young ones," some say. Not true. My students who are meeting the endorsement requirements of our state to become teachers of the gifted and talented tell me that yes, indeed, the K–12 students that they work with can begin to see the creative process as something that is, at base, an emotional journey as well as a cognitive one. Every week some of them try out the activities we have done in class, modifying them for their own use. I always ask them how they would apply the concept we are trying out in class, and I have collected these suggestions in my book, *Creativity for 21st Century Skills.*[10]

Creative Process of a Scholar/Writer

My big discovery as an artist during the past 20 years is that you don't have to write literature—fiction, poetry, or drama—in order to be creative as a writer. In writing the three big and detailed nonfiction books (two of which went into three editions—*Talented Children and Adults: Their Development and Education* and *Understanding Those Who Create/Understanding Creativity*), and a third, *"My Teeming Brain": Understanding Creative Writers*, I followed a creative process very similar to that which I use in writing literary works, except for the massive reading I had to do for these big nonfiction books. I had to laugh when a novelist was recently quoted saying that she had begun a biography of a famous person but when she went to the archives and figured out that she had to reference all these letters, books, and sources, she gave up and just wrote a novel, as the detail impending in writing nonfiction was overwhelming. John Grisham wrote a nonfiction book, *The Innocent Man*, and said, never again, after he experienced the perils of annotation and after he was sued for defamation. He'd stick to fiction, he thought, where you don't have to check your facts.

I read and read, organized, thought, walked, swam, obsessed on, and dreamed these big nonfiction books. I used four of the Five Core Attitudes. The core attitude of self-discipline became necessary. I would write for about an hour or two every day, 7 days a week. The core attitude of openness to experience or naïveté helped me to see the field as new, and to explore new theories and ideas and to come up with The Piirto Pyramid of Talent Development and the creativity theory discussed here. The core attitude of group trust was not very evident, as I worked alone and did not consult with anyone as I wrote and researched and synthesized. The core attitude of risk-taking became operant later, when I overcame my shyness (who, me? Little Janie Piirto from Ishpeming, MI, make a theory?) and dared to use my own theory of the Pyramid of Talent Development as an organizational framework for the second and third editions of *Understanding Those Who Create*, and *Talented Children and Adults* and for *"My Teeming Brain."*

The core attitude of tolerance for ambiguity was operative as I tried to reconcile conflicting ideas, especially those of the trajectory of talent development from predictive behaviors in childhood to dominance of the gatekeepers who rule domains. I publicly wondered whether a high IQ is necessary for the realization of talent potential, and concluded in the negative, settling on the importance of personality attributes and environmental "suns," noting that different domains have different IQ thresholds necessary for working in the domain.

In writing scholarship, I used the Seven I's, also. As a conscious decision I did not use other synoptic textbooks as models, but began anew, organizing the texts *improvisationally*. My *intuition* was to create my own texts rather than be overly influenced by others. My *inspirations* came piecemeal, but were often intellectual, bouncing off the ideas of others—the Sun of Community and Culture. The *incubation* was constant; I walked around in a state of trance, thinking about that day's writing and while I slept, the ideas for what I would write the next day were brewing. The Pyramid was an example of *imagery* to illustrate what I had learned. I did not use *imagination* as I do in thinking of plots as such, except in imagining the imagery. My *insight* was the importance of personality and environment rather than test scores.

In the General Practices for Creativity area, the use of ritual was constant, especially as I set myself up to write in the mornings. I have already made a conscious decision to live a creative life and my friends and lifestyle could be called an example of that. Exercise always satisfies and provides a place for meditation and for inspiration. Walking my dog in the woods or on the empty old running track at our university's baseball field are daily opportunities for solitude and meditation.

As I mentioned above, I write not only such synoptic texts, but also literary work—I write a couple of poems a week, I suppose, early in the morning after dream images arrest me or late at night, or on my iPod, or in a Thoughtlog in my purse as I travel about in my life. The inception of these is often a vague inner feeling, an intuition, that there is some truth here in what I am experiencing or observing, and I scratch out notes to capture its essence, and then spend days, weeks, years, revising and tweaking. I always work on several projects—such as this—often in the same day. I dream whole novels and read about two novels a week. If only I'd write these dreamt plots and characters down, I'd be rich. My writing practice by now is well-established and my only regret is that my products as a literary writer are less well-known than my products as a scholarly and educational writer. I would have wished it otherwise, but I keep plodding (pun intended) along—on both, the literary and the scholarly.

This Book

After thinking and dreaming and meditating for a few weeks that summer of 2012, I took McIntosh up on his query. Under my personal Sun of Community and Culture, I know a lot of people and I began to think of certain thinkers who could speak to the intuitive—and who live by teaching and working in this way. I began to put together a list of subject matter experts who use intuitive practices in their teaching and creating. These chapter writers have true expertise in the classic sense—most of them have practiced their teaching and work for more than 10,000 hours, the thumbnail advice given by the expertise researchers. The authors of these chapters have, in total, more than 500 years of teaching experience, both with K–12 children and with undergraduates and graduate students. They are mostly educators in arts and academic domains and not psychologists, who are asked to tell educators how to teach but who often have limited experience in the classrooms for which they are giving advice.

Those whom I queried responded with enthusiasm, saying they felt the time had come for an emphasis on the intuitive as well as the cognitive in creativity. They also expressed dismay at the way that teachers are currently being treated—and at the climate of multiple-choice assessment that prevails through the federal government's mandates of No Child Left Behind and Race to the Top, wondering why anyone would want to go into teaching these days.

First intuitively and then consciously, the authors seem to adhere to what Pasi Sahlberg described as necessary in his recent book, *Finnish Lessons*[11]. Sahlberg decried what he called the Global Educational Reform Movement (GERM), which calls for narrowing the curriculum and relentlessly drilling even small children to take high-stakes tests in reading, mathematics, and science, ignoring social science, the arts, physical education, vocational subjects, and other necessary areas of study.

Like Sahlberg and other holistically minded educators, the writers in this book call for authentic teacher-created assessment; they say that the work of childhood is play; they teach for excellence through equity and fairness. Most of them teach or have taught or been administrators in public schools—urban, rural, suburban—to students of diverse backgrounds, and they have differentiated and do differentiate by noticing and teaching to their students' strengths. They love the subjects they teach and have over the years developed and tweaked their teaching practices for maximum benefit for the students they love and serve.

The result of my thinking, dreaming, and querying is this informative, readable, and insightful collection of sort-of creative nonfiction essays from teacher experts in their domains about how they teach their subject matter and simultaneously emphasize creativity. It differs from many edited books—at least the ones in which I've published chapters—in that I did not discourage the word "I." I also discouraged extensive use of references, preferring personal stories, case examples, and tales of teaching. (Sometimes we scholars overreference, obscuring our personal, intuitive, intrinsic, and experience-gleaned knowledge with deference to sometimes questionable authority.)

The title suggests a way of thinking about creativity and doing creativity that is holistic, natural, and instinctual. The term *organic* means what it says; that creativity doesn't need to be proscribed, but can emanate naturally and intrinsically from within the process of learning and educating, and that it occurs with mutuality in a congress of respect between teachers, students, and administrators. The term *intuition* was left to the contributors to define; some practiced the intuitive as related to the new age philosophy having to do with a spiritual cast, and some as simply "a gut feeling."

Teaching, itself, is an intuitive practice, despite the attempts of federal and state bosses to make it concrete and accountable. The experienced teacher constantly intuits, reacts with her instincts, recognizes rapidly what the student is attempting to explain, and answers instantly with a response that is organically apt. Teaching is improvising and reacting on the spot. The more one teaches, the more intuitive one is; a deep knowledge of the techniques of pedagogical interaction is embedded into the teacher's repertoire by the time she has been teaching for awhile. No lesson plans for how to teach will suffice; teaching well also needs gut reactions and intuition. Christopher Bache spoke about how intuition feeds upon synchronicity while teaching is happening. He called it "a mysterious interweaving of minds," and "the magic." [12]

> When the magic happened, the walls of our separate minds seemed to come down temporarily, secrets were exchanged, and healing flowed. When the magic happened, my students and I tapped into levels of creativity beyond our separate capacities . . . If I cut myself off from my intuition . . . I would also be cutting myself off from a creativity that was benefiting my teaching in very tangible ways.

This book is being published by a house that began as a place where teachers, researchers, parents, and administrators of programs for gifted and talented children could find materials. This book contains essays in which the term *gifted* was deemphasized, and in which test scores were not important, but in which case examples were of students who, according to the authors who observed their behaviors, had high potential. The science of identifying the gifted relies mostly on IQ scores at this historical time—however, in various domains, IQ scores are not adequate. You will recognize these students by what they do, not by how they test.

The Authors and Their Essays

Because these authors are by and large so very experienced, their advice is probably solid, based on many years in their professions while they progressed from novice to expert. I thought readers would be interested in what such experienced masters of teaching had learned through study and through trial and error, rather than read what Dalton characterized as "convoluted manuscripts destined for arcane periodicals." [13]

I tried to include experts in each of the domains usually taught in K–12 schools. Perhaps this edited book with its authors who teach and do science, mathematics, literature, foreign language, social studies, creative writing, dance, music, visual arts, theatre, school administration, preservice education, educational psychology, gifted and talented pull-out resource rooms, and school counseling will move you, startle you, engage you as a reader, and prompt you to think in new ways, led by our award-winning, well-published, well-spoken, expert authors.

The description/abstract for each chapter is in the Table of Contents. Before each chapter is a brief biography and a photograph of the author.

What follows are some relevant quotations from the authors about how they practice organic creativity.

- ☙ **Todd Kettler and Laila Sanguras in Chapter 1:** "We teach literature creatively in hopes that our students will catch even a momentary glimpse of the sublime—a brush with truth so pure that it takes one's breath away. The glimpse of the sublime frames meaning deep within our intellect. The sublime is pursued with reason, found in imagination, and verified by intuition. "

- ☙ **Erin Daniels in Chapter 2:** "In the best of worlds, students would be given options in math class from the very beginning. Teachers would present different ways to solve problems, allow students to choose their best method, and then learn how to get to the solution in the way that best suited the individual. This path to the solution may also be something the students discover on their own, following their intuition. This should be the goal."

- ☙ **Daniel Peppercorn in Chapter 3:** "Some of the more palpable forms of creativity are new exercises that link seemingly unrelated topics, lessons that give students an opportunity to be imaginative, discussions that are conducive to an exchange of fresh ideas and humor, and hands-on assignments that foster critical thinking, problem solving, creating, and presenting."

- ☙ **Keith Taber in Chapter 4:** "Scientists often rely upon this kind of intuition or tacit knowledge in their work in science, and it no doubt operates in all areas of expertise. Scientists and teachers alike are only explicitly aware of some their knowledge, and often have to trust and follow their intuitions because they cannot rely on using logic when they are not actually aware of the basis for their judgments."

- ☙ **Kristin MacDowell and Rodney Michael in Chapter 5:** "Throughout these experiments and projects, the students must use their intuition, visualization, imagery, and creative abilities to transform ideas into plans, then build actual devices using their plans . . . The creative thought process is encouraged, exercised, and celebrated from beginning to end."

- ☙ **F. Christopher Reynolds in Chapter 6:** "Cultivating creativity through feeding back brings students' passionate interests out into the open. Those passions provide inspiration to connect to like-minded others in the Francophone world. Intuition is the faithful guide to this path of the heart, and encouraging the students' devotion to their intuitive inner knowing makes a world of difference."

- ❧ **Barry Oreck in Chapter 7:** "Clearly *Artistry* (*A*) is deeply interconnected with creativity. It is almost impossible to imagine an aspect of artistry that would not be considered creative. *A* encompasses ways of being and learning, artistic attitudes and curiosity, appreciation of beauty and qualities of things, a need or drive for expression, an emotional connection. Perhaps the most accurate definition of *A* would be *access*: access to one's inner voice, to the intuitive, subconscious, connected self."

- ❧ **Jessica Nicoll in Chapter 8:** "Our instincts, impulses, and intuition are the most precious resources we have as artists, and our inner critic is what causes us to second-guess them and undermine ourselves. The trick is to keep ourselves from blocking them, to condition ourselves to recognize our instincts and immediately give them voice, before the critic has a chance to shut them down."

- ❧ **Jeremy Dubin in Chapter 9:** "Once we have given ourselves permission to follow through on our intuition, then true artistic exploration can begin. With a safe environment around us, and an open channel to our intuition within us, it's time to dig in and start working on some scenes; and in my experience the indisputably best tool available to developing actors is Shakespeare."

- ❧ **Tarik Davis in Chapter 10:** "It's about standing up against the system that keeps them mindlessly filling in the bubbles with a No. 2 pencil, being a statistic taking orders at McDonald's, and not ever tapping into their own artistic souls. It's about engendering a culture that champions creativity, curiosity, and intuition. I teach this culture."

- ❧ **Sally dhruvá Stephenson in Chapter 11:** "There is a subtle difference between leading the musical line and following it, and the direction can shift back and forth seamlessly when players are sensitive to this dynamic and have established group trust. Intuition plays a big role in learning to relax into this conversation of listening and answering musically."

- ❧ **Branice McKenzie in Chapter 12:** "I saw what one little song can do, and how it can transform a child's spirit in the course of a 50-minute workshop. I literally saw children turn around and become changed, transformed . . . It's a matter of spirit and it's also a matter of the amazing learning and teaching potential that music has."

- ❧ **Stephanie S. Tolan in Chapter 13:** "I have not only engaged in a purposeful exploration of the nonrational aspects of consciousness, I have actively worked to learn how to use my intuition more effectively not just in writing, but in the rest of my life as well. The exploration has become a spiritual journey as well as a way to increase my own creativity."

❧ **Carl Leggo in Chapter 14:** "I am always seeking to attend to my writing as an intuitive process that is full of mystery, a process that I do not consciously determine or control. Instead, I remain open to the writing that emerges, listening constantly and carefully to the heart's rhythms, to the possibilities of intuition. Therefore, my writing and I are always in flux, always changing."

❧ **Charles Caldemeyer in Chapter 15:** "I ask students to just 'follow their paint,' meaning to let their intuition guide them from mark to mark, the previous step determining the next. This old abstract expressionist trick allows a student who is clearly on to something, but is not yet able to articulate it, the freedom to discover ways to express aspects of his or her life."

❧ **George Johnson in Chapter 16:** "Here is an activity I have used to develop intuition. It requires a temporary suspension of disbelief, a type of naïveté that younger students are better at than sophisticated high school students. Take an artifact, something old with a history to it, and place it in the student's hand."

❧ **Diane Montgomery in Chapter 17:** "I place high value and importance on intuition as a mechanism to unite what sentiment and logic reveal to us. Graduate students who have studied these developmental areas separately often are relieved that their implicit theories are valuable to their practice in education or psychology—receiving the academic permission to trust intuition, insight, and imagination in practice."

❧ **Celeste Snowber in Chapter 18:** "The body is the canvas for creativity. We paint with our hands, dance with our feet, sing with our breath, and sculpt with our palms. Our very beings are creative— we are made with the glorious impossible—ears that hear, flesh that remembers, pulse that regulates, and hair that protects. As the visceral imagination is opened up, the intuition is given muscles, and we can teach on our feet, and be informed by what has great capacity to guide us."

❧ **Jennifer Groman in Chapter 19:** "I believe that organic creativity as a life practice transforms and deepens our understanding of ourselves and those around us. The creative products we generate as we work in this way act as a mirror, reflecting our transforming identity back to us and out to the world. The work is intuitive. The work changes us. It grows us."

✥ **Cyndi Burnett in Chapter 20:** "I suddenly realized that intuition was wholly missing from the CPS process, and that I had been deliberately silencing one of the most important aspects of my natural, organic, and creative process! I immediately knew this was where I needed to focus my research."

✥ **Maria Balotta in Chapter 21:** "The incubation period for creative solutions is frequently seconds long, but as I look back at my journey as a school counselor, I cannot think of any story where intuition did not play a significant role."

✥ **Rebecca McElfresh in Chapter 22:** "Years of standardized practice lead both students and teachers to be limited in their capacity to take risks and to move into any activity that is open-ended in its possible outcomes. . . . Experiences with organic creativity open us to different ways of working in which we must, in a sense, find our own way as we begin to recognize and depend on our intuitive sensibilities. Therefore, initial guidance provides enough scaffolding for the organic nature of the work to unfold."

Dear reader, my hope is that you open up to the insights in this book, are inspired, incubate, engage in improvisation, trust your intuition, free your imagination, and create an image.

Jane Piirto
2013

ORGANIC CREATIVITY IN ACADEMIC DOMAINS

Figure I.1. *Rodney Michael gives a physics master class.*

Chapter 1

NAÏVETÉ, IMAGINATION, AND A GLIMPSE OF THE SUBLIME

Organic Creativity in Teaching Literature

Todd Kettler and Laila Sanguras

The reader became the book; and summer night
Was like the conscious being of the book.—Wallace Stevens[14]

I stole my first book when I was 8. Mrs. Booth lent it to me, and I read it. The story took hold of me, wrapped itself around my mind, and whispered its siren song softly to my soul. It was the first time I fell captive to a book, the first time a story in my mind hummed the soft harmony of truth. To return it would have been like losing a part of who I was. I don't even remember the name of the book, but I remember Mrs. Booth's name written in ballpoint pen across the cover to remind me of my juvenile crime. I apologized 34 years later when our paths crossed at a funeral. I told her the book was still on a shelf at my mother's house,

Todd Kettler, Ph.D., is an assistant professor in the Department of Educational Psychology at the University of North Texas. He teaches courses in gifted education and creativity. Dr. Kettler was a contributing author on *Using the Common Core State Standards for English Language Arts With Gifted and Advanced Learners* (Prufrock Press, 2013), and in the fall of 2012, he was honored with the Advocate of the Year award by the Texas Association for the Gifted and Talented. In addition to his work as a teacher and researcher at the University of North Texas, Dr. Kettler spent 17 years as an English teacher and gifted and talented program administrator.

Laila Sanguras has been an English/language arts teacher for 14 years. She taught in Oregon at the beginning of her career and then moved to Coppell, TX, where she currently teaches language arts to gifted eighth graders and was awarded Teacher of the Year. She is also an instructor for the Gifted Students Institute and the Girls Talk Back program at Southern Methodist University. Laila is a regular presenter for the National Association for Gifted Children and Texas Association for the Gifted and Talented conferences and is working toward her Ph.D. in research, measurement, and statistics at the University of North Texas.

her name still inscribed on the cover. And I told her I had since accumulated about 1,500 others just like it, most of which I respectfully paid for.—Todd

Not to give you the impression that we are a literary version of Bonnie and Clyde, but I feel compelled to confess that I, too, was once involved with stolen books. As a child, my mom took me to two kinds of swap meets in southern California: One sold new, shabby-chic items to women looking for a good deal— furniture, clothing, and a fresh Farmer's market. The other kind boasted flea market items—used tires, mismatched dishes, and books . . . overflowing stacks of coverless books with stamps on the front pages labeling them as stolen, warning the person holding them that neither the publishers nor the authors had received any payment for them. They were cheap, as most stolen goods are, and I couldn't wait to see how many my allowance would buy me.—Laila

Literature is quirky. It's art. It's history. It's philosophy and psychology. We learn about love through literature before we have our first date. We learn temperance and restraint. We confront injustice, mystery, and wonder. We open doors we have never seen, and we stand in landscapes of our own imaginations. Books, stories, poems, and lyrics shape us. Across our lifespan, from childhood through adulthood, literature is a source through which we continue to find meaning in our lives and our worlds.

School curriculum has reserved a place for literature study for as long as most of us can remember, and perhaps longer. But time marches on, and things change. It seems unlikely that we study the same works today as our parents did, or our grandparents did, but it turns out things have not changed much. It seems reasonable that we still read those great texts today. Perhaps the way we teach them has changed; perhaps the why and the how we teach literature has evolved as we've put almost half a millennium between Shakespeare and ourselves.

We find ourselves in a 21st-century world focused on the production and distribution of knowledge and information. The knowledge economy is vastly different from an industrial economy and has distinctly been considered a creative economy;[15] yet, very few schools actually teach students how to be creators of knowledge. The task of teaching students to be creators of knowledge seems buried under the politics of 21st-century education—scripted curriculum and standardized accountability testing. Many of the current features of school seem obsolete given that they were features designed to prepare students for an industrial economy.

Although literature's long-secured position in the standard curriculum received a contract extension with the Common Core State Standards for

English Language Arts[16], it's time to ask the critical question. How do we teach literature in a way that helps students become creators of knowledge? How do teachers of literature work as creators of knowledge? In what ways does the literature curriculum remain viable as preparation for a knowledge economy driven by creativity and innovation?

Sometimes in sincere efforts to teach literature, teachers fill students with knowledge of genres, definitions of literary forms and devices, and background on authors. Although those may be well and good, they can become baggage standing in the way of the reader's personal experience with the text. Today, when a simple Google search can turn up thousands of summaries and criticisms on any literary work in a matter of seconds, more than one of our students have asked, "Why do I need to read the book? I read several commentaries about the book."

In our work as teachers of literature, we have been carving out a creative pedagogy of literature—a model of teaching that places priority on the reader's personal experience with the text as a starting point for the generation of ideas. We want to make a distinction between analyzing literature and responding to literature. Responding to literature nurtures the creative self while analyzing literature appeals to the rational self. Ask any group of students to talk about their favorite song or their favorite movie, and you may have to interrupt the conversation just to bring it to closure. "Why do you like that song? What does it make you think of?" But suppose you asked students to describe the meter of the song or its harmonic function. There is a good chance silence would follow. Certainly meter and harmony are worthy of study by those pursuing music theory, but that's a small segment of the population. The vast majority of people enjoy responding to music. It enhances their happy times, and it gets them through struggling times.

Too often, literature is studied in school as if our goal were to train the next generation of literary critics or prepare students for a TV game show of interesting but trivial details. Students are told to analyze theme, tone, and mood. They write papers on plot structure and irony. They memorize definitions of limerick, sonnet, and haiku. They Google the theme of *To Kill a Mockingbird* on their smartphones minutes before class and walk in with the persona of the well-prepared student.

A Different Approach

Jesse was a mediocre student in my ninth-grade English class for academically talented students. In his unorganized backpack he carried several spiral notebooks, well-worn and tattered around the edges. He wrote in them regularly, even if he was supposed to be doing class assignments related to daily objectives on literary elements or genre characteristics. One day, he finally agreed to let me read from the stack of notebooks he carried. After several minutes, I commented to Jesse that he'd been writing poems and stories all this time. He said, "No, those are songs."

"What's the difference?" I asked.

Jesse said that poems and stories are all about metaphors and allusions, or irony and imagery, boring stuff like that. "But songs," he said, "mean something when you hear them."

Like any well-trained English teacher I quickly replied, "Oh, but stories and poems have wonderful meanings too. Don't you remember when we talked about theme back in September?"

"Sort of," he frowned. "I just remembering you telling us what the theme was while we wrote it down."—Todd

It may have been the most disappointing moment of my teaching career. I knew that Jesse was right. He called me out for teaching literature as if it were dead. I had become the enemy of intellect, the Green Knight of imagination. I blamed the standards movement, the California Achievement Test, and even Shakespeare himself. How did I get here? How did I not remember how my own eyes had frequently drifted out the window when I sat through English classes in high school? Had I really become the teacher determined to beat the theme of "The Rocking-Horse Winner"[17] into my students whether they liked it or not? Jesse's comment was an existential moment to this teacher of literature.

I reflected on why I loved literature. I thought about my favorite stories: Oates's "Where Are You Going, Where Have You Been?", Carver's "Where I'm Calling From," O'Brien's "Sweetheart of the Song Tra Bong."[18] I recalled the marvel I sensed the first time I read *Who's Afraid of Virginia Woolf*[19], and I remembered how as adolescent boys we loved reading *The Hobbit*, until the teacher ruined it by lecturing on its pseudogenre plot structure. There had to be a better way. Surely John Keating (*Dead Poets Society*[20]) was right when he said, "We don't read and write poetry because it's cute. We read and write poetry because we are members of the human race." Thus began the journey to a creative pedagogy of literature.

Creative Pedagogy of Literature

At its heart, a creative pedagogy of literature is one that asks students to be creators of knowledge as a result of meaningful interactions with literary texts. It is a constructivist pedagogy taking seriously the idea that learning and creating are similar processes.[21] To learn is to generate and construct ideas and then to defend those ideas with argumentation, reason, and evidence. The creative pedagogy of literature sees creating as one of the fundamental acts of learning as opposed to a nonessential activity completed after learning.

To create is to make something new and novel. The ability to create is not limited to the mad scientist, or the genius, or the artist in his studio. Rather, creativity is developed skills that can be nurtured and taught to all students and adults—and creativity is fundamental to success in the knowledge economy. Thinking creatively and developing new ideas or improving existing ideas occurs in the kitchen, in the garage, in corporate boardrooms, and certainly in classrooms. The creative pedagogy of literature uses the literary text as the launching point for the generation of ideas. The reader is taught to respond to literature in an attempt to make meanings about life and our place in the human narrative. Responses to text are oral and written, both personal and collective, imaginative and insightful; responses make connections between the ideas of the author and the experiences of the reader.

We have identified four facets of the creative pedagogy of literature: (1) teaching as disciplined improvisation, (2) centrality of imagination, (3) modeling and developing creative dispositions, and (4) problem solving. These four facets have implications for instruction, curriculum, and feedback/assessment. They do not replace curriculum standards such as the Common Core State Standards for English Language Arts; rather, they complement standards and provide direction on how a teacher can teach students to create knowledge.

Disciplined Improvisation

Improvisation is a natural aspect of childhood play, an authentic feature of jazz music, and an emerging business practice in some of the most successful and innovative companies in the United States. Improvisation implies freedom. Children play freely without restriction or convention. Peanuts become boulders along a rugged terrain; plastic fruits become baseballs in the backyard. Rules are vague and adaptable and rarely discussed, if at all.

Jazz musicians famously make up the music as they go; they do it with such amazing skill that improvisation is a hallmark trait of jazz performance.

But what might improvisation look like in the act of teaching? When we improvise as teachers, we are sensitive to teachable moments while maintaining the overall focus on our learning goals. We enter the learning space of the classroom with a broad idea of where we are headed, but retain the flexibility to emphasize ambiguity and possibility. Do not take improvisation to represent poor preparation or lack of skill as a teacher. The jazz musician must practice his craft for years before he is ready to improvise on stage. The teacher must know the stories of the literature curriculum deeply to be able to improvise. Those who are ill-prepared try to hide it by reading from PowerPoints or lecture notes. The committed improvisational teacher creates open-ended inquiry and an environment of exploration. To the improvisational teacher, the learning is in the process, not the predetermined answers. The improvisational teacher hopes that in the middle of the learning, there is serious debate on whether Billy Budd was a hero or a scapegoat.[22] Then in the midst of the debate, she pushes students to clarify, retell, and extend their thinking about Billy Budd to a person facing similar circumstances in real life. That's improvisation. The opposite of improvisational teaching is ending the debate to finish the slideshow before the bell rings.

Disciplined improvisation requires the teacher to be prepared to explore the literature of study but intentionally flexible to various interpretations. The *discipline* qualifier is a commitment to see where learning is headed and contributes to the flow in a supporting role. The archetypal example is the piano player at the jazz club on Monday night's improvisational session. The piano player sets the tone, then lightly fades into the background while the other players take turns leading the music. The piano player accompanies and enhances the show; likewise, the teacher practices disciplined improvisation when she keeps the goal of creative idea generation at the forefront of learning. She sets the tone, then accompanies the students on their journey to generate ideas and personalize the meanings of the literary texts.

By modeling the art of improvisation, the teacher creates an environment where students can freely explore their responses to literature. In doing so, students learn to value the process of learning and the power of creativity, oftentimes without recognizing what is happening. At the beginning, the girls may laugh about how the class discussion strayed from the initial talk of irony in Mona Gardner's "The Dinner Party"[23] to the discomfort of hearing boys at lunch tell sexist jokes, perhaps suggesting that their teacher is so easy to distract, but then later realize that the straying is the point. After experiencing the creativity of an improvisational classroom, students eventually resent the crushing of their ideas in classrooms where the teachers refuse to nurture idea generation and interpretation. Improvisation, and the creativity that is born from this purposeful teaching approach, becomes the pulse of learning.

Teachers who want to teach literary improvisation should purposefully design learning experiences to give students opportunities to improvise. An example may be to ask students to perform a dramatic reading of a poem. In order for the dramatic reading to be meaningful, students must understand the poem's mood and tone, as well as the syntax and poetic structure. This understanding may be informal or even innate, but it must be practiced. Students could be asked to interpret a poem's meaning. In an effort to make sense of the poem, students could choose to analyze significant poetic devices, examine the poet's life, or study world events during the time of the poem's publication, emphasizing how this external information contributes to the overall understanding of the poem. Improvisation requires an initial structure so that it can eventually be removed, furthering the ultimate goal: to make meaning from literature. Creativity presents itself in the disciplined improvisation, the student who is aware of the possibilities and purposefully chooses a path.

Centrality of Imagination

A few years ago I had the opportunity to hear Tim O'Brien deliver a keynote address to a regional conference for English teachers. O'Brien has long been among my favorite authors. I sat at the front of the ballroom, overcome with excitement to hear him speak. He began with a story about himself and his wife and child. He talked about how they experience life with tails. The story went on for an extended period; I kept thinking that he would soon get to the heart of serious fiction writing. After I was thoroughly confused whether he meant tail or tale, the award-winning writer of fiction finally revealed the secret: imagination. He said the fiction writer employs imagination when using the extraordinary to illuminate the ordinary. He told a room full of teachers that if we want to make a difference for our students, nurturing and fostering the imagination would be at the heart of our enterprise.—Todd

It is possible that had I heard this message from anyone other than my iconic favorite author, the genius behind *Going After Cacciato* and *The Things They Carried*[24], I would not have even taken note. But on that morning with a little awe and disbelief, I did take note, and the new pedagogy began to emerge. I found Kieran Egan's *An Imaginative Approach to Teaching* and saw O'Brien's idea through the eyes of an educator. Egan pointed out that imagination was too often seen as a secondary concern in classroom, as peripheral to learning—at best a reason to allow kids an opportunity to express themselves. Furthermore, while imagination may be peripheral to elementary education, it may have been completely antithetical to the curriculum and instruction of high school education. Instead, Egan argued, "imagination is at the center of education; it is crucial to any subject, mathematics and science no less than history and literature." [25]

Readers of fantasy are typically comfortable stretching their imaginations for the sake of an afternoon lost in an unknown world, but it takes more effort to convince realistic fiction lovers to suspend disbelief—not because we lack imagination, but because we prefer the comfort of realism. Stephanie Meyer, Suzanne Collins, and Marie Lu recognized this, spinning supernatural and dystopic tales that, while they demand a belief in the surreal, are rooted in the complexities of realism.[26] They navigate their readers through complicated familial and romantic relationships, sacrifice for family and community, and expose the dangers of intolerant power. Although these contemporary authors may be seen as "fantasy-lite" writers by the strictest of fantasy fans, they have created a portal from the classroom to an imaginative world.

In his wordless graphic novel, *The Arrival*[27], Shaun Tan demands imagination from readers of all ages. Readers of this story become archaeologists, using the author's carefully created artifacts to build the story: the protagonist's angst at leaving his family, his discomfort at adapting to a strange new world, and his discovery of what it means to belong. It's a collage of unique images that mean little without imagination. By assigning "reading" such as this, teachers guide their students through the portal, allowing them to wield the great power granted by imagination.

Perhaps it is our interest in psychology, but we often ponder the motives of the people in our lives and of the characters in our books. This curiosity is one that can be fostered in our students, if only we take the time to imagine the possibilities. Students in an eighth-grade English class may agree that Gene from *A Separate Peace* is selfish, insecure, and generally messed up; however, they may disagree when asked to dissect his character, divining what life events could have possibly led him to that fateful jounce of the tree limb. Depending on their personal experiences and worldviews, perhaps they envision an absentee father, or a series of academic failures, or even a chemical imbalance. The product students create (i.e., an essay, a scrapbook, a series of Facebook posts) is secondary to the true purpose: melding life experiences and imagination to create deep, personal meaning of literature.

This idea is not a new one—just read Geoffrey Maguire's *Wicked: The Life and Times of the Wicked Witch of the West*—but this use of imagination to build empathy and understanding is often superseded by multiple-choice questions that, at most, may require simple inference. Teachers who value creativity in the classroom use imagination as a force to push students beyond the simple and the basic to the sublime.

Modeling and Developing Creative Dispositions

My ninth grade teacher was one who understood what it meant to creatively interact with literature. I don't remember his name or the novel we were studying, probably because I was too intent on trying to be invisible to my classmates, but I do recall the assignment: present the internal struggle of two characters in a creative way. We could work individually or with partners; but, as is often the case, the invisible ones work alone. This was fine, because I was a girl with a plan. I set to work on my idea—sewing, gluing, pinning into the night. The final product was me—small, timid me—revealing my left profile to the class, describing one character's angst and then rotating to show my right profile, a different character wearing different clothes speaking with a different voice, revealing her lamentations. I think my peers were shocked, probably wondering where I had come from and if I had just moved here. But my teacher, my wonderfully supportive teacher, applauded and praised my performance, specifically noting my creative interpretation. I spent the remainder of the year contentedly unnoticed, with the firm understanding that my originality (and persona as a wallflower with a closeted dramatic flair) was welcomed and encouraged.—Laila

The literature on creative individuals includes a number of personality dispositions associated with creative thinking or production. In our approach to developing a creative pedagogy of literature, we have focused on three particular dispositions to nurture and develop in our students: (a) a tolerance for ambiguity, (b) naïveté or openness to experience, and (c) risk-taking. We model these regularly as teachers, and we create situations in which students can practice these dispositions in a safe and supportive environment.

Tolerance for ambiguity. Creative people have been known to tolerate ambiguity in ways that less creative people do not. Creative people prefer complexity and asymmetry. Tolerance for ambiguity is both an acceptance and preference for situations without frameworks, rules, and known procedures. Getzels referred to this as "openness to the world."[28] If the teacher assigns a project that is open-ended with few rules and guidelines, no model exemplar, and no specific requirements for length or format, student reactions will range from terrified and anxious to pleased and excited. Ambiguous situations lend themselves to creative responses, and creative people find pleasant challenge in bringing order to disorder.

Because tolerance builds with increased exposure, it is important to provide students with multiple opportunities to confront ambiguity in literature. Remember the frustration when reading Frank Stockton's "The Lady or the Tiger?"[29], especially upon realizing the intentionality of the ambiguous conclusion and that "the answer" didn't exist in the teacher's edition? Pleasure can be derived from arguing over Robert Browning's choice of diction in "My Last Duchess"—is the speaker referring to his previous or final duchess? The distinction is significant, and absolutely worth debating, highlighting the nuances of language that make the study of literature so timeless and beautiful. In fact, one could argue that the critical and creative thinking that results from tolerance for ambiguity is what a literature teacher should emphasize.

Naïveté. Piirto described naïveté as a core attitude for creativity, clarifying naïveté as openness to experience, one of the Big Five personality attributes.[30] Perhaps naïveté is not perceived as a positive or desirable trait by public perception—we don't want to go to a naïve doctor or a naïve accountant. However, naïveté, openness to the new, is a disposition that supports creative responses. Creative persons may be more open to experience and accepting of new information. Naïveté is the willingness to see things in a new way—to embrace the perhaps, the what if. We demonstrate naïveté when we approach literature with openness to interpretation, a hope that the text will present an idea or a description in a new way. Through the interpretive process, the naïve disposition absorbs the new with hope and wonder—expectation that my view of the world may well change or expand because of this interaction with text. Creative people read seeking the possible, not the definite.

In *Looking for Alaska*[31], John Green creates quirky and lovable Miles Halter, a young man in search of the "Great Perhaps." He is naïve and unwavering in his quest, determined to live a life full of rich experiences. Teachers should perhaps encourage students to approach literature with an innocent yearning for understanding, becoming a modern-day Socrates, asking challenging questions and playing devil's advocate, reveling in the discomfort of evolving beliefs. They could dare third graders to suggest that India Opal from *Because of Winn-Dixie*[32] would have been better off had she not been abandoned by her mother. They could ask their high school students to wonder at the significance of the hand washing motions in Tim O'Brien's "Church,"[33] visibly curious about this striking allusion. They practice the art of questioning in order to foster creativity, modeling their quest for understanding after Miles' quest—after all, there is never disappointment in the what if or what could be, only in the what might have been.

Risk-taking. Risk-taking is the third disposition of focus in the creative pedagogy of literature. Generating and sharing new ideas is risky. Developing new products, posing new interpretations, and asking new questions all involve taking a risk of rejection. Risk-taking is a courageous activity and necessary for creative response.[34] The most creative responses are unique and novel, and inherently involve the students taking risks that their ideas will be rejected or ridiculed by their peers. In a creative pedagogy of literature, not only are those types of assignments typical, but the disposition of risk-taking is nurtured and rewarded.

Students' willingness to take risks often varies depending on their confidence in their ability to generate new and interesting ideas. When examined conceptually, students of all ages and abilities can articulate what a specific story or poem can teach them about life, friendship, or truth. We recently designed a yearlong ninth-grade English curriculum addressing the essential question "Who Am I?" The purpose of literature became for students to define themselves in terms of relationships, politics, and their responses to personal failure. Our high school students no longer saw *Romeo and Juliet* as required "because every freshman has to read it," but as a vehicle to further their understanding of relationships and what it means to love. Similarly, middle school students use *The Giver*[35] to help define themselves politically, solidifying their beliefs about the role of government. Elementary students discuss Wilbur's challenges in *Charlotte's Web*[36] as a way to consider how they respond to failure in their lives. At every level, students take risks when they choose a stance, but now when they argue that love is, indeed, worth fighting for, they have their own experiences coupled with the wisdom of Shakespeare's characters to support their beliefs. Students become philosophers, gleaning wisdom from literature about life's great profundities.

Problem Finding and Problem Solving

If you were to ask my mom to describe me as a teenager, she would probably characterize me as a good girl: an honors student, cheerleader, and student council officer. I didn't do drugs, go to wild parties, or run away from home. However, this good girl's favorite novel was Go Ask Alice[37], *an edgy book published in 1971 that remains popular today with teenage girls. While tucked safely under the covers of my bed, I tried LSD, learned to survive on the streets, and waded through the muddy waters of complicated family dynamics. Literature has always been my avenue for experimentation, and as I have gotten older, has provided answers to some of life's toughest problems.*—Laila

We have both been teachers of literature for years, and have seen our share of teacher training and professional learning on teaching English. Almost never has problem solving been discussed as the methodology of teaching literature. Problem solving is frequently lauded and recommended as a methodology in math and science but not often, if at all, in literature. However, we find ourselves in a new era of education with new emphases and radical changes in knowledge and information. Thinking differently is perhaps necessary, including thinking differently about teaching literature.

It is difficult to make the case that stories and poems are the materials best designed to solve problems. We are not saying never, but we are claiming that literature was not intended for nor should it be seen as a solutions tool. It seems unlikely that a business looking to expand into a new market would turn to the works of Twain or Conrad for guidance. It seems similarly unlikely that a medical researcher would look to the works of Fitzgerald or Orwell for elusive cures to pediatric cancer. Literature has not, and will not, solve the most complex problems of the day. In fact, some of us may recount situations in which our problems actually grew while we fed our insatiable appetite for reading.

However, literature, like other art forms, may be fertile ground for problem finding.[38] Literary texts illuminate life's problems. In some stories, like *To Kill a Mockingbird* or *Romeo and Juliet*, the problems are illuminated with a bright spotlight. In other stories, like *The Absolutely True Diary of a Part-Time Indian*[39] or *The Stranger*[40], the problems are lightly hinted at. The potential of problem finding is not limited to prose, but includes poetry as well. Surely, Frost's "The Road Not Taken" can be seen as an illumination of problems. When Poe's "The Raven" ceases to be seen as a Halloween poem and is seen instead as a lament of love lost, students approach it completely differently. At that point, they begin to make personal connections about love and remembrance. Ask them to talk about the complex problems that Poe describes, and creativity begins to bridge the text to their lives.

Middle school students may never have considered the issues that can arise when one person in a relationship is deeply religious while the other publicly challenges the gospel, yet the division rises to the surface in class discussions of the relationship between the main characters in Heiligman's *Charles and Emma: The Darwins' Leap of Faith*[41]. Students use Charles and Emma to voice and problem solve potential issues related to giftedness, religious conflict, and the illogical nature of love. Hemphill's *Your Own, Sylvia: A Verse Portrait of Sylvia Plath*[42] can also address problems that arise with giftedness, in addition to issues related to gender inequality, mental illness, and fidelity. Literature provides a safe environment for students to employ problem-solving and problem-finding skills, not only strengthening their ability to define problems but also to creatively respond to them. The self-awareness that students gain from literature studies centered on the principles of creativity is unparalleled in classrooms that do not foster creative thinking.

A Glimpse of the Sublime

The ancient Greek writer Longinus wrote about the effects of good writing in his epistolary essay, *On the Sublime*[43]. For Longinus, the sublime was a momentary evasion of reality—the power of the text to arouse emotions of awe and wonder in the mind of the reader. That which is sublime is beautiful, mysterious, and boundless. The sublime is pursued with reason, yet found in imagination. Immanuel Kant[44] argued that which is sublime is so revered that by comparison all else is small. Wordsworth romanticized the concept of the sublime in his "Lines Composed a Few Miles Above Tintern Abby":

Of aspect more sublime; that blessed mood,
In which the burden of the mystery
In which the heavy and weary weight
Of all this unintelligible world,
Is lightened.[45]

The concept of the sublime weaves its way through the history of literature, and its mysterious fascination with imagination, beauty, and truth provide a hopeful aesthetic for our creative pedagogy of literature. We make it a habit to ask, to what end? Why are we doing this? Why teach literature at all? Moreover, why teach literature within this framework of creativity? We teach literature creatively in hopes that our students will catch even a momentary glimpse of the sublime—a brush with truth so pure that it takes one's breath away. The glimpse of the sublime frames meaning deep within our intellect. The sublime is pursued with reason, found in imagination, and verified by intuition. Longinus even claimed it touched our soul. It's intoxicating and addicting. Once one catches a glimpse of the sublime, he will long for more.

What does it feel like to glimpse the sublime? It's the feeling an 8-year-old has when he reads the book that he can never return to the teacher. It's the fantasy that if I keep the book and read this story over and over, I'll continue to find that feeling. But glimpsing the sublime is not that predictable. The sublime sneaks up on the reader even as he collects and reads hundreds of books in hopes of the occasional glimpse.

As an adult a few years ago, I sat in the Denver airport awaiting a flight back home. I was reading Sherman Alexie's The Absolutely True Diary of a Part-Time Indian. *I was near the end of the book, reading the part where* (spoiler alert) *Arnold's sister died. There was something about the way Arnold waited in the snow for his father, pleading with God not to let his daddy die too. It's hard to describe exactly what the glimpse of the sublime feels like. My breathing grew rapid; I could feel the droning of my own heartbeat. I could only imagine the love and fear of loss that all families must feel, even drunken, dysfunctional families deep on Alexie's made-up Indian reservation. I thought of the potential loss of my own father. Tears welled up in me, I sensed my embarrassment as a supposedly serious adult—a business traveler—weeping in the Denver airport as I read a book written for young people.*—Todd

That's why we position ourselves within a creative pedagogy of literature. We seek meaning, beauty, and truth. We seek them for ourselves, and we seek them for our students. Not so we can tuck them safely within the pockets of our minds, but in order to rearrange our world in some way. Meaning, beauty, and truth don't rest well inside us; they are meant to flow through us, joining hands with our imagination, emerging as new ideas.

Chapter 2

THE MESS OF MATHEMATICS

Organic Creativity in Teaching Advanced Mathematics

Erin Daniels

What does creativity mean in math? Do students have to write a poem about the number 3? Or how about an essay on the importance of significant digits? In our verbally oriented schooling society, too often teachers feel this is their only resort if they want to incorporate creativity into their classroom. In the truest sense of the word, as many have pointed out, creativity is to make something new. That something could be a new solution, a new method, or even a new outlook. The written word may not even enter the equation.

Many of the Five Core Attitudes, Seven I's, and General Practices for Creativity as described by Piirto can be seen and enhanced in math and in the mathematics classroom.[46] Just as these features are present in a poet or a jazz musician, they are present in the aspiring mathematician, but how they are manifested may look differently. Many approach math as a subject in which you must find the one road that leads you to that one accurate, if not elusive, right answer. This does not have to be the case, though. I venture to say that math is not linear, and there are many different interweaving avenues that can get you to the correct ending. In fact, much to the dismay of many math teachers, some students will not arrive at a solution simply by following the steps taught, and they may rely on intuition along the way—yes, even in the logical, rational world of mathematics.

Erin Daniels is a high school math teacher in Mount Vernon, OH. She received her undergraduate degree from Mount Vernon Nazarene University in integrated mathematics education. As an undergrad, Erin completed research and did a thesis on instructional methods in the mathematics classroom. She recently completed her master's degree in talent development education at Ashland University. Erin teaches geometry and AP calculus classes. She has served as a math club advisor at the high school. She has served on her school district's virtual curriculum committee, and presented at a technology conference in central Ohio.

Risk-Taking

Let's first consider risk-taking as a creative component in the math classroom. Besides the risk of entering a math class and not coming out alive, which many people experience in the school years, risk-taking can be a beneficial skill to practice and teach when learning mathematics. Way too many times, the task of finding the precise sequence to get a correct answer is imposed upon the unsuspecting math student, where the exact process becomes more important than the overall goal and answer to the problem. It starts at a young age and continues through high school and beyond. The instructors of algebra are notorious for their steps that must be followed: First, you must get your variables to one side, and then move your constants.

Now, granted, there are certain rules you cannot break or math is no longer math, but there are also different possibilities and routes to take. It's actually acceptable to get your constants on one side of the equation first, and then get your variables together on one side. But too often, students are not shown the options and forced to regurgitate the steps they have been told. In the class of geometry, after taking algebra, students are often at a loss when many options are presented in the case of a proof. They are given the start and the finish of the problem, and must come up with everything in between. Here is where creativity can flourish, and it is also where the students begin to really fret. *What step do I do first? How many steps are in between? Do I have to use this theorem?* These are just the beginning of the questions the students ask, but it is also, sometimes, the first time they have had to take a risk.

In the best of worlds, students would be given options in math class from the very beginning. Teachers would present different ways to solve problems, allow students to choose their best method, and then learn how to get to the solution in the way that best suited the individual. This path to the solution may also be something the students discover on their own, following their intuition. This should be the goal. And the real show-offs, and that is said with true affection, will answer the question showing their answer with three different methods of getting that answer. Even though I jest about this, it is wonderful to see this work that is not required but part of the student's desire and thorn to pursue his or her mathematical talent.

A word of warning does follow. If you thought grading was time-consuming before, this does not alleviate the problem. In my calculus classes, we discuss concepts and meanings along with our practice problems. Students do not have to follow standard steps to get to the end result; they just have to show their work of how they got there. With a class of 15, I can have

15 different paths, all of which lead to a correct solution on a quiz. It takes me a long time to grade these papers. Of course, I am looking at their final answer, but I am grading the process they took as well, which can be quite varied. This is creativity at work. Students are presenting a novel approach to a problem. Most of the time, the solution process looks nothing like what was modeled in class. However, students took a risk and solved the problem in a way that made sense to them.

For those with perfectionism, an attribute of some academically talented students, the core attitude of risk-taking seems like an impossible feat. When facing the decision between possible failure and one more A to maintain their GPA, which could be worth thousands of dollars at college, perfectionist students will probably choose the latter. Risk is not something they can afford with such high stakes. This is why finding those avenues as a classroom teacher becomes all the more pressing. In one of my calculus classes, I start a unit with a common word that has a meaning in the everyday world and a mathematical meaning. I have students create posters using the term in a phrase just from their everyday knowledge of the word. I pull out all of the stops. I give them blank pieces of paper, colored pencils, markers, and even glitter crayons.

Every year, it takes a good 5 minutes to convince these high-achieving, point-counting students that this is not for a grade, and there is no right answer. Then the creativity starts to blossom. I see a side of the students that has not had the chance to bud. I get everything from the comedic to the philosophical in their approach. After sharing (and laughing), I then have the students turn over the page and jot down how this everyday term might mean something mathematically. I want them to make connections between what they know and what the math could be. It never fails that I get much more involvement and a more meaningful discussion after the students have had a risk-free chance to shine. The students are more willing to give opinions with a new sense of freedom, knowing they may be quite wrong. However, they have had the chance to relax, show a new side, and they now are willing to share regardless. Perfectionists have taken risks.

Resilience

Another dilemma for the perfectionists and the faint of heart in this creativity journey is finding the ability to be resilient. The time-honored saying "If at first you don't succeed, try, try again" has a lot of truth in it. There is something to be said for the creative who are only considered masters in their domain after 10,000 hours of practice. Resiliency has been linked directly to the uncovering and fostering of talent. Students who have had to work for their success exhibit a sense of mental toughness. Most of the time, anything that is great must take some work. Those who are resilient know the importance of hard work and the results that come with this strong work ethic. Of course, there are the cliché examples of telling students how many lightbulbs Thomas Edison went through before he was successful and how Michael Jordan did not make the basketball team as a youngster. These are familiar, though, because of the truth that reverberates with each individual. Hard work and trial and error unlock so much more than what can happen if something is only tried once.

This year, I have become aware of the effect of a lack of resiliency in my calculus class, full of self-proclaimed "slackers." They want to beat the system. They will answer just enough questions on the quiz to pass. They will complete just enough homework to be able to get the grade for the 9 weeks that they need. They are brilliant in math and brilliant at doing just enough to get by. To try or show effort would be horrible for the image they want to portray, which means they cannot show they care. If they come to a problem that is difficult, they give up. If they make mistakes (in pen) on their quizzes, it takes too much effort to fix it.

At first, I thought their brilliance would overcome their laziness, but I did a study comparing their scores to another calculus class, and the class of "slackers" was way below the other, even when just comparing ability level. I thought that at least on tests and quizzes they would be comparable because their IQ levels are even higher than the other class. However, I think their lack of resiliency has harmed them. They have not practiced the mantra of "try, try again," and therefore, they have trouble succeeding in understanding the concepts deeply.

Incubation

For the creative in any domain, allowing time for incubation is key. This allows the students to wrestle with the problems and let things rise to the surface. Modeling the benefits of incubation can be an invaluable tool for young minds. If a question ever arises in class, especially a conceptual question in calculus, that is new and that I have not thought of before, I try not to answer blindly without complete confidence. Sometimes I have to tell the students that I will think about it and get back to them with the right answer to their question. I then ruminate and let the question work itself out in my brain, as well as maybe do some research, until I can give the students an accurate example. As a math teacher, teaching and doing math is part of my creative product, and the process by which I do both of these is being closely watched each day. One of Piirto's guidelines for enhancing creativity in students is to do your own creative work and let the students see you doing it.[47] As a human, I will not be perfect in my math and teaching abilities, but it's something I like to do, and this backdrop is a great way to teach students how they can perfect their own creative abilities without feeling worthless for not having reached excellence or eminence right away.

Many math classrooms are based on efficiency and accuracy, sometimes to the detriment of allowing students time to process the new material in a way that makes sense in their brains. Providing time for incubation can give students the time for better conceptual understanding. An idea that changes the usual framework of the math class is to give students a few days to complete each homework assignment. In my calculus class, the students have anywhere from 3–5 days to complete an assignment. As they work away at the problems, they can bring their questions in as they are grappling with the material. Sometimes they have been working on the assignment and turn it in, and then they want to redo it of their own accord because the process has become even clearer through the days they have had to think about the concept. Instead of worrying about getting 40 problems done in the 2 hours they are home one evening, they can spend time thinking about the math. It is not about rushing to get something done, but working to understand with time to think. This incubation period allows the concept to change and evolve through the wait time.

By allowing time for incubation, a collaborative process also begins to take place. No longer is the teacher just pouring knowledge into the unsuspecting and unprepared students, but rather, students are able to take control of their own learning as they have time to process what is going on. Many creative ideas have come after students take the concepts and work on them for a day or two, and then I, not one to pass up a great idea, incorporate them into my teaching each year. One year we were discussing the volume process in calculus with the shell and disk methods. It is overwhelming at first, with many nuances to differentiate within the two methods. One of these differences includes the fact that *parallel* rectangles are used in the *shell* method, and *perpendicular* rectangles are used in the *disk* method. After a few days of practice and dialogue, we were discussing the need to remember the key distinctions, and one student piped up with his idea. He said that he had come up with new words to keep the methods separate—the paraSHELL method and the perpenDISKular method. Lightbulbs—the aha's of insight—could almost visibly be seen turning on over the students' heads.

To aid in this incubation practice, the advantages of self-discipline cannot be overlooked. This is where math teachers are doing quite well—they assign homework. Not only does this help students get into the routine of working at something consistently and frequently, but it is a great benefit in the creative process. In order to add something unique and new to the field of math, you must be familiar with the very basics. This happens through repeated individual practice, which often comes in the form of homework.

The new push this year in our school is to align our curriculum with the new Common Core State Standards and to prepare our students for the new performance assessments that will replace the Ohio Graduation Test (OGT). This emphasis alone brings in several of the blocks that harm creativity, such as time limits, performance pressures, and organizational rules and regulations. I am not here to argue, right now, about the presence of standardized tests in the school at all, but the sheer volume of new data, information, and assessments that are entering our schools has become all encompassing. We now are administering five benchmark tests throughout the year to begin preparing for what the statewide test will be. We spend most of our professional development analyzing the data and preparing for the next influx of assessments. Teachers are now complaining about all of this extra work that is taking away from their true love—teaching and having their own unique style to share with their students. This can even change into causing the teacher to do work he or she hates, and for students to do work they hate, which is another block to creativity.

Intrinsic Motivation

With all of these mandates being pushed down from the top, it is more important than ever to be able to infuse students with the freedom to be creative and to exhibit what is lying somewhere in between. This can come in the form of allowing intrinsic motivation to lead the lessons or to find the sources of inspiration for the students to be able to follow their passion, both of which are possible in the world of mathematics.

Students are usually motivated by something, and part of the goal for mathematics is to find that motivation and build upon it. For many, the idea that math is fun happens to be the farthest thing from the truth. Little things can start to change this mindset. On my desk at school, I have games, puzzles, brain teasers, and more in a basket. Of course, there are the toys you can "beat," such as finding a way to get the wooden pieces to form a cube. There are also the toys that are just for fun—a magnetic base with nuts, bolts, and outlines of people. You can't win; you can't beat them. They are just fun logic toys. They enhance the creative flow. My students will beg to be able to play with these after they are done with a test. They don't ask if they can sleep or go to their locker, but if they can get into the basket of toys (which, of course, are all masked as toys but are mathematical traps!). Students will then start to bring in their own games they discarded long ago. My box will begin to fill up as students donate what treasures they could find that would be worthy of the basket. No grades are attached, no requirements are established, and yet this little side activity has infiltrated the math classroom to spark creativity.

Whatever the subject matter at hand, motivation is key for the students to really take the material and run with it. One of the arduous tasks of a teacher would be to somehow turn the ability and desire to learn from that of having an external locus of control to an internal locus of control. If a teacher can figure out those inner tickings of a student and work with them, the sky is the limit. Some of my calculus students countered the lesson we were going over with an inquiry about a related theoretical framework that was far beyond the scope of the lesson, but it was related. As a class, we set up a problem to be solved that would help us understand this inquiry. Now, the question was something that I am almost sure would be worthy of a Ph.D. dissertation, but these students had the mind to solve it. We would spend a few minutes at the end of each class for a few weeks pondering the dilemma we had set up. The students would ask their other teachers for advice and input and spend hours at home coming up with additional background work. They had found something that interested them that was not forced upon them. They were working solely through intrinsic motivation.

Now, if we take this down a level from that of conceptual mathematical problems, there are still other areas in which to work with students without doing a dissertation. My work in progress this year has been to find ways to word my queries and challenges so they pique the students' interests. I have sometimes had to forget about the grades I would assign and put the problem sets in a new light. Because of the fact that several of my brilliant students are getting a D- on a good day, I knew grades were anything but motivation for them. They do, however, want to show off their mathematical prowess and they take pride in solving tough math problems. So on days when students work in groups or individually on the concept of the current day's curriculum, I challenge some of these pods of students with the "tough" problems that not everyone can do. That's all that is needed to get their interest. Their intrinsic motivation has set in because this pride to excel above and beyond is what drives them.

Openness to Experience

Recently, I have been actively trying to promote an atmosphere that allows students to engage in the material in a personal manner. This allows them to work creatively in their best light. In one of my classes, I have students who are very interested in formulating the theorems of the unit before I actually teach them. If I am going to teach the Quotient rule in calculus on Thursday, they work all week to analytically and intuitively figure it out before the unveiling in class. This becomes a whole side project in my lesson plans. They tell me their deductions and ideas, and I give them a counterexample to work around; thus they gradually get closer to the correct theorem. These students are not doing this because it is an assignment or a grade. The students have not yet had the formal instruction, but are letting intuition have space in their work. In fact, they could easily look the theorem up in their books or on the Internet, but they have tapped into an intrinsic motivator that causes them to push into the unknown. At the end of the day, my boards are full of ideas and trials that have occurred from students in this class.

One day, I decided to have the students come up with their own problems to solve at the end of a unit on related rates. Our problems in class had all been nicely worded problems about a ladder leaning against a building falling down at 5 feet/second and finding the rate at which it was being pulled away from the building. Mathematically relevant to the curriculum, yes. Creative and original, no. So with students having their own say in the process, creativity entered the math arena. One student created a problem with different sized cylinders stacked on top of each other and asked about the rate the water was flowing into them. Another student took up the entire chalkboard to write his problem on the rate the distance was changing between Einstein and Hawking. He included black holes, rates of acceleration, and a reference to pi (a tribute to my love of the number) into the problem. He then proceeded to take the remaining 20 minutes and other board space to work on this problem. At the end of class, he was not done, so he came after school to work on the problem, was late to band practice, and still not done. He then took the problem home and came in the next day with a page full of work to show the solution. Interestingly enough, this assignment was completely optional and no grade was given. He was inspired, though.

If you are willing, this approach can transform your mindset, your classroom, or your mathematical pretenses. The idea is to be open to something new, the very heart of creativity. One day in class, we were studying absolute value functions, the standard v-shaped graphs that can be shifted in numerous ways. The question arose about what would happen with a mixture of variables inside the absolute value sign. Now, admittedly, I normally would disregard the question with the greatest of comments, such as "I'm not sure where that will take us, we'll have to look into that later." "Later" meaning after all of the standardized tests had been given, all of the benchmarks had been achieved, and all of the students had shown growth by some measure. However, with the mindset of leaning toward incorporating creative thought, we pursued the question right then and there. We actually found a really neat looking graph with our exploration, on which we imposed the name of the "Argyle Relation." Through the process, we actually met our standards and understood the concepts, but we went further. We created something new, by the fact that we did not study someone else's work but did it ourselves. You will not find the "Argyle Relation" in any textbook, nor will anyone outside our four walls have a clue what this is in reference to, but our class participated in the creative process together.

These applications do not always have to be for the mathematically inclined students. Students who are in math because they have to take the class to graduate can still find some inward motivation or inspiration. The nemesis of many math teachers is the question, "When am I going to use this?" Now, it is truly important to be able to relate the mathematical content to applications for the students. However, most of the time, the students who are asking this question will not be persuaded, no matter how you respond to the query. Hope is not lost, however. In my geometry class, we learned how to do a six-step problem on finding the distance between parallel lines. I promised the class that this would be the longest problem of the year, and we discussed the importance of being able to follow through and check work along the way. I, of course, knew this problem was not for the faint of heart, and I fully expected some to give up, the same ones who always question, "When am I going to use this?" However, to my surprise, it was one of these such students who was totally enthralled by the question. He even completed more practice problems than required and showed me his solutions with little tweaks he had made to the process. Sometimes, the challenge can be enough of a motivator to see the inspiration at work. All that this student needed was something that inspired him and tugged at him to let creativity begin to take place.

Passion

For creativity to truly blossom without being forcibly constructed, the true passions of the students must be tapped into. The concepts and the work will not be work but an expression of themselves being able to delve into something that is interesting to them. Now, not everyone is born with a propensity toward math, but the outright aversion to math may be lessened for these students. If we are truly going to find the creativity of our students in math, it must seem like play to them. Our job is to help the students find and enjoy the fun that is available.

With this mindset, many days may be filled with cleaning minuscule amounts of play dough out of the carpet (and apologizing to custodians), but it represents a classroom where the students got to experiment and play. This could be seen in the building blocks that are used in my geometry class to really see and comprehend the polyhedra in a three-dimensional way. Students may create their own board game with all of the odds and ends they find in the classroom to learn the background of postulates and theorems in the framework of geometry. Students may form their own cross sections of a solid using play dough to truly grasp how to find volume. Or my favorite is when the classroom is full of honeycomb decorations for students to graph and find the volume of using statistics and calculus while making comparisons to water displacement principles that they learned in science. It is hard to end the units when doing this because the toys have to go away, which is usually sad for all.

All of this play in math class also helps the students employ the benefits of imagination and imagery—something that often gets lost in a sea of x's and y's on the page. I remember the first time I realized I was deep in my mathematics journey was when I looked at a page in my math notes and saw a page that had almost all letters and no numbers. I often have my students take a step back and look at their notes; our minds sometimes get so caught up in the moment of the next step, that we miss the big picture of what is conceptually going on. Play allows us to step back, process ideas, connect our ideas, and put images to the page full of formulas.

The looming factor, though, that is on everyone's mind is how creativity can be worked into the curriculum when everything is so standardized and success is based on how well students fill in the bubbles on a test. This is something that everyone in education is going to struggle with, and I see the differences in my own classes. In my geometry classes, I am constantly pushing students so they will do well on the Ohio Graduation Test (OGT). In Advanced Placement Calculus, we are not only hurriedly making our way through the concepts to get done by the beginning of May, but we are also spending much precious time on test preparation, including discussions on the best way to simplify, the best way to approach multiple choice, and even the best way to guess.

Freedom

On the other hand, my calculus class that is not part of the Advanced Placement program is my only class where a standardized test is not impending at the end of the year. There is so much freedom in this class. Piirto wrote, "The idea that teaching is meandering pleasurably with students in a river of knowledge, where the ideas to be pursued arise from the context of the discussion, supports the idea of teaching as a creative activity."[48] When I first read this, I highlighted and marked this passage because it described my calculus class very well. If we do not reach section 3.2 by next week, it is OK. We will probably have more rich discussion and follow through than if we had to work with imposed timelines. It ends up that when we go off on a tangential discussion we learn the intended objectives and more—most of the time.

It is the possibility of not meeting the standards, though, that keeps most teachers captive to the strict timeline and routine approach of teaching. As one person quite aptly put it, the Advanced Placement students must work harder to achieve, not necessarily with time to think about the material. They must work hard enough to get the best score possible, whereas the regular calculus students get time to think and ruminate on what is truly going on with the mathematical concepts. This time of freedom, however, is where students are allowed to express themselves, when they can add new outlooks and new ideas to the curriculum in place.

And honestly, with the best intentions, these ideas may fall flat at any given moment. Intuition has a place, and rational thought can be set aside for a moment. Part of the appeal of creativity is that there is no set formula to apply to get a creative work. This can be extremely frustrating for the mathematically inclined who love to follow steps 1–6 to get the promised result. For as much success as some of these students have brought me, there are still plenty of days where they leave class feeling like they have gained nothing new from the lesson. There are days when only one person may catch on to the vision you lay before them.

As a teacher, I feel that I have gotten more creative every year, and, along with this, many processes have gotten to be more habitual. In my first year of teaching, I made so many split-second decisions in the classroom that I later regretted, but I have learned from my mistakes (and am still learning) and now good decisions come more automatically. I can be more creative and novel in my approach to teaching when some parts come more quickly and effortlessly, such as the right thing to say to discipline a disruptive student, or the best way to question a struggling student, or even the right example to give for an individual learning the material. My overall process of teaching becomes much more effective when I don't have to put extensive thought into each and every decision I make.

There is not a handbook that comes with each creative product that explains all that goes into making a new advance in a field. However, by carefully studying creators, several characteristics seem to always arise, one of which is automaticity. When people can spend their energy on something besides the foundational part of their domain, they can then work on adding something new to their domain. It also follows the guide of self-discipline, which is a key feature of the creative process. I have personally seen the benefits of automaticity in my own students' math ability and my personal teaching ability. Automaticity affects the creative product in many worthwhile ways.

Resilience and Perfectionism

The key is to not lose heart, keep trying, keep experimenting, and, in doing so, you will be modeling your own creativity for your students. In a quest to open up the pathways of creativity for all of my students, I am on my own journey of molding something new in my students. My teaching is my own creativity. I must be resilient and willing to take risks. I must not allow perfectionism to hinder progress. I must find my job a time of play and passion if I expect it in my students.

Creativity is quite elusive and unexplainable. Many have researched and started to put parameters on this interesting topic. To muddy the waters more, each domain has its own set of creativity factors and products. The subject of math with its analytical, step-oriented, logical processes does have many ways in which creativity can abound and intuition can be appreciated and cultivated. One does not have to reach the lofty heights of adding something new to the field that has never been thought of before; rather it could be something such as adding a new outlook or a new path to a solution. I see creativity at work every day in my classroom.

One of the keys to pursuing and fostering this creative process is to step outside the all too familiar linear landscape of mathematics. Instead of allowing one path to get to one solution, encourage the discovery of as many different avenues and detours as possible to get to that same solution. It allows the students to break free from the mentality to just follow the rules, giving them the chance to make their own assumptions and predictions about the beauty of math. Only after these constraints have been broken will true creative products begin to appear.

Chapter 3

THINKING OUTSIDE THE BLOCKS

Organic Creativity in Teaching Social Studies

Daniel Peppercorn

Writer Victor Miller said, "School is like theatre. Teachers are like directors, students are like actors, and classes are like theatrical presentations."[49] I've adopted Victor's philosophy, and, as a social studies teacher, I try to bring out my students' creativity and make my classes interactive, meaningful, and engaging. In addition to Victor's presentation, I've been inspired by movies like *Dead Poets Society* and *Ferris Bueller's Day Off,* my favorite teachers, my parents, and my students. In this chapter I'll discuss these influences, give examples of some of my most imaginative activities, offer the 6 C's for getting the most out of our students, and explain why we should listen to Matt Damon and Sir Ken Robinson by developing creative lessons and condemning the reform efforts that are leading to the McDonaldization and MBA-ification of our schools.

Before a big high school basketball game at my alma mater, Lincoln-Sudbury, my coach said of an opposing player, "He's very creative." One of my teammates looked at me and said, "What does that mean? Does he do finger paintings during halftime?" Although creativity in an athlete is hard to define, it's easier to pinpoint when you see it in a classroom. According to Steve Jobs, "Creativity is just connecting things."[50]

Daniel Peppercorn, Ed.M., is an eighth-grade teacher and social studies curriculum coordinator who graduated magna cum laude in history from Harvard College and received his Ed.M. from Harvard's Graduate School of Education. He is a former all-state athlete and coach who performs improv, makes films, and recently completed a creative nonfiction comedy and a parody of a Dr. Seuss book. He is the author of *Creative Adventures in Social Studies: Engaging Activities & Essential Questions to Inspire Students.*

In social studies, creativity involves connecting history to current events and students' lives. Some of the more palpable forms of creativity are new exercises that link seemingly unrelated topics, lessons that give students an opportunity to be imaginative, discussions that are conducive to an exchange of fresh ideas and humor, and hands-on assignments that foster critical thinking, problem solving, creating, and presenting.

One reason I enjoy working with adolescents is that while they may not know as much as adults, they're often more creative, spontaneous, enthusiastic, humble, and funny. As business innovation speaker and consultant Stephen Shapiro declared,

> To quote Einstein once again 'Imagination is more important than knowledge.' Unfortunately, society and our educational systems have put a premium on knowledge rather than imagination. Schools teach the regurgitation of facts rather than thinking and creativity. Studies show that 98% of 5 year olds test as highly creative, yet only 2% of adults do. We don't lose our creativity, but we learn habits which stop it from emerging.[51]

Inspirations

I once worked at a private school where the principal told the graduating class of eighth graders that his wish for them was that they wouldn't lose the enthusiasm and creativity that they had in middle school. When I was hired, he encouraged me to design creative lessons and try to "get my students to love learning." On the door to his office he had the quote from Apple Computers' "Think Different" advertising campaign.[52]

My principal's approach reminded me of the methods of Robin Williams's character in *Dead Poets Society*[53], John Keating. Fittingly, he sent me to a seminar at the Westtown School, which is in the same league as St. Andrew's School, where *Dead Poets Society* was filmed. Although this movie gives viewers an entertaining escape into some compelling conflicts, it also made me want to be a teacher. I admired how Keating showed his students the importance of being creative, motivated them to pursue their dreams, and gave them confidence in their ideas. After seeing the movie, I hoped I could one day teach a class that would empower students, spark their intellectual curiosity, and cultivate a spirit of creative thinking, teamwork, and respect.

Organic Creativity in Academic Domains

Similarly, seeing *Ferris Bueller's Day Off*[54] caused me to gravitate to the world of education. Several of writer and director John Hughes's films, like *The Breakfast Club* and *Sixteen Candles*, capture the angst felt by disenchanted teenagers in school; however, Ferris Bueller embodied the ultimate fantasy of many young people in America. When I first saw *Ferris Bueller's Day Off* as a 12-year-old, I laughed at the funny lines, rooted for Ferris to outsmart his principal, and lived vicariously through his pranks and misadventures. Seeing the movie later in life, I realized that I wanted to teach a class that students would look forward to attending. I thought school should be a place where you bolster students' academic skills and help them grow as human beings, but also show them that learning can be fun.

In addition to being creative, one of the best attributes of John Keating, Ferris Bueller, and my favorite teachers is their ability to make people laugh. Comedians are inherently creative because they transmit unique ideas that surprise listeners, and their self-deprecating humor can make people comfortable. Class comics are valuable in that they keep their peers engaged and can provide teachers with a foil.

During our annual Curriculum Night, I try to incorporate humor into the presentation to give my students' parents a sense of what my class is like. For example, sometimes I give them current events challenge questions and they win bills from our classroom currency for answering questions correctly. One question was: "According to a study by psychologists, do our memories get more or less positive over time?" After a parent correctly answered that our memories get more positive over time, I said, "Hopefully your son or daughter will really like my class. But even if they don't, in 10 years they'll love the class."

Furthermore, I've done an activity called Celebrity Conventions in which students portray historical figures. Sometimes two students portray the same historical figure as part of a "Celebrity Duel" and then the class decides who was the "real" person. I once had two students portray Charles Lindbergh and after the second one spoke, their classmate asked, "If you're really Charles Lindbergh, how come you didn't mention that your baby was kidnapped?" Rather than acknowledging the oversight, the student portraying Lindbergh looked down and said, "It's just too painful for me to talk about that."[55]

Many of my students have entertained their classmates with their comedic abilities. In our activity called "Musical Acts With Newsical Facts," two boys did a parody of Michael Jackson's "Thriller" that was called "Slater." It was about Samuel Slater's contributions to industrialization in America. Another one of my students wrote and recorded a song called "I'm Dreaming of an Industrial Revolution" that was sung to the tune of Bing Crosby's "I'm Dreaming of a White Christmas."

Ultimately, my students, favorite movies, and best teachers helped me realize that comedy, laughter, and having fun are important ingredients in the development of a creative atmosphere that's conducive to learning. I've coached varsity basketball and baseball, and I once attended a coach's clinic at Harvard that was run by head basketball coach Tommy Amaker. His guest speaker was Larry Brown, who's the only coach to ever win both an NCAA championship (with the Kansas Jayhawks in 1988) and an NBA title (with the Detroit Pistons in 2004). Coach Brown said he writes the following words on the board before games: "play hard, play together, play smart, have fun . . ."[56]

Two teachers I had in high school, Mrs. A-B and Bill Schechter, transmitted these values every day and they inspired me to be a creative teacher. Florence Aldrich-Bennett (Mrs. A-B) was my third-grade teacher and some of the innovative activities we did in her class have shaped the way I teach. For example, a fantasy world of trading goods that we created in Mrs. A-B's class sparked the idea for the simulation of the American colonies in which students earn "money" from King Pepper, pay taxes, create laws, and bid on prizes in an auction. Mrs. A-B also had profiles of different monsters on the walls of her classroom, and we got to make up stories about these creatures. Mrs. A-B's classroom was a forest of creativity (which was actually filled with hanging and potted plants).

Bill Schechter was my high school teacher who taught a class about post-WWII America and the originality of his teaching style rubbed off on me. In Bill's class, the creative activities involved: (a) practicing stream of consciousness writing like the Beats; (b) building a cabin like the one Thoreau built in Walden Woods; (c) painting murals of scenes from *The Catcher in the Rye*; (d) practicing Cold War era bombing drills by sitting under our desks during some of our classes; (e) taking part in a mock hearing that was like the McCarthy hearings; (f) simulating a Civil Rights protest march after the Rodney King ordeal; (g) studying rock and roll, Chuck Berry, and Elvis, and analyzing the politicized music of Bob Dylan; and (h) writing a paper about the Harvard Strikes.

In the spirit of Bill's class, I incorporate experiential learning exercises into my curriculum and try to bring history to life by bringing in guest speakers. The list of people I've invited to speak includes: (a) Ruby Bridges' first-grade teacher; (b) a student's dad who is a veteran of the Vietnam War; (c) a student's grandfather who helped release concentration camp inmates during

Organic Creativity in Academic Domains

WWII; (d) a Holocaust survivor; (e) a Civil War expert who portrayed an officer; (f) a friend who directed an award-winning documentary about the Palestinian-Israeli conflict; (g) a friend from Nigeria who offered the African perspective on the slave trade; (h) a college professor who's an inventor; (i) a soldier who served in Afghanistan; and (j) a three-time world Irish step-dancing champion who overcame learning differences. We've also used Skype to talk with my student who was traveling in India and to learn about the North Korea conflict from my friend who lives in South Korea.

Incredibly, 15 years after I was in his class, Bill recently talked to my five classes about the impact that activists from the 1960s have had on American culture. He led my students in a "No sitting in rows" movement and helped them analyze songs like "For What It's Worth" by Buffalo Springfield. Bill would be proud to know that the desks in my classroom are now arranged in inside and outside layers of rectangular shaped horseshoes so students can see their peers and me.

The couches that Bill had in his history lounge at Lincoln-Sudbury inspired me to let one star student each week sit on a couch in my classroom at the private school I taught at after college. The principal helped me lug a light green couch (that was donated by a parent) from a high-rise building into my classroom and the students were motivated to win the honor of sitting on the couch for a week. I don't have a couch in my public school classroom, but my students earn the privilege of sitting in an ultra-comfortable luxury chair.

Although they're not physically in my classroom, there are other people, like educator Erin Gruwell, who are there in spirit because they've influenced the way I teach social studies. A family friend gave me tickets to the premiere of the movie *Freedom Writers*[57] in which Hilary Swank plays Gruwell. The film is about Gruwell's ability to motivate her students by thinking outside of the box. Gruwell connects the topics she teaches to her students' lives and she eventually publishes a book of her students' writing called *The Freedom Writers Diary*.

While watching the movie I realized that, like Gruwell, I'd developed creative lessons and resources that could help teachers and students. Fittingly, Gruwell wrote one of the endorsements that appears on the back of my book *Creative Adventures in Social Studies: Engaging Activities & Essential Questions to Inspire Students*. When I started teaching, I kept looking for a book that had a year's worth of meaningful and creative social studies activities that I could incorporate into my curriculum. In the end, I decided to write the book I was looking for that would help teachers make learning exciting by connecting history, American culture, human behavior, and current events to students' lives.

At the same time, my parents have had a positive impact on the way I work with adolescents. My dad is a doctor and my mom is a pediatrician turned animal rights activist, but they're also teachers who made interactive and experiential learning a big part of my upbringing. My dad would take my brother and me for walks on the Freedom Trail and to the Peabody Museum, where he'd challenge us to see who could find certain types of sharks or apes the fastest. Similarly, my mom brought us to every farm and zoo in New England and we grew up on a pseudo farm with horses, geese, and dogs.

At our house in Sudbury, Mom even made our family holidays interactive. At Thanksgiving we'd say "We're Thankful For . . . " poems for everyone at the table, and we'd wear pilgrim hats and bonnets and Native American headdresses that we made out of construction paper. After dinner, my brother and I would grab a dictionary and lead everyone in a game of Fictionary, which is like Balderdash.

As a teacher, I sometimes do an activity at the beginning of units that's similar to Fictionary. I have students get in groups and write down definitions for historical figures they've never heard of, like Sybil Ludington, James Armistead, and Deborah Samson. I'll mix in their definitions with the real one, read them out loud, and students will try to guess the real definition and try to get their classmates to guess their fake definition as correct.

In addition, the way I design my curriculum has been influenced by my poet grandmother; my family friends who are educators, like Monica Steinberg and Eric Gruenstein; the administrators in the district where I work; and my colleagues. They have all played an important role in fostering my creativity.

My 6 C's for Social Studies Philosophy

Based on my experiences, the six most important ingredients for engaging students in social studies are creativity, competition, comedy, camaraderie, connections, and chinos. The lessons in my class are intended to create an atmosphere in which students:

1. are imaginative;
2. take part in benign competitions;
3. feed off of everyone's use of humor;
4. display teamwork;

5. feel connected with their teacher; and

6. try to win chinos, which is the name for our classroom "money"/ currency.

Here's a brief explanation of these elements.

♣ *Creativity.* Most of my lessons, activities, and assignments are designed to give students an opportunity to be imaginative, make interesting connections, and create something that they can be proud of producing.

♣ *Competition.* Many of my activities give students an incentive to do their best work. For example, the students form groups/colonies and earn "money" by correctly answering current events challenge questions or winning review games. We also form teams for debates about controversial issues, and I give students prizes for the most creative and practical entries in our invention contest.

♣ *Comedy.* Giving students opportunities to display their sense of humor and laugh helps create an environment that is conducive to learning.

♣ *Camaraderie.* Students are often motivated to do their best work when they're working in teams because they don't want to let their teammates down. Students also enjoy group projects because they can interact with their peers, trade ideas, and collaborate with their classmates in order to present their skits, films, PowerPoints, artwork, or models.

♣ *Connections.* One way to help students feel connected is to simply enjoy teaching the class that they're attending. By being enthusiastic about their participation, you can draw them out and encourage them to be an active participant.

Another way to connect with students is to talk with them about a topic they're interested in that's not directly related to academics. For example, my family had four horses as a kid in Sudbury, so I can bond with students who are into horseback riding. I also can connect with students who play sports because in high school I played varsity basketball and was an all-state tennis captain, and at Harvard, I broadcasted football and played JV baseball. Furthermore, I try to use sports analogies when I teach. I mention that the Patriots had home field advantage over the British, and I say that just as a hockey player's check on an opponent can stop his forward progress, the branches of government have checks and balances that keep one branch from becoming too powerful.

Although I'm not a fashion guru, I recently bonded with some of the girls in my class who love shopping. My dad and I used to give each other the initials of baseball players and then try to guess the player on our car rides into Fenway Park to watch Red Sox games. So I used this game with the girls by coming up with the initials of famous designers. CK was Calvin Klein, VW was Vera Wang, and RL was Ralph Lauren. I stumped them with TB, which was Tommy Bahama.

❧ *Chinos.* This is the name for the bills that are part of our class currency when the students are in colonies. In our colonization unit, students meet King Pepper after they create brochures about their fictional colonies. The king gives them a charter and then they earn chinos (i.e., "money") for answering questions correctly and doing good work with their teammates. The king also makes new laws that mirror the Proclamation of 1763, the Stamp Act, the Tea Act, etc.[58]

In our chino reward system, students can get taxed for not having their homework or breaking a "law," but they win chinos if they bring in current events questions, e-mail me an article that we use for a debate, or are one of the winners in our Halloween costume photo contest.

We have a scoreboard that shows the number of chinos each "colony" has and the groups eventually use their chinos to bid on prizes in an auction (or they use their chinos to win prizes through a lottery). In the end, the colonies rebel against King Pepper, form a class country, and compete against the other social studies blocks/countries.

Examples of Creative Activities

I try to develop exercises that incorporate the 6 C's, enhance my students' intellectual curiosity, and improve their analytical and creative thinking skills. My favorite activity name is "Musical Acts With Newsical Facts." For this assignment, students select an existing song that has rhyming lyrics and they write an original song that incorporates current events or history facts. Then, they record their song or make a music video and play it for their classmates.

Other activities involving music keep students engaged and interested in what we're studying. For instance, we've explored how Civil War music reflected American society and military practices in the 1860s, and we've examined how "Yankee Doodle" was originally sung by the British to mock the colonists' style and uniforms, but the Patriots ended up singing the song to mock the British.

In general, students like activities that enable them to see social transformations. We do content analyses of advertisements and they examine how the portrayals of African Americans and women have changed. Another exercise involves looking at how comedy has evolved from the days of Charlie Chaplin to today. We do a content analysis of the laugh tracks and gender roles from clips of *I Love Lucy* and *Seinfeld* and students look at how comedy has changed on TV sitcoms. I also have an activity in which they interview their grandparents or other older relatives and ask them about the biggest social changes they've seen in their lifetime and the positive and negative aspects of these developments.

One of the most practical activities is the one called "College Admissions Interview" or "Job Interview for Historical Figures." Students create a mock interview write-up or mock resume for a prominent person and then they act out the interview in front of their classmates. Students learn about the college admissions process, acquire job interview skills, and examine the lives of historical characters. One pair of students had Dr. Phil interviewing Ben Franklin for a job, and Dr. Phil ended up helping Franklin with his family conflict that revolved around Franklin's daughter Sarah marrying a Loyalist.

Ultimately, students enjoy hands-on activities that involve simulations, role-plays, and live action. For example, during our industrialization unit, they like the paper airplane assembly line activity in which they get to work in assembly line teams, make paper airplanes, fly them, and discuss the benefits and drawbacks of mass production.

Students also like the interactive lessons in which they write political satire, have a political cartoon contest, build architecture replicas, study portraits, and have debates about controversial issues. In general, I strive to incorporate art into lessons because it's been proven to narrow the knowledge gap between students, and I try to integrate movement into my curriculum because it's been shown to improve the brain's ability to absorb new information.[59]

At the same time, students enjoy activities that are connected to their life and interests. Our assignment called "You're the Hero" involves students picking a current or historical event, writing answers to questions about the event, and then creating a Photoshopped picture in which they're heroes who change the outcome of the event.

By incorporating pop culture, sports, and movement into lessons, I use things that students enjoy and are familiar with as a hook for getting them interested in social studies. For instance, we sometimes have a Home Run Derby or 3-Point Contest to review unit content. I'll put sticky notes on the floor, one student at a time will get out of his or her seat, and if he or she answers the given question correctly, he or she gets to try to throw an orange Nerf ball into the blue recycling bin that's on a desk at the front of the class-room. Above the bin, I draw a baseball field and a scoreboard.

In Four Corner Debates, I make a controversial statement about a topic and then students go to the corner that reflects their opinion on the issue: Strongly Agree, Agree, Disagree, or Strongly Disagree. We also do traditional debates in which the class is divided into two teams and students debate back and forth as if it's a ping-pong match. Sometimes we do Fish Bowl debates in which students get into two opposing teams of three students; I put two seats at the front of the class, and they tag the shoulder of their teammate who's sitting in the "hot seat" for the right to enter the one-on-one debate.

Some of our Four Corner Debate topics have included:

- Are modern superheroes good or bad role models for kids?
- Is it ethical to make and sell Ugg boots and NBA leather basketballs?
- Should males be allowed to play on girls' sports teams and should females be allowed to play on boys' sports teams?
- Should the toys in McDonald's Happy Meals be banned?
- Are Native American sports mascots racist?

The College Thesis Paper (or outline) is an independent project in which students learn research techniques, explore topics that interest them, and come up with a creative way to teach their classmates about their topic. The topics range from the meaning of dreams, to the violence and sexism in classic fairy tales, to the ways in which foods and holidays reflect different cultures.

Here are some more activities and assignments that have been effective (with explanations for each):

- *Personal Chronology With News Connections.* Students list the 10 biggest milestones of their life on one side of a piece of paper and then, without showing them their timeline, the student has a parent or guardian write down what he or she thinks are the 10 biggest milestones in their son or daughter's life. The student and their parent also try to remember any news stories that happened around the same time as the milestones. In class, we talk about why one history was written differently by two different people. Our discussion about values and biases is a good springboard for talking about historiography.

✣ *Looking at a Presidential Campaign as if It's a Reality TV Show.* Before we studied the presidential campaigns, I asked my students, "How many of you follow politics?" A couple of hands went up. Then, I asked them, "How many of you watch reality TV?" All of their hands went up. We decided to look at the presidential election as if it were a reality TV show and the winner earned the right to be the leader of the United States and live in the White House. One of my more creative students came up with a name for our show: *Keeping Up With the Kandidates.*

✣ *Fantasy Senate Races.* This is a political election version of a fantasy sports league.

✣ *Satirical Campaign Ads and Mock Debates.* Students created PowerPoint presentations and iMovie films in which they made satirical attack ads and mocked *Saturday Night Live* presidential debates.

✣ *Federal Government Budget vs. Your Personal Budget After Winning Prize Money.* We pretended that students won $1,000 and they created a pie chart to show how they were going to spend their money (e.g., on clothes, video games, sports games, food, movies, charities, a college fund, etc.). Next, students looked at the president's proposed budget and analyzed the benefits and costs of adhering to his proposals.

✣ *Create Your Own Current Events Assignment.* The group of students that creates the most creative current events assignment gets to have their classmates complete it while they have a night off from homework.

✣ *Political Cartoon Golf.* Students walk around the classroom with a scorecard/graphic organizer and they analyze the following elements of 18 political cartoons: exaggeration, ridicule, the cartoonist's opinion on the issue, and caption.

✣ *Gender Stereotypes in Ads That Target Children.* Students read an article about gender bias in ads that target kids and then they do a content analysis of ads that appear during children's television shows on PBS and Nickelodeon.

✣ *Environment and Architecture: Comparing the Anasazi Indian Cliff Dwellings and Frank Lloyd Wright's* Fallingwater. Students look at photographs of these two structures, examine how both homes are connected to their natural surroundings, and analyze the similarities and differences between the two creations.

❧ *Puritan Punishments and Enhanced Interrogation Techniques.* Students act out some of the Puritan punishments by wearing letters that represent crimes (e.g., "A" for adultery, "B" for blasphemy, "D" for public drunkenness, and "T" for thief). The class discusses how the nature of punishments has changed in America from Puritan times and students look at the differences between the effectiveness of public and private punishments. Eventually, we compare Puritan punishments to the CIA's use of enhanced interrogation techniques and they have a debate on whether these methods of "torture" should be used on suspected terrorists.

❧ *Joint Stock Company Simulation.* In this activity, blindfolded students try to get from England to the New World and groups of students "invest" in their classmates' voyages.

❧ *Overcoming Adversity in Early American History, Current Events, and Your Life.* This involves studying how the U.S. learned from the mistakes that were made under the Articles of Confederation and created a strong Constitution. Students write about how they've overcome obstacles and turned a negative into a positive, and they write a mock letter from a celebrity about how overcoming challenges made them stronger in the long run.

❧ *Debate about the 1st Amendment and Violent Video Games.* In preparing for the debate, students watch an episode of *The Simpsons* called "Marge vs. Itchy and Scratchy," they create a survey, and we stage a situation in which a student is kicked out of class for wearing a controversial "International Terrorist" T-shirt, which has a picture of George W. Bush. (This is based on a real situation in Michigan in which a student wore an identical shirt and was suspended, but had it overturned with the help of the ACLU.)

❧ *Then and Now Dialogue With Slang.* Students create a conversation between a 1920s figure and a modern celebrity.

Other activities we've done include:
❧ presidential candidate social networking profile;
❧ analysis of televised political debates;
❧ analyzing the extent to which Disney's *Pocahontas* is educational and fictional;

- ❧ real estate agent contest for the colonial regions;
- ❧ review game shows with lifelines in which students can call relatives, and vocabulary challenges, which are like a social studies version of *$25,000 Pyramid*;
- ❧ a famous painting of Washington Crossing the Delaware versus a modern painting that's more historically accurate;
- ❧ Bill of Rights skits (with awards for Best Actor, Best Actress, Best Supporting Actor and Actress, etc.);
- ❧ simulation of how a bill becomes a law;
- ❧ strict versus loose interpretations of the U.S. Constitution skits;
- ❧ invention contest;
- ❧ Bloomers versus Flappers debates;
- ❧ slave versus free states in Congress simulation;
- ❧ reading chapters of *The Cartoon History of the United States*;
- ❧ jazz discussion and Charleston dance moves;
- ❧ class propaganda posters (after learning about American and Nazi propaganda during WWII);
- ❧ baseball card archaeology dig; and
- ❧ writing relay with transitions.

Significance and Conclusion

Using creative approaches to teaching social studies has become even more important in recent years because of the school reform movement that's based on using standardized assessments to measure teachers' effectiveness and students' knowledge. Matt Damon made a powerful case for why it's dangerous for our government to use standardized tests to measure students' abilities and keep teachers accountable.[60]

Essentially, Damon said that we shouldn't apply business school principles to teaching and learning because the MBA-ification of schools is interfering with teachers' ability to inspire their students, help them discover their talents and interests, and let them showcase their creativity. By putting so much emphasis on standardized tests, we're losing sight of the importance of developing students' creative thinking skills, and we're killing students' intellectual curiosity and love of learning. We should develop students' academic skills, help them figure out what they're good at, and give them opportunities to be imaginative.

My favorite high school history teacher, Bill Schechter, one of my inspirations described above, called the school where President Obama's girls go and the school where Secretary of Education Arne Duncan's kids are enrolled. Bill asked them if they use students' standardized test scores to evaluate teachers, and both schools said that they don't believe in that kind of assessment and evaluation system. How ironic.

Although it's not part of the state standards, in the spirit of Bill's approach to education, I often incorporate clips of people who used their creativity to improve American society. For example, students can be inspired by seeing clips of Louis Armstrong, Ray Charles, Jim Henson, Maya Angelou, Rachel Carson, and Maya Lin.[61]

Sir Ken Robinson gave a poignant and humorous talk about how schools kill students' creativity.[62] His warning about what's happening to students' innate love of learning reminds me of what I've read about the McDonaldization of society.[63] Essentially, in our standards-based academic culture, promoting creativity and originality are secondary to churning out large quantities of students who perform well on identical tests. I agree with Robinson's assertion that, "Creativity is as important in education as literacy, and we should treat it with the same status."[64]

Ultimately, designing creative lessons is an important ingredient for making a social studies class engaging and interesting. Young people have a better chance of excelling in school when their teachers give them opportunities to be imaginative, infuse creativity into their classrooms, and make connections between history, current events, and students' lives.

Chapter 4

ONCE UPON A TIME, THERE WERE NO ACIDS

Teaching Science Intuitively and Learning Science Creatively

Keith S. Taber

The purpose of this chapter is to encourage teachers to adopt an approach to teaching science that values creativity, given that both scientific discovery and learning are intrinsically creative processes. The chapter draws upon my professional experience as it has shifted through a number of phases—from teaching science subjects in secondary schools and college; through working with graduates preparing to become teachers; to now supporting graduate students in education (often, but not always, teachers themselves) who are learning to undertake original research into teaching and learning. It also draws on my experience as a researcher interested in the learning of science.

Science as a teaching subject (or the sciences as teaching subjects, depending upon the level of the course) present some particular challenges to the teacher who wishes to teach creatively. To some extent, these challenges relate to common perceptions of science and science education, although in some teaching contexts there may be very real constraints imposed by curriculum requirements and assessment regimes. My intent in this chapter is not to undermine the importance of learning canonical knowledge in science lessons, but rather to make a case that imagination and creativity are inherently

Dr. Keith S. Taber is a former secondary school and further education college teacher of chemistry and physics, and was the Royal Society of Chemistry's Teacher Fellow in 2000–2001. He is Reader in Science Education, and Chair of the Science, Technology & Mathematics Education Academic Group in the Faculty of Education at the University of Cambridge, England, where he teaches educational research methods to graduate students. He is editor of the journal *Chemistry Education Research and Practice*. His research is primarily concerned with aspects of conceptual understanding and student learning in science. He has written a number of books and a good many articles and research papers on science education.

part of science and of learning, and so should be acknowledged and emphasized more in science teaching.

My argument is that science is inherently a creative activity, and any
science education that does not reflect that cannot be considered authentic,
as it will not provide learners with a valid image of what science is about. In
making this argument, it is important to acknowledge some of the common
perceptions of science as a subject, as these will need to be either challenged
or accommodated in developing a more creative approach to teaching and
learning science. These key common perceptions are:

- science is a difficult subject, only suitable for the most able;
- science is about facts—and teaching needs to transfer scientific
  knowledge to learners;
- in science, answers are right or wrong, and the important thing is to
  get the right answer.

In this chapter, I will suggest these myths are dangerous, as they misrep-
resent the nature of science.

Science for All

The first perception, that science is primarily for nerdy geeks who are the
only people clever enough to understand it, is actually an issue of policy, and
so depends on what we want science education to be about. It is certainly
true that in many countries, science curricula have traditionally tended to
be informed by top-down rather than bottom-up thinking. If we develop
science curriculum starting with the needs of those who will go on to be
professional scientists and asking what college education prepares them for
higher study, and then asking what high school education prepares them for
those college courses, and then asking . . . then inevitably the science courses
studied by everyone will be most suitable for a minority.

In the past, even on these terms (that is, if we did think we should plan
all science teaching primarily for the few who will become professional scientists!), we have often got things wrong by overemphasizing the "knowledge" that is needed by future scientists rather than focusing on the types of
thinking skills that are most useful for those going into science. That is, there
has been a tendency to think that schoolchildren need to know something
about all of the major areas of science—even if that has been at the cost of

producing a breadth that is not supported by any depth, or indeed any real understanding of how all of the different topics fit together.

In recent years, there has been a strong shift in thinking about the purposes of science education, to recognizing that what might be termed scientific literacy is an essential part of the education of any citizen in a technologically advanced society, and especially one that considers itself a democracy. Citizens need to be able to make informed decisions about their consumption choices, their civic roles, their judgments in supporting—or opposing—various pressure groups, policies, and political parties. They need to understand the advantages and risks of nuclear power; the level of consensus about, and the potential risks of, global warming; and indeed whether it is worth paying a premium for a shampoo that is claimed to be better for their hair because it contains various nutrients.

The kind of science education that best supports future citizens certainly would include basic knowledge of core scientific concepts and ideas. Equally important is critical thinking, and an appreciation of *the nature of* science. A major misconception of science is that it produces knowledge that is known to be correct because it has been tested and "proven." This is totally against the modern understanding of the nature of scientific knowledge—which is considered to be provisional, and *always open to further questioning if new evidence comes to light.*

The challenge for learners, and their teachers, is appreciating how science can produce knowledge that is not absolute, *but yet* is robust enough to inform decision making. This is crucial, because there are many areas of science where most scientists are very confident that current understanding—if perhaps not the final word—certainly does a good enough job to treat it for now *as if* it is certain knowledge. Yet there are many other areas—and these are often those that make headlines in popular media—where scientists have strong disagreements, with different groups making contrary claims, each claiming that their view is supported by the best available evidence. Understanding this apparent enigma is incredibly important if science education is to support future citizens as they make sense of public debate about environmental, energy, health, and other science-related policy issues.

The challenge for teachers here is underlined by a famous research study carried out by William Perry, who interviewed students at Harvard and Radcliffe Colleges about their conceptions of their studies.[65] A key feature of Perry's results was the long and difficult path to developing an understanding that although there may not be clear evidence to support a single perspective or opinion on some issue, this need not prevent us from adopting a stance *on a principled basis*, having evaluated the different alternatives.

In effect, students started college expecting there to be clear answers that their teachers would direct them to. When it transpired that academic life was not so simple (and teachers had the cheek to ask them to read diverse texts offering inconsistent views), the natural shift was toward relativism: a view that all possible positions are defendable and therefore there is no basis for choosing between them. So—to take a topical example—for a student at the relativist stage, if not *all* scientists can agree that human activity is causing climate change, then the best response is to adopt a view based on personal preference. Where there is no clear canonical view to adopt (the relativist will think), then my view should be considered just as valid as anyone else's (regardless of the evidence and arguments on which different views may be based)—because we are all entitled to our opinion. We are indeed all entitled to opinions, but that is not what is meant by scientific literacy, which involves being able to *entertain different views* (using our imagination!) and evaluating the basis on which each is proposed.

Teaching About Science as a Creative Activity

Key to addressing this challenge is for us to emphasize in our teaching how science is a creative human activity. Certainly science depends upon the careful collection of evidence in the laboratory and in the field, on the analysis of data (that may sometimes involve complex mathematics), and in drawing logical deductions from evidence. Yet, it is just as true that science depends on human creativity. All scientific discoveries are creations of the human mind. For what science does is take evidence (the hard facts) and fit it into patterns.

We might think that this means finding the patterns that are in nature (and that is how many scientists conceptualize their work), but in terms of cognitive processes, this means *inventing* patterns that can make sense of the data. Scientists *imagine* possibilities to best fit data, and then *invent* ways of testing those imaginary possibilities by doing further data collection.

The patterns scientists work with are of different types, but may generally be considered models. So scientists invent typologies (classification systems) such as Linnaeus's system for classifying livings things, or Mendeleev's periodic system of the elements. These inventions are creative acts of imagination, and these creative acts are absolutely essential to science. As models, they can be developed as new evidence comes to light, and as other new understandings are developed. There are now five kingdoms of living things (not just "plants" and "animals" as was taught when I was at school), as scientists have imagined new ways of thinking about the variety of living things. This is not because the natural world suddenly became more diverse during the 20th century, but rather new evidence supported new ways of imagining the possible patterns. The new ways of thinking only become adopted in science when they are seen to have greater value for explaining data, approaching problems, etc. by others in the scientific community.

Here's a little thought experiment for you to try out. If you asked your students *how scientists know* what an acid is, what do you imagine they would say? They probably think that acids have always existed in nature, and one day a scientist discovered them. However, that is not the whole story. For one thing, many acids that are known today never existed on Earth until chemists made them. Having decided what an acid was, they were able to imagine how they might synthesize even stronger ones—including "superacids" that are said to be billions of times stronger than normal acids! Moreover, chemists have changed their minds about what counts as an acid several times, not because they "got it wrong" before, but because they decided a new way of thinking about acids was *more useful* in doing chemistry. (That's a bit like you deciding to redefine your class without the stroppy students—or your students deciding to redefine the school day as finishing at noon—because it was more convenient.)

There are now a good many different forms of the periodic table that can be found in laboratories, textbooks, and on Internet sites. This is not because we are not sure which is "right," but because chemists have many different interests, and different forms of the table support different perspectives or research topics. There are many possible imaginings here, and a number of them have been found useful by different groups of chemists.

One further example, to ensure physics does not get left out, might be magnetic field lines. We are all familiar with diagrams of magnets surrounded by lines representing the magnetic field. We may even know (and teach) students some "facts" about these lines. We might know they go from north to south, that the density of lines drawn reflects field strength, and that they never cross each other. But do we stop to ask students how we know these lines exist? Or how we know they go from north to south and not the other way around?

The typical learner brought up on standard texts and teaching will likely tell us that a scientist must have proven the lines exist, and that experiments must show the lines go from North to South, because that is how science is commonly understood—as factual outcomes of empirical investigation. Yet *there are no* magnetic field lines around magnets (even though there are ingenious ways to use iron filings to "demonstrate" them!): They only exist in our imaginations.

Magnetic field lines go from North to South for the same reason that electric current goes from positive to negative in a circuit: because someone made up a convention. Generations of school children have asked in vain why we do not simply change the electric current convention now that we know that current is (nearly always) a flow of electrons moving from negative to positive. The logic of the question is that (a) scientists guessed, (b) they got it wrong, so (c) now they should correct the mistake. *Why teach that current flows from positive to negative if we know that it is really electrons going the other way?*

However, from the scientific perspective, there is nothing wrong with the convention, because science is about creating useful mental models of the world. The mental model of "conventional current" flowing one way around a circuit "works." It is a useful thinking tool that helps scientists make sense of circuits. If we think science is about providing an objective account of how the world really "is," then conventional current is an anachronism. But science can never provide an absolute account of things: rather it offers imaginative creations as thinking tools to help us find ways to *make sense of* nature, and, in those terms, conventional current has been a useful creation. Making sense is a creative process, using our imagination.

Michael Faraday, likewise, invented magnetic field lines to help him think about his experiments on magnets. He did not "discover" the lines, as they never existed before he thought of them. They proved to be very useful thinking tools, and now they are reproduced in textbooks and student notes the world over. As we have made up the lines, and the rules about them, we could choose to change the rules if we decide that would be helpful. So although magnetic field lines do not normally cross each other, in modeling the intense and violent magnetic activity on the sun, scientists think of the lines crossing, cutting, and reconnecting in the process of producing solar flares. To ask whether the lines *really* cross is like asking if Santa Claus *really* lives at the North Pole—the real question is whether it makes sense to think that lines might cross in certain physical scenarios.

The challenge here for the teacher is to shift the emphasis from science as finding out how the world is to science as the process of constructing models to help us make sense of, and think about, aspects of the natural world.

That is the shift that occurred among academics in understanding the nature of science in the 20th century, and teaching according to the same vision opens up possibilities for teaching science more creatively. Yes, it is important that students know about and understand some of the important models and theories developed in science, but if we see them as creative products of human imagination, then there is plenty of scope to look at how those ideas originated, how they have developed, and how we might even look to modify them for our own purposes—to find ways to put learners in the position of creative scientists, as imaginers of possibilities, as well as testers of whether those possibilities can do useful mental work for us.

Learning Science as an Inherently Creative Process

My second dangerous myth about science education was that "science is about facts—and teaching needs to transfer scientific knowledge to learners." I hope readers will accept my argument that science is not primarily about facts. I am not suggesting that "facts" are unimportant, as they do have an important role to play, and there are certainly lots of them that we might consider in science classes: the melting temperature of tin, the crystal structure of a diamond, the list of essential amino acids, the strength of the Earth's gravitational field at the orbit of a geosynchronous satellite, the distance to Alpha Centauri, etc. However, none of these facts are scientifically interesting or important outside of a conceptual framework—a way of thinking about a topic constructed through human imagination—that gives them meaning and allows them to be used in explanations or technological applications.

My reference to "transferring knowledge" in the myth is a deliberate curveball, because although we commonly talk of teaching as transferring knowledge, we know that "transfer" is the wrong metaphor, as nothing is "transferred" from one place to another. Indeed, even if we adopt a metaphor such as "replicated" or "copied" (as surely "faxing" is a better metaphor for a naïve notion of teaching: making a distal copy of our original knowledge) then we fail to acknowledge what we understand about learning and cognition. Learning, especially learning of concepts and complex ideas, is a process of *constructing an understanding*, of *making* sense of what we see and read and are told.

Sometimes learning seems straightforward. This is most often the case when what is to be learned is simple, and the learner already has in place the interpretive resources to make sense of teaching in much the way intended.

So if the teacher is talking about an example of oxidation, and the learner already has a mental model of the topic of oxidation that is pretty close to what the teacher is assuming, then there is a good chance that the learner (provided she is paying attention and is motivated to learn and can hear clearly, etc.) will construct a meaning of the example that pretty well matches what was intended.

However, we know that often this is not what happens. Students may lack the necessary interpretive resources or simply misidentify which prior learning they are meant to bring to bear, and often a learner's intuitive understanding of the topic is actually at odds with canonical knowledge. This issue has probably been the subject of more research in science education than anything else, as so often teaching does not go wrong simply because learners fail to learn, but rather they acquire their own alternative conceptions that do not quite match what was intended! Indeed there is a massive literature reporting the alternative understandings of science topics that learners have been found to hold, both before and after formal teaching.

This catalogue of misconceptions is clearly seen as a problem in teaching the accepted models and concepts of science. However, it is also a reminder of how every act of learning is a creative process. Every student who has to make sense of teaching about evolution or acids or magnetic fields is using the same kinds of cognitive processes as the scientists who first imagined the same ideas: just like those scientists, the learners are constructing new (for them) ways of imagining and making sense of the information available. Whereas the original scientists were often making sense of laboratory or field data, the classroom learner is often relying more on the information from teacher and textbook or website, but in essence he is involved in the same kind of "making sense" process.

This leads us to ask if it really matters if the sense made by our students is somewhat at odds with the sense offered by the currently accepted theories of science. I wonder what readers think, having read this far, and what you expect my answer to be.

Is Science About Getting The Right Answers?

My third myth about science education was that "in science, answers are right or wrong, and the important thing is to get the right answer." Of course, there are right and wrong answers, and—all other things being equal—right answers are better than wrong ones. But there are assumptions here about what we want to assess. We do want students to know certain things; for example, it is useful to know that water has the formula H_2O. But much knowledge of this kind can be acquired incidentally while teaching more conceptual material, and as there are an enormous number of such facts that might be useful, it is usually more important that students know where to find out such information from reliable sources. It would be more import-ant that students could explain what is meant by H_2O, and how it links to the particle model of matter and the key chemical concepts of "substance," "element," and "compound." Even in this example, it may be reassuring if a learner could select an appropriate verbal definition of an element in an objective test, but this may not reflect deep understanding.

A student could recognize a statement that an element is, say, "the sim-plest kind of substance that can be formed by chemical means" without hav-ing developed a meaning for such a statement reflecting its significance for chemistry. Arguably, we should be more impressed by the student who can devise a role-play, or develop a graphical representation, or construct a narra-tive, or build a model that shows some understanding of the concept of ele-ment, than the student who can select or even regurgitate a formal definition. We should be more impressed both because this indicates and gives us insight into the learner's own understanding, and because in the act of constructing some kind of representation of their understanding, the learners are involved in an activity parallel to that of the scientists who developed our canonical understanding of the concepts.

Now, "element" might be a challenging example to start with this kind of work, but the same principle applies across most of science. If we want students to appreciate the components and structure of a cell, then why not have them build a model? If we want to see if students have made appropri-ate sense of the idea of a "couple" in mechanics, then set them the task of working in groups to devise a set of representations of forces some of which are, and some of which are not, couples. Then groups swap examples and see if they can identify examples and nonexamples from the different stu-dent-devised representations. This involves dialogue in working with peers (and so having to explain ideas, and consider those of others), formation of new forms of symbolic representation, interpretation of the formalisms of others, and application of a concept to novel examples.

We might provide a formal definition as part of setting up this process—a couple is comprised of two antiparallel forces that are equal in magnitude and do not act along the same line of action, say—and *perhaps* students will come away from the activity remembering the definition. If so, it is unlikely to be just rote learning, as they have worked with the definition and applied it both in devising original representations, and in interpreting the representations of others. Something that could be quite "cold" and "dry" has become something that can be engaging and even fun.

Teaching as Building Bespoke Bridges

Some students, perhaps those who would sometimes be labeled as nerds or geeks, might be very happy to learn a formal definition of a couple, but this is the kind of task that many students might think difficult, and even boring. Yet the kind of activity described here shifts the focus from the abstract concept to the construction of something more substantive in the form of a set of diagrams and provides a challenge that allows learners to explore the idea and come to make sense of it (while working cooperatively in a team). This type of activity also highlights how teaching, just like scientific discovery, and learning itself, is very much a creative process.

Most teachers have more limited subject knowledge than the writers of the best textbooks, and we know that subject knowledge is important to good teaching. We also know that teachers make mistakes or are sometimes not as clear as they intend to be. So we might wonder why we bother with the expense of teachers when good textbooks probably offer better scientific accuracy and should contain carefully thought-out, checked, and rechecked presentations of the material. A cynic might argue the teacher's job should be to assign the reading and exercises from the textbook, and to monitor the students and ensure they remain on task. That may be how some teachers work, but that is not likely to be considered good teaching by those choosing to read this book. Teaching is an interactive process that involves moderating between curriculum and learners.

Part of the teacher's job is to understand the science at least at the level that is being taught (and hopefully somewhat beyond). But, just as important, the teacher's job is to know the learners, and to try and help find a route to progress from current knowledge and understanding (which may often be flawed and idiosyncratic) toward the target knowledge set out in the curriculum. This involves the teacher being able to examine how things appear from where the learner is, and to find ways to bridge between current knowledge and target knowledge. In other words, the teacher's job is to make the unfamiliar ideas of science become familiar for the learners: that is, presenting the science in ways that can be interpreted by students in terms of what they already know and think.

Teachers have various tactics they use, involving the use of words, diagrams, gestures, demonstration, models, and so forth. But the key strategies involve modeling processes: forming models of the curriculum knowledge that are more accessible to learners than the target knowledge itself. One of these strategies is simplification. This involves stripping away what can be considered as nonessential complications to reveal the essence of an idea. It may well be that some of what is stripped away is important, and needs to be reintroduced later, so decisions need to be made about what is essential, and what can be put to one side *for now* without undermining the core ideas. This requires judgments—and sometimes quite nuanced judgments—and the ability to imagine what the *essential* aspects of a complex idea might be understood to be.

The second major tactic involves developing metaphors, similes, and analogies between the target knowledge and what is already familiar to learners. These devices are also types of models, and as models, they are limited representations of what we are asked to teach, but often they provide suitable starting points for linking up with students' existing experiences and ideas, and so provide a base for building new knowledge. The atom is (in some ways) like a tiny solar system; the nucleus is (in some ways) like the control center of the cell; an electric current in a circuit is (in some ways) like a continuous loop of rope being pulled as it is loosely gripped by a ring of students. There are many popular, even standard, examples that teachers can learn—but the teacher's real expertise comes to the fore when these are not working, when the students are still not getting it. This is when the teacher digs deep and tries out new comparisons, tentatively at first, and then following through on those that students respond to because they are making sense to them.

Teaching as On-Line Problem Solving

This suggests that teachers are able to offer something textbooks cannot: flexibility in interaction. The textbook writer uses simplifications and analogies, designed to suit the grade level of the reader, but every student is unique, with his or her ways of understanding topics, and his or her own wealth of personal experience upon which to ground scientific knowledge. The teacher develops a dialogue, exploring student thinking and finding points where it might be possible to anchor new knowledge. Doing this well requires expertise that derives from knowledge of the subject matter, preparation in the pedagogy, and a good deal of insight into learners and their ways of thinking. Part of that insight comes from interacting with the current class, but experienced teachers are informed by past experiences of working with the ideas of many other students before. Good teaching is highly creative, as the teacher works in real time to create bridges from where the learner's thinking currently is, to where the curriculum suggests his or her thinking needs to go.

Although we can plan a lesson in general terms, it is only when we get in the context of the classroom that we find where we have to start modifying and augmenting our presentation as it becomes clear which students are not following ideas—and we start exploring how to help make the unfamiliar familiar for them. Given the size of classes, and the diversity of levels of understanding, and the unique set of interpretive resources brought by each and every learner, it is not surprising that this is challenging work. If anything, it is a mystery how we manage to do such a decent job as often as we do! The teacher's craft relies on myriad small decisions made during the class in response to the clues and cues we are able to abstract from often noisy, busy classrooms.

If as teachers we were to be asked to explain in detail how we make those decisions—why we decided to ask Julie that critical question, why we suggested that particular comparison to Ahmed, why we thought that odd gesture might convey something useful to Susie—then it is quite likely that a lot of the time we might simply feel we relied on inspired guesswork, and in a sense this is probably so. A large part of expertise depends upon tacit knowledge, things we have learned at an implicit level of our cognitive systems (our preconscious thinking), of which we are not directly aware, yet which we can apply in making decisions and solving problems: the teacher's intuition.

There is nothing mystical about such intuition. Indeed the chemist-philosopher Michael Polanyi described the importance of such tacit knowledge in scientific work.[66] Scientists often rely upon this kind of intuition or tacit knowledge in their work in science, and it no doubt operates in all areas of expertise. Scientists and teachers alike are only explicitly aware of some their knowledge, and often have to trust and follow their intuitions because they cannot rely on using logic when they are not actually aware of the basis for their judgments. Scientists are expected to offer justifications for their conclusions and to go back and test their intuitions and present evidence to make a strong case for their claims. The final results often look tidy and logical, but the starting point is often intuition and expert judgment that is better characterized as inspired guesswork than cold logic.

Go, Teach Science Creatively

Science then is an inherently creative activity that relies upon scientists developing levels of expertise, aspects of which can only ever be accessed through their intuitions. Formal reports of science focus on the logical justification of ideas in terms of hard evidence, but usually such tidy accounts are only possible after a great deal of work that started with imaginative guesses and creative hunches. An authentic science education should emphasize that what science produces is theoretical knowledge: conceptual frameworks, models, typologies, explanations, and so forth. All are initially the products of human imagination, which are then selected according to how well they help us think about the actual evidence available.

Authentic science education should give learners the opportunities to develop their own ideas, and test them against data of various kinds. If learners explore their ideas in dialogue with others and try to represent them in models, and similes, and new forms of representation, then they are acting like scientists. This is true even if they are wrong: and indeed one of the most influential philosophers of science (Karl Popper) suggested that the crux of scientific activity was not being right, but setting out your ideas in such a way that they could be tested and shown to be inadequate.[67] Odd as it seems, having an idea you can then demonstrate as wrong can be seen as very good science!

Good science teachers are inherently creative: We draw upon our experience in the classroom to be sensitive to clues about when we need to change tack, simplify more, offer a new analogy, take on and develop an initially incongruous simile suggested by a student, and even when it is best to admit defeat for now, and return to a problem afresh on another occasion. What we are often not so good at is ensuring that students themselves appreciate the creative aspect of science. Yet science teaching that asks students to use their imaginations to make sense of new experiences or ideas, to find creative ways to represent and model their thinking, and then to explore the strengths and limitations of their creative ideas as part of a community of peers, is not only likely to be more engaging and accessible for most students, but also to actually offer a more authentic image of the creative processes so essential to science itself.

Further Reading

On Creativity in Science

Taber, K. S. (2011). The natures of scientific thinking: Creativity as the handmaiden to logic in the development of public and personal knowledge. In M. S. Khine (Ed.), *Advances in the nature of science research: Concepts and methodologies* (pp. 51–74). Dordrecht, The Netherlands: Springer.

On Teaching for Student Construction of Knowledge

Taber, K. S. (2011). Constructivism as educational theory: Contingency in learning, and optimally guided instruction. In J. Hassaskhah (Ed.), *Educational Theory* (pp. 39–61). New York, NY: Nova. Available at https://camtools.cam.ac.uk/wiki/eclipse/Constructivism.html.

On Students' Own Ideas About Science Topics

Examples of learners' own ideas and understandings in scientific topics can be found at: https://camtools.cam.ac.uk/wiki/eclipse/topics.html

On the Nature of Science

Chalmers, A. F. (1982). *What is this thing called science?* (2nd ed.). Milton Keynes, England: Open University Press.

Teaching About the Nature of Science

Some principles and activities for teaching academically talented senior secondary students about the nature of science can be found in:

Taber, K. S. (2007). *Enriching school science for the gifted learner*. London, England: Gatsby Science Enhancement Programme.

Chapter 5

BEGINNING WITH THE TOTALLY UNEXPECTED

Organic Creativity in Teaching Physics

Kristin MacDowell and Rodney Michael

Today's students bring with them fantastic access to information and a background rich in technology. Effectively teaching these students requires innovative methods and a willingness to encourage creativity in the classroom. Edward Redish commented that

> Physicists are consistently among the most creative and inventive of all scientists . . . But as teachers, we tend to be among the most conservative, repeating the content and methods that we had received as students from our teachers and that they received from theirs. For the coming generations of students, that's not going to be good enough.[68]

Great teachers have always used an element of creativity in the classroom. But with the information-rich environment of today's world, an interactive

---

Kristin MacDowell, M.Ed., currently teaches physics at Wadsworth High School in Wadsworth, OH, where she resides with her husband, Robert, and three children, Tyler, Keira, and Joseph. Earning both her undergraduate and master's degree from Ashland University, she completed her B.S. in comprehensive science for secondary education in 1999 and her master's degree in talent development education in 2010. In addition to the current physics assignment, Kristin has taught a variety of courses including chemistry, geology, applied science, honors physical science, and honors physics in her career.

Rodney Michael, Ph.D., is an associate professor of physics at Ashland University. He received his Ph.D. from Ohio University in medium energy nuclear physics. He has done research in the field of neutrino physics and held grants in the field of nuclear and particle astrophysics. Dr. Michael also spent more than a decade teaching in summer honors institutes for academically talented high school students and has worked on curriculum development for a local private independent middle school.

relationship between the teacher and student, which fosters creativity in both, is necessary for a quality education.

Traditionally, people report physics as their hardest course. Even though the field involves many abstract ideas and concepts, many of which may seem counterintuitive, the vast majority of students in an introductory physics class already have at their command the basic tools necessary for grasping the difficult concepts. We then must ask the question, "Is there a way to teach that will allow these students to enjoy the course and leave with a mastery of the basic tenets of physics?" The answer to this question has been the subject of much research and has led to many publications over the last 50 years.

The research shows that the teaching of physics has better results, both in understanding and retention, when the student is actively engaged in the process. The modern pedagogy in physics falls under two equivalent titles, interactive-engagement, and active learning. Hake gave 6,000 students pre- and postcourse exams utilizing both conceptual tests and mechanical baseline exams. Students who participated in an interactive-engagement course did two standard deviations better in the normalized gains over students taking a traditional lecture, laboratory, and textbook problems course.[69] Teachers and professors in the active learning classroom try to inspire students to develop their own questions, collect and analyze data, and form their own conclusions. This method depends on interaction with peers and instructors, instant feedback from observation, and significant opportunities to express their reasoning process via spoken, written, or experimental methods. There are as many ways to create an active learning classroom as there are teachers, and it is reasonable that the classroom may still involve many traditional elements. Courses being taught with an active learning pedagogy share most if not all of the following characteristics, according to Metzler and Thornton:

- ❧ Specific student ideas are elicited and addressed.
- ❧ Students are encouraged to "figure things out for themselves."
- ❧ Students engage in a variety of problem-solving activities during class time.
- ❧ Students express their reasoning explicitly.
- ❧ Students often work together in small groups.
- ❧ Students receive rapid feedback in the course of their investigative or problem-solving activity.
- ❧ Qualitative reasoning and conceptual thinking are emphasized.
- ❧ Problems are posed in a wide variety of contexts and representations.
- ❧ Instruction frequently incorporates use of actual physical systems in problem solving.[70]

Organic Creativity in Teaching Physics

Through trial and error, the authors have each developed a method of teaching that is a balance between the traditional classroom and an active learning classroom. The style of teaching required in the active classroom needs to be very fluid. The Socratic method is applied to help students find their own answers, and often students observe results, or have ideas that cause instructors to step back, do some problem solving of their own, and rethink their own understanding. It is a style of teaching that requires thinking on your feet, a bit of courage, and the patience to allow the students to question and explore. It is also a very gratifying and stimulating way to spend your time in the classroom. What follows are the personal stories of the authors and their creative endeavors of developing an active learning classroom.

Kristin MacDowell's Story

At 36 years old, with three children of my own, and in my 14th year of teaching high school physics, I am continually trying to think of innovative ways to encourage creativity in my classroom. As I have made my journey through undergraduate courses and graduate courses, and each year of classroom experience, I see the need for creativity in my classroom becoming increasingly important. I have always known that for me, personally, it is the best way to teach and have always believed it is the best way for students to learn. I am thankful to have had undergraduate and graduate professors who understood, encouraged, and validated these same ideas.

During my undergraduate studies, Dr. Rodney Michael encouraged us as students to create our own laboratory investigations on a certain topic or idea. After designing the lab procedure, we then had to design our own lab reports. It was also necessary for us to use our own visualization methods and intuition, especially when attempting to understand upper level physics. As I listened to lectures and tried to understand the concepts in quantum theory, Dr. Michael would often ask us to imagine or visualize the ideas presented. In all of my teaching courses, I needed to find exciting and interesting ways to present lessons. Ashland University professors, in general, were very encouraging in the area of developing creativity and finding their own unique ways of doing so.

When I began teaching at Wadsworth High School, I used original ideas for laboratory investigations, and I searched for unique and exciting demonstrations and labs that I often modified. The students then appreciated both the demonstrations and the labs, and students today still display enjoyment, learning, and creative growth as a result of the exposure and experience with these lessons. As a teacher, however, I have been questioned both directly and indirectly on the educational value of my lessons. Although I taught honors level courses, with many talented students, I was questioned by staff members, parents, administrators, and even some students. They expressed concern, dissatisfaction, or a general disapproval of my laboratory investigations. At a level where creativity should be explored and encouraged, the "fun" part of learning and exploring was misunderstood. The lessons had been viewed as meaningless activities that removed the expected rigor of an honors level course.

I learned in my master's level work that my lessons not only had educational value, but also were critically important to the development of talented students who intended to function and compete for careers on a global level. Piirto explained,

> The world needed a polio vaccine, a phonograph, a steam engine, a theory of evolution. The world needed geometry, calculus, quantum theory, and computers. The world needed space travel and will need time travel. Scientific creativity has invented these when they were needed.[71]

With the validity of my ideas on the importance of encouraging creativity in my lessons being confirmed through research and completion of a master's degree in talent development education, I have continued to use my lessons and to create more lessons that encourage creative thought. I now have the knowledge necessary to defend the importance and need for such lessons when I am questioned on their educational value.

Approaching the idea of encouraging creativity at the high school level for any subject area presents problems for any teacher today. In Ohio, we are currently aligning our curriculum with the Common Core State Standards. Because we are held accountable for covering these standards and ensuring that our students have mastered the associated concepts within the limited schedule of the school year, adding creativity into lessons may seem impossible at times. My approach is to encourage bits of creative thought, imagination, intuition, visualization, and imagery throughout the year as often as I can.

Organic Creativity in Academic Domains

I have had several years of experience teaching honors level physics and conceptual level physics courses, which I am currently teaching. The main difference between the two courses is the math content and difficulty. The honors physics course requires more calculations and mathematical analysis of content. In both courses, I have found it is necessary to implement activities in which creativity is encouraged. Without such activities, the honors level physics students tend to become overwhelmed with the math portion of the course and lose interest overall. The conceptual level students, most of whom struggle with the minimal math concepts in the course, look forward to the activities and ask frequently when the next one will be taking place. The products from these activities created by students from both levels of physics courses are equally impressive. Although I have experienced teaching more mathematically and scientifically talented students in the honors physics course, I have encountered several students with talents in the vocational-technical areas and artistic domain. In both physics courses, it is refreshing to see the students proudly display their abilities and apply their specific talents to products from our activities.

When studying concepts in physics, it is often necessary to use visualization and imagery. Although it would be a great experience to take students into a car or ride simulator and actually allow them the opportunity to feel the inertia of their bodies, it is not practical or affordable. Similarly, students could feel apparent weight loss or apparent weight gain if taken into a pool or quickly moving elevator, but time does not allow for such adventures. Placing force sensors on a dummy and simulating car crashes without a seatbelt or airbag, then with a seatbelt and/or airbag, would demonstrate several physics concepts. However, this again is not possible in most high schools.

For these examples, and many more, I ask the students to imagine how they would feel. I ask them to close their eyes and think about the situation, and then visualize what they would see, how they would move, and what they would feel. Although I give notes and lecture over these topics, and may show a few demonstrations, I find that the students gain a better understanding of the concepts from visualization and imagery. If the students are unable to do an experiment or demonstration that allows them to see, hear, or feel the properties of concepts being studied, their own imaginations can be used to aid in a clearer understanding.

Because I am a physics teacher, I encourage my students to use their intuition and creative thinking to design and build several devices throughout the year. Some examples of laboratory investigations in which students are required to perform these tasks include designing and building cars and ramps, projectile launchers, and Rube Goldberg devices from various junk found around the home. They also design and build egg drop devices using only a limited number of craft sticks and glue. One of the most popular projects is designing and building a house, car, boat, or other approved item and then having the students wire them with simple circuits to produce required lighting and rotation of an object. Throughout these experiments and projects, the students must use their intuition, visualization, imagery, and creative abilities to transform ideas into plans, then build actual devices using their plans. This process allows all students with talents in various areas to contribute to the project in different ways. The creative thought process is encouraged, exercised, and celebrated from beginning to end.

I intentionally plan these investigations so that the students will need to use either junk or limited supplies to build the items needed for data collection. Research has been done on products to be created and judged based on creativity.[72] This research has shown that people generate the most innovative solutions when both the objects they had to work with and the category of the product were selected randomly. By beginning with the totally unexpected, the participants in this research were forced to stretch their creativity to the highest degree. When requiring students to build a car designed to collect time and distance data in order to calculate speed and acceleration, I encourage students to look at things sitting around their homes and garages. Students become innovators and creators. Suddenly an old rolling chair becomes four wheels, and a soccer shoe becomes the body of a car. Old Barbie dolls become passengers, and old plywood or extra gutter pieces become ramps. The relatively useless junk they find is used to create the vehicle and ramp needed to collect their data.

Similarly, when the entire laboratory investigation and report is based on examining the functioning of each part of a Rube Goldberg device (many simple machines that work together in a complex manner to perform a simple task), then analyzing the overall successful or unsuccessful functioning of the device itself, students must use imagery, imagination, and often times, intuition in designing, building, and analyzing such a device. Imagery and imagination must be used by students when they are generating an idea for the main purpose of a Rube Goldberg device. After drafting an overall idea and plan, they must build the device. Oftentimes, one or several parts of the original plan do not function as the students had hoped, and they must be changed. At this point, both imagery and intuition play a major role. Some students will look at the partially completed device and use imagery or visualization to "see" how to fix the problem. As an observer, I can watch as these students think through their ideas and then proceed with whatever solution came to their minds. This is the problem-solving method I most often witness.

However, some students will act solely on instinct and use their intuition to begin fixing the problem. Usually, the other members of the group will complain or question the student who begins fixing impulsively without explanation. Adams explained this behavior in stating, "The intuitive person distrusts the facts if they conflict with intuition. The thinking person prefers to make decisions by logically extrapolating from data, whatever the source."[73] It is pleasing to see that oftentimes, despite questioning, the intuitive solution by the assumed impulsive student fixes the problem and allows the device to work properly. The nature of these projects encourages creativity for all group members.

Additionally, the projects allow all to participate and collaborate toward a common goal. Science classes, especially physics, can be challenging and frustrating for those who lack a more analytical thought process. In the investigations performed in my classroom, all students are able to contribute their ideas and talents. When students are building and wiring a car, boat, house, or other building, those who may not fully understand the wiring aspect are still critical in the design efforts. The placing of lighting and rotating objects is just as important as the actual connection of the wires in the functionality of the project. In this project, as well as all others, there is always room for students to add personal touches. For example, in a mini-mall designed by a group of four female students, four unique and personal ideas were connected within the project. A candy store from the sugar-loving student was connected to a dance studio designed by the dancer, a coffee house with wallpaper made of real coffee beans for the coffee drinker, and a sporting goods store created by the athletic girl. Not only is this fun for the students, but it also celebrates their individuality and unity as a group. All of these aspects encourage creativity in my students.

Not only do the projects encourage creativity, but also they allow for a break from intensive calculations or lectures, notes, and homework cycles that can become mundane and boring. For instance, when studying the concepts of momentum and impulse, the concept of impulse is completely foreign to most students. As a result, any associated concepts and calculations can be very difficult for students to manage. After a round of notes, lectures, and a homework assignment, we begin planning and building the associated "Egg Drop" laboratory investigation. This is a classic laboratory investigation of impulse-momentum theorem that has been done for years. I try to refresh it by creating a new set of rules for the kids to follow so that they must use original ideas. I only allow the students to use 150 craft sticks, 20 hot glue sticks, and hot glue guns. No glue may be attached to the egg itself, and there may be no other items used. As of right now, there are no "answers" online for the kids to find. They must come up with a way to save the egg using their supplies in a unique way to create flexibility or break-away systems.

A break from the pencil and paper part of the learning process can give a fresh perspective on the associated concepts. When we return to another homework/classroom assignment after one day of planning and one day of building, most often the students are refreshed and can focus on the concepts and calculations again. The students also tend to find a better understanding of concepts related to impulse-momentum theorem through the experience of building an egg drop device. This makes future assignments less complicated and aids in reinforcement of correct processes for calculations.

Many times students will utilize a break-away design with loosely connected craft sticks arranged in a random fashion with the egg positioned in the center of the configuration. The intention is that the outer sticks will break away, allowing more time for the egg to come to rest, thus reducing the force on it. A unique design used this year created a bottom heavy tunnel with break-away sticks inside, allowing the egg, which was cradled loosely inside the tunnel, to move downward through the break-away sticks as it landed. Another interesting design featured a nearly circular outer frame made solid and sturdy with multiple craft sticks and melted hot glue. On the inside of the frame, the egg was held in a craft stick cradle which was suspended by partially melted hot glue sticks attached to the outer frame. When it landed, the sturdy frame held its shape and the egg in its cradle safely bounced to rest due to the flexibility of the partially melted hot glue attachments.

Some of my favorite Rube Goldberg devices resulted in stapling papers, taking a picture, and filling a balloon with carbon dioxide from a chemical reaction. These all involve several steps, so I will not explain them fully, but I will comment on a portion of each. The paper stapling began with testing the safety shower in the room and filling a bucket on the end of a lever. Utilizing something in the room that itself was a lever system was quite unique. Taking a picture of the lab group that created the device at the end showed perfectly how the device, once started, could complete the function on its own and provided proof that the device did indeed work. Filling a balloon using a gas created during a chemical reaction is impressive in many aspects, and seeing it function perfectly was phenomenal. I enjoy all of the projects that my students create, but these were some of my favorites.

My sincere hope is that my physics class will be considered both fun and memorable and, more importantly, aid in the development of the creative nature of my students. By using imagery, visualization, imagination, intuition, and, in general, collaborative creativity, my students will be problem solvers and innovators. These are critical qualities in preparation for any career. Businesses all over the country are seeking innovative and creative minds. In STEM (science, technology, engineering, and mathematics) careers, innovation and problem solving are keys to success. Along with the formal education and career preparatory courses that my students will complete, they will have developed additional skills. No matter what career option my students choose, I know that the problem solving, innovative, and creative methods practiced in my classroom can give them the edge for attaining positions and excelling within those positions.

Rodney Michael's Story

I first stepped into a classroom as a graduate student almost 25 years ago. I was taught to teach physics in the traditional manner of lecture, recitation, cookbook laboratory, textbook problems, and written exams. Although I still utilize all of these resources, I have broadened my approach to include many inquiry- and activity-based projects. From a personal standpoint, I find the process of creative interaction in the classroom setting to be very stimulating and rewarding.

In physics education, when students get involved in independent research projects, they start to develop the ability to think and solve problems using the tools learned in class. I have also noticed that students who are involved in these projects tend to be more excited about what they are learning and enjoy the process because they have taken ownership of their education. I started wondering, *How can I bring that sense of discovery, excitement, and student ownership into the introductory classroom?*

I started the process slowly, by introducing an open-ended laboratory experiment into the first-year physics curriculum, one for each of the first two semesters. In these laboratories, I ask the students to identify a topic relating to class but which was not specifically covered in class or the book. The students then need to design a way to explore that topic, design an experiment, and collect and analyze the data. After a couple of years of finding the pitfalls and learning how the students can best be escorted through the process, this endeavor has developed into a favorite part of Introductory Physics, for both the students and myself. The project has been such a success that I have now given the entire second semester laboratory over to self-guided exploration.

Trying to carry the excitement of learning into the lecture hall for an introductory course is more of a challenge than it is for the laboratory. The typical introductory, calculus-based physics course at our small liberal arts university consists of chemistry, education, mathematics, biology, and physics majors. Each of these students needs to take away something different from the class. The mathematics and physics majors need a strong computational understanding, whereas the biology and education majors need a strong conceptual understanding. The problem for the professor is then to be creative in providing both the computational and conceptual foundations in the classroom.

Even though I still use traditional lecture, it seems like every year more and more time is given over to group activities and questions. I keep a small toy box on the windowsill of the classroom, filled with springs, masses, gyroscopes, tops, and other small toys. Lectures will often start with the observation of some phenomenon involving one or more of these toys. The traditional lecture is then mixed with asking and answering questions while explaining the computations for the observed phenomenon. When new methods of computation or new algorithms are introduced, the students will break into groups to work together on problems, which are often inspired by the students' questions. Because in some lectures the content can be driven as much by the student as by the professor, this method of teaching keeps me engaged while forcing me to be creative and think on my feet.

Much of the impetus for my moving away from more traditional methods of teaching physics came from my many years of experience teaching in a summer honors program. In this program, I worked with rising sophomores and juniors from high schools around Ohio, all of whom had been identified as academically talented. Coursework with the students included 3 hours in the morning, a break for lunch and study, and 2 more hours in the afternoon for 6 consecutive days. It quickly became evident to me that I could not expect a group of 14- and 15-year-old kids to be passive learners for those extensive periods of time. Everything I had done with my college classes up to that point had to go out the window.

Few of the students in the program had taken a physics course prior to attending, but most showed a deep curiosity and a greater enthusiasm for the subject than did my liberal arts core college students. The course offerings alternated between years and included quarks and leptons one summer followed by string theory the following session. All of the students were unfalteringly grateful for the opportunity of discussing the ideas presented in class with like-minded peers and their professor. Several of the students went on to study physics in college, and I know of two who have attained or are pursuing a Ph.D. in physics.

As it turned out, these high school students who came to learn about physical theories ended up teaching me how to be a better educator. I observed over the course of several years that the more freedom I gave them to explore the subject in their own way, the more they learned and retained. Two examples I would like to relate involve two best friends and an entire class.

One particular pair of young women bonded and became best friends for the next few years during the summer program. They would stop by and visit the honors program for several yeas after they were no longer able to participate in it. In one of the string theory classes I had, the students examined waves on strings. By posing a problem and allowing them to explore in the laboratory for answers, I had the students animated and engaged. Midway through the activity, one of the girls spotted a small laser in the cabinet and asked if it was possible to measure vibrations with the laser. So I pulled the laser down and told her to find out. These girls proceeded to spend every spare minute in the laboratory. They would eat their lunch in the laboratory, spend their study time there, and even spend their evenings working on their experiment. By the end of the week they had found a method for measuring the vibration of a string with a laser, and it was a method I would have never dreamt of.

Another year I had a particularly active class and trying to control the chaos of an open laboratory just became untenable. So I gave them a group project with the hopes that peer pressure would help keep them focused. The students needed to form what they learned in class into a performance. The project brought about the creation of Captain Physics. The group would refer to the reference book and look online for the details about fundamental particles and particle interactions. They worked hard to figure out how to convey the world of particle physics in a play that others could understand. Come the last night of the program, they had Captain Physics running around on stage guiding the gluons and helping hold the quarks together. As he built up the protons and neutrons, in came the electrons, and Captain Physics then helped the photons hold the nucleus and electrons together. By the end of the play, the group had built an atom, founded on solid scientific principles, made out of people and props. The kids had a blast and learned a great deal about the subatomic world in the process. Jane Piirto wrote a poem about that and also about the String Theory class.[74]

STRING THEORY

We thought we'd climb a tree
Because Newton is our god
And you know the story of the apple
And gravity.

String Theory and eleven dimensions.
the three of space and one of time of which we are aware.
What was the universe like
In the seconds after the Big Bang?
Try to comprehend the 4th dimension.

We blew up coke and Mentos

In the parking lot.
Our Big Bang.

The most creative teaching that I do is inspired by what I learned from the academically talented high school students in the honors program. I have taken the freeform activity-based learning that I used with the high school students, added a little college-level rigor, and developed a core course for nonscience majors called Origins of the Universe. It is a class on cosmology for students with no science or mathematics beyond the secondary level. When designing this course, I noted from my other core classes that science exams are a huge stress on nonscience majors. In my Astronomy and Science of Sound core classes, students would cram for the tests and then by the final they would have forgotten the material. With Origins of the Universe, I wanted to create a course that would leave students with a fascination for physics and a curiosity about what physics can tell them of the world. While designing the course, I came to the decision that there would be no exams or quizzes. I felt the topics alone were enough of a challenge without trying to memorize facts or figures, and I could find other methods for gauging student understanding.

I wanted to get across, as Gribbin said,

the beautiful simplicity of the quantum theory's explanation of atomic spectra, and . . . the revelation that the best things in science are both beautiful and simple, a fact that all too many teachers conceal from their students, by accident or design.[75]

In this course, I wanted to find a way to share Gribbin's "beautiful simplicity." I divided the course into four parts:

1. Einstein's special and general theories of relativity;
2. quantum mechanics;
3. particle physics; and
4. cosmology—where we apply the ideas and concepts of the first three parts to understand the Big Bang theory.

I found several books on the subjects suitable to a layperson's interest and developed a class around those books. Students are required to take notes and write down questions while they are reading the material assigned each week. Then every class starts in the same fashion. I ask the question, "What do you want to know?"

Students are eager to get answers to their questions and to express ideas they have formed and oftentimes state their disbelief. Depending on what questions are asked, each class is distinctly different. Some classes turn out to be students working in groups to answer each other's questions and to make proposals on what might be developing in the theory they are studying. Sometimes the entire class is a back and forth between the professor and the students, and oftentimes the class will move into the laboratory where students are led to answer their questions through observation and experiment. My personal favorites are the days when the class writes a science fiction story based on the scientific knowledge they have gained from the reading and discussions. They are then graded on how accurately the story uses the science and how creatively they illustrate the ideas contained in the theory.

It is easy to walk into a classroom and tell the students what you know, but it takes a lot of courage to walk into a classroom and to let the class be led by the students and to follow them as the professor. It requires a confidence in your understanding of the material and a certain willingness to grasp the material deeper than you may have in the past. In teaching this Origins course, I have gained a much greater depth of understanding of relativity and quantum mechanics by being willing to openly discuss the concepts and predictions in an open forum with nonscience students. I find this method of teaching to be incredibly gratifying and also find that the students respond very well to the course, and many continue exploring the world of modern physics as a hobby long after the class is over.

One question that is often asked about this kind of learning is, "How can you afford the loss of lecture time?" In my experience, students in many science courses will just read the chapter summaries and trust the professor to tell them in lecture what they need to know for a test. For an activity-based classroom, the students must be active participants. Just like in a philosophy or literature class, students need to read the chapter before class and come prepared to class. There are several ways to lead a class to this kind of study habit. In the introductory courses, I give random pop quizzes, which count for extra credit; in my core class, students hand in a set of questions based on the reading for that day. Once the students are coming to class prepared, the lecture is no longer needed to introduce material but can be used for clarification of concept and methods or enhancing the material in the chapter, examples, group problems, and experimentation. In other words, nonpassive engagement of the students.

As a departure from the traditional methods of teaching physics handed down from mentor to student for the last century, one needs to ask, "Does it work? Is the activity-based classroom giving the students a firm conceptual base and the quantitative prowess of the traditional classroom?" The research all says that activity-based learning is doing a better job. One study in particular performed at California Polytechnic State University shows significant improvement in both qualitative and quantitative understanding. Students were allowed to register for one of three studio classes or one of three recitation classes. The classes were taught by three professors, where each professor taught one recitation section and one studio section. Students in all of the courses showed similar scores on the pretests. All of the 225 students took the same traditional quantitative final, written by an outside professor. The students in the activity-based studio class scored better than the students in the traditional lecture at a 98% significance level.[76]

Involving a student in a creative and active environment forces the student to focus on the lesson being taught. How often does a teacher in the middle of lecture look out on a class and see half of the audience mentally absent, daydreaming about something else? An active classroom from the outside often seems like chaos, and in many cases is the loudest room in the building. If, however, you stop to listen to a well-run active classroom, and take the time to hear past the chaos, you will find students focusing on learning, enjoying the process, and developing critical thinking skills. This type of engagement has benefits over the rational passive classroom. Often missed is that this style of teaching has an added benefit; it keeps the teacher engaged also. It allows the teacher to apply his creativity on a daily basis and ensures that every time he walks into the classroom, it will be a new experience. Imagine that. Such methods are better for the student, better for the teacher, and better for student comprehension, all rolled into one.

Chapter 6

LET THE BEAUTY WE LOVE BE WHAT WE DO

Organic Creativity in Teaching World Languages

F. Christopher Reynolds

Bonjour. By the time you read this, I will have completed my 30th year as a French teacher at the middle school and high school levels. Although what follows is embedded into French classes, the teaching strategy below has worked in Spanish and German classes too. Because of that, I am confident that the practice below has a global application for world language classes. Joseph Campbell named the guiding mythology of our times the Creative Mythology. For him, the great gift of our Western culture was the value given to the sovereignty of individual hearts. Campbell felt that the roots of the Creative Mythology were in southern France in the 1200s when a culture of mutual respect between men and women, *la courtoisie*, became the guiding principle. At the heart of this tradition were the stories of the Holy Grail.[77]

Each seeker of the Grail entered the forest where it was darkest. Campbell noted that this meant that each of us has to find our own way into the mystery of the path of the heart. Intuition is the faithful guide to that path of the heart and devotion to our intuitive inner knowing makes a world of difference. Should we walk on someone else's path, we will fail to secure the treasure. In a high school French class, the darkest entry-points into the forest of the Grail adventure are where the room is frailest and most isolated. Those entry-

F. Christopher Reynolds, M.Ed., is a teacher, musician, and shaman. He teaches French and is world language co-chair at Berea-Midpark High School. He has won the Cleveland *Plain Dealer*'s Crystal Apple Award. He is an adjunct professor at Ashland University and Ursuline College. Christopher is a pipe-carrier who facilitates the Earth-based practices at Angel House in Strongsville, OH. He founded the Urrealist art movement. Topics of his published writings include depth psychology, giftedness, holistic education, and the psychology of shamanic awareness. His teaching, singing, and healing are dedicated to assisting in the transformation now occurring in Western culture. He is the proud father of Isaac and Ana. His website is http://www.urrealist.com.

points are within the students themselves. It is in their originality. Although what follows may seem like I am teaching art, music, poetry, and prose, my deeper intention is to leverage the students' creative self-expression, or—in Aristotle's term—*poesis,* in order to give them a template as to how to respond to the creativity around them for the rest of their lives. Knowing a courteous response to originality gives students the chance to experience and to witness each other in a learning community that nurtures the greatest resource in life—their creative and receptive capacities.

Creativity in the High School World Language Class

A student sits in front of the French 4/5 class. He's singing a song that he's written in French:

Chante du coeur de la nature
Qui nous réveille des rêves
Sent nos coeurs qui bat si purs
Ta vision s'achève . . .

When he finishes, the teacher asks: *Qui pourrait repondre à la chanson que David a écrite?* (Who can feed David back?)

Student 1: *Pendant qu'il chantait, je me sentais la frisson sur mes epaules.* (While he was singing, I felt the chills over my shoulders.)
Student 2: *J'ai aimé comment sa voix et j'ai vu dans mon esprit un image d'une plage.* (I liked his voice and I saw an image of a beach in my mind.)
Student 3: *La poésie de ses paroles était bonne.* (The poetry of his lyrics was good.)
Student 4: *Sa chanson m'a fait penser au chanteur, Iron and Wine.* (His song reminded me of the singer Iron and Wine.)
Student 5: *Pour moi, sa chanson ressemblait à une chanson de Françis Cabrel.* (For me, his song sounded like a Francis Cabrel song.)
Student 6: *Je veux essayer de jouer du piano avec le refrain.* (I want to try to play piano with the refrain.)

In the above vignette, the students were engaged in *feeding back.*[78] It took them 3 years to reach that level of interaction. In the previous years, the students were taught to feed back, first in English, next using a blend of English and French, and then full-on immersion. When I write of developing creativity specific to a French classroom, there are three capacities. There is a first capacity to create music, art, poetry, prose, and international relationships using French, as in David's original song. There is a second capacity to personally respond in French to the creativity of another person, as in how the students here responded. Finally, there is a third capacity. It expands beyond cultural creative forms into the engendering of authentic future lives in which the French language and culture play an enriching role. The most important moment to begin the journey is during the first year, using English, when the first original work enters the classroom.

The Teachable Moment

Each year, with groups of students who are new to me, there comes the teachable moment of the first original drawing, poem, or song (written in English). Every group has its own manner of timing, so this moment is not to be forced. Yet, one day, it appears. At that moment, I teach about feeding back. There are three layers of awareness, scholarship, and strategy that inform this way of original response to creativity in a French class. You could imagine the classroom space as multilayered, like a Russian nesting doll each inside the next. The outermost layer is the teacher worldview. The middle layer is the psychology and the innermost layer is the teacher strategy in the day-in, day-out direct student contact. The middle, psychological layer offers the easiest entry into our subject.

I am first a high school French teacher, and I teach adolescent students. A holistic psychology that regards humanity, the Earth, and the cosmos as physical, emotional, spiritual, ecological, and cosmological works best because only the most expansive awareness is able to account for all of the ideas, dreams, feelings, and life experiences that occur during the American rite of passage of high school. Within that psychology is a recovered primal attitude toward the teen years that informs traditional rites of passage.[79] Most important in that primal attitude is the role of the human heart in learning. A proper rite of passage during the teen years marks youths with indelible courage toward life. What this means for us as teachers is to remember that when a child is young, the rule is to move away from pain and to cry out for emptiness to be filled by others. However, during the teen years, this flips and the opposite is true. Where it hurts most indicates the place where the emotional path seems darkest. Within the creative mythology of our era, it's where the heart's journey into adult originality begins. Also, emptiness is to be filled by giving. We are filled by our acts of loving service. The first original work to enter the classroom is most often from a student who has realized those two ideas. That's why it's so valuable and why setting the ground rules for responding to originality right away sets the tone for not only the first poesis, but originality in all its forms. This year, the first original work to enter the room was a set of poems written by my student, James. I let him know that I wanted him to share his poetry with the class because I wanted to teach a lesson on the importance of creativity. To prepare for this lesson, I have artwork from previous students to share.

I still have work and sketchbooks from Pete, a former middle school French 1 student, who won an art scholarship 4 years later. The sketchbooks are an object lesson of self-discipline in creativity over a period of years. They are also a testimony to oceanic consciousness and flow more than immediately apparent raw talent.[80] By evidence of oceanic consciousness and flow in Pete's work, I mean that you can see page after page where it is clear that it is a series of attempts, all made in one sitting. In fact, the first time he shared his sketches in class, when I asked him what it was like to do the drawings, he replied that when he was working, he lost track of time and skipped dinner. I also have art from students who demonstrated a remarkable inborn talent for drawing. Without any practice at all, it's as if there is a mini-Matisse inside of them. Finally, I have a third kind of student art from those who instinctively used the creative process as their way to cope with life as teens and continued to do so from then on. A learning space that nurtures creativity dissolves stereotypes with authenticity, nurturing, and knowledge. In particular, to prepare this foundation, it's vital to empower those students who come with an understanding of originality based on life experience and to marginalize those students who put on the appearance of knowledge.

There is a remarkable synchronistic resonance to the first original work that comes into the room. I strive to respond to the piece as soon as possible. The day of the first sharing, I teach about the flipping of the heart and go on to say that classmates who don't know about the adult heart respond with violence to the frail and original around them. I stress that attacks against originality are attempts to fill emptiness and sooth heart-pain by stealing the inner value of others. Next, I share the works of art from the three different categories, but I don't tell them who is who. I ask them, "Who do you think is the person who is going to have a career in art in the future and what are your reasons?" I give them 3 minutes to think about it. After 3 minutes I say,

I'm not going to ask you to share your opinions, but see how you did based on what I'll share next. First, it's good to know that there is a difference between a talent and a gift. Talent comes from a word related to money and worth. A gift is different and the word has a hidden double-meaning. The Germanic root of gift is the word *poison*. Your talents are yours to develop or not, but your gift is something you cannot not do in your life. Not living your gift hurts.

I then reveal who continues on with a life that includes art-making and offer that we don't really know the future of someone sharing their creativity with us, so, when we respond best, we do no harm.

I then hold up one of Pete's early drawings of his face and put behind it one of his self-portraits drawn 4 years later. The difference is striking. I tell the students,

Who here could have seen this (holding up a beautiful self-portrait) hiding behind this? (I hold up a first attempt by a 13-year-old Pete.) I can tell you that when Pete was in my middle school class, it was the so-called "coolest" student who made the first comments about Pete's work, attacked him, in fact. Now that you know the whole story about who Pete is going to be, can you get a sense of how violent that is, to attack someone's life in that way? You can be sure that I shut that down immediately. I asked Pete how he felt when he was drawing and he told the class that he lost track of time and skipped his dinner.

Let's move to James' poetry. They are song lyrics. There has only been one James in the history of the universe and these lyrics have never existed before now. There are two kinds of responses that are not allowed. The first one is to tell James that you could never write like he does because you are not as good as him. The second is to tell James something like he should stop writing now because his lyrics aren't cool like Taylor Swift or someone like her. The reason those responses are not allowed is that here you are presented with something original and honest and your response is to talk about yourself? James is not sharing his art with you so you will talk about yourself. He wants to know, do his words reach you?

We'll practice first with Pete's first drawing. Imagine it's 1985 and you are Pete's friend. He tells you he spent last night drawing and puts these drawings into your hands. How would you respond so he knows that his work had an impact on you? More importantly, how could you respond so he feels strengthened and inspired to do more? You want to have him keep coming back to you and sharing his work because he knows you are a friend to gift and his life.

I allow the students to try responses and accept all of them, but I hold students accountable about keeping the focus outside of themselves. We are lighthearted and playful.

With the responsive mood now present in the classroom, I say,

So that you'll be ready when creativity comes your way, I'm going to teach you about how to feed back. What this is like would be, say, a child learning to speak. He looks at you and says, "Bla, bla, bla, bla." Would it make sense to respond, "No! That's wrong! You have to pronounce the words this way!" No, the child is looking for a response, so maybe you'll say, "Blip, blup, blup!" Now look! The child is smiling and says back, "Bla bla blip!" What you have going now is a conversation. Feeding back is how you have a conversation using creativity. What do I mean? I'll show you. There are four levels of response that are possible when someone shares an original work with you. They are:

- Reminds me of . . .
- _____ occurs to me in response to your art
- Art answers art
- Silence

The Importance of Your Worldview

At this point, let's pause the lesson in progress in order to shift to the outer layer of the creative classroom, the layer of metanarratives or world-views. We are in a period of Western Renaissance.[81] The rebirth is a cultural rite of passage out of the modern, Cartesian, mechanistic, and patriarchal worldview and into an emerging, participatory, holistic, and quantum world-view. As early 21st-century educators, it's a form of neglect to not understand the differences between the two worldviews presently in play. The students we teach will live in a universe that is much more participatory than the 20th-century universe of their elders. Because to participate in the creative act is to merge into the transpersonal, it is the emerging, holistic worldview that is spacious enough to comprehend the spiritual and psychological wholeness of it. For example, a recurring driving force for decisiveness in my students' lives comes from their dreams at night. One student dreamed she was walking in Paris, another dreamed he was on a train speaking French. This year, a student kept having dreams of being independent in a big city. To me, there is nothing more original than my students' dreams. I am able to value their dreams the way I do because for me they are more than chemical activity of the sleeping brain. The holistic path of a deeply fulfilling life has room for the spiritual dimension and my response to the dreaming aspect reflects that.

Another quality of the new worldview is that there is a greater esteem for the feminine-toned, receptive, nurturing, and primal, responsive other-half of the creative act. In the I-Ching and in the new worldview, creation is a wholeness made of a complementary pair. The Creative, primal yang is partnered with the Receptive, primal yin. Translator Richard Wilhelm described the Receptive as "devotion; its image is the earth. It is the perfect complement of the Creative—the complement, not the opposite, for the Receptive does not combat the Creative but completes it."[82]

Feeding Back

To feed back, then, requires a radical receptivity rooted in the emerging worldview within the teacher and classroom. The worldview we bring into the classroom with us has a fundamental impact on how well feeding back will occur.

Level 1: Reminds Me of . . . : The Importance of Lifelong Learning

The first level of feeding back is the response: *reminds me of . . .* This level invites you to allow the creativity to inspire you to remember and to share your memories. In the opening vignette, students who spoke of the musicians Iron and Wine and Francis Cabrel fed back from this first level. It helps if you are a lifelong learner and your memory is wealthy with ideas, life experiences, and resources. To be a good creativity teacher in a world language class, it helps to be devoted to international travels. A second language is meant for life experience, so listening to the world's music, reading the books, tasting the foods, dancing the dances, singing the songs, participating in the ceremonies, seeing the art, watching the films, taking in the feast of Earth with our own eyes, all can be brought to enrich the creativity of our students. Certainly, the possibilities multiply exponentially with the foreign tongues we master. A well-lived life makes for the best feeding back. During the time of this writing, Andrew, a former student, shared his manifesto with me. It reminded me of the moral theology of Alasdair MacIntyre.[83] I printed out a page and we looked at it together. I think I learned more than my student did as we moved more deeply into issues of economic justice inspired by his manifesto. It was meaningful for me to feed Andrew's work back in a way that inspired him to follow his passion more deeply. When I was starting out in 1984, I didn't have the knowledge I have now, but acquired it over time. MacIntyre was writing back then too, but I didn't know about him. There is no prerequisite knowledge to begin feeding back at the first level, but there is an expectation of lifelong learning and a heart for adventure.

Level 2: _____ Occurs to Me: Sensual Virtue and the Thought of the Heart

I chose a scenario in which a student shared an original piece of music in the opening because music most often offers the easiest entry into this second, deeper level of feeding back. At the level of ___ occurs to me, when you listen, listen with your entire body because our bodies are *sensually responsive to virtue*. As you listen to a student's song with your whole body, all that is required is to notice and report the responses. The closer the song was written and performed from the heart of the student, the more you will feel. It can feel like warm chills passing over you. Your heart may warm, even shake in your chest. Sometimes the warm chills will be in just your knee or along the side of your face. Sometimes, you will weep. Inwardly, you may see images in your mind's eye. Those *thoughts of the heart* that were inspired by the song, when shared with the creator, have a surprising impact. Even more so, when the bodily sensations inspired by the song are shared with the singer, rest assured that more music will soon be arriving through your classroom door. All you must do is report what you experienced. In the dialogue, Student 1, who said she felt the chills over her shoulders, and Student 2, who shared the image of a beach in his mind's eye, were both responding at this deeper level. If nothing occurs to you, revert to the first level of feeding back and search your memory for what the song reminded you of. The day David sang his song, I was reminded of a French female singer, Zaz's, melodies.

The practice of whole-body listening that helps my creativity teaching most comes from a Lakota-style sweat lodge and from ritual with the medicine wheel. In both, I perceive with my entire being, especially through my body and with my heart. The French painter, Paul Cézanne, would walk the land around Aix-en-Provence, paying attention to what he described as *la petite sensation*. He would walk until the beauty of what he saw tingled in his body and then he would stop and paint in that spot.[84]

Level 3: Art Answers Art: Synchronistic Enactment

The Monday after December's Sandy Hook school shooting in Newtown, CT, in 2012, one of my creative French 3 students brought in a narrative she wrote based on her emotional reaction to the tragedy. Berea High School on Monday, December 16, 2012, felt much the same way it did on the day after September 11, 2001. There was a constant, quiet tension. Shelly showed me her text, but it was too raw to be read to the class that morning. I asked her to let me take it in and respond. I read it, and it was a narrative of a grieving mother. Letting the emotion move into me, as the students were taking a quiz, I wrote a brief poem inspired by her words. At the close of the class, I explained how Shelly had written a work in response to Sandy Hook, how it was too raw, but that I wanted to respond to acknowledge her feelings. I read the poem out loud to the class and handed her the original. That was art answering art. I made a work of art to answer hers.

When you or a student responds in this way, what is most original in you speaks to what is most original in the creator. In the opening vignette, it was the sixth student who heard in her imagination a piano part that went along with David's song and who fed back at this third and deeper level. In class that day, David sang the song again, this time with the second student adding her piano. At the level of art answers art, a remarkable event occurs. (I can attest to this because of my years of sweat lodge experiences.) A perceptible ritual space is conceived in the classroom. Although what I am describing may sound unusual, the new paradigm sciences that are rooted in quantum physics name this kind of space as a *morphogenic field*. What I am describing is also understood in transpersonal psychology, archetypal psychology, Jungian psychology, and spiritual psychology. In the historical record, André Breton, the "pope" of the Surrealists, described this space coming forth during their games of imagination.

Chris Bache named such morphogenic fields in schools as *mindfields*.[85] When art answers art, a mindfield is conceived that can be strengthened and grown the rest of the year and student creativity flows steadily through your doorway, lands on your desk, hangs from your walls, and fills your room with music, tears, laughter, stories of international friends, plans for global travel, and songs from all over the world.

By enacting immediate art answering art and conceiving the mindfield, the members of the class begin to experience a quantum leap in the appearance of synchronicity into their lives. Synchronicity was a term C. G. Jung first wrote about in 1928 in a seminar on dreams.[86] A good working definition of the phenomenon is this: *a meaningful coincidence in which two independent events having no causal connection nevertheless seem to form a meaningful pattern.* Since 1928, there has been long enough study of the phenomenon that it is considered a psychological fact. At the mature stage of the acceptance of synchronicity, synchronicity is an accepted fact of life, part of life's intelligence and artistry. The world is talking to you all of the time.

Art answering art gives students an experiential education in synchronicity and in that way, it guides them through direct experience into what it's like to live in a participatory worldview.[87] The synchronistic moments do not come as a constant state, but organically, when the timing is right. During those weeks when the classroom mindfield is flush with original activity, it is as if the walls of the classroom dissolve and dreams that the students never imagined possible start coming true.

Level 4: Silence: Attending to the Beauty

The deepest expression of receptivity is silence. When you are completely stilled by beauty, it is a type of aesthetic arrest. You become silent and have been opened to awe. First expressed by James Joyce, it was Joseph Campbell who delivered the concept into American culture on public television through the "Power of Myth" series with Bill Moyers.[88] I can tell you that to be stilled by an authentic and original work happens in public high schools. Epiphany does not come only from the grand masters after years of study, it comes often from adolescent artists making their frail creative first steps. In *The Power of Myth*, Campbell offered room for the aesthetic effect of a raw but authentic work when he described the sublime. I think he's also getting at an authentic experience of someone at the extremes, an adolescent. Something that may feel itself ugly, even monstrous, still has the capacity to open the heart. For our classrooms, I am asserting that honoring the unsure and even the ugly keeps the space open for the unexpected radiance that makes everyone's day and subtly changes your life. Teenagers become gentler and more open to the wisdom of life when they have opportunities to be arrested by beauty. At this point in my career, I think being aesthetically arrested is a life necessity.

I must add that the possibility of offering silence gives persons a way to feed back if they truly feel nothing in response to someone's creativity. Offering silence in response to the creative gives you a way to do no harm. When you draw a blank in response to someone's work, then kindly offer silence.

Creativity in French Class

I described the outermost container of the classroom, which is the world-view of the teacher. For the middle container, I stressed the importance of the teacher's awareness of adolescent passage into adulthood. As with the world-view, a holistic notion of life is most receptive when it responds to the wholeness of the students. Let's focus now on the development of the three creative capacities in French: (a) the capacity to create using French, (b) the capacity to respond to originality using French, and (c) the capacity to move beyond school into an authentic, original life enriched by Francophone culture.

We'll go back now to the introductory lesson on feeding back James's poem, the first original work to enter the classroom, that we have on pause. I explain each level of feeding back and give examples of how it is done.

Reminding them that we will do our best to feed James back and to do no harm, I have James read his work again, in order to get a fresh, immediate response. In a class of 28, I have at least 3 students feed back. I always feed back the creator too. James reads his poem and I invite his classmates to feed him back, getting these responses:

Student 1: Wow, I never knew you were that deep, it's weird, but I feel it in my stomach. My stomach feels warm.
Student 2: I like how your words fit together. It's a love song.
Student 3: I think it could be a real song.
M. Reynolds: Something I'd like to try is to let me play some chords while you read it again.

I fingerpick a chord progression and James reads the poem again.[89] When we finish the performance, there is a stillness and warmth in the room. The presence of stillness and warmth that seems to soak into everyone in the classroom is how a classroom mindfield expanded by creativity feels. When the bell rings to end fifth period, the students seem reluctant to leave the room.

The day after, two other students bring in their drawings, taking 8–10 minutes at the end of class. In the beginning, creativity in the French room is founded upon valuing the original by establishing the practice of feeding back. As you continue to develop the practice, it becomes more clear that what at first appeared as a development of *poesis* also functions as a unique collection of metaphors about living life rooted in the reality of the classroom. The many metaphors nourish a dedication in each student to trust the unique beauty that they love and to follow their hearts into life. Flow and oceanic consciousness are the evidence of an inner guidance that encourage a sense of direction. Over time, a genuine deep respect toward self and others results.

In the second year of French, the students already have experience feeding back and can move into the next level, where I use a *pause* and a *playback*. When you pause, you stop to teach the students the vocabulary they need to express in the target language that matches what they just expressed in English. They take notes on this and what comes forth is a capacity to speak of emotions and insight. I make sure that the responders have the words to express the desired response. To play back, I have the student share the original work again and continue on after with everyone in French. I continue to stretch the amount of French conversation as far as I can. Near the end of the third year and from then on, there is near total immersion, along with a remarkable level of trust.

The most rewarding experiences of development of creativity in my French classes have taken place when we were in France itself. It has been such a wonderful opportunity to begin with students who only know how to count and name colors in French and witness their growth into international travelers walking down the Champs-Élysées together. They savor it all and it shows. In 2011, after our first day in Paris, we were gathered at the statue of Charlemagne in front of Cathédrale Notre-Dame. The students were taking turns talking about their experiences when suddenly, the large bell of the north tower, le Bourbon, began to ring. Mark, who was talking, began to weep for the beauty of it. We all did. He couldn't speak for a while. Moments later, Aly came up to our group with tears in her eyes too. She said that she was inside the cathedral and the beauty affected her in such a way that she felt energy move upward in her body into her throat and pour out her mouth. She gestured with her hands as she explained. With any other group of persons, such a sharing might have invited less than receptive responses. With that group of students, a few began to weep as well. Mark told her that he felt the tingles on top of his head. I shared that what her experience reminded me of was images of the Green Woman and Green Man, who are carved into pillars inside the cathedrals. Those images have plants pouring up through their throats and out of their mouths.

Figure 6.1. *Painting by Megan Tatnall. Poetry by Caitlin Hiatt.* Pas tous les anges viennent du bonheur *(Not all angels come from happiness). Used with permission.*

Expansions Outward

At Berea-Midpark High School, art and visual effects teacher, Jim Bycznski, with whom I've had an ongoing conversation through our creativity for the past 12 years, founded the Creative Collective, which is a forum of art answering art. We have the first-ever program for art answering art as part of world language instruction and global awareness. Students in French, Spanish, Mandarin Chinese, German, Greek, Russian, Latin, Norwegian, Italian, and Albanian responded to images from the art students. Figure 6.1 shares an example.

As in the arts, there are talents and gifts in world languages. There are those who seem like reincarnated Ducs and Duchesses and it's more like they are remembering a language they already speak. There are others who fall in love with the sound and even though they are not immediately good at it, go on to live international lives. Cultivating creativity through feeding back brings students' passionate interests out into the open. Those passions provide the inspiration to connect to like-minded others in the Francophone world. Intuition is the faithful guide to this path of the heart, and encouraging the students' devotion to their intuitive inner knowing makes a world of difference. Brian, who wants to be a doctor, is talking to his French e-pal about Médecins sans Frontières (Doctors Without Borders). My student Andrea, who is going into fashion design, has been searching online for as much as she can find about the prêt-à-porter (ready-to-wear) side of fashion. In a remarkable feat of international-mindedness due to French class, my student Rachel used e-mail, Skype, and the strategies she learned in French class to make friends with an Italian family, learn Italian with their assistance, and then visit Italy.

The Importance of Closing the Space

In closing, I invite you into the practice of feeding back in your world language classroom. I am confident that the devotion to bringing forth the original in yourself and the students will deepen the meaning in your life as it has mine. In traditional ritual space, there is time spent "closing the space." A traditional ritual ends by a sharing of gratitude and then a release of all that was done as a gift for the good of the world. I have had the experience that my students come back to see me. Teaching in this new paradigm requires just as much care about closing as is taken in traditional ritual space. It's not hard to do. When I close the space of the classroom, I ask the students to share something from the year for which they were grateful—not for long, maybe 1–2 minutes. After the students share, then I do the same. To consciously close the space, I say, "So, we'll let go of all we've experienced together this year and imagine that all the good is a gift that we are offering the world." After that, we sit in complete silence for a minute. After the minute is up, I usually say something like, "OK, we're done for this year, get out there and have some adventures so we have something to talk about when we meet again!"

I'll close this space with the poem by Rumi that gives this essay its title:

Today, like every other day,
We wake up empty and frightened.
Don't open the door to the study and begin reading.
Take down a musical instrument.
Let the beauty we love be what we do.
There are hundreds of ways to kneel and kiss the ground.

Au revoir.

ORGANIC CREATIVITY IN THE ARTS

Figure II.1. *Chapter authors Barry Oreck and Jessica Nicoll in performance.*

Chapter 7

LOOKING FOR ARTISTRY

Barry Oreck

As with many people, my career path retraces my own childhood. I was one of those squirmy kids in school. My interests bounced around; I got good grades in the subjects I liked, lousy ones in things I didn't. I had trouble sitting still; lived for recess and arts classes. In high school, I arrived before 7 a.m. for choir rehearsal and stayed most nights until at least 8 p.m., after whatever team practice or play rehearsal I was involved in ended. I was editor of the school newspaper and started an underground film series. Thankfully my mother didn't pull me out of those activities because of my dismal grade point average—perhaps she knew that was why I was even a little interested in school. My success in "extra"curricular activities didn't impress my teachers, however. The theme running through all of my report cards was: "Barry has a lot of potential but is not self-motivated. He always needs to be pushed." Even then that seemed ironic.

Now after a career built, to a great extent, on my artistic interests and ability to collaborate on complex group projects, those comments seem particularly paradoxical. I greatly appreciate the quality academic foundation I received at my progressive private school—writing and math (and certainly science, social studies, and history) have been extremely important in my life and career. But the fact that my teachers were unaware, unwilling, or unable to connect my intense interests and deep motivation in the arts, sports, journalism, and film to anything that was going on in the classroom is a telling commentary. I was extremely fortunate to go to a school that offered an out-

Barry Oreck, Ph.D., directs professional development in the Schoolwide Enrichment Model and teaches at Long Island University Brooklyn and SUNY Buffalo. From 1983–2001, he directed ArtsConnection's arts-in-education programs in more than 150 New York City public schools and has consulted in curriculum, assessment, and program development for the Ohio Department of Education, the Mississippi School of the Arts, Shakespeare Theatre Company, Young Playwrights Theatre, Lincoln Center Theatre, the Metropolitan Opera Guild, and Young Audiences, among many others. His research on artistic talent, self-regulation, and professional development has been published in the Champions of Change research compendium, *Arts Education Policy Review, Journal of Teacher Education*, and *Teaching Artist Journal*, among other publications. His own work as a dancer and choreographer in the duo Nicoll + Oreck has been produced in New York and around the country.

standing arts and sports program. If I hadn't had those, I'm really not sure I would have made it through high school. For students in schools with shrinking or nonexistent arts programs, limitations on involvement in extracurricular activities, and narrowing curricula driven by high-stakes standardized testing, opportunities to find their strengths and passions are severely limited. My history and my concern for students like myself in schools around the country led me into the world of the arts and the field of the education of the gifted and talented—an intersection of two marginalized areas of education focused on identifying and developing the strengths and interests of students who often don't excel on tests and may struggle with the linear, sequential, strictly verbal rules of the typical game of school.

Perhaps predictably, I cycled through seven different majors in my 4 (or 6, depending on how you count it) undergraduate years of college. I continued to act and dance (hundred of hours for each credit) but had not found a way to merge my interests in a single field. Finally working with my dance mentor, Gerrie Glover, an accomplished multidisciplinary artist (dancer/choreographer, concert pianist and organist, and painter), I began to teach, choreograph, and run a dance company. I was thrown into teaching like many of my contemporaries in the heyday of arts education—we had the National Education Association (NEA) Dance Touring and Artist in the Schools programs and other grants to actually pay dancers to dance and teach. Gerrie's approach in all art forms was deeply creative, aesthetic, and often overlapping. Her interests in dance/theatre and in teaching were scientific and somatic (30 years before the term was applied to dance), psychological, and political. As I learned to teach by doing, with a range of students from young children to university students, and performed with and recruited dancers for our dance company, New Mexico DanceWorks, I found a question that fascinated me.

What makes certain performers extraordinary? I could see in dance that the difference between very capable, technically proficient performers and those working at the deepest levels of artistry was small but obvious. It had little to do with specific skills or physical characteristics such as flexibility or strength, body type, or physique. There was something else—something about the ways in which the charismatic performer communicates, the level of focus, a connectedness to an emotional source, a sense of calm amidst great effort—that made specific dancers stand out to experts and untrained audience members alike. These are aspects of creativity, communicated absolutely clearly, without words. What were the physical manifestations? What was happening just before the movement, during it, and during the learning process?

Organic Creativity in the Arts

Trying to uncover some of these subtle differences, I started a master's degree in neuromuscular physiology to study physical and emotional responses of dancers as they learned and performed movement. This was the 1970s and, unfortunately, the technology to capture movement in real time was very primitive. The bundles of wires protruding from my subjects prevented them from moving freely and me from measuring subtle differences. The experience did shape my thinking, however, about the nature of artistic ability and creativity. I observed ways we teach that can either nurture the characteristics of the most outstanding dancers or that can ignore or even deaden these aspects of artistic development in a daily routine of repetitive, imitative training activities. How do exceptional artists like Mikhail Baryshnikov, Judith Jamison, or Gregory Hines endure and thrive in a demanding training regimen and emerge with their own style and personality intact? Are there things we as teachers can do to nurture the artistry in all of our students?

Finding Artists

My move to New York City to pursue a dance career was hastened by the sudden end of the arts education boom upon the election of Ronald Reagan. I quickly altered plans (by luck and coincidence) to take a job at a remarkable arts-in-education organization, ArtsConnection, where I was to stay for the next 19 years. I directed a program called the Young Talent Program, which sent professional artists into elementary schools to identify students for advanced instruction in dance, music, circus, and theatre at professional studios such as the Alvin Ailey Center, Manhattan Theatre Club, and the Big Apple Circus. A panel of artists would see each third-grade class for one period, then confer and select students for arts classes in school and in professional studios. Time after time, classroom teachers who witnessed the audition but had no role in the selection process, when presented with the final list, would say, "You've picked all my worst kids." Virtually every time, in all sorts of schools, in all parts of the city, in all art forms, the talents of students who appeared to the teaching artists to be the most creative, smart, expressive, and cooperative were not recognized by their teachers or were seen in a negative light. In fact, we consistently selected a number of the top academic students as well as the lowest achieving, but those struggling students were the ones who stood out most to the teachers.

It was clear that we were seeing a distinct and important target group: students with outstanding artistic ability whose talents were not only not recognized in school but often got them into trouble. Many of the same talent characteristics most appreciated by the artists made some of these students playground leaders among their peers, for better or worse. In the mostly low-income neighborhoods and underserved schools in which we worked, many of those playground leaders were labeled highly at-risk and our program was funded in part by the Department of Juvenile Justice in the years when they still had a focus on prevention over incarceration.

In 1990, the U.S. Department of Education awarded ArtsConnection the first of two 3-year Javits grants to study this group of students and the phenomenon of gifted underachievement we had observed. We designed the Talent Beyond Words program to create a systematic process to identify potentially talented elementary school students who had little or no prior instruction in dance, music, and theatre. The new process involved the classroom teachers in the assessment to see if greater direct awareness of artistic behaviors would alter their perspective on their students' abilities.

First we brought together panels of artist/teachers in each discipline (dance, music, and theatre), representing a wide range of styles and techniques[90], to develop selection criteria. We asked the artists to describe the behaviors of the most successful students they had taught and the situations or activities in which they might see those behaviors. The criteria each panel developed independently fit into three general categories—Skills, Creativity, and Motivation. Although the arts experts were not versed in the field of the education of the gifted and talented, the categories they'd identified clearly matched Renzulli's Three Ring Conception of Giftedness—Above Average Ability, Creativity, and Task Commitment (see Figure 7.1).[91] I pressed the experts to define underlying natural abilities that were more important than the rest (e.g., a strong speaking voice for an actor; flexibility, balance, good feet, or posture for a dancer; strong rhythm or hand-eye coordination for a musician), but the panelists consistently resisted these seemingly obvious prerequisites, saying that all of these areas could be developed with motivation, creativity, and practice, and citing numerous examples of outstanding artists initially or permanently lacking these characteristics. The artists were convinced that no single category could be deemed essential or most important, but rather that talent was defined by the totality of the behaviors or, as Renzulli put it, the overlap of the rings.

The process we developed, called the Talent Assessment Process in Dance, Music and Theatre (D/M/T TAP), is described in detail elsewhere.[92] Many things distinguish D/M/T TAP from a typical assessment or audition. Two arts instructors (alternating leading and watching) and a classroom teacher

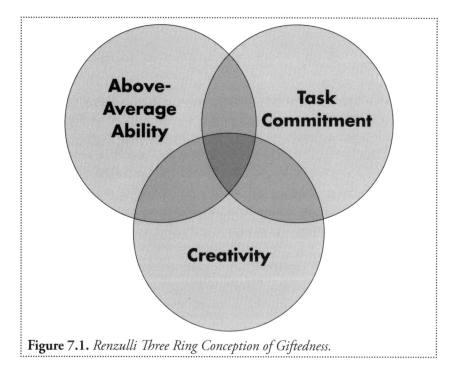

Figure 7.1. *Renzulli Three Ring Conception of Giftedness.*

observed students in a variety of activities over five class sessions. Many of the experiences involved group work and problem solving in a safe, fun atmosphere with lots of interaction with teachers and peers. In order to see creativity, imagination, and sensitivity at work, we wanted to see students deeply engaged in artistically authentic and satisfying experiences, not put on the spot to perform under pressure. Because motivation characteristics take time to emerge, we offered students challenging tasks that take some perseverance to master while trying not to discourage them. The creativity and motivation criteria (some of which could easily overlap, such as the ability to focus) proved to be vital information in the selection process and were a central feature of student evaluations throughout the 3-year program.

That creativity and motivation were considered essential to artistic ability and success is not at all surprising. When discussing the roots of their own success and that of their most promising students, accomplished artists often mention attitude—of curiosity, openness, risk-taking—as key to their development. Many professional artists with whom I have spoken over the years have readily admitted that growing up they were far from the most "talented" person they knew but either (a) worked harder, (b) came up with their own

way of doing things, (c) found a teacher/mentor who inspired them to perse-
vere, or (d) some of all of the above.

Two stories will help illuminate this idea. On the first day of the third-
grade music assessment process, Jason struggled. He seemed uncomfortable
and was slow to pick up on the call and response clapping rhythm games led
by the instructor. The second session was not much better as the students
sang and learned a simple tune on the recorder. Things began to change
when percussion instruments were introduced, and Jason had the chance to
play a part on the bass drum. As other students had trouble staying with
their parts, Jason stubbornly kept on the beat, holding the entire ensemble together. His concentration and determination were clear in his face and
body. He had the simplest but most important part to play, and he was rock
solid. When his mother was informed that Jason had been selected to be part
of the advanced group, she asked, "Are you sure you picked the right Jason?"
(There was another Jason in the class.) She had not recognized musical talent
in her son but was excited for him. Throughout the 3 years of the advanced
instructional program, his determination to improve, along with his concentration, listening skills, and teamwork, made him a key member of the group.

Tiffany was a large 9-year-old girl with an imposing presence. She looked
glum for the first three quarters of the initial dance assessment workshop.
Toward the end of the class, students were given the chance to go across the
floor with their own dance. She exploded with power and focus, moving
fully, her face showing her pleasure in the movement and music. Her classmates and teacher watched with surprise and delight. As one of her classmates
bluntly said, "Tiffany's fat but she sure can dance." Her teacher did not previously know of her abilities or interests in dance or music. Selected for the
advanced dance program, Tiffany later got a role singing and dancing in an
off-Broadway play.

Who else in school is specifically looking for creative, expressive, kinesthetic, spatial, or nonverbal abilities in students? Possibly the art or music
teachers (if they see students frequently enough). But art and music teachers
rarely work alongside the classroom teacher, so discussions about individual
students and detailed observations are rare. It's safe to say that Jason and
Tiffany would not have been identified in a one-time assessment. They would
have been unlikely candidates for a selective arts program. They might not
have been noticed if there were not a variety of activities reflecting different
styles and cultures. They needed to be in a setting where their expressiveness,
interest, and creative risk-taking could be observed.

My initial question about charismatic performers came back to me in a new form—what is it about certain people, in this case, children with no prior arts training, that makes them stand out as artists? If it is not a specific characteristic, physical attribute, or recognized interest, then what is it?

The Existence of A

Among the most accomplished performers, where everyone is trained to their physical limits, almost all of the difference between people is considered artistry. We can see and hear it most easily at a high level of performance. But artistry is also obvious in untrained children working in the arts, as in people in every walk of life and activity. An artistic attitude, emotional connection, and aesthetic appreciation signal the artist at work. The charismatic performers I was interested in so many years ago may have greater access than others to their artistry, but I believe it is something everyone is born with and something that can be tapped into in innumerable ways at any time in one's life.

This is not to say there are no differences in specific talent characteristics or appropriate physical attributes needed to excel in a given domain. Maslow calls these differences "special talent" creativity.[93] To pass the domain's gatekeepers, a specific attribute such as a powerful tenor voice, extreme size in sports, or striking good looks in theatre can overcome limitations in creativity or motivation. Just as we look at "Big C" and "little c" creativity,[94] a continuum exists from specifically prized characteristics of a domain to general artistry that can exist in any domain. We might refer to this general artistry as an *A factor*—a range of abilities and attitudes that can explain and predict outstanding performance in a variety of artistic experiences and settings. It is crucial to recognize that *A* is equally important at both ends of the continuum—from Carnegie Hall to the gym at P.S. 130.

Clearly *A* is deeply interconnected with creativity. It is almost impossible to imagine an aspect of artistry that would not be considered creative. *A* encompasses ways of being and learning, artistic attitudes and curiosity, appreciation of beauty and qualities of things, a need or drive for expression, an emotional connection. Perhaps the most accurate definition of *A* would be *access*: access to one's inner voice, to the intuitive, subconscious, connected self. *A* is also integration in the sense of connecting the physical, emotional, cognitive aspects of our being. Lev Vygotsky described the artistic act as a synthesis, essential for catharsis and emotional integration. "Art is the social technique of emotion," he said.[95]

The idea of a general construct of artistic talent would likely seem natural and obvious in cultures where dance, music, theatre, and visual art are woven into daily life and ritual, as opposed to within Eurocentric systems featuring separate domains and training programs. I'm not suggesting that the arts are interchangeable or that any one art form can stand in for the others. People are drawn to their preferred form, style, or technique by a host of factors. I do believe, however, that the characteristics of *A* are similar across artistic endeavors; artists bring many of the same qualities to their art in whatever form it is in. John Dewey described art as a quality of doing and what is done.[96]

In New York City, each school we worked with had the assessment and advanced classes in only one art form. After 3 years of testing and expansion into 10 New York City public schools, we had the chance to export the program to Ohio where a new law had required the inclusion of the arts in gifted and talented identification and the Ohio Department of Education and Ohio Arts Council wanted to use the D/M/T TAP. A Javits grant gave us the chance to recruit and train teaching artists, work with school-based music and art teachers, and devise a visual art component that relied on a portfolio, a drawing test,[97] and work created in a workshop setting.[98]

In a small town and large urban district in Ohio, we were able for the first time to compare the same students across the four art forms. Many of the students excelled in more than one art form, which was not terribly surprising. What was striking was the magnitude of the statistical correlation among the art forms—almost perfect across the three performing arts and just a bit lower when visual art was added in. The statistics provide further empirical evidence[99] for the idea of a general talent in the arts, or artisticness, or artistry, or *A*.

Developing A In School

One of the most striking outcomes of both the New City and Ohio projects was a change in the cultures of the schools. Academic classroom teachers, parents, and family members were all essential participants, along with artists, students, and arts programming staff. Together, each community developed greater awareness and appreciation for artistic abilities and increased opportunities and outlets for students, both in and outside of school. The unusual longevity of the Young Talent Program (1978–present) has given us an excellent vantage point to study the impact of this culture-shift on students who previously had few opportunities to find or develop their artistic abilities and interests.

The most direct and immediate result was the response of classroom teachers involved in the observational assessment process. Teachers don't usually get a chance to see their students work in the arts, which normally happens during their preparation periods. In this carefully orchestrated observation process, they saw new abilities in all of their students, *whether they were identified as ready for advanced instruction or not*. Teachers were excellent observers of artistic behaviors when given clear criteria. Their comments in the postworkshop discussions (a key feature of the process) consistently highlighted surprises and new awareness.

The students who *were* identified, particularly those struggling in school or on tests, made significant and, in some cases, striking improvement in the classrooms of teachers who had participated in the assessment process.[100] Teachers also participated in professional development workshops, which gave them new insights about the artistic process and some arts-based teaching strategies. In my 2004 study of classroom teachers' use of the arts in their teaching practice,[101] the strongest motivator for teachers to use the arts in the classroom was their awareness that they have students who need it—who learn best that way, who need to move, act, draw, sing, to learn. It didn't matter whether teachers had had any formal arts instruction in their own background. Those who used arts strategies the most tended to think of themselves as creative people. Their own artistry in teaching allowed them to learn and use arts strategies in their practice and better connect to the artistic abilities of their students.

More than 15 years after the end of my U.S. Department of Education-funded research, I still get calls and e-mails saying, "I hear you have research showing the arts can improve test scores." "Yes," I say, "we did have evidence of that, but it's a much, much more complicated story."

A in the Classroom

I don't see much convincing evidence for a direct correlation between arts instruction and academic improvement (i.e., music training improves math performance or visual art affects spatial reasoning, etc.). Students' successes in our studies grew from a web of factors, starting with high quality, challenging arts instruction; without that, it is unlikely the other outcomes would have followed. They were pushed to work hard for something they cared about. Looking back at her elementary school experiences in the Young Talent Program, Angela, a high school student, recalled,

> When someone pushes you and you find that you improve, you learn to practice. Because you know if you practice it, you get it. So they gave us that start-off push. You didn't want to. You were tired. And then the next class, you didn't need the push anymore . . . when you actually see it physically happening, . . . then you know that 'if I can do this with my body, then I must be able to do this with my mind.' I may not be perfect, but I am getting better.[102]

When my coresearcher Susan Baum and I watched students in their arts classes, we were struck by the effectiveness of their intuitive learning behaviors: They found personal strategies to learn and remember new material, practiced on their own, worked well together, and took and used feedback to improve. We wanted to look more closely at these self-regulatory behaviors to see if they could help students academically as well.[103]

Watching the same students in their academic classrooms, we saw little opportunity for this type of self-regulation. We realized that the pedagogy of the arts classes provided the model for the students' success. In the arts, students were physically active. They often saw or experienced new material *before* discussion or explanation. Teachers encouraged students' questions and even their odd-sounding ideas. Students, knowing that everyone was expected to demonstrate new skills frequently, asked clarifying questions and practiced in and outside of class rather than avoiding or delaying the task. In the arts, self-evaluation, peer feedback, and shared goal-setting with the teacher were common. Students often moved to another part of the room to see or hear better or to avoid distractions, and we saw them complete tasks or practice on their own, even when the teacher wasn't looking.

The structure and pedagogy we saw in typical academic classrooms neither encouraged nor allowed most of those behaviors and, in fact, student creativity was most evident in off-task activities. Although students may have been aware of some of their successful learning strategies, they were unable to apply them in the classroom. When asked how she remembered a long, complicated dance phrase, fourth grader Maria replied,

> When you learn a new dance you learn the first four counts, then the next four and then you go back and do the first and second fours

together. Then you learn the next four and it just keeps going like that—adding and going back to the beginning.

We asked if it worked like that in math and she quickly responded, "No—in math if you miss the first step, you're lost forever." If she didn't know something in dance, Maria said she'd asked her friends to work on it with her at lunchtime or in the playground. In math, she said, "My friends are probably as confused as me so I don't ask them."[104]

For students to apply their arts-based learning behaviors in the classroom, we realized two things had to change: Students had to become conscious of their successful strategies *and* teachers had to provide opportunities for the students to apply them. Teachers began working with teaching artists to create and teach arts-infused academic units. The lessons succeeded not only in increasing students' self-regulatory behaviors but also improved their writing and science and social studies understanding.[105] When teachers saw typically disengaged students take leadership roles and excel in class, they were motivated to continue using the arts. Although most students enjoyed the arts-infused lessons, the identified students made the most improvement in writing and content understanding.

To further help academically struggling students, we created MAGIC (Merging Artistic Gifts Into the Classroom)—weekly, small-group sessions to help students apply arts learning strategies to specific academic challenges. A MAGIC teacher recruited from each school worked with students to adapt a range of strategies—including drawing and visualization for sequencing and problem solving, rhythm and song as mnemonic devices, physicalizing and dramatizing events and characters from books, and creating mental pictures and movement games to estimate and calculate math problems—that called on students' particular abilities and learning preferences. During MAGIC, students also wrote in journals and reflected on their strengths, building metacognition and confidence to apply their abilities in new settings. Probably most important was the MAGIC teacher herself, who supported and positively reinforced students' efforts and became an advocate within the school and with parents.

Developing A

The academic improvements, while impressive, were not the motor for this project; sustaining students' successful artistic development throughout elementary and into middle and high school was our central goal. In the New York City communities in which we worked, elementary school arts programs had steadily declined, most middle schools had cut back or suspended band and orchestra programs, and few had dance or theatre teachers. Many former community-based arts programs had changed their focus to academic assistance or other services. And for our students and their families, New York City's wealth of high-level arts training and educational resources were tantalizingly out of reach.

The Young Talent Program students we followed in our study had to be highly creative and resilient. Maintaining arts training through middle school and high school required the support of parents, family members, and others in the community. As Elnora Powell, the mother of one YTP student, Troy Powell, who had an illustrious career with the Alvin Ailey American Dance Theatre and is now the director of the Ailey II company, reflected on Troy's time in the program, "It took *this* village, to raise *this* child. Out of the hundreds of people that helped, if just one wasn't there, I think maybe Troy wouldn't be here."[106]

Young Talent Program students received scholarships to attend the Martha Graham School, Alvin Ailey Dance Center, Dance Theatre of Harlem, Harlem School of the Arts, the Juilliard School Saturday Program, the Brooklyn Conservatory of Music, the Walt Disney Youth Orchestra, and many other local arts organizations. The arts organizations enthusiastically welcomed and supported these students from across the city, but without transportation or supervision, none of these connections could have been established or maintained. Groups of family members, organized by an ArtsConnection parent liaison, accompanied students to performances and auditions, arranged for afternoon travel and pick-ups at studios, and spread information about arts magnet schools, summer opportunities, and scholarship applications. The school-based family groups provided the safety and familiarity essential for students' continued arts involvement.

The students knew all too well how difficult and challenging a career in the arts could be. The idea of waiting tables and auditioning was not an appealing (or feasible) career aspiration for most. Even though Simone wanted to become a singer, she knew that she needed to choose a career that would enable her to have a more secure life. "We have a lot of money problems—money, it's all about money." But she explained,

> Music is a part of me. I can't not do it. I don't think that I could ever
> lose touch with music . . . Even if I don't end up as a performer, I

can always encourage my own children to play music. Or I could be a music teacher and encourage children to want to play music. I want to give them the feeling that I had that made me want to play music.[107]

Despite financial hardships, most families were highly supportive of their children's artistic development for its own value. As middle school student David's mother said,

My two kids were good at academics, but the music and singing were such an important part of their lives that they couldn't function without it. I feel that it helped them express themselves and look outside of the academics and get an understanding of life.[108]

Life for many of these students now included taking classes in a professional studio outside their immediate neighborhood and alongside other motivated students from a range of backgrounds. Suddenly, arts professionals and older peers were part of their world. Angela remembers performing in a celebration honoring Martha Graham at Lincoln Center, "Just being there, just being in the Metropolitan [Opera House] was something I never thought I would do in my entire life and to actually perform there was like big time for me."[109]

Virtually every student in our study faced some combination of family hardship, immigration issues, or housing displacement, and contended with their parents' very real concerns about their safety. Most had responsibilities in their homes and cared for younger siblings. But their resilience and creativity was fed by their artistic involvement. Carmela had a scholarship to dance 3–4 days a week after school at the Martha Graham School. In her first 5 years after moving to New York from Venezuela, she and her sisters relocated repeatedly from borough to borough and school to school with her single mother. As her mother described,

Dance has given her the emotional stability that she needed. Because Carmela now, after everything that we've been through, is more peaceful. Her self-esteem is greater and she is a happier child. Because she's so in tune with dance and that's all she wants to do. If it were up to her she would do it all the time.[110]

Randall, studying design in college at the Fashion Institute of Technology, had been a struggling student, considered highly at risk for failure when he first entered the Young Talent Program in third grade. He attributes his current work habits and dedication to his involvement in the arts:

> If ArtsConnection never came into my life . . . I don't know. I'm still pretty much trying to pick out where I would be today. Like what would I be doing to kill all this empty time that I would have if I wasn't dancing?[111]

Still Looking for A

It's odd to look back at my life and be able to trace such a direct trajectory of interests and pursuits, from middle school onward. At the time, it never felt direct; each turn opened up new questions. Although my situation was very different from that of the students in YTP, I feel a kinship in having had artistic interests and skills that went unappreciated when I was viewed through a narrow academic lens. My own subsequent path—trying to wire up outstanding artists to see what makes them special, then assessing artistic behaviors carefully with many sets of eyes and points of view, and then using those insights to try to open up arts and educational opportunities for young artists—makes an interesting kind of sense now.

When we see qualities of ourselves in others, our empathy is heightened and we are moved to action. In a meeting with almost 100 teaching artists at ArtsConnection, I once asked, "What or who inspired you to become an artist?" The most common answer was that there had been someone in their lives who noticed and inspired them—who saw their talent and pushed them to pursue it further. To the question "Why do you teach?" the most frequent response was, "I want to be that person for someone else."

I have tried hard to reconcile my conviction that *A* is a universal quality of all people with my observation that some people display it, or have access to it, more readily and more often. All students need and deserve the arts in their education. But for some, art will be a primary force in their lives—the way they learn, a key part of their identity, and a necessary means of expression—if they know it is there. With music and art teachers spread ever thinner in U.S. schools, most of whom lack even basic dance or theatre instruction, the creative and artistic abilities and interests of many will never be uncovered. This problem is most acute in underserved schools and economically disadvantaged communities where out-of-school arts instruction is often unattainable and success in school is critical for future educational and career opportunities. We need to change the culture of schools to value artistic abilities as highly as the narrow range of abilities currently prized and tested. It seems obvious that recognizing and developing artistry should be a central goal of all education.

Chapter 8

LEARNING TO
BE A CAIRN

Jessica Nicoll

Every day we slaughter our finest impulses. That is why we get a heart-ache when we read those lines written by the hand of a master and recognize them as our own, as the tender shoots which we stifled because we lacked the faith to believe in our own powers, our own criterion of truth and beauty. Every man, when he gets quiet, when he becomes desperately honest with himself, is capable of uttering profound truths. We all derive from the same source. There is no mystery about the origin of things. We are all part of creation, all kings, all poets, all musicians; we have only to open up, only to discover what is already there.—Henry Miller[112]

Those words bring me back to Saara-Maria and Teija, dance students who are learning about teaching. We sit in a dance studio in Turku, Finland, reflecting on what happens when teaching children dance. Saara-Maria and Teija speak with a kind of awe when they say, "Sometimes creativity comes right from the students; it's like it arises from them." *Yes*, I think, and *take care*; constructing too many exciting ways to push or pull it out of them can take away the space in which children's creativity arises. Tricks and techniques offered to student teachers—ways to draw their own students into "being creative"—sometimes, without anyone noticing, get in the way of the very thing they hope to nurture.

How, then, do I help my own dance students, particularly choreography students, "be creative"? I don't think I do help them "be creative." I start with

Jessica Nicoll, on faculty at Hunter College in New York City, has performed with Kei Takei, Phyllis Lamhut, Claire Porter, and others and choreographs and performs in New York City as part of Nicoll + Oreck. A public school teaching artist, Nicoll also teaches at the 92nd Street Y Harkness Dance Center and Spoke the Hub Dancing and leads professional development for teachers and artists through ArtsConnection, New York City Center, and the Metropolitan Opera Guild. Nicoll presents her work nationally and internationally and writes frequently on arts in education. She has won the following awards: 1999 Off-Off-Broadway Review Award; 2007, 2008, and 2012 Boulder International Fringe Festival Encore Awards; 2004 Linda LeRoy Janklow Award; and 2007 BAXten Award for teaching artistry.

the belief that they *are* creative. I try to help them notice what intrigues them and trust themselves to play and follow where their own creativity leads. It's a process of looking and listening, more than teaching—or at least more than teaching in the manner of instructing. And the looking and listening is the process we go through together. My students and I often look up from our observations with raised eyebrows and open mouths as if to say, "Huh! Who knew that was about to happen?" We may say nothing in those moments, but we do start to laugh. The mysteries are so funny.

This makes me think about Alex. At 15, she'd been dancing for 6 years, but had never choreographed and emerged a little shocked from her first choreography class. I hadn't laid out a step-by-step procedure. I didn't say, "Make an 8-count phrase, use three levels, and have a beginning and ending shape." I neither gave her a theme nor asked her to name one. I might have said, "Listen to your body and notice how it wants to move." Perhaps she improvised, following one impulse to the next and the next and the next . . . Somehow—by magic?—her body, her mind, and her creativity (that thing she'd brought with her into the studio) devised a "something." A something for her to chew on.

In the second class, the dancer/choreographers improvised ("messing around," I sometimes call it) while I asked from time to time, "Does somebody have a 'What if . . . ?'", listening hard for someone to say, "What if we fell down at the end?" or "What if we couldn't move our arms?" or whatever else they—not *I*, but *they*—thought of. Soon I asked the students to brainstorm privately some "what if" possibilities for their own work that evening. Later Alex read from her list: "What if someone else danced my phrase at the same time but reversed? Huge? Small? Slow? While making sounds? Wearing a rainbow?" She looked at the group with surprise. "What does that mean?" she asked, laughing. Yes, the mysteries make us laugh.

Lately, I picture myself as a cairn on the side of a mountain. I love stepping out of the deep woods, off a winding trail, onto a rocky mountainside, not quite sure where to go next, but with a general sense that I am at least on the mountain I meant to be on (although that's not always true; I occasionally find myself on a different mountain than intended). Proceeding slowly, I scan the terrain and enjoy the new, open view, noticing a shape of cloud mimicking the rocky promontory just ahead. Then, with a burst of delight, I see, there in the distance, a small pile of stones—a cairn—telling me, "Yes, this will do." I approach and admire the cairn's combination of stability and delicacy. It is not a worded sign listing possible destinations and mileage, with arrows indicating steeper or gentler ways up or down the mountain. It is just a small, quiet, wordless pile of stones. I move on, chancing out another set of steps, and study my surroundings carefully, trusting that in time I will find another cairn, similar but distinct, a little ways up the mountain.

If someone has placed the cairns too close together, I am disappointed: too much information, too soon. Part of me disengages; I stop noticing the details of this place. Someone has mapped my route too tightly. My wandering now lacks a feeling of discovery and the possibility that my path differs slightly from that of those who came before or will come after.

This becomes my goal as a teacher, maybe especially in choreography: to be a cairn, just one small, quiet pile of stones that tells a student, "You're doing fine. You choose where your next steps lead. I'm sure you'll find another cairn along the way."

This is not how it is usually done. I've been hired, after all, to "teach" choreography. Aren't there rules for this sort of thing? Don't students have to be taught how to deal with space and time and music and movements that will look good? Don't they need to learn the craft first, to be shown what kinds of ideas will work, what sorts of problems are interesting, and then later—when they're ready—they'll find their own promising ideas? Couldn't they—thinking again of the cairn—get frustrated wandering around or, worse, fall off the mountain? I used to think that. Then I met Allegra.

Allegra changed my life but I don't think she knows it. About 29 years ago, she was 9 and I was a 25-year-old artist in residence, teaching dance in her public school gym in Queens, NY. Allegra asked, 20 minutes into a 45-minute class, "When do we get to dance?" My standard responses— that this *was* dance, that warming up was part of the practice, that there are many perspectives and ways to dance—were all of the rationales I'd absorbed through my own training, as a dancer and teacher. Even as I spoke, I knew I was failing her. If she didn't feel like she was dancing from the moment she walked in the door, then I was missing something. I was not tapping into something deep and true about Allegra's own dancing self. Something she brought with her into that space.

I went home that day distraught. It was true that we needed to warm up the body and that I should structure a developmentally appropriate progression for young dance students, engaging 25 or 30 energetic children with some semblance of control and focused, productive effort. There was truth in my own experience and my own passions about the dance training I could offer and my expertise in sharing it. But I could not run away from Allegra's truth. Her inner guide told her this did not quite feel like dancing. And she

hooked me when she tucked her frustration into the most delightful, innocent question: "When do we get to dance?"

That was it. One sweet, honest question tripped me up on my own desire
for students to experience dance the way I did, love it like I did, see it like I
did. I could not *not* bring those passions into the classroom; they were me,
and at the essence of my teaching. But I had to learn to share the space. And
if I shared the space, I had to share the power. Allegra's question gave me a
new direction: What was the *least* I could do to make room for each student
to discover his or her own feeling of dancing? How did the passion I brought
to my own choreography resemble and differ from the passion I brought to
another art I practice—the art of teaching?

Listening and Watching

I suppose Allegra was testing whether I was listening. Doing so became a
key to opening the space. If I could listen well, students' passions, questions,
and what I began to call "what ifs?" could shape the dance; we would start
to recognize and experience the creativity hiding just below the surface. I did
not come in empty-handed, but neither did the students; that belief had to
walk in with me. I could no longer roll out a fully designed class not suscepti-
ble to change—change specifically provoked by students' ideas. I began to see
class design as a process of selecting choreographic structures in which I and
the students stayed alert for shifts—in attention, in spatial design, in energy,
in timing, in just about anything we could imagine in the physical world.

My take on Allegra's challenge—to get out of her way so she could experience her own sense of dancing—applied to every class I taught, from big
classes of 10-year-olds, to intimate groups of teenage choreographers like
Alex, to, most recently, diverse collections of college students who may or
may not be dance majors. Being a cairn meant being present and minimalist.
Offering a little something, without saying or doing too much. I walked into
one class with Kevin, my drummer, and said to the fourth graders, "What
do you know about time, or what do you think about time? Or what do you
think you know about time?" The first tender offerings focused on telling
time—by clock or calendar or season—and then someone said, "Time flies."
"When?" I asked. "When you're having fun," another answered. "What does
that mean?" I asked. Before I knew it, 25 children were excitedly pondering
whether time ever stopped, what would happen when they died, how reincar-
nation and déjà vu worked, and after about 5 minutes I said, "Well, Kevin's

going to tell you something he knows about time and he's not going to say a word." Kevin had not been in on my preparatory musings, but he grinned and began to play. The children gasped and began to rock to Kevin's beat. "Oh," they said. "Oh. That's time too." What a dance class we had after that.

Allegra's question didn't suddenly make me stop planning. In fact, planning became a more intensive process. I spent hours imagining every student and digging around in my memory for what I heard and saw in their dancing. I started hauling notebook and pen around the studio with me, scribbling notes about what students were doing, what questions they asked each other, what thoughts they expressed. Studying the notes later, I asked myself questions. When did this or that student get excited? What did he or she say, or was she mostly silent? To whom should I pay special attention so I would catch that little smile or glimmer in the eye and be able to say, "What was that, Stephanie, it looks like you had an idea?" My goal: to pay very close attention and turn the students on to themselves.

The scary part was—still is—the not knowing. "Where will this lead? Is there time?" I've learned that if I'm afraid, I'm probably on the right track. This part *is* like my creative struggle when making a new dance: that inner voice saying, "This will probably stink." Taking that risk with my own artwork, I realize, involves only me. Jumping off a cliff with a group of students, though, could have heavier consequences.

It's How I Am

Sometime around 2000, I read Seymour Sarason's *Teaching as a Performing Art*.[113] Sarason describes the work of his mentor, a visual artist and teacher, Henry Schaefer-Simmern, whose own book, *The Unfolding of Artistic Activity*,[114] documents the extraordinary artwork of "non-artists" whom he taught in a particularly nondirective way. Schaefer-Simmern and Sarason both were committed to individuals' innate capabilities and questioned the assumptions behind a uniform imposition of teachers' rules. They sounded like kindred cairns, inspiring me to go further out on the edge of my thinking about students' choreographic capabilities. By chance, soon after discovering these works, I was invited to try some of my ideas with a very small group of teenage choreographers in a program called Young Masters.[115]

I had been taught to begin with improvisation, followed or accompanied by training in compositional forms, after which comes choreography, when students get to make "real" dances. That is stated too simply. Still, the overall concept is that improvisation opens a creative channel to use when learning compositional rules and then it all comes together in the choreographic process for which students have been well prepared. I kept getting hung up on a variation of Allegra's question: Who gets to have the idea?

In most improvisation classes, a teacher poses prompts, side-coaching students who physically explore the ideas, imagery, or limitations the teacher offers. Improvisations often follow game structures or "scores" and are designed as open-ended, creative explorations. Students don't usually propose the prompt, nor do they side-coach or direct other students' explorations. Although students improvising to a teacher's prompts do experience certain creativity, if they never initiate or direct, the teacher remains in command and, thus, holds the creative reins. Alane Starko, writing about visual arts teaching, says, "Rather than shielding students from the frustration of seeking ideas, teacher-structured problems rob students of the art making process: looking for ideas; choosing materials, tools, and forms; visualizing a variety of possibilities."[116] Starko talks about problem finding, not just problem solving; this was where I wanted to go.

I checked my thinking with friends from college. Was there a missing link in our education, wonderful though it had been? Had our training—to respond to improvisational commands and construct compositional studies along a uniform progression—accidentally overlooked what we might have offered: interesting problems or intuitions that the existing structures didn't accommodate? Did inattention to our own impulses make us stifle some tender shoots long ago? One of my old friends nodded and said softly, "Yeah, I got an MFA but I can't say I ever really knew what *I* wanted to say with my dances." I longed to find a different way in with the Young Masters choreographers.

The first day of the experiment, I rode the subway to the studio, nervous about my plan for the 2-hour class. I intended to ask Anna, Lydia, and Indira, the only choreographers who had enrolled in Young Masters thus far, to create a "something," then to show and discuss the work, and to identify their own goals for the course. I had narrowed the tasks no further. My training suggested I offer a starting place—a theme or a concept, some structure for them to follow. Out on the mountainside, one might erect the occasional signpost saying something like, "If I were you, I'd turn left here. You don't have to, but *I* might do that, based on *my* experience with this trail." I was working hard to try another way, to be a cairn.

As the train pulled into the stop before mine, a woman rose and stood by the door. I was surprised the woman beside her didn't rise also; I had thought they were together. Just before the train arrived at the station, the standing woman said to her seated friend, "You're going to stay there until the doors open?" The friend nodded and said with a shrug, "It's how I am." The train stopped, the doors opened, and the seated woman stood, following her companion onto the platform, both women gently laughing. I laughed too; they'd given me the idea I'd been looking for.

In the studio, I met the three choreographers and we talked briefly about goals. Then I told them my subway story and said, "So that's it—'It's How I Am.' Whatever that means to you. How much time do you need?" Anna suggested half an hour and the others agreed. Then Lydia said, "Do I have to *think* about 'how I am' to create the dance, or could I just start to move?" "Great question," I said. "Moving can be a beginning. Follow wherever that leads."

The three dances made that day were startlingly different from one another; each choreographer found form, process, and content that seemed necessary to her own creation. Picturing those dances now, nearly a decade later, I see them whole, each with its own rhythmic, spatial, and dynamic structure and growing out of the "am"ness of each young artist. What those students and others created over the next 3 years changed my understanding and my process. David Bohm wrote about an artist creating "his own order of necessity. Different parts of the form he is making must have an inner necessity or else the thing has not really much of a value."[117] I did not arrive empty-handed to my first meeting with the three teenage choreographers. Nor did they.

Going to College

Teaching at a college upped the ante. After teaching technique for three semesters, I was invited to teach improvisation in an undergraduate dance program in the fall of 2011, 4 years after the end of the Young Masters experiment. I read up on different universities' approaches to the choreographic process to see if anything had changed since my undergrad experience. Studying course descriptions and articles in professional dance education journals, I was struck by the uniformity of the choreographic progression described: improvisation (with primarily professor-designed prompts, I'm guessing), composition, and, at long last, choreography. The dance education field seemed quite certain this model was still best. I thought of Ben Shahn, recalling a young poet who had given up writing poetry because in college he discovered that "there's so much that you have to know before you can write poetry. There are so many forms that you have to master first." Shahn wondered,

> whether it was made clear to him that all poetic forms have derived from practice; that in the very act of writing poetry he was, however crudely, beginning to create form. I wonder whether it was pointed out to him that form is an instrument, not a tyrant.[118]

As I prepared to teach improv, I realized there was no turning back; I had to see if my approach would work on a bigger mountainside. Now, instead of three or six or eight teenage girls dedicated to dancing and to each other, I would face college students who had enrolled for a host of reasons, including, for some, that it was a requirement for the dance major. Nearly 20 of them, ranging in age from 19 to 37, with vastly different experiences in dance—from some who had barely taken a dance class to those who had had professional dance careers—filled the roster, all of them essentially new to improvisation. And instead of 2 or 3 hours for each session, this would be a 50-minute class, three times a week. With grades. Ready? Jump.

The first class assignment, due the next day, was to write an honest answer to two questions: (a) What do you hope to get out of this course? and (b) What will you have to bring in order to get that out of it? Every student returned the next day with a response, as did I. Most were handwritten and each told me something valuable. I was already learning what made my students tick. In the fourth class, at the beginning of week 2, I threw the improvisers into one of the simplest structures I've found to trigger a series of "what if?" questions. Twenty students count off around a circle, from 1 to 10 and 1 to 10 again, to create pairs who share a number across the circle. Silently, without visible or audible cue, the dancers, in order from 1 to 10, change places on the circle—1s, 2s, 3s, etc. Each pair must feel the moment to change. That's it. My job is to watch and to listen. Always—always—something shifts and people notice. A near collision, a change of energy or timing, an unexpected relationship and the implication of a narrative—people notice and gasp and laugh and say, "Oh." That's when I say, "What? What happened? What do you want to do next?" In that simple, minimal structure, students start tuning in to their innate understanding of form, noticing what intrigues them in action, and saying things others hadn't thought of. They begin to notice what already exists in their imaginations and bodies to manipulate space, time, dynamics, and other choreographic structures. My almost wordless message to my students: "You have it within you."

Sometimes, out on the mountain, you see a pile of rocks that's just a pile of rocks. You move toward it because you think it's a cairn. You gradually realize that it's not a cairn, but also that it brought you to an interesting place you wouldn't have otherwise gone. One day, I asked the students in my improvisation course to start with breath and heartbeat, seeing where that led. I watched Neela, pressed against the wall, barely moving, looking grim. Inside, I panicked. I wrote myself notes: "Neela looks frustrated. It does look a little like a loony-bin. People are rocking like Dustin Hoffman in *Rain Man*. Oh no." I contemplated stepping in, offering a new path, jolting them out of their go-nowhere breath/beat explorations. Then I remembered a colleague leading a workshop about "chance dances," tossing coins on the floor to establish, by chance, where the dancers' starting positions would be. Except she didn't like where the pennies had fallen, so she scooped them up and said, "That's no good—let's try again." No, I couldn't jettison this empty-looking wandering; I would have to live through the pain of it. I scribbled on and remembered something Lawrence Stenhouse wrote: "Through self-monitoring, the teacher becomes a conscious artist. Through conscious art he is able to use himself as an instrument in his research."[119]

I made a note to lead a reflection in the next class so students might air their frustrations about the open-ended structure and subsequent lack of inspiration. I prepared to apologize to Neela for putting her through that undirected tedium. It hadn't been a cairn. It was just a pile of rocks.

But when Neela spoke the next morning, she took me where she'd been—a place I couldn't actually see from the outside.

> I feel like the beginning yesterday was made just for me. I had a horrible morning and didn't want to dance. And you said to just focus on our breath and our heartbeats. I noticed myself start to change. What I was feeling on the inside shifted to the outside and started to move. When we were done, I was in a new place—and I realized my own breath had gotten me there.

Others had different experiences, of course. Molly, for example, never found her pulse, so finally she gave up and started to go with others' rhythms, which she described as fun, "like changing personalities." Steven spoke of becoming obsessed with the smallest motion of his toes. I listened. When I finally spoke, I was laughing. First I read from my notes: how unsatisfying the improv had appeared, how like a loony-bin. Then I told Neela I'd planned to apologize for putting her through that. She stared, wide-eyed. Eyebrows raised, mouths open, we thought but didn't say, "Huh! Who knew that was about to happen?" The mysteries are so funny.

Choreographic Projects: Facing the Fear

A year after teaching that course, I was asked to direct the dance program's Choreographic Projects. I said it was impossible: 29 choreographers in 50-minute classes, three times a week. It was nuts. Too many artists, too little time for each one's problem finding in the process of creating 29 distinct group works. I couldn't run away from the challenge.

There was a lot of fear in the room. My own fear about failing at what I'd declared was impossible. My students' fears; most had never choreographed a group work and were holding in their heads all of the composition rules they'd learned while making solo works the previous spring. And the fears of my colleagues, who, having entrusted me with this mission, had their own anxieties. What, after all, could emerge from a class led by someone who just wanted to arrange some rocks along a mountain trail? How would these choreographers learn how to make good dances if I didn't steadily point them in the right direction, calling out mileage and indicating better routes from time to time? If I insisted, as I did, that my job was not to *fix* the works, but rather to have the students study their own work, find questions, and conduct experiments, how would we explain ourselves to a paying audience? Previous concerts, directed toward a modern dance aesthetic and subjected to costuming and music approval by the faculty, had been presented as essentially "finished" products. This concert, too, would undoubtedly be taken as a reflection of the faculty's skill in developing accomplished artists; what faculty member wouldn't be nervous? How many people was I willing to drag up the mountain trail with me? All of them.

The hard part of being a cairn is being as watchful and patient as you need to be. People approach and you think, "Yes, yes, this is good." Then they start to veer off because they see some odd rock formation or tree branch over your left shoulder and you think, "Uh-oh. You are definitely headed off a cliff there." But you can't really say anything. You can concentrate your energy: Be more present, more solid, perhaps, so that after an explorer has spent a little time looking at something interesting, he or she will become aware again that you are there and that another promising pile of rocks might sit somewhere nearby.

This is where it gets tricky, as an artist who also teaches, to know which part of the art you're in: making your own choreography (or painting or poem or film) or making your own teaching. The intuitive visions kick in no matter what. But there's a difference. When you're looking at another artist's work thinking, "Wouldn't it be great if they huddled in the corner a little longer and then maybe one person bursts out first? Or how about you use this piece of music—I *love* this piece of music—this would be *perfect*!", little red flags should be popping up all through your consciousness. Those would be your art ideas—seeded with a student's beginnings. Those responses can't—and shouldn't—be shut off; you're seeing something, being inspired. Write that down in your notebook—and then focus your attention on that artist over there and what's taking shape under her hands. What is she saying or not saying? Can you tell what she's thinking about? Are you puzzled, intrigued, frustrated? How is she working with her dancers or the materials? What problem is she trying to solve? That's how my notes look when I'm thick in the art of teaching. It's not a different process, but it is a different intent. It's also a different content: student's work, not mine.

As a cairn, I should be honest. I shouldn't scatter myself into the brush and see if my students can find their way alone. I plant myself at the edge of the studio and watch, intently. I take notes. I write down what choreographers say and read it back to them later, asking, "Did you know you said that?"

In the moment, my questions are usually echoes. "How do the opposite rolls look?" Joan asks. "How do the opposite rolls look?" I ask back. She wants to strangle me. "I can't see!" she says, infuriated. "Why can't you see?" I ask. "I don't know!" she wails. "How will you see?" I say. Now she pauses. "Maybe . . ." She chews a fingernail. "Maybe," she goes on, "they have to roll the same way, then opposite, and then I can compare." The dancers experiment while she side-coaches again and again. At last Joan cries, "I know what it is. I figured it out! There you go, now it looks like something."

If a student doesn't ask a question, it's on me. "Give me an example," my friend Fran, a dean at a school of education, said as I described the process to her over dinner one night. I offered this: "Is the ending taking the time you want it to take?"

"That's a terrible question," Fran said. "It's a yes or no question. I'd ask the student to explain why it's taking that time, so she'll understand her choices better."

"I don't want her to explain," I said. "I want her to look." Fran's automatic rejection of a "yes/no" question had an educator's rationale. I wanted students to stay in the artistic process. Asking them to explain—particularly to someone in power—would take them out of the artistic process. They would begin rationalizing. As we talked, I realized that explaining was helping me—in *this* situation. But if Fran asked me to explain my choreography while I was in the midst of it, I'd refuse. What student—pressed by a teacher—would claim that right for herself?

Fran asked why I didn't just suggest the student look at the ending; why pose a question? "It's the quality of a suggestion," I said. "She'd start trying to figure out what *I* thought was wrong. Asking if the ending does what she wants keeps me out of it. I could have asked something else, like 'Does the end happen where you want it in space?'" Before posing any questions, I told Fran, I tell students not to answer, to just look and take notes, and to disregard questions that aren't useful. Suggestions have a different power. Where the questions lead is none of my business. We sit together in the art of it, following where it goes. Listen. Play it back. Watch. Ask a question. Be still. Trust.

Trusting myself can be harder than trusting students. As Jen rehearsed her trio, I puzzled over the opening shape—dancers' arms flung overhead. Wanting to ask, "Why are their arms up there?" I instead wrote in my journal. I wondered how to help Jen focus on the opening without saying, "I think the arms are weird." I asked Jen if I could address her dancers. "Before you start, is there anything you're confused about?" They identified a problem with counts. Nothing about arms. While Jen clarified counts, I wrote my disappointment: "Nobody confused by arms."

Soon Jen cued the dancers, then stopped. "Wait a second. Now *I'm* confused. What's that arm doing up there?" Jen guided her dancers through a number of experiments with different arm motions, finally saying, "Try that." We watched her revised opening and she clapped her hands, delighted. "That's so much better!" she cried. "I fixed it!"

Baffled, I also felt guilty. Talking with my partner Barry [Oreck] later, I worried that I'd unintentionally manipulated Jen to deal with *my* problem, not hers. "I'm not sure why I asked the dancers about being confused. I was desperate." Barry listened, then said, "Maybe it was intuitive. You turned to the material—the dancers—instead of the choreographer and helped Jen look at the work from inside. Maybe digging into it, instead of thinking about it, gave her time to wonder if anything confused *her*."

Barry set out a cairn, reminding me how much of value happens on an unconscious level. All I "knew" was to let the writing slow me down and to stay out of it when the dancers' problem differed from mine. I like to think that if the arms had remained "weird," that would have been all right too. Looking back, Jen's discovery of her power to make her piece "better" according to her own criteria was the prize. It was what Schaefer-Simmern might say was evidence of artistic unfolding.

Who Shouldn't Be There?

I taught improvisation along with choreography that semester. Lee, a senior pharmacology major, had not danced since her childhood in Korea and saw this as her last chance to dance in college. Enrolled in the beginning level technique class—a prerequisite for improv—she came to improv through a scheduling miscommunication. By the time we figured it out, she was committed to our improvisation class and we to her. I skirted around the rules and Lee stayed.

On the day of Lee's "what if"—a day every slightly petrified improv student faced, charged with directing half the class through an improvisation he or she had designed while the other half watched—she rose and took a deep breath. In halting English, she said, "I want—watch my hands." She started to delicately paint the air. Immediately the dancers on stage mirrored her gestures. Lee stopped, dropping her chin to her chest. She took another breath. "No," she said. "How can I say?" Slowly she moved her hands again. The dancers on stage watched, rapt, and then, almost as one, smiled, nodded, and began to move, independent of one another, each responding uniquely to Lee's hands. Dancers traveled, dropped to the ground, reached and spun, each finding his or her own way to interpret Lee's intent. As they moved, her hands changed; she picked up on dancers' actions and experimented with new gestures, watching the result and shifting again. The cringe I felt initially ("Oh dear, a miming conductor routine") eased as I opened my eyes to the beauty taking shape. This was like an improv teacher's side-coaching. But it was a student, not a teacher, and she had found another language for leading. Those watching, puzzled at first, turned to each other, asking, "What? How?" Soon they, too, began to smile and say, "Oh, oh . . ."

At the end of this silent, breathtaking symphony of motion, Lee as conductor and dancers as her instruments found stillness. Every dancer in the audience and on stage erupted with an ecstatic cheer, on their feet, applauding the most extraordinary improvisation of the semester. Lee stood speechless, hands to her mouth: What had she done? Stunned, I tried not to cry, aware of my power as a teacher and that my own celebration or emotion might suggest this was the kind of work the other 18 should have been doing all along—a message I didn't want to send. How does a cairn silently cheer?

Every student in conference with me after that day mentioned Lee's improv and how it had changed them. Lee too, spoke of being transformed. "I made it up," she said, "because my English is no good. I asked myself, 'How can I say what I want to say?' I went home that day to my aunt and told her everything. She was so proud. It changed everything. I think now I am a dancer." Lee was the one student who did not have the prerequisite, who was not "qualified" to be in that class.

There is no way to know, teaching this way, if you really get it "right." There are signs though. Anna, of the Young Masters experiment, said when it was all over, "It really felt like it was ours, that it had emerged from something we already had inside of us—not that it had been "taught.'"[120] That small cairn continues to beckon me forward.

Chapter 9

EMBRACING VULNERABILITY

Organic Creativity in Teaching Theatre

Jeremy Dubin

There is a quote attributed, perhaps apocryphally, to Lawrence Olivier. When asked why actors act, he said it could be summed up thusly: "Look at me, look at me, look at me." The reply is witty (in that enviable way that all old British actors seem to have of speaking) and at first glance might appear glib; but the capriciousness of his response perhaps belies the caustic depth of the sentiment. It is, in truth, an insightful and almost painfully honest remark. Is it an oversimplification? Yes, but any performer who says it doesn't ring at least a little true is a liar. Or in denial. Or possibly just a much better person than I am. On the surface, the statement suggests nothing but egotism, but just a dash more scrutiny and the plaintive, pleading quality, the emotional neediness, the downright desperation becomes evident. It encapsulates that incongruous concoction of confidence and insecurity, of inhibition and exhibition, of hunger and chutzpah that constitutes the enigmatic psyche of those driven to perform.

I know of what I speak. I have spent nearly my whole life performing, well over a decade of it as part of a professional resident ensemble producing up to 10 productions each year. I don't think I could begin to conjecture exactly how many performances I've turned in, but I think it's safe to say that over the past 10 years I have spent more nights on a stage than off. I've received acclaim, awards, ovations, and national recognition, and every single time I walk off that stage I still anxiously wonder "Did they like me?" Sickening, isn't it?

 Jeremy Dubin, M.F.A., is an Artistic Associate with the Cincinnati Shakespeare Company (CSC), where he acts, directs, and serves as resident text coach. He is also the director and curriculum designer of the CSC Shakespeare Summer Camp and the CSC Groundlings Program (a yearlong Shakespeare intensive for talented high school students).

Now, it may be that not every student drawn to theatre is saddled with that kind of insecurity, but speaking anecdotally, a lot more are than aren't. Of course, the way in which that insecurity manifests can vary wildly. Sometimes it is through overcompensation, the upshot of which is the type of personality generally associated with theatre students (for better or for worse)—big, boisterous, the first to volunteer for any class exercise, anxious for any opportunity to be the center of attention. For these students, the real trick is getting them to stop performing, to open up and share themselves simply and honestly on stage, to convince them that the real person is actually much more interesting than the persona it's hiding under. Just as common, if not more so, is the introvert—sometimes painfully shy. At first I was baffled by the presence of these students in my classes.

My programs are not affiliated with any school; subsequently there is no course requirement they fulfill. They are strictly voluntary, and, in fact, cost money. So why would these students, to whom it seems utter agony to have to open their mouths and speak in front of a group, voluntarily sign up for a performance class? I eventually came to realize it's because it is utter agony for them to have to open their mouths and speak in front of a group. They are seeking to find their voices and to blast through whatever blockages they have imposed upon themselves. And for these students, the trick is convincing them that they have as much a right to be heard as anyone else (which can be very difficult for them to believe), and to get them to stop apologizing, be it consciously or unconsciously, for wanting attention. Ultimately, for both these types of students (and the thousand gradations between), it comes down to the problem of vulnerability.

Rosalind Russell once said, "Acting is standing up naked and turning around very slowly." (Conversely Sir Ralph Richardson called acting "merely the art of keeping a large group of people from coughing," so you see what I mean about those Brits). But I think I have to side with Rosalind on this. It is taking the most intimate and private parts of life and putting them on display. It is the art of public vulnerability. But that vulnerability, which is so integral to good acting, is also delicate and volatile. Being vulnerable is terrifying for anyone, let alone adolescents (the age I primarily teach) whose bodies, voices, and hormonal balances are changing by the day. Add into that mix the insecurities I talked about above, and you've got a situation fraught with perils. When one is feeling vulnerable, one tends to either withdraw and wall up—which makes it virtually impossible be creative, to share, to take risks, or to collaborate—or else to lash out and try to tear down others, which makes it virtually impossible for anyone else in the vicinity to be creative, to share, to take risks, or to collaborate. The tricky part is not overcoming vulnerability (I would think that much easier—to just never take any risks), but learning to embrace, indulge, and celebrate it. For that to be remotely possible, it is imperative to establish a group trust.

Risk-Taking

Risk-taking is an inherent part of the creative process. If students are to realize their potential, to develop the skills in which they are the least confident, to step outside of what is comfortable, they need to have the freedom to indulge in unfettered exploration. They have to be willing not only to go out on a limb, but to leap, hop, and jitterbug on that limb. What stands in the way of their arboreal Lindy-Hopping is that ubiquitous question "What if I fall?" Unless these students are attending Shangri-La High, they have been conditioned to fear failure. That fear becomes all the more acute with the possibility of public failure, which performance-related activities, by their nature, must include. If fear of failure is not to preclude risk-taking, it is necessary to have a safe environment—an environment in which failure has been destigmatized, in which it is encouraged and even celebrated. In such an environment, one can fail without fear of judgment, one has permission to be bad at things—it's pretty incredible just how liberating that idea can be. If embraced whole-heartedly, then failure ceases to be something to be avoided, and becomes what it should be: an invaluable and illuminative tool of learning and growth. This is the first thing that I discuss at the beginning of any course, and I have found that it is a notion that appeals universally. Students are hungry for the opportunity to create such an environment, and all it takes is the decision to do it. Of course there are some things that can help that process along the way.

I begin each class with a little ritual (or exercise, or warm-up, whichever vocabulary jibes with you). Everyone stands in a circle, closes their eyes (whether or not we take hands is dependent on if it's flu season), and takes a couple of deep breaths together as an ensemble. Then I ask them to flip whatever switches they need to flip in their brains to put them in a positive mindset, to commit to creating a supportive and safe environment, and to decide one thing they are going to try that day that scares the hell out of them. We take a couple more breaths together and pump some good energy into the group, and then we open our eyes. Just that simple, but it serves as a sort of mini-meditation and an effective reminder of the safe environment that we want to create.

I like to spend the first part of any course with a combination of trust exercises and games. I won't detail all of them here, as there are almost endless resources for such things, online and elsewhere, but I would like to discuss the one I always begin with: the trust walk. You may be familiar with it, or some variant of it. The class stands in a wide circle; one brave volunteer enters the circle, stands in front of a classmate and closes his or her eyes. Said class-mate exchanges a silent communication with someone across the circle and then gives the volunteer a gentle nudge in that direction. The volunteer then simply has to walk across the circle in that direction with eyes closed and without slowing down, until he reaches the other person (or someone nearby if he has drifted off course). He is gently caught and then sent to someone else in the circle, etc. It is a simple exercise, but one that is both beneficial and revelatory, and a patent embodiment of risk-taking. It requires the vol-unteer to put herself blindly into the hands of her classmates—I know, the metaphor alone almost knocks you over, doesn't it? It is the "without slowing down" instruction that becomes the vital one, for inevitably there will come a point in the crossing when she will think she has gone too far, that she should have been caught already, and her body will scream at her to stop; her panic reaction will kick in and she will slow down, or lean back, or bring her arms up, or in some other way attempt to protect herself.

Sometimes it is subtle, sometimes it is overt, but it is almost always there. You point it out to the student and ask him to try to push through that moment the next time—the feeling of vulnerability and panic will still be there, will always be there, but the important thing is that we can learn to control how we respond to it. They also, if they pay attention, will learn where within their bodies their panic reaction manifests, where they feel most vulnerable. For some, it's in the stomach, for some the face or shoulders, or elsewhere, but it is the place they will instinctually try to protect in their moment of panic. Knowing where that is can be incredibly useful informa-tion for both student and teacher. Those standing in the circle are entrusted with the safety of the person in the middle, and being given that trust, I have never seen anyone fail to rise to the occasion. It is a concrete illustration of how important it is to support each other, and just how easy it would be to cause irreparable damage. Incidentally, I have always found it fascinating that after the first volunteer walks the circle, almost every hand shoots in the air to be the one to go next.

Games

Games are equally important. Even the simplest games, something like Duck, Duck, Goose, can illustrate beautifully such fundamental acting concepts as Objective, Tactic, and Obstacle, while at the same time helping the student to reconnect to a childlike state of mind, one that is playful and receptive. Games can acclimate students to feeling silly or foolish in front of one another, and can be pivotal in circumventing that formidable obstacle of learning, the ego.

These activities and exercises can go a long way in helping students deal with the anxiety of external judgment; however, the much more insidious demon is internal judgment. The single greatest detriment to the creative process is the inner critic—that voice that suggests an idea we have isn't good, or isn't clever, or isn't worthy of being put out into the world. It is a voice with which every artist has at some point been intimately familiar, and it is heartbreaking to think of the number of masterpieces and strokes of brilliance it has barred from the world. There is a quote of Martha Graham's I'm very fond of; Agnes de Mille had come to her after the opening of *Oklahoma!*, concerned at the high praise she was receiving for work she considered only mediocre. Martha replied to her,

> There is a vitality, a life force, an energy, a quickening that is translated through you into action, and because there is only one of you in all of time, this expression is unique. And if you block it, it will never exist through any other medium and it will be lost. The world will not have it. It is not your business to determine how good it is nor how valuable nor how it compares with other expressions. It is your business to keep it yours clearly and directly, to keep the channel open.[121]

Our instincts, impulses, and intuition are the most precious resources we have as artists, and our inner critic is what causes us to second-guess them and undermine ourselves. The trick is to keep ourselves from blocking them, to condition ourselves to recognize our instincts and immediately give them voice, before the critic has a chance to shut them down. To facilitate this, I like to use improvisation.

Improvisation

Improvisation is an activity that can be abjectly terrifying, again because of the element of vulnerability. The fear is that one might open one's mouth and say something that will reveal one to be stupid, or unoriginal, or insane. The beauty of improvisation is that it emphasizes the idea that that's okay. Whatever comes out of one's mouth is valid, even if it's stupid, or unoriginal, or insane. The most basic and most important tenet of improvisation, the first thing they will teach you in any improv class or book is always say yes, never deny. This means saying yes to other people's ideas, and also to your own; because you never know where an idea (be it stupid, or unoriginal, or insane) might lead. And interestingly enough, having permission to be stupid, unoriginal, and insane can allow the imagination to flourish. Consequently, many improv games and exercises are designed to help blast through the inner critic, or at least circumvent it.

I begin with structured games that are goal-oriented. One of my favorites is a game called 5 Things, which is a kind of variation on charades. One person leaves the room, and the rest of the group comes up with five unusual activities (i.e., playing hockey with a turtle instead of a puck). The person is called back into the room, and his teammates, using mime and gibberish (a made-up nonsensical language), have to get him to perform each activity and guess correctly what he is doing. There is a 5-minute time limit, and the team receives one point for each activity that is correctly guessed.

Not only is this highly entertaining to watch, but it has multiple benefits. First, all of the players have a specific goal they are trying to accomplish, and this tends to make them think less about the fact that they are performing in front of people. It doesn't matter if their ideas are silly or stupid, as long as it helps their teammate guess. Also, their focus is on their teammate, not on themselves, which tends to make them less self-conscious. Lastly, the obstacle of a time limit means they have no time to second-guess themselves—the circumstances of the game necessitate that they act on their intuition and first instincts. And a periodic bonus is that those silly, ridiculous ideas, the ones they might deem too stupid to try if given any time to consider it, often are the ones that get the biggest response from those watching. This can be a wonderful validation and an incentive to keep sharing ideas.

The next stage involves games with less structure and more freeform improv. A very basic one I like to use is called Expert. One person gets up in front of the group and is provided with some ridiculous topic on which he or she is the world's leading expert. The rest of the group then asks questions that the expert answers. The only rule is the expert must answer with complete confidence and surety. The actual content of the answer is irrelevant; he could answer in complete gibberish (which I have seen happen more than once), as long as it's done with utter conviction. The rest of the group is empowered as "snipers" and if they detect the expert hesitating, or displaying verbally or physically any sign of uncertainty, they can shout out "Bang!" After an allotted number of "bangs" the expert is out, and someone else steps up. The beauty of this game is that it not only requires the student to give voice to his first instincts, but also to do so confidently and assertively. Far too often we torpedo our own ideas, instincts, and intuitions by presenting them in a way that is apologetic; our body language, or phrasing, or vocality screams out "I'm sorry, I know this is terrible, please shoot it down." This cannot help but influence how the idea will be received by others, and in turn what we will think of it ourselves.

These games, and hundreds of others like them, are designed to keep students from judging their own work, to prevent them from getting in the way of their own creative process. As Martha Graham suggested in the quote above, we ourselves are often the least qualified person to judge our own work. That's not our place. Our place is to stay open to our intuition and our instincts and to get our ideas out there. Once we have given ourselves permission to follow through on our intuition, then true artistic exploration can begin. With a safe environment around us, and an open channel to our intuition within us, it's time to dig in and start working on some scenes; and in my experience the indisputably best tool available to developing actors is Shakespeare.

The Importance (Still) of Shakespeare

Over the past few generations, there has been a subtle but unmistakable shift in our relationship with the spoken word. As Kristin Linklater keenly observed in *Freeing Shakespeare's Voice*,

> The industrial revolution, the technological revolution, the rapid growth in literacy and the influence of print have diminished the need for the human voice over the past one hundred fifty years, and we are moving at breakneck speed, in evolutionary terms, further and further away from tens of thousands of years of oral/aural civilization.[122]

The advent of e-mailing, texting, and tweeting has accelerated this process by making brevity and expediency the new gold standard. In addition, our cultural mores have also undergone a shift. Outside of sporting events, full-throated expressions of passion are generally frowned upon. From early childhood onward, we are systematically taught to temper our responses, to be moderate and reasonable, and to avoid getting worked up. These are, of course, necessary social skills in any civilized society, but we are also, as a consequence, getting accustomed to choking off our feelings. This can result in not only emotional blockages, but also vocal ones. There are times when getting worked up is appropriate, when a passionate outburst is exactly what's called for. Being able to do this, at least in any sort of articulate way, is something we are in danger of losing. And, as art serves to reflect the society that creates it, this trend has also become evident in our performance aesthetic.

Most modern schools of acting will tell you, it's all about the subtext. It's not what you say, but what you don't say that really matters. We convey more through the "meaningful look" than through the words we speak. The technology of film and television and the advent of the close-up has allowed this to flourish. Words seem superfluous when we can see the nuances of a thought played across a face 20 feet high, and should we miss it, the underscoring (a very effective emotional shorthand) will tell us exactly what we're supposed to be feeling, and so the words become almost secondary—it is what is underneath those words that matters.

The society in which Shakespeare lived, the society which he reflects in his plays, had a very different relationship with language; the language itself may not have changed much since the Elizabethan era (the occasional thee, thou, or prithee notwithstanding), but our interaction with language certainly has. In Shakespeare's England, literacy was still far from widespread; for most, there was no communication through writing, no entertainment through reading. They had to rely solely on the spoken word.

Consequently, the oral tradition was much more vital. A good story that could be passed along from mouth to mouth was highly valued, and the more colorful and descriptive the language, the better. And this is where Shakespeare excelled. His language drips with texture and color. His imagery is vivid and evocative. The very sounds of the words themselves create an almost tactile sense to his work. In addition, in Shakespeare's society, uninhibited expressions of passion were not considered unseemly. In fact, thy were valued—especially when it came to theatre. Direct and spirited speech was what was required to make a play popular, or even heard, in the theatres of London. Shakespeare was contending against the rowdy (and often illiterate) crowd, the shrill shriek of the vendors, the honest-to-God bear baiting going on right outside the gates.

If he wanted to have any hope of his story being understood and followed, he had to do it clearly and overtly with the words. Truth was conveyed by the words—characters spoke exactly what they were thinking, what they were feeling. There was no subtext or unspoken motivations. Even deceptive characters (Iago, for instance), would announce to the audience that they were about to be deceitful. Subtleties and implications, significant looks, a quirked eyebrow, or slight upturning of the corner of the mouth (tropes that speak volumes in modern media) meant absolutely nothing. It all had to be conveyed clearly and unequivocally through the words.

So, is Shakespeare some sort of panacea that will obliterate harmful vocal habits, cure all modern neuroses, and return us to the golden age of literary eloquence? Probably not. However, the fact that he was writing in a different time, a time when the spoken word was a more vibrant and vital part of the human experience, when unabashed expressions of fervent emotion were not a societal taboo, means that his use of language is different from what we are accustomed to today, and performing it requires a slightly different set of tools. Becoming acquainted with those tools can immeasurably enrich young performers' palettes, capabilities, and whole experience of the art. It can put them in better touch with their instrument, broaden their scope and range, allow them to even become more comfortable with vulnerability, for Shakespeare's language supports vulnerability and gives it a voice. It provides a tenable framework for the naked expression of heightened emotion. And when a student experiences the power of that kind of expression, it can be absolutely transformative.

Carrie's Story

One summer at Shakespeare camp, we had a student named Carrie. She was in seventh grade and well-entrenched at the introvert end of the spectrum. She was quiet, self-conscious, incredibly smart, and somewhat embarrassed about it. She would undoubtedly be described by teachers as a model student, polite and well-behaved, yet during every class exercise her mannerisms and body language were protective and apologetic. She had been cast as Marc Antony in a scene from *Julius Caesar* (the ratio of male to female students compared to the ratio of male to female roles in the canon means that we often employ cross-gender casting—in this particular case it resulted in a coterie of female conspirators rising up against a male Caesar).

The scene was the assassination. In case anyone should be unfamiliar, a small cabal of senators has decided that Caesar is in danger of becoming a tyrant, and so they surround him and slaughter him on the senate floor. In the aftermath, Marc Antony, Caesar's close friend and ally, arrives and sees what has happened. After pretending to make nice with the conspirators, he is left alone with the still bleeding corpse of Caesar. The speech that follows is as potent as any in the canon—deep mourning for a slaughtered friend, damning condemnation of the conspirators' betrayal, avowal of vengeance, invocation of spirits and gods, and prophesying of the bloody consequences and harrowing chaos to come. I'm going to include the text here, because reading it will provide a better idea of its potency than any description could.

> O, pardon me, thou bleeding piece of earth,
> That I am meek and gentle with these butchers!
> Thou art the ruins of the noblest man
> That ever lived in the tide of times.
> Woe to the hand that shed this costly blood!
> Over thy wounds now do I prophesy,
> —Which, like dumb mouths, do ope their ruby lips,
> To beg the voice and utterance of my tongue—
> A curse shall light upon the limbs of men;
> Domestic fury and fierce civil strife
> Shall cumber all the parts of Italy;
> Blood and destruction shall be so in use
> And dreadful objects so familiar
> That mothers shall but smile when they behold
> Their infants quarter'd with the hands of war;
> All pity choked with custom of fell deeds:
> And Caesar's spirit, ranging for revenge,
> With Ate by his side come hot from hell,
> Shall in these confines with a monarch's voice
> Cry 'Havoc,' and let slip the dogs of war;
> That this foul deed shall smell above the earth
> With carrion men, groaning for burial.

To illustrate my point about Shakespeare's language, I want to take a small detour here and try a little exercise. Read the piece out loud (unless you are in a coffee shop or something, in which case enjoy your latte and do this when you get home). It's important to remember that Shakespeare wrote his plays to be performed, not read silently; the sounds of the consonants and vowels he employs in any given speech both clarify meaning and help the actor with his emotional journey. Now I'm going to throw you a couple tricks of the trade. Read it again and really indulge all the sounds, especially alliterated sounds ("fury and fierce civil strife," for instance). Already you may notice the speech become more vibrant and visceral. Next we're going to add onto this something called a tonal build.

You'll notice that after "costly blood" the entire rest of the speech is only one sentence (another challenge that Shakespeare offers the modern actor, who lives in a world of soundbites and quippy one-line exchanges). The energy should keep building and building with no release until the very end. This does not mean to do it all on one breath; you need breath under you to support the language. Instead, begin each new thought (or each new verse line if you prefer) on a higher pitch than the last one. You'll want to begin low to give yourself room to climb, and increase in small increments to prevent ending up comically high in the stratosphere (which even if you do, is fine for the purposes of this exercise). Notice how much more active the piece becomes, how the rhythm starts to assert itself, how the inherent build comes into focus, and how the potential energy contained within the words starts to become kinetic. Cool, right? Okay, enjoy the rest of your latte, and we'll get back to Carrie.

Carrie understood the speech perfectly. As I mentioned, she was extremely intelligent. She was also incredibly insightful; she could answer any question about the meaning of the text and the purpose it was meant to serve within the larger story. She delivered the speech in a way that was absolutely comprehensible—and very, very polite. Which, even with a cursory glance at the text, one can see is problematic. This is not a polite speech. Politeness has no business anywhere near this speech. It requires exactly all of those things we are taught are distasteful, and are conditioned to repress and squelch—especially in any quasiacademic setting. For all of its eloquence (and it is eloquent—viciously so), it is raw and it is visceral. It is ugly, and it is, above all, passionate. It comes from the depths of the self and embraces an absolute belief in the power of the spoken word to conjure events into being, to curse foes, to call down gods and to shape the destiny of the world. In order to best take advantage of the limited rehearsal time available, we split up. While the conspirators worked with a fight choreographer on stage combat (always a favorite), I took Carrie off to work the speech. We found an unoccupied dressing room, fashioned a substitute corpse from some cushions and towels, and went to work. The first time through, it was very tentative. Her eyes would periodically shift from the "body" to me, silently asking, "Was that okay?"

The next time we went through it, we engaged in a simple volume exercise. I'd say a line of the speech and have her repeat it, challenging her to top my volume. We'd go back and forth until we were both bellowing at the top of our lungs. A little silly perhaps, but it often serves to make the student less self-conscious when she sees her teacher is willing to scream like a maniac—it also often shows students that what they thought of as a 10 on their dial is actually only a 3. Once she was comfortable using her outside voice inside, we started applying the exercises detailed above. We went through line by line, making sure she was indulging every sound. Then we went through and made sure she never backed off the tonal build. This was harder for her; as you may have noticed when you did the exercise, as it gets higher and higher in pitch, it feels more out of control—which can be a little scary. Her voice kept wanting to settle back into a "safe" more comfortable range. But she fought the good fight and kept at it until she was able to do it. Finally, after taking it apart and looking at it in pieces, it was time to put it all back together again.

She began one more time, kneeling and focused on the makeshift rag doll corpse. She breathed a couple deep, easy breaths, and the text started coming. It was quiet, but it was connected to her. It had that quality that actors all strive for—it was a memorized speech, but she was discovering the words as they came. It felt immediate, urgent, and alive. There was a full force of will behind the words, investing them. She reached the word "butchers" at the end of the second line and spat it with such vehemence that it visibly rocked her. There tends to be a sort of tipping point at moments like those; the violence of the moment can cause us to retreat, to instinctually back off, for the intensity can be frightening, or else give in to it, ceding control to the text. She ceded. It was a moment of true inspiration; the language took her and lifted her, inspired her to find whatever she had to find in order to meet the needs of the oratory. Her politeness and propriety crumbled, as the words insisted on being heard. The cadence and the rhythm carried her inexorably forward, not allowing her to back off, the pitch rising and building with each new thought. She rose up from the ground, and her protective, apologetic body language was gone.

Suddenly she just opened up, whatever blockages and vocal inhibitions she had imposed upon herself fell away, and for the first time in who knows how long, she had direct clear access to her entire instrument. Her voice took on a depth and resonance, and all of the energy of the speech, the relentless cadence and rhythm, the tonal build, culminated in a blood-boiling "Havoc!"

that seemed all but impossible coming from her frame. The speech came to its conclusion. There is something that happens after a truly remarkable performance; you've probably experienced it in a theatre, a concert hall, or elsewhere. The room has changed, the air is different, something outside our routine realm of experience has occurred. Carrie was actually trembling, and looked a little dazed. She looked at me, and after a couple of beats said, "Was that okay?"

A door opened for Carrie that day that challenged her notions of herself and her capabilities. I'm not going to say that the experience instantly obliterated all of her insecurities and banished forever all of her physical and vocal inhibitions; these things don't work that way. After moments of breakthrough, our old habits and tendencies reassert themselves, sometimes with a vengeance, and it is the work of years to overcome them (should you be interested, Carrie took on that challenge, coming back year after year, becoming a leader among her peers, then a camp counselor, and eventually going on to study theatre at college). But experiencing even once what the payoff can be, knowing that it is possible to shatter what we conceive of as our limitations, makes all of the difference, and provides the impetus to keep fighting.

Can all of what Carrie experienced that day be attributed to Shakespeare? Undoubtedly, a tremendous amount of it had to do with what a remarkable young lady she was, but there is no question in my mind that it also had a good deal to do with the tools she was using. Inspiration can come from anywhere, but it certainly helps to be working with material that is itself inspired, that asks great things of you, and will give you great things in return. When inspiration arrived and the moment came to let go, to cede power to the language, to do a trust fall, she had text that not only caught her, but lifted her and allowed her to soar. I don't know that you get that with Neil Simon (I do not mean in any way to cast aspersions on Mr. Simon, whose works I absolutely adore). If we want to challenge students, challenge them to find what their instruments are capable of, challenge their notions of what language is capable of, challenge them to embrace whole-bodily the vitality and the potency of the spoken word, then why not give them every advantage? Cook with the best ingredients, build with the best tools, and act with the greatest playwright in the history of the English language.

Vulnerability Is Scary

Vulnerability is scary. Especially in front of strangers. Especially in front of large groups of strangers, which is, God help us, what actors have chosen to do for a living. But vulnerability goes hand in hand with honesty. And without honesty, theatre can't perform its most valuable function—giving society the opportunity to see itself. Of course theatre involves artifice, but if that artifice is not used to express truth, it is mere mummery. "Look at me, look at me, look at me!" the actor cries—and then is faced with the decision of what to do when people actually look. He can bluff, bluster, and hide, or he can do the terrifying thing: Stand there exposed, in direct contradiction of all common sense, conventional wisdom, and every screaming instinct of self-protection and preservation, in order that he may "hold, as 'twere, the mirror up to nature, to show virtue her own feature, scorn her own image, and the very age and body of the time his form and pressure."[123] Nice turn of phrase, but what did you expect? He's British.

Chapter 10

INSIDE THE TARDIS, OUTSIDE THE BOX

Organic Creativity in Teaching Theatre and Improvisation

Tarik Davis

"People are creative; you've got to allow them to do a lot of things that don't fit any kind of system. You've got to have a lot of deviation. That's what enriches life."—Myles Horton[124]

I remember the first time I heard the theme music and saw the opening credits. A black hole opened into a psychedelic portal and the name appeared in bad 1970s graphics. I had to be no more than 5. This BBC show was old, the special effects were laughable, and the subject matter was well over my head, but for some reason I couldn't stop watching. I didn't want my parents to change the channel.

An eccentric looking man, with an incredibly long scarf dragging on the ground, a crazy (almost afro-like) curly mane, and a gentlemanly English accent appeared with a grin of excitement out of a blue police box. He would show up to save the day, defeating the terrifying monsters again and again, using only his creativity, intuition, and his sonic screwdriver (like a magic wand, it can open doors, take measurements, and save lives). He made this 5-year-old kid from New Jersey say, "That's me. I'm Doctor Who."

Doctor Who, the popular science fiction television character from the U.K., is the last of the Time Lords, his alien species.[125] He also happens to be my favorite doctor. He freely travels through time and space in a small blue police box called the TARDIS (Time and Relative Dimension In Space)

An avid believer in people's affinity and necessity for expression through imagination, **Tarik Davis** is a teaching artist in New York City. With a long history performing improv and writing comedy, he strives to crosspollinate performance styles and audiences in all his work. Tarik performed regularly at The Upright Citizens' Brigade. In 2003, he moved to Amsterdam to work for Boom Chicago. Back in the states in 2007, he performed for The Second City on Norwegian Cruise lines before returning to NYC to write and self-produce his own video projects, teach improv, direct theatre, and appear in commercial spots.

seeking adventure. In his ability to jump backward and forward, see all sides of an equation, and change forms, he has the ultimate freedom: Doctor Who is completely unclassifiable. There is no system in which he fits. More than a childhood fantasy, Doctor Who became my dream role.

I've been a professional actor for the last 10 years and because it's hard to make a consistent living at it, I supplement my income teaching improvisation to people of all ages, directing plays, and illustrating. The majority of this supplemental income currently comes from teaching for ArtsConnection, a New York City organization that sends professional teaching artists into public schools. Some classes are "pure" theatre classes and some emphasize English language learning. Most of the schools are in communities at the lower end of the economic spectrum and most are in buildings that house more that one school. English language learners are often given a separate curriculum and spend much of the school day separated from English-speaking peers. I teach from three to five 45–60 minute classes per day. At one point this year, I was working 6 days a week as a teaching artist. I'm an actor.

The picture I want to paint is of the faces of children ages 7–18, of the lives they lead, and their dreams. Not of the system that surrounds them. This is the system that rewards the "best" teachers and "best" students and says to everyone else, "Work harder." When I hear that we need to "fix schools," I think of the buildings, and yet that's not what is generally meant. Most talk about fixing education is about the system of schools. To be honest, I don't know if our education *system* needs saving, although I see a lot to be fixed.

On February 12, 2013, like millions of Americans, I watched President Obama deliver his State of the Union address during which he outlined a perfect American curriculum: math, science, technology, and engineering. Where in that system for America's future is dance? Theatre? Visual arts? Music? Hell, where is civics? An effective doctor, using a holistic approach to heal a patient or prevent disease, takes into account age, weight, family history, gender, and race, and myriad other things that combine to impact our physical well-being. Rarely does just one thing make us sick. If we're truly concerned about the future of our children then why not take a similar, holistic approach to their education? If we want our future citizens to acquire healthy educations then we should approach the problem like effective doctors. Math and science alone will not save our schools. And they certainly will not be solely responsible for saving the children in them.

In the media sound chamber, a lot of blame is placed on teachers: "The teachers are failing our kids!" "There aren't enough good teachers!" "The union makes it impossible to have teacher accountability!"

In a War Zone Behind Enemy Lines

Until I started working in the schools, I agreed with most of these sentiments. I get it. I get why people are quick to blame teachers when something goes wrong in the classrooms. They are, after all, the adults in the room. Yet, after dealing, alone, with 30 kids, none of whom speak English, some of whom are in gangs, most who don't want to be there and yet they have to listen to me, I realized I was in a war zone behind enemy lines. I'm the guy pushing, persuading, convincing, coaxing, tricking, pleading with them to do something embarrassing, something they are almost too scared to try. So, instead, they put on the "apathetic cool-guy façade." It's not about good teachers or bad teachers, it's not about a Race to the Top for more money or college acceptance letters. It's about standing up against the system that keeps them mindlessly filling in the bubbles with a No. 2 pencil, being a statistic taking orders at McDonald's, and not ever tapping into their own artistic souls. It's about engendering a culture that champions creativity, curiosity, and intuition. I teach this culture.

On Wednesdays, I'm in a middle school in Crown Heights, Brooklyn. I have four classes, 20–30 students in each class. It's a struggle to make a connection, especially with the 12–14 year olds. Too much is going on with their bodies, they're agitated and aggravated, and they simply don't want to be there. Their "real" teacher can't get them to sit down and take off their coats. There are numerous faux fights on the verge of becoming real fights. Students take out various sugary snacks while I stand on stage, silently, and patiently waiting for them to collect themselves. I don't raise my voice. I'd rather let a whole class slip by just to focus on patience and self-control. Students skeptically leer at me as if to say, "I know I'm supposed to be sitting and waiting for instruction but I'm not going to."

Their "real" teacher is exhausted and sits in a chair. She takes my artist residency time as a respite. Eventually, dissenting voices of students yell, "Sit down!" "He's waiting!" "Why you being stupid!? You messing everything up for everybody!" Ten minutes later, one by one, the students sit and wait for instruction. I call them all up to the stage and I ask them, "What's your dream?" Standing in a circle they respond:

"I want to play in the NFL."
"I want to be rich!"
"I want to be a veterinarian."
"I want to live to 20."

Imagine a tall, athletic, charismatic 13-year-old girl (Akila), wishing to live for another 7 years. Now imagine the room of kids nodding in agreement. The reality that separates my students and a majority of Americans is that an early and gruesome death is not only common but often expected for this bunch of seventh and eighth graders. If your primary wish as a 13-year-old is to live to 20, is there anything a public school can provide that doesn't seem like an utter waste of time? Standardized tests? More math and science? Tired teachers and an indifferent school board that's dissolving your school and merging it with another at the end of the year? What about a chance to act out any scene that's in your head? Become any character you want? Work on writing a scene to perform on stage in front of your class?

Doctor Who Throws Out The Lesson Plan

I thought, "I have to deal with this now." I threw out my lesson plan and asked Akila, "What's something you really like doing?" She said she liked to play basketball. "Great," I said, "Do you see yourself playing professionally?" Akila thought about it for a second and then looked at me. "I'd like to . . ." she said. Suddenly I felt like The Doctor, whipping out my sonic screwdriver and assembling a complicated device to scramble the Cyberman's mind control waves using only scraps of broken kitchen appliances and whatever other odds and ends were lying around.

"Okay," I said, "let's imagine you keep playing basketball and you play all 4 years in high school and you're so good you get a scholarship to play in college. How old are you when you graduate high school?" "Eighteen," she said. I continued, "Okay! So you're the star forward in college, you play all 4 years, and you even win a championship your senior year. How old are you when you graduate college?" She thought about it. "Twenty-one or twenty-two?" "Are we past 20?" I asked. Akila smiled as if I'd tricked her into living for at least 8 more years. "Okay," I said, "pull up those two chairs. Everyone else have a seat and watch." I then began a structured improv scene with Akila.

"You're playing professional basketball, you're on the team. But here's the thing, you're not the starting forward, you're the rookie. There's another player who has that spot and she's a star. I'm the coach and I'm in my office. Do you think you could walk in and convince me to start you?" "Yeah!" She enthusiastically replied. "Okay," I said. "You have to walk in and convince me to start you. Is this what you want?" "Definitely!" her enthusiasm unfettered.

Organic Creativity in the Arts

Akila then walks into my improv office where I sit drinking improv tea and reading the improv sports section of my newspaper. Hesitant, like a human stepping into the TARDIS for the first time, she approaches my chair, sits down, and says quietly, "Hi . . . um . . . so, like, you should start me."

Her teacher and fellow students begin to shake their heads in dismay.

I say, "I'm sorry, I have an important call." As I walk away from the scene, Akila's jaw hits the floor. "What's wrong?" I ask.

The other kids begin to shout, "I wouldn't do anything for you if you came into my office like that!" "She was too quiet, we couldn't hear her, it was like she didn't want it!"

I ask, "What would you like to have seen?"

They respond, "I wanted to see her be more confident!"

I look at Akila, who's still sitting in my improv office, "Do you want try again?"

"Yes!" she eagerly responds, "I want this!"

We begin again. She knocks on an imaginary door. She struts in and she begins to make her case. Passionately, looking me right in the eye, she says, "I can make the team play as a whole; I can lead them on the floor!"

I look at the rest of the class which moments ago was refusing to invest in the class; they all nodded with pride. "Well done," I say.

The entire class raises their hands, "Me next!" they shout.

Doctor Who always throws out his plan. Things never go smoothly and, as an audience member, you constantly feel like this time might be the time he loses. Not your typical superhero, he stumbles along the way quite a bit and sometimes even dies. Along with his ability to regenerate (handy!), his faith in humanity (a race he's sworn to protect because he sees their beauty and potential) gives him the ability to keep fighting. He never stops.

My improv training in the United States, Europe, and on a cruise ship has become the foundation for my teaching, as I believe in fully allowing students to mine their own creativity—creating scenes, characters, and whole worlds of their imagination. To be a successful improviser there are two things one must absorb into one's core. The first is saying "Yes, and . . .", thereby always accepting the reality that you're thrust into. Saying, "Yes, and . . ." provides an implicit forward momentum that can help get you through the roughest of patches and proves an invaluable tool in creating a cohesive team with your scene partner(s). Another thing one must be able to live and breath is the ability to make connections. This is possibly one of the hardest things to grasp when learning improv due to the fact that everything is happening in the present. You can easily lose focus, forgetting what's happened before and therefore not be able to connect it to what will happen next. Once you hone your focus and start to make connections within your improv, you cannot help but make connections with everything else in your life. This meditation on the present, and total focus on those around you—what they thrust upon you and how they wait for you to volley—is what forces me to recognize the similarity between the dysfunction I see in the education system and my career as a professional actor. At times I don't know where one starts and the other ends.

One day, while working with high schoolers in preparation for their upcoming performances of *12 Angry Men,*[126] a student asked me, "What kind of actor are you?" The kids would go to my website, see my resume, look at my reel, and sometimes call me "the Verizon guy" because they remember the commercial I was in from a few years back. Although flattered that they looked up to me as a director and were having a good time in rehearsals, the question haunted me. I didn't give the student an answer because I couldn't come up with a satisfactory one. I didn't know what kind of actor I was; I felt like a fraud and that I was doing these kids, and every kid I've taught, a disservice. "They shouldn't be learning from me!" "What right do I have to try to instruct these kids on what it is to be an actor?" "I'm not on TV currently." "What was the last role I booked?" "When was the last role I booked?"

All of the anxieties that come with this profession were weighing on me. Living in NYC and getting by paycheck to paycheck, I was getting sick and tired of seeing numerous friends and colleagues "get ahead" as I made no progress. I listened to my friend's advice to get new head shots and send them out to casting directors, agents, and managers in time for pilot season. The last thing I expected was to actually get a reply. A week or so after I expected the envelopes to land on desks, my phone rang.

I had just finished teaching a class. "Hi, is this Tarik? Look, I never ever do this, but after I looked at your headshot and resume I decided to give you a call. Can you come in for a meeting on Thursday?" This was someone who could be the person I needed to take my career to a place where I could confidently answer the question, "What kind of actor are you?"

I meet my potential new manager at her office, where the walls are lined with photos of the famous actors she represents. "Where do you teach?" she asks. I begin to tell her about the numerous schools I teach in when she cuts me off. "You're a very serious person." "I'm sorry?" I reply. She continues, "I called you in because everything about you says you're a comedy guy but your voice is deeper than I expected and you carry yourself in a very serious manner. This is a business and we're about making money and if we choose to represent you, you essentially represent us, and when we send you into a room you have to be larger than life, you have to own the room, and frankly the guy I'm seeing right now isn't going to get anyone to notice him." She continues. "I mean I want you to be yourself and all but if people are expecting a comedian they need to see a comedian."

I tried to explain that I thought we were just chatting about where I taught but when I'm on stage or in front of the camera I can "turn it on." The words hurt coming from my mouth but there I was, saying them. I didn't want to blow this chance. So not only did I say those words, I did indeed "turn it on." I changed my personality and became the comedian she wanted to see and sure enough, it changed to, "Now this is a guy we can send into a room." She told me she needed to see more from me and couldn't sign me based on her impression of me during the meeting. She gave me a script for a new sitcom and asked me to self-tape my audition and send it to her. She liked it but she kept saying that she "needed to see more." She sent me a second pilot script. The part I was asked to read was totally against my type but I thought, "So what? I'm an actor! You ask me to become a fire hydrant, I'll become a fire hydrant."

All the while she made it very clear to me that I had to be a comedian and a big personality when I walked into the room. She also made me drop by her office and preaudition for her before the actual auditions. Each time I went in I thought, "Be likable!" "Smile!" "Don't mess this up!" "Turn it on!" The last of three auditions was actually a room that I'd spent the better portion of my career trying to get in. When I arrived, I found a tired looking young man who sat behind a large computer screen. He put a mic on me, went back behind the computer screen, and told me to speak to an empty chair. He barely looked at me. Despite the fact that I was talking to an empty chair and a computer screen, I felt good about the audition. I even made the computer screen chuckle.

The potential manager had gotten feedback from the big network I auditioned for. They told her that I "did a fine job." Before I could speak, she said the management company couldn't afford to send me into rooms for a year until I did better than fine. Instead of a system that responds to the people it is set up to serve, the entertainment industry—and the typical interactions that exist within it—are based on preconceptions about what makes a good investment. It felt like I had failed a test that was designed for me to fail.

Soon after, I had dinner with my cousin who owns her own fitness center in Brooklyn. She's always been one of my biggest fans. She comes to all of my shows, tells her friends about the commercials or the web videos I've made, and constantly pushes me to make my own stuff. After I told her about the experience with the potential manager and the fast and furious pilot auditions, she said, "You know Tarik, I don't think I'd know where to cast you on television. There's nobody like you on TV." I'm supposed to play the not-really-necessary Black sidekick, or a drug dealer, or a stuttering werewolf-slave (a part I was actually asked to read for). Not a wizardly British guy who flies in a police box.

The idea of making people think, engaging with them, and tapping into their own creativity are considered liabilities in my chosen profession. Schools, similarly, with so many standardized tests, are being designed not to engage or to encourage a creative spirit but to commodify the students' progress. Today, if a school isn't "working," it's shut down. If a manager sends you into an audition but you're too complex to cast, you're dropped. Pass or fail.

Zach, a student at Essex Street Academy, where I've taught improv and directed theatre, e-mailed me and asked for one-on-one advice about being a working actor. When we met, he told me he was thinking of auditioning for the school play that year. He had never performed in front of an audience before but as he told me, "I know this is what I'm supposed to do. It's all I think about." His plan was to start in commercials, then work his way up to television. "I'd love to be on a sitcom like *Two and a Half Men*." Then he would graduate to film. I said he should focus on the audition for the upcoming play and that I'd be here if he needed any help.

So here's a kid who sees me as a "working actor," as someone who can tell him what's coming down the road. After we met, Zach auditioned and got a great part in the play. And after working with him for a few months in rehearsals, I could honestly say that performing is something he's supposed to do. There have been many students that profess a love for the craft. I encourage them to love it, to practice it, to dream about it, and to make it their own. And then the problem—the system of it all—begins to rise. I hear the words my father spoke when I told him I wanted to be an actor: "Tarik, I know you have talent but you have three strikes against you: (1) It's a tough business, (2) we're not rich, (3) you're Black."

To be fair, that's not simply an argument parents use to discourage their children from pursuing the arts. I've heard those sentiments echoed from numerous artists who say, "I wanted to be an actor, I just couldn't handle being cast as a token all the time." Do we just accept that? Do I discourage students from pursuing this dream because of my own personal battles with the industry?

We Are Teaching Them to Give Answers But Not to Create Answers

In a 6-hour meeting with teachers, I find their predictions of what their students will face as they get older just as grim. "We're only teaching them to take tests." "They can't do anything without being told exactly what to do because we aren't allowed to let them try things." "We're not allowed to fail." Another teacher added, "Because of the tests they can answer questions but they can't create an answer." She was talking about seeing in her own students a decline in their creative and imaginative problem-solving abilities: "We're not preparing them for the world, we're preparing them for McDonald's."

Zach and his fellow castmates worked on improvising for those moments when they forgot a line in the play. "You can't freeze in front of an audience," I'd say, "you have to learn your lines and more importantly you have to learn what the lines say, what the scene is, who your character is, and who's on stage with you. That way, if you forget (which you won't because you'll learn your lines) you'll be able to keep going. Listen to what is being said and use it to get to the next action." The system might threaten to recast in order to get the actors to get their act together but the theatre program in this school was barely 2 years old and getting kids to actually show up was a battle in itself. When performance time came and the curtains opened, then closed, the cast was greeted by an overwhelming standing ovation. Theatre wasn't just an idea; it was a living and breathing thing. They dropped their lines and did not freeze. They did not let on that they were lost; they supported each other, and they found new moments in the story within each scene. And they had fun. What would have happened if the play had been a multiple-choice test and each line was a question? Instead of filling in bubbles, they created the answer and convinced the audience it was the correct one. In the process, they learned that they could in fact accomplish what they had set out to do.

After the show, another student in the play, Stephanie, told me that being in the play and having her English teacher and me keep on her to show up and dig into the experience "changed my life. No one ever challenged me to be good at anything." No system she encounters can take that experience away.

A different school, on the brink of being shut down, in Corona, Queens, is home to overstressed teachers who are afraid of losing their jobs. Many of the kids come to school underfed and under threat of gang and/or domestic violence. I was asked to teach improv in this school with the hopes that it would help the kids develop the confidence to participate in class and try something scary like speaking English. This is another planet, and I'm an alien. The absolute last thing anyone in this school wants is an energetic, blah, blah, blah actor telling them to take "playing around" seriously. At times—many, many times—I dreaded going to work. I was fighting a losing battle, I thought, becoming cynical like all the other teachers. What's the point of trying to get kids who don't speak English to improvise and then turn their improvised scenes into written material that they'd then perform in front of an audience? What was the point? The kids had way more important things to worry about than the merits of improvised theatre.

And then there was Maurice. Maurice, from the Dominican Republic, was 17 years old and in the seventh grade. He spoke a little, very broken English and because of No Child Left Behind laws, he could not graduate to a higher grade because he kept failing the English proficiency tests that would let him move up. In every class I had with him, he gave his all, even reprimanding other students when they began to misbehave. He was a foot taller than all of the other kids—heck, he was even taller than me. Maurice's teacher told me that before he moved to the United States, he was a baseball star in the Dominican Republic. Unfortunately, here he couldn't play baseball because he was so much older than the other seventh graders. (I still have to pause here for a second. A kid has a talent and a passion that he's not allowed to use because he doesn't meet the requirements of a test that has nothing to do with that? How many professional baseball players in Major League Baseball can't speak enough English to give an interview? They're allowed to play baseball because the two things aren't related! Anyway.) Maurice being a former athlete told me something about him: He liked, and understood, the need for practice. He knew that in order to get better at something you have to try again. He applied this to my improv class; he wanted to get better. His teacher explained to me that every year, he studies very hard for the English test but due, in part, to the fact that his parents and his friends don't speak English, he fails. If he hung out with kids who did speak English, either by being in a classroom with native speakers or by playing on the baseball team, his practice would be organic. Basically, in order for Maurice to be able to play baseball, he'd have to be on the team already.

When I started the residency in Corona, I made a promise to the class after a particularly trying day in which the kids refused to participate in the activity. "Why we doing this anyway, mister?" one student asked. "Because you're going to perform it in the auditorium to a room filled with people," I responded.

Everyone's face went white with terror. "In the auditorium? In front of the whole school?" "Yup" I replied. In reality, I didn't know if this would be possible. I'd stopped asking the school for things after being yelled at for asking if I could make copies of scripts for my students. Somehow, I had to follow through on my promise. Suddenly the improv that this alien was teaching them was a "big deal." When I ventured to ask the very tired and war-worn vice principal if I could use the auditorium for my final class, I also asked if he could get other students to the performance as an audience. Before he could answer, his walkie-talkie blared about a fight breaking out, and he rushed out to deal with the situation.

A week before the last day of my residency, the kids were taking it upon themselves to run their own rehearsals, working on their diction and correcting and helping each other when they would mispronounce or misuse a word. I wasn't doing anything except observing. The only thing they asked me was, "Are we still performing in the auditorium next week?" "Yes," I said. "We're still performing in the auditorium next week."

A whole week went by and I still didn't receive a reply from the vice principal, and now the day of the performance was upon us. On my hour and a half commute I was sweating bullets—what was I going to do if we didn't get into the auditorium? The kids put their trust in me, and I let them down. When I arrived at the school, the project coordinator was waiting for me. "We're in the auditorium!" he exclaimed, and we happily scrambled to get the kids into the space to squeeze in a rehearsal. As other classes from the school began to take their seats, my kids realized what was about to follow. One said out loud, "This is happening."

The students were sensational, and the audience of their peers loved them. Maurice's scene got a huge reaction, and it was clear to me that he loved the attention. At the end of the day, I told them how proud I was and what good jobs they had done all year, and when I looked up, I saw that that they were crying. Seventh and eighth graders who are "the hard kids" because they don't care about anything were crying because an alien who might as well be traveling in a blue police box put the tools to discover what they did care about in their hands. Two girls came to me with tears in their eyes demanding that they be allowed to do it again. "We want to try again, we know we can be better next time!" One said, "I want to be an actress, how do I act more?" The school's theatre teacher said, "That was incredible; they did amazing work. You should be proud." I was, and I recommended that students wanting to pursue this beyond my residency join her program, which is when I found out that their theatre program was reserved for "higher achieving" students proficient in speaking English and that the school was most likely going to be shut down because it was falling behind.

Daleks, The Doctor's mortal enemy, look like floating trash bins with plungers for lasers (they actually were plungers due to production costs in the 1970s). Their harsh robotic voices repeat "Exterminate!" Motivated by the idea that all non-Dalek life forms are imperfect and therefore should be exterminated, they've had every emotion erased from their bodies except for hate. To me, the Daleks are perfect representations of the systems I fight against. Inorganic, emotionless, uncreative, and continuously striving for preconceived notions of sanitized perfection.

Facing overwhelming monsters, like the reality of a school closing now that the kids within it have a newfound sense of passion, is extremely depressing. There seemed to be far too many monsters compared to every victory I thought I had won. Both the battles I fought—as a teacher and actor—felt like part of the same war. So, I decided to quit both teaching and acting. I didn't want to tell anyone because I didn't want the sympathy. I had no idea what I was going to do instead, but I couldn't deal with the lose/lose politics of it all. When told I can't use the stage for my students, I hear, "Exterminate!" When a kid is 17 years old in seventh grade and isn't allowed to move up, I hear, "Exterminate!" When I'm told to be more "urban" in an audition, I hear, "Exterminate!"

Reflections on the Artist As Outsider

I got an e-mail from John, one of Zach's classmates who graduated high school a year ago. He had been cast in an independent film, and he wanted to have lunch. He thanked me for inspiring him and asked how I was doing. "Okay," I said. Without hearing a single detail about my career, John asked, "You're not thinking of quitting, are you? You can't quit! I need you to keep acting!"

When John said, "I need you to keep acting!" I heard something quite different. I heard instead, "I need you to keep fighting!" I was confused. Why was it important to him whether I acted or not? Whether I kept fighting or not? I wasn't his teacher anymore; he was a young adult going after his dreams and I would still be there, helping him realize it was a possible path. And then it dawned on me that I was being an idiot. John is a fellow artist! What message would I be sending if I gave up my dreams while still in my early 30s? Here I was getting taught one of the most valuable lessons in my life by one of my former students outside of the classroom with no tests, no metrics, and no system telling us what to study. It was at a diner. We were outside the box—which of course is what I always use to provoke students to look at their work in new ways: "Can you take a different approach or come at it another way?" "What happens when you stand on the outside and look in, be the outsider?"

I was so wrapped up in my own sorrows I wasn't taking my own advice. I was getting depressed and angry by not fitting within the confines of the systems in which I was trying to exist. I forgot that I'm an outsider. I forgot that I always have been an outsider in every single setting and situation in my life. I forgot that being an outsider means that I'm also a fighter, standing up to the systems of power over and over again. And being an outsider who is an actor is wonderful because I bring a different perspective to roles and force people to think about what they're watching. And if I'm getting people to think, ultimately I'm teaching. As an outsider who teaches, I recognize other outsiders and I can help them find their voice. If I help other outsiders find their voice they will ultimately take action, they will act. And on, and on, and on.

> "The way you educate is by example. You educate by your own life. what you are. I'm interested in people learning how to learn. The only way I can help is to share my enthusiasm and my ability to learn myself. If I quit learning I can't help."—Myles Horton[127]

My heroes are outsiders. They inspire me as an artist, teach me to engage, challenge, improvise, and play. Doctor Who keeps fighting to save the universe using only his wits and boundless curiosity. The students I teach show me a limitless world of hope and imagination and fill me with endless energy to keep fighting.

It may be foolhardy to demand that two large systems—American public education and show business—change to benefit the people they serve, but I'm only doing what I know my heroes would. And I continually ask, is it truly unreasonable for me to think I can effect positive change in a life, as well as in the systems through which that life must navigate? Isn't that the righteous thing to do?

Chapter 11

TAPPING INTO THE SOUNDS OF THE UNIVERSE

Organic Creativity in Music-Making and Songwriting

Sally dhruvá Stephenson

Sound . . . vibration . . . music. As far back as we can remember, there has been sound. Three-thousand-year-old Vedic scriptures of Hinduism, passed along by oral tradition, give us "om" as the original sacred vibration of the universe. The book of John in the Bible says, "In the beginning was the Word." The baby in the womb hears the rhythm of the mother's heartbeat. Even before the presence of man, wind whistled through canyons and bird-song echoed off the hillsides. And astronomers now claim to have discovered the sound of a black hole, and it's supposedly a B flat, 57 octaves lower than middle C.[128]

For every human being with normal faculties, sound is the key to language and communication, and in all cultures, music seems to share the functions of marking the important passages of life—the tender lullabies of birth, the joyous celebrations of union, the grief-filled mourning of passings. The most basic of human expressions, sound and music are invaluable in fulfilling universal human needs.

Fast forward 5,000 years to one of the many developed societies on the planet. Music can be manufactured by machines, even synthesizing the human voice; transmitted, stored, and duplicated electronically; and dis-

Sally dhruvá Stephenson, Ed.D., is an associate professor in the Department of Educational Professions at Frostburg State University with an interest in arts in education. She is an advocate for international education and recently taught as a visiting professor at Hunan Normal University in Changsha, China. Prior to receiving her doctorate at West Virginia University, she taught elementary gifted and talented students in Braxton County, WV, and was involved with the Landmark Studio for the Arts. She is a performing songwriter and has released several CDs under the name "dhruva'." In addition to sharing music, she enjoys photography, traveling, and growing sunflowers.

tributed across the globe, virtually instantaneously. Music collectors hold thousands of digital compositions in their libraries, and debates rage over the "ownership" of music property. In modern form, nearly unrecognizable from the striking of an animal skin stretched tightly over a log frame, music is nonetheless as integral to 21st-century humanity as it was to primitive man sitting hunched around the campfire, drums echoing into the night. Recognizing that music is an essential part of the human experience, we as educators and aspiring artists can and should recognize and foster opportunities through music and sound to discover our own inner selves and to connect us meaningfully with others.

My own journey began as a child in a music-loving household. Both my parents sang to me and played recordings of Beethoven, the Boston Pops, and the blues. Riding in the car with my father, we would play the "radio game": He would improvise different radio stations—reporting the news, giving me a play-by-play of a football game, or, best of all, singing various songs that would change when I pressed the button on the glove compartment to switch the "station." I learned to love Chopin and Mozart as my older sister practiced the piano, taught myself folk guitar at age 11, and was given the gift of being taught to sight-read choral music using numbers[129] by my eighth-grade choir director, Nat Frazer—a technique that has been the foundation for all subsequent formal music education throughout my life.

I sang in school and church choirs and performed in musical theatre productions. And, as an adult, I began dabbling in other instruments and discovered that I, too, could write songs. "How many instruments do you play?" I often get asked. My reply is, "Oh, hundreds, if you include all the percussion instruments!" Do I count the potato peeler, the railroad spike, the bird call? These are all sounds I have used on recordings to embellish my songs. Discovering my own voice through songwriting has been particularly rewarding, and sharing live music—collaborating and improvising with others, whether adults or children—is one of the most cherished experiences of my life. I believe with my whole being that *everyone* can have a personal experience with creating music if they want it. Helping people to open up to this possibility is my greatest joy, and I recognize that it is part of my purpose in life.

Another of my mentors and teachers, Paul Reisler, is the Artistic Director of Kid Pan Alley, an organization that teams up children in classrooms with professional songwriters for a cowriting experience. The Kid Pan Alley motto is "Inspiring Kids to Be Creators, Not Consumers."[130] Music consumerism has become rampant in modern society. Although music listening can be very enjoyable, it is a passive experience and does not have the same impact as when someone personally engages in the creation of music. Music from the radio, an mp3 player, or other external source vibrates the ear, but the vibration coming from a participatory music experience resonates through the whole body and beyond.

Once, at a songwriting workshop, one of the participants said he was there because he just didn't "get" music. This stunned me. How could anyone not "get" music? I understood that people have different tastes in music— country versus opera, for example—but to "not get" music altogether? One day during the weeklong workshop, we were given a task to write a song in 20 minutes with the idea-starter of "Don't make me stop this car!" I was part- nered with this individual for the exercise, and as I frantically searched for a usable idea, he casually mentioned that once he drove nine kids in a pickup truck to the Grand Canyon. Fifteen minutes later, a song was born, and guess what? The next morning, when I delivered a recording to him at the bed and breakfast where he was staying, he proudly introduced me to his hosts and fellow guests as his "cowriter"! I think he "got" it. But it took a personal cre- ative experience for him to make a connection with music.

This personal creative experience is what is sometimes lacking in today's world. Lucky youth with supportive parents or forward-thinking school dis- tricts that have maintained—or, even more rare nowadays, nurtured—their music education programs have the good fortune to study an instrument, play in a band or orchestra, or sing in a choir. But for many others, music (and her sisters, the visual arts, drama, and dance) has become something someone else does, something to be consumed, something to view, and not something to do. But it doesn't have to be this way.

In my college teaching experience, for that is what I now do, I have taught courses in creative expression for elementary classroom teachers. I begin these courses by surveying my college students about their comfort level in self-expression for each of the art forms. And their responses often distress me. Student after student has told me that they don't sing anymore because someone, perhaps back in the fifth grade, said something negative about their voices or their singing ability. And they promptly shut up and have never sung in public since that time. There are a few individuals who would technically be considered "tone deaf," but relatively few.

Most people who have issues with singing either have never learned to match pitches or have a limited vocal range. There are strategies for dealing with these problems. And even if a person has a pitch problem, he or she gen- erally can speak in rhythm, such as in the currently popular hip-hop style of music. There is never an insurmountable problem that will prevent someone from engaging in a personal experience with music. Even a deaf person can follow along to clap or play a percussion instrument and can feel and enjoy musical vibrations.

There are simple methods of creating music. Many people have the idea that one has to read music and study for years in order to be a musician. I believe that we are all born to make music and that we never lose that potential. Yes, the greatest instrumental virtuosi are those who started as young children and have practiced intensely for years. But even individuals who are not polished musicians, who have not developed automaticity in music, being able to do something without thinking, can dive into music and begin to find their own musical voices. So many people tell me they wish they could play an instrument. "Then try it!" I tell them. "There will always be someone better than you—and someone worse than you," I say, and generally folks agree. The secret to feeling successful is to make comparisons only with oneself, not with others. The artist in each of us is a child, one that we must find and protect. We need to be gentle with our inner children, be patient, and allow ourselves the freedom to make mistakes. We wouldn't criticize a child for hitting a wrong note; we should be as kind with ourselves.

Taking the First Steps

Everyone will determine his or her creative musical direction on his or her own. What is easy for one person can be a huge challenge for another. For a person such as I described above, learning to release her singing voice may be the goal; for someone who has formally learned to play an instrument, it might be putting down his sheet music and discovering the instrument anew. Some of the readers of this essay, I hope, will be inspired to write a first song; for others, the focus may be to turn off the classroom CD player and interact with the children with live singing and movement. Regardless of the direction each individual takes, the common thread is maintaining an openness to new experience. Being engaged in the creative process is often likened to wearing two hats: one for the creator's role, the free-flowing hat of inspiration, and a second for the editor's role, to analyze and critique the work in progress. It is essential, when entering into a mental space with creative intent, that one defers the use of the editorial hat. Useful indeed for reworking and improving on the raw material, the critic's hat very much gets in the way when connecting with the creative flow and should be set aside for later use.

Organic Creativity in the Arts

One must also be in a psychologically safe place. We spend our lives becoming experts at something and wanting to be viewed as authorities. Opening up to new creative experiences requires that we dive into uncharted waters, ones in which we are not the experts. Always traveling through familiar territory is comfortable but does not bring with it the rawness, the uncertainty, the disequilibrium of which Piaget speaks, which is the fertile ground for inspiration and insight. To welcome in a new creative experience, we must step out of our comfort zones and dare to be risk-takers.

Finding that creative space is not always easy. The demands of reality, a scarcity of time or space, or the need for particular materials or supplies can all be viewed as barriers to creativity. But if the desire to engage in the creative process is there, the possibilities are infinite. Listen for triggers of creativity: Do ideas come in the car when the radio is turned off? In the shower? Upon first awakening in the morning? How about while taking a walk? Many people find that putting the body into motion frees the mind to open up creatively. If solitude is needed, why not get up 20 minutes earlier in the morning for some quiet space? Many creatives are "night owls" who prefer to make time for their creative work when the rest of the world takes a rest. Once there is a creative commitment, start looking for the avenues that will facilitate movement along the path.

Songwriters often get asked whether they write the words or the music to their songs first. There are as many different methods of songwriting as there are songwriters. But for me, I have observed that my process takes a fairly consistent form. First and foremost must come an inspiration. This can and often does come from a personal experience, but may also result from hearing or reading a story or news event or observing a person or a scene, and often is initiated by hearing a spoken phrase that strikes me as interesting. (A recent example of this is when someone used the words "breathing space" in a conversation with me, which gave inspiration to a song by that title.) So from somewhere the idea is born. That germ of a song usually has an incubation period of no more than a few days. If I can't find or don't take the time to work on it shortly thereafter, it will cease to be interesting to me and the song will never be written. Believe me, I have tried going back and writing out some ideas I've found scribbled on old scraps of paper, but it never works. So I am aware that for the inspiration to come to fruition, I must find some writing space within a few days.

Sometimes the need to write is more immediate. If the initial idea stimulates lines or a verse or chorus right away, it is necessary for me to stop what I'm doing and capture it or the lines will be lost. I have written in shopping malls, at rest areas along the highway, walking along the beach, and on park benches. Oddly enough, public places can be good spaces to write (if not filled with distracting piped-in music); the more public the place, the more anonymity one has and can disappear into the background of humanity. If I am composing without paper handy, I can keep a certain amount of material in my mind via repetition, but not enough for a complete song without really working hard to remember it.

Generally, the writing takes place at home, when I am alone and have a couple of hours free. Out comes the yellow pad, pen, and, most of the time, guitar. I draft the first verse and/or chorus, usually both, and then pick up the guitar or sit down at the piano to see what melody comes to me. Then it is simply a back-and-forth process of trying out words and music, going back and making changes, until an hour or so later, I emerge from my trance with a song. It literally feels like I have been submerged in the depths of some intangible waters and lose all track of time, so it is important that I know I have a clear schedule before I sit down to write. Csikszentmihalyi calls this experience "flow," a subjective state involving focused concentration, a loss of awareness of self, a suspension of the normal sense of time passing, and a feeling of intrinsic reward for the experience. He describes the experience of flow that occurs during the creative process as "a sense of being part of an entity greater than ourselves."[131]

Creative Music-Making

Following are some ideas and strategies for music making. I hope readers will wear the lens of possibility and imagination, not the filter of negativity, full of reasons not to try something. The strategies can be adapted for different situations—the age or attention span and skill level of the participants, the materials and time available, and so on. But regardless of circumstances, the most important goal is that everyone involved experiences the act of creating music.

The Art of "Jamming"

I used to live out in the country in a rural part of West Virginia. Folks would get together on the weekends to share a potluck dinner and play volleyball. Later on, the guitars would come out and the evening's entertainment would begin. I desperately wanted to be a part of the musicians' group, but I was too timid and insecure in my abilities at the time, even though I played a little guitar and some flute "by ear," self-taught. At one of these gatherings, I noticed that on the outskirts of the circle was an oboe player, playing on the sidelines. "An oboe!" I thought. "If he can join in, surely so can I!" And so, 20 feet further back, literally at the edge of the woods, I took out my flute and played along softly and simply. I was far enough away from the crowd that only I could hear what I was playing. But I was jamming along, making music with the others. It took many sessions of playing on the fringes before I grew bold enough to step in close, but over time, it happened. I developed the creative courage needed to be a musical risk-taker. And now, as often as not, I am the instigator, the initiator, the encourager. But I know what it feels like to have to work up the courage to play that first note.

Tips on learning to jam. Many people have at some point in time studied an instrument, usually in school. But most of them need written sheet music in order to play. Here are some suggestions for learning to improvise, to play along with others "by ear."

- Simplicity is the foundation. Find the "home note" of the song (generally the key in which it is played) and become very secure playing there. Just like a toddler extending his territory bit by bit, musically step away, see how it feels, and then come back home. Always know where "home" is—and when in doubt, go home.

- Listening is the most important tool. Some notes sound good together; some don't. (This depends on the style of music being played. Some forms of jazz, by nature, are extremely liberal in this aspect, and music born of different cultural traditions may have different tonalities.) Listen to what others are playing and what the notes sound like in combination. In Western music, our ears have become attuned to certain combinations of pitches that we call chords or harmonies. Learn to listen for these combinations, for sounds that fit together in a way pleasing to the ear.

- Rhythm creates structure. Does the song have a beat? If so, find it and internalize it. Take it into the body—tap a finger or toe or gently pat a leg. Be careful to follow the rhythm, not try to drive it. If there is a particular rhythm, there will be a set number of beats that repeat. Look for patterns, most of the time in groups of three or four. Sometimes songs are free of a beat and simply float along in a very relaxed manner; in this case, avoid adding any rhythmic structure. The ultimate in a rhythmic experience is to participate in a drum circle, a legacy from the rich African musical tradition that is becoming increasingly popular in the Western world.

* Jamming, or improvisational playing with others, is a musical conversation. It demands of the players that they both speak and listen. There is a subtle difference between leading the musical line and following it, and the direction can shift back and forth seamlessly when players are sensitive to this dynamic and have established group trust. Intuition plays a big role in learning to relax into this conversation of listening and answering musically.

Group Songwriting With Children

Writing songs with children can be a profoundly rewarding experience, both for the children and for their adult cowriters. As we well know, the spark of imagination is alive and well in children and their enthusiasm can be boundless. The vehicle of songwriting is one that really excites young people and gives them a novel way to express their feelings, tell their stories, and share their sense of humor. And the rewards of having written a song can go beyond the immediate satisfaction, as expressed by this fourth grader who participated in a songwriting residency: "It will help you because some people don't think you can do it, and then if you write a song, they'll believe you and think that you're doing something better with your life."[132]

The value of being able to express one's feelings through music, even for children, is inestimable. In one group songwriting experience I conducted with a group of third graders one November, the children were writing a song entitled "I'm Thankful for Thanksgiving." Of course, some humor crept in, with lines like "I'm thankful for my messy room; dirty socks hang on the wall." But so did pathos with the line "Feeling strong and healthy with no more medical bills." A surprising sentiment coming from a third grader, one would think—until learning that its author was a young leukemia survivor.

> I'm thankful for food, water, shelter, and air
> They meet my basic needs
> I'm thankful for my family, two dogs and three cats
> They keep me company
> I'm thankful for my roomy house
> It keeps me cozy warm
> Going places, running bases
> Pumpkin pie and corn

And I'm thankful for my messy room
Dirty socks hang on the wall
Being bigger than my little sister
Makes me look so tall
Going to the circus where the clowns make me giggle
They honk their horns, stick out the tongues
And make their ears wiggle
>   Thanksgiving, Thanksgiving
>   The relatives all come
>   Thanksgiving, Thanksgiving
>   The turkey's almost done![133]

In another session, a fourth grader writing a song about a school dance disappointment said, when interviewed afterward about the songwriting experience, "It felt good to let my feelings go. I haven't let them go, and it seems like they stayed inside my body all my life. It made me feel better."[134] This sense of wellness through insight as one possible outcome of songwriting is common to young people and adults alike.

Tips on writing songs with children. Here are some tips for writing songs with young people:

- ♫ Solicit ideas from the children, both for the theme of the song itself, and for words and phrases to include in the text. Write the ideas in a place all of the children can see. If needed, the group can vote on its favorite song idea. For the first part of the session, accept and write down all of the ideas given. It is important to keep all options open, to maintain a tolerance for ambiguity and not to settle on a direction for the song lyrics too soon in order to build a rich and varied collection of potential ideas and imagery for later use as the song develops.

- ♫ After developing a large set of words and phrases related to the theme of the song, ask the children for suggestions for a first line, and lines to follow. It is surprising how easily this comes to children—rhythm and rhyme are their natural languages. With some gentle guidance and shaping, the children will happily put together verses that tell the story and, most likely, a chorus with a refrain that emphasizes the theme of the song.

- ♫ Decide whether to create the music, solicit melodic ideas from the children, put the original lyrics to a familiar tune, or create the song as an unsung rhythmic spoken word piece. My preferred style of collaboration is to invite the children, once part or all of the lyrics are created, to sing a possible melody for each line. The children will eagerly provide musical suggestions, and the group can experiment with them by echo-singing to choose their favorite. If the children come up with the melody themselves, it will be in their vocal range (an important consideration for young voices). Those comfortable with playing an accompaniment instrument, generally guitar or piano, will probably be able to harmonize an appropriate chord progression. But the children's melodies can be utilized and the song sung *a capella* even without such accompaniment.

♪ Plan a way to record the finished song immediately upon completion. This will serve to capture the musical ideas before they can be forgotten, and gives the children immediate positive feedback for their creative work. It will likely be the first time they have ever heard the sound of their voices recorded, and they will be delighted and proud of their accomplishment.

Music to Enhance Learning

Educators are always searching for ways to make learning more meaningful, to deepen the connections between the content material and the students. Music is an ideal vehicle for doing so. Who can ever forget their ABCs after learning the alphabet song? But in our segmented educational system in which each subject is taught in isolation and music is relegated to the domain of the specialist, the value of utilizing music in learning can be overlooked. One teacher who watched her class collaborate with a songwriter made the following observation:

This class likes music and they don't even realize they're writing. To me, they're doing skills that sometimes might be dreaded, whereas right now; they don't even realize what they're doing. They're having fun. And I think, if you can present anything they need to work on in a fun, interesting way, that's over half the battle.[135]

Tips on Integrating Music Into the Curriculum

Teachers looking to integrate music into their everyday curriculum/lessons may find these suggestions helpful:

- ♫ Begin with looking for obvious connections. Social studies themes dealing with periods in history or peoples of the world, for example, naturally lend themselves to including folk songs such as Civil War ballads, sea shanties, and work songs. There are many good resources with countless songs available, often including recordings.[136]

- ♫ Utilize rhythmic speech for a mnemonic aid in learning and remembering concepts. Small groups of students can each take a few terms or ideas and formulate a two-line couplet or four-line verse that can be compiled together into a longer poem. Remember "In fourteen hundred and ninety-two, Columbus sailed the ocean blue"? When students are engaged in creating and repeating their own rhymes, the learning connections are deepened.

- ♫ Develop a collection of small, inexpensive percussion instruments for classroom use. This can include everything from an empty plastic pill bottle filled with an inch of unpopped popcorn to an African bamboo shaker purchased from a supplier of world music instruments. Many stores selling toys for young children now have an inexpensive rhythm band package for sale. Full classroom sets of items are not necessary, nor does every student need to play at once. Many teachers hesitate to utilize classroom instruments for fear of noise chaos, but this can be prevented by managing the number of instruments distributed and by teaching students to respond to direction cues. These percussion instruments can be incorporated into many activities and will always get the students' attention!

- ♫ Bring language arts activities to life by adding elements of sound and music such as interesting sound effects, a gentle underlying rhythm to add tension to a dramatic story, or simple gestures and movements. Both curricular reading materials and original writings by the students can be embellished with the addition of musical elements. For a special occasion, try recording students reading aloud with sound effects such as in the old "radio dramas."

- ♫ Tap into the natural creative impulses of the children. Add one or two specific soundmakers to a reading center; ask students for ideas on how they can demonstrate a science concept using sound and motion, or how they could demonstrate a math fact musically. (For example, fractions could be expressed using a hand drum playing every fourth beat, rhythm sticks every second beat, and a shaker on each beat.)

✷ For a teacher who is interested in learning to using music naturally and holistically in the classroom, I highly recommend training courses in Orff-Schulwerk.[137] This approach to teaching children music, developed by German composer Carl Orff, builds children's skills in creating and performing music in a very natural, beautiful way beginning with speech rhythms and "body percussion" and evolving to ensemble playing facilitated with five-tone pentatonic scales using easy-to-learn repetitions of melodic and harmonic motifs.

✷ In this technological age, many programs are available for production and recording of music on computers and other electronic devices. Students growing up with advanced technology will readily develop the skills needed to utilize such programs for creative music-making. Having digital files of original music creations facilitates sharing these with others. Taking the concept of digital sharing even further, there are now online virtual worlds where people in different countries, represented by animated avatars, create and perform live music in real time.

The Journey Continues

One of the truly great things about music in our lives is that there is no expiration date, no time at which we need to put it aside and leave it behind. Even those of us in our final days can find peace and solace with the addition of music to our environment. Live therapeutic music played on the Celtic harp by certified music practitioners in the hospital acute care setting has been found to have benefits in pain reduction and reduced stress and anxiety for patients and their families. For all of us, the experience of music is as close as the beating of our hearts and the rhythm of our breathing.

I hope something in my ramblings has touched off a spark, a desire to reach beyond current self-perceived musical limits, whatever they are. Some, no doubt, are already accomplished musicians. For them, perhaps, it is a renewed commitment to the self-discipline required to hone their craft and take it to the next level.[138] For others who may not have thought of themselves as musicians, it is time to free themselves from that misconception. For as surely as the waves lap against the shore, as the wings of the hummingbird vibrate in the air, and as our footsteps resonate against the Earth, we are musical beings. It is our birthright. Embrace, enjoy, and share!

Here is a song I wrote that illustrates the joy of songwriting:

Song of the Earth[139]

I want to sing the song of the Earth with my soul, with my soul
I want to sing it for all that it's worth, let it roll, let it roll
The mother needs her children now to love and make her whole
I want to sing the song of the Earth with my soul, with my soul, with my soul

La Canción de la Tierra (Spanish)

Quiero cantar la canción de la tierra con mi alma, con mi alma
Quiero cantar con todo mi corazon, escuchadla, escuchadla
La madre necesita a sus hijos ahora para amar y sanarla
Quiero cantar la canción de la tierra con mi alma, con mi alma, con mi alma

Une Mélodie à la Terre (French)

J'aimerai chanter une mélodie à la terre,
avec toute mon âme, avec toute mon âme
J'aimerai chanter toute sa splendeur à tue-tête,
allons tous chantons, allons tous chantons
A présent la maman aime ses enfants, pour l'aimer et la combler
J'aimerai chanter une mélodie à la terre
avec toute mon âme, avec toute mon âme, avec toute mon âme

Das Lied der Erde (German)

Ich möchte das lied der erde singen,
mit meiner seele, mit meiner seele
Ich möchte es für alle singen, es frei lassen
aus meiner kehle, aus meiner kehle
Die mutter braucht die liebe von ihren kindern jetzt
um wieder gesund zu werden
Ich möchte das lied der erde singen,
mit meiner seele, mit meiner seele, mit meiner seele

En Sang om Jorden (Danish)

Jeg vil synge en sang om jorden med min sjæl, med min sjæl.

Jeg vil synge den for hvad den er værd, lad det rulle lad det rulle.

Moderjord har brug for sine børn nu til at elske og få hende til at hele.

Jeg vil synge en sang om jorden, med min sjæl, med min sjæl, med min sjæl

Chapter 12

I CHANNEL A CHILD IN ME

Organic Creativity in Teaching Music

Branice McKenzie[1]

Introduction

I was born in Pennsylvania and raised in Washington, DC. My biological mother was a theologian and the woman who raised me, my second mother, was an administrative secretary for the government. My father was a concert tenor. I was raised in a home where music was a big part of my upbringing. I used to rehearse with my father; he sang European Classical music. I was always taken to the theatre from the time I was a little girl, and my father was singing, doing concerts, singing in church. I was a piano student from ages 6 to 12 years. I did a full piano recital, memorized, at the age 11. Those 6 years of piano study have served me quite well and have taken me really quite far in my singing and music career as a whole (composer, performer, teaching artist).

I was raised listening to Paul Robeson singing Negro spirituals; Lena Horne; Harry Belafonte; Peter, Paul, and Mary; Leontyne Price; and artists of that ilk. I come from a family of educators; my mother had three sisters, and all of them were Black women born in the early part of the 20th century. My mother graduated summa cum laude from Brooklyn College, and she was the

1   This essay comes from three 90-minute interviews conducted by Jane Piirto with Ms. McKenzie when she was a teaching artist in New York City. The words come from transcriptions and are presented here with slight revision. She has given permission to use her real name.

Branice McKenzie, M.A., is a singer, songwriter, music minister, and teaching artist. Her career spans concert artistry to musical theatre to touring with such notables as Harry Belafonte, Gregory Hines, and Hugh Masekela. Her recordings of original compositions include *Branice McKenzie; Music Is; Am Me: Melodies, Lyrics and Lessons for Children;* and *I Fly.* Branice is a member of the vocal faculty at Oakland School for the Arts, taught as visiting faculty at Brown University, and conducted master classes at the Shanghai Institute of Visual Arts. She has a B.A. from Brown University and an M.A. from New York University.

first African American woman to graduate from Union Theological Seminary with a master's in Christian Education from both Columbia University and Union. Her sisters were all college-educated women, and all except one of them also had master's degrees.

There are four generations of just women. My biological mother passed when I was 3, and I was raised by my father's second wife, the second of my two mothers, and she was an educated woman also, a college graduate, and a teacher in the South, and when she moved to the North, she worked for the government during World War II. I had all of these role models of these women who were college-educated, and therefore, I followed in their tradition. There were certain things that were givens: "You're going to college and you're going to finish there, because we've already set the way and outlined the path for you." I went to public school, and I was valedictorian of my class.

I loved music and respected the musical theatre, and I was thought of as an instrumentalist as I was growing up all through high school, but in my soul knew I had a voice—literally and figuratively. I went to Brown University with a full academic scholarship. I had never done a vocal solo before. I was working for the Chaplain, and I cofounded and directed the Black Chorus of Brown University, which initially started as a choir for the church services that we had for the African American community on campus. The choir developed and ended up recording albums, concertizing, and touring and representing the university around the country, and as the choir director, I developed into a singer, a vocalist. It was a late start for me. I had a professor who was also a professional jazz musician who encouraged me to go into a career as a professional vocalist. His uncle was a voice teacher at Carnegie Hall, and my professor told me I had to go to New York and go for it, and I followed his direction and instruction and advice.

When I came to New York, I embarked on a career as a jazz vocalist, and to quell all the angst of my parents, I went to grad school so that they would feel that I had all the education that I needed to make it in the world. What if this singing doesn't work? What are you going to do? So I went and got a master's degree in music education. My bachelor's degree is in psychology. I have such a love for education, such a love for the process of learning and teaching, and for how people learn and how to help people learn, so if I hadn't developed my career in music, I was going to go ahead and continue with graduate study in education and psychology.

Then I had my master's, my parents were fine, and I embarked on a professional career. I married a professional musician, and we were young, and we were just doing what we did and I got a lot of wonderful opportunities. I was one of the principals in a show that was an off-Broadway show and critically acclaimed, and we had an extended run at the Village Gate. I was one of the stars, if you will, and I got good reviews and that kind of launched me, for while I was doing that show, the vocal director for Harry Belafonte came to see the show, and literally called me the next morning and hired me to work with Belafonte. So I took off from the show, and worked with Belafonte. I ended up working with him as a backup singer for 10 years.

Harry is known in every corner and crevice of this world. It was a great experience, and he still remains a friend. I met a lot of musicians who are major players in my musical and professional life right now. As a matter of fact, the music director for Belafonte, who was with him for 20 years, who wrote all his arrangements and conducted the band and the singers, worked as my coteacher with ArtsConnection, Richard Cummings.

Also in the off-Broadway show, the drummer for the show was Gregory Hines' best friend, and when Gregory decided to add vocalists to his show, I auditioned and ended up working with Gregory for 17 years. Belafonte and Hines were two of my main professional jobs. Both of those opportunities came out of that show. That show, *Shades of Harlem,* went to Lithuania to represent the United States in a theatre festival. One of the odd things that happened was that most of the people, and literally, the children, had not seen African Americans in person. They would run up to us because they'd only seen African Americans on television.

In the midst of all those things, I've worked as a solo artist, a jazz vocalist, and I embarked on a career as a composer that was reignited because of my work with children. Now, really, I'm as much of a composer as a vocalist in terms of what I do as a professional performing artist. I work on songs, I sing my songs, and I record my songs. I write all of the music that I use with the children, which is how the igniting happened. I didn't want to use the traditional children's music; I wanted the children to be excited, and to have to hear different things to be motivated to want to sing this music, and so I said, "Let me write it, let me write a funky tune, let me write South African tunes; let's do a jazz suite."

My spirituality and my love for knowledge, theology, spirituality, and metaphysics is from my biological mother; she was a theologian in the Baptist church. If she were living now, of course she would be clergy—she would be a pastor. But at that time, she was a woman with a master's from one of the finest universities, and all she could do in the church was be a church secretary and head of the Christian Education Program. But my father was a musician and my mother was a theologian, and I am a church musician and someone who thought for many years that I would be going to divinity school, so I literally have my mother and father in me, and I combine that in my work a lot. If you hear my music, you will hear a lot of that in me.

In my first children's CD, the spirituality is about me always being attracted to the study and knowledge and the presence of God in life, and how that looks and how we make that happen—the mystique of it—it is about all of the things that we can't see but some of us know, or think we know, all of the miracles and the synchronicities, and the serendipities—spiritual things that happen in people's lives. I am a Christian, and at the same time I spend a lot of time studying metaphysics and the science of mind. What it is essentially is a very clear acknowledging that God is in us; you find God in each person, and we, as opposed to seeking God as someone or something external, can find God within each of us, and we can call on God in us for all of the things that we give over to God outside of us. God can do all of these things through us because God is in us. You change your thinking, you change your life. That's what Science of Mind is about and I wholeheartedly believe that.

My Work With ArtsConnection

One of my best friends, a college roommate, was a teaching artist with ArtsConnection for many years, and she said "They're looking for a music/vocal teaching artist." This was in 1993/1994, and she said, "Why don't you go in and interview and speak with them?" I have been working with them ever since. I never used my music education, my degree, or knowledge, at all, and I started to remember how much I loved music education and working with children. I just had not been working that muscle. I became a certified teacher as a part of getting the master's. I used what I learned; I pulled out my books, referred to my notes. The more I taught children, the more I realized that I loved the work. I realized that this is something I was supposed to be doing. My challenge is that because my voice is my main teaching tool and because my voice is also my instrument, that's become an issue for me. I can't do as much teaching artist work as I would like—or, I can't do as much performing work as I would like because it takes such a toll on my voice.

I use my voice to talk to the children, and then I use my voice to sing with the children. And then, I'm expected to go to a club at night and use my voice to perform. The voice needs care just like everything else, but it's part of my body, and it happens to be my instrument. It would be a lot easier for me if my instrument were something that was not a part of my physical body, but it happens that it is. Working on the balance of that is a challenge for me. I do the best I can. I've worked on my teaching procedure so I don't use my voice as much, and I do a balancing act to the best of my ability.

Seeing Transformation

When I was teaching children, I saw transformation. Literally. Our children aren't children anymore. We require so much of them that they grow up too fast. They don't have a childhood, they don't have a glimmer in their eye, that sparkle. They don't have a sense of joy, and while that is obviously a gross generalization, I saw what one little song can do, and how it can transform a child's spirit in the course of a 50-minute workshop. I literally saw children turn around and become changed, transformed into child wonders. It's a matter of spirit, and it's also a matter of the amazing learning and teaching potential that music has. Music is the universal language.

The school where Barry [Oreck] and I worked, P.S. 130, had 38 different ethnicities. We all understand the language of music. Let's talk about singing a song in English, which is a new language for you who have been in this country merely 8 months. Let's talk about the facility that that brings in terms of speaking the language, understanding it because you are singing it with other children around you, and let's talk about how that propels you in the classroom and in the entire educational environment.

I really actually approach my work with the children in a motherly way, so the academic learning is no more important than the social skills learning. I'll spend half a lesson dealing with the children in terms of how they treat each other because that's our only hope. So we spend a lot of time learning how to say, "Pardon me," "Excuse me," when to say it. I also really work hard to dialogue with the children individually to honor what they have to say. I don't want them to feel dismissed because they are children.

As an African American woman, I think I can relate better to African American children. I don't think I am any better of an educator for them. But I can approach a Black child, and we have unspoken cultural things in common in terms of what I know. If your mother's raising you, there are certain things I know your grandmother has taught you. There are certain things I know that are not accepted in your home. Now I'm not the same generation as your mother—I could be your grandmother—but I know culturally things that go on in your home or don't go on in your home and I know that the way you're acting right now, that's not acceptable in your home.

I treat White children just like I would treat Black kids. The Black kid knows that I know that he or she knows better. Generally, many times White children are not as disciplined as our children because they don't have to be. It's a different standard. We historically have had to make sure our children know how to behave and handle themselves because their lives were in danger, their lives depended on it. It then comes down historically through the generations—"You've got to listen to me. If I tell you to come here, you can't even look at me and say, 'Why?' Because you might end up injured or dead." Now realistically, White American children have much more freedom; they dialogue with their parents and essentially they are raised into their "entitlement" in this country and in the world. Sometimes the respect for me doesn't happen, because of my color, from White American children; there's a split second when we get to know each other and they see I love them and we're going to have fun and then we're fine. But initially, it's almost like there's less respect; it depends on the school and circumstances, but I've encountered that.

All the children like to do the same thing. They like a game we play called "Name, Name What's Your Name." They love to sing the songs, they love me, I love them. There is a difference, for a lot of children, in the level of musicianship—raw, rugged musicianship. Because of the music that most African American children listen to, because of their experience in church, if they attend church, or because of certain styles of music in their home, they've been tapping their feet and bopping their head longer and hearing rhythm and syncopation that they have been translating into their bodies. So they have more experience in recognizing specific kinds of rhythms and syncopation and "blues-ed" notes. It's just the most interesting thing and it has to do with the music they're exposed to, and not necessarily with any kind of innate talent; it does have to do with their environment and their culture.

I can have 7-year-old African American children learn a song and pick up the rhythm quicker than some other children. They all get it, but I've noticed that an African American kindergartner might be more adept in hearing that rhythm/syncopation and be more adept at imitating it, and in being able to reproduce it, echo it, than a child from another culture. And again these are gross generalizations—you have children who are studying music, listening to it—I find that across the board that is the case many times.

I loved the opportunity to "save" some children through the Young Talent Program. I loved the idea of thinking beyond usual boundaries, in terms of how we auditioned children, how we assessed them, and how we brought them into the program. I enjoyed that because I think that's what we're supposed to do, especially as artists; and, not to incite classroom teachers, we teacher artists may be freer thinkers. We also may be a little bit more liberated. Classroom teachers are so bogged down, having to fit into the requirement of their particular Board of Education, they don't have the opportunity to be creative, as teachers used to be, and I felt like we could save a lot of children and I felt like we did. I was introduced to it by Barry [Oreck]. What Barry explained to me was not a difficult concept to wrap my brain around because it was what I think about children. We're not trying to catch fame; we're trying to use art in children's minds to help them academically, to give them a way, a path, to academic achievement.

Tapping Into the Creative Spirit

My goal in the classroom and in these workshops is to get children to tap into their creative spirit. My belief is the more they create, the more they use their brain and their thinking in a different way. My belief is the more they create, the more they see that they can create something wonderful. When they see what can come from them, they feel better about themselves; they are tapping into a part of their brains and experiences that they have not used before. It gives them confidence; it encourages risk-taking skills. It transforms how they think and read and function in the academic arena. Process is much more important than how many songs they learn. I'm much more concerned with what happens when we go around and do, "Name, Name, What's Your Name," the first time and the fifth time. How has their risk-taking expanded, how many more improvisations are present, how much wider and deeper are their self-expressions?

If they're going to be musicians, though, it's very important that they learn to read music. The written music is the representation of the art and the more you know about the art, the better you can be "in it". Many people think they are less creative as musicians if they have to read. They think that the improvisation is more creative if you're not able to read, but improvisation is nothing to dread. Being able to read and understand the language, the symbolic language, the written language of the art, is not stifling. It's a tool. I read music. I had to learn how to play by ear. If you put anything in front of me I can read it. Well, that's exciting and it gives me more room to express. It also makes a big difference because a lot of the jobs are studio work where they need somebody who can read music. Children should start to read music as early as they can open their eyes. That's what I think.

But in these circumstances and these music workshops I do, that's not what I'm concerned with. I'm concerned with them being able to hear the song and sing it correctly, and with reading words, because I want them to have that academic and literary experience. When I ran a music school for children, one of the ways we were learning about music was reading symbols. They weren't the traditional music symbols, but symbols that represented sounds.

We were studying the community, so what do we have in the community? Trains, buses, people walking, motorcycles, etc., and we had sounds that we made with our mouths and/or with our feet, then we created a symbol that represented that sound. Then we created a music suite that was called "Our Community," and we put the sounds together the way we wanted, which is what written music is: symbols that represent sounds. So they then are learning to read symbols that represent a sound which is prereading, or coreading, which is helping them to recognize how symbols represent sounds in music. It was great fun, and we had the visual/written symbol for the sound. You see a motorcycle, and that one motorcycle represents "zoom." And you see four? That represents "zoom, zoom, zoom, zoom." There might be four motorcycles, three birds, and it goes on like that and you create a piece, and then you and the class perform it.

I must do this work. I have not been given this gift for no reason. I have more children's songs than I could teach in a year, and they keep coming to me. I've been given this music. I've been given the gift of being able to relate to children. The children like me, they receive me, they're happy to see me the next time. I believe in discipline and fun with children, I require a lot of them, and I always hold high expectations. But I really try to make sure they know it's because I love them. I had a challenge initially when I started working as a teaching artist; I felt I was so harsh with them and so rough on them that I didn't have enough of a balance in terms of my loving way and intent with them.

My favorite grade level is second grade, 7-year-olds, but kindergartners, first graders, I'm so in love with them also. There's so much in them, so much feeling, so much wisdom, so much observation, so much joy, so much love. So much intuitive "stuff." I really work hard to just validate what they have to say. It fuels me. "Children, kindergartners—we're going to write a song about New York. How would you like it to sound?" I'll play a particular feel on the piano. First I say, "Will it be fast or slow or medium?" They have opinions. And they have thoughts about how they want it to sound. "Do you like that? No, do you like that? Yeah. Come on."

As I said, I like the young ones the best—all the way up to sixth grade. After sixth grade, you won't find me—junior high, high school, no, because I have to work too hard to get through their stuff. It's a harder road. That's not where I'm led. I'm led to work with the young children. I have kindergartners who will say to me, after we finish a class or something—and this will be in the regular music class, where I teach them children songs, melody, rhythm, pulse of the song. We just learn these songs and have fun making body sounds—Children will come up to me and say, "You know, Miss McKenzie, when I go home at night, and I'm not feeling good, sometimes I sing that song and I feel better." The song is taking them out of where they are and the music transforms them and brings them what it is they need.

Talent

Talent is what we all have. It's a matter of figuring out where yours is and what mine is. Everybody's got a gift. I think that it goes across the board. Somebody might have a talent for talking to people or creating a dance, and my feeling is, I'm very disgruntled with the educational system because there's this wasteland of children because they're all being relegated to sit the same way, and to sit in these classrooms and we're not addressing who they are, so they're missing it, and only the children who can adapt, or who our particular teaching system addresses, get it. Everybody else is considered wrong.

Here's a perfect example. I was doing a jazz workshop with second graders. There was a kid, a discipline challenge, and so the teacher had him sitting over there in a corner, drumming with a pencil. My accompanist went over there and had a conversation with him. This was an African American little boy. My partner is Black and a man, so an African American male going to speak to a Black little boy was powerful. He went over and the next thing I know, the little boy was sitting next to him, playing the drums. My accompanist was showing him the keyboard and the rhythms on the keyboard. That was all the boy needed. Then he could go anywhere. The teaching artist had addressed this hole in him and filled him with this wonderfulness that is just going to permeate his whole being.

First of all everyone can sing—if you can speak you can sing. Does everyone want to hear everybody sing? No. Can everybody sing? Yes. Should everybody sing? Sure, why not, because singing is not just about performing art, singing is about expressing yourself using an instrument that you have. It's your body, a part of your body, and I always say that the voice is the horn of the soul, and all of us would love to amplify some of the things in our soul. Why not take a walk and sing songs? Why not sit in your home and just sing to the rafters? Why not join a community choir if that's what makes you feel good?

I think we laud the media performing arts so much because we don't have as much art in the school as we used to. Since the advent of television, we're done to. Now singing is relegated to a stage, the mastery of the performing art. Everyone is afraid of judgment. Car radios stopped us from singing in the car. Church is one of the few places people do sing nowadays. I think the judgment piece in terms of singing in public is very, very big. For children, creating on any level is like exposing themselves. Everybody's editing themselves because everybody's talking about everybody—about what they have on, what they're wearing, what they look like, what they sound like. It's a cultural pastime. We have magazines that are literally based on judging other people's personal choices and behavior. It has a very big impact on undoing the pop culture and collapsing the authentic culture of this country.

Perception of Sound

I find perception of sound to not be a difficult or challenging aspect in any child. I think that one of the advantages of this talent assessment program [YTP] is that the child doesn't have to have lessons before you see them.

One girl, Christine, 8 or 9, sang wonderfully. We worked on two lines, and spoke them in time, and sang them, went over the words again and we were singing a line in the song, and the line in the song was: "You've got to take a little risk, make a little fist, push the bad away and look at what will happen each and every day." Christine had two comments. Her melodic memory and ability to reproduce a melodic phrase was impeccable. Her pitch was impeccable. She had a sense of music. Every time she raised her hand, I had to call on her because I was just fascinated with what she had to say. One time she raised her hand and she said, "You know what, when we get to 'push the bad away,' we get to do this." She demonstrated a dance move. And I said, "Well you know what, Christine, that is exactly what we do in the choreography." And she raised her hand again and she said, "So when we sing 'Take a little risk,' it's just like we're saying 'Take a little chance.'"

This was a girl whose perception of sound transferred to her perception of the music and her understanding of the lyric. She had arrangement ideas, movement ideas. It started with me noticing how quickly she was able to sing—and when she sang, she was singing it pitch perfect; she knew when to come in, and to hear what she had to say about music and perception was extraordinary. I don't know if she studied music, I don't know if she was singing in a choir in church but I do know that she had all these things, specifically perception of sound, which was the first thing that made me notice her.

When they are moving and coordinating, they're moving to the music. It has to do with how they're taking the music in aurally and how it is speaking to their bodies. First of all, it has to speak to their brains. It does have an effect, and I know that the closer you are to understanding and being able to deliver the pitch and the melody, the easier it is for you to move to. As they say in the business, *we love a singer who moves well.* In other words, someone who moves well might not have perception of sound at all. But I've noticed that if they have a perception of sound they don't have difficulty just moving to the music. But that coordination, that's a difficult piece.

It's a little more difficult to get a sense of that rhythm and perception of sound because it is dance, because it is movement and someone who sings well and who even has good rhythm might not move or be coordinated enough to move like a dancer. That would be somebody who I would really have to work on, but it doesn't indicate that they don't need to be in this music program. I like to root for the children who seem to take on a new persona in the presence of the teaching artist. Maybe they come into the classroom and give the teacher a hard time by being difficult but the kid would do anything to make sure that he or she is in the workshop. Missing out on that workshop is not something that he wants to happen in his life and it's like it becomes his savior.

The experience for those 50 minutes with the music makes him literally become a different child, because he gets it. This kid notices how he is able to be a star in this particular realm and he gets another kind of respect and positive reinforcement, even from his classmates, because this kid knows the answer. This kid was listening; he knows how "Take the A Train" goes and can sing the bridge; he remembers Duke Ellington's name. What happens is it is an enthusiasm and interest in the subject, so then this kid, all of a sudden, is paying attention, and loves to sing "Take the A Train," and this kid is reading because we have the lyrics up there because he wants to sing!

Music Talent Is Miraculous

I've noticed that in children with talent, who have such an interest in music, their talent is waiting to unfold. You can see it because it's miraculous. It's really miraculous. For example, I was finishing up a jazz program with the second graders; we were singing "Stomping at the Savoy"—and these second graders were moving to the music and the rhythm—being uninhibited, feeling safe enough to really respond to the music. Nobody was saying, "What you listening to that funny music for?" Because everybody was listening to it and these children were singing the music; they were getting it; they were feeling the whole character of this particular music. We haven't had time to do the history of jazz and listen to a lot of different jazz songs. They may have only heard two songs. They got the music; they got the style; and when they have a chance to hear jazz again, they are ready to receive it again. There's something about it; they get it.

I think that is talent because there are some kids who you can see—they're the next Wynton Marsalis or something because they're hearing it and it's touching them in a different way. It speaks to them. There's no way to explain it. Jazz is just for them. The other kids might be listening and enjoying it, and they love singing the song but they're not like a boy I taught—let's call him Jordan. Every time the music came on, he was right on it, snapping fingers—it was in his posture; it was like he was being channeled or something.

They got up and danced. And they danced. And they danced. They didn't think it was silly. Something happened. Music is powerful. They can learn about the history of New York City, the subway system, how it works, they learn about all that just from learning that song and singing "Take the A Train." In that song, we have the history of Harlem, the history of New York City, we have the physics and science of how trains work, how subway trains work, the jobs that people do. You could use that one song for a unit.

Conclusion

I wouldn't be happy as a regular music teacher. I would not be happy because I would feel like a bird in a cage, and that would translate to the children. I would resent being there because I like the freedom of a workshop. As I'm developing curriculum I think in terms of those Talent Assessment Program (TAP) assessments. As I'm observing children, always in my mind and in my brain, I'm looking to see in this particular child more risk-taking, and I'm seeing creative thinking, and I'm seeing many more children who are not copying children next to them, and I see a child who takes a long time to answer a question but he is willing to raise his hand, and she's willing to take a chance that children might laugh at them if they try to get it out.

I'm observing other children being appreciative of their peers' artistic offerings, creative offerings, so I really use that as a foundational piece in my teaching.

I don't say that was right, that was wrong; I always say across the board, "Thank you." Whatever the child offers, I say, "Thank you." In terms of creative offerings, I'm really into thank you. And I'm always saying to the children, "Wasn't that a great offering? Let's give them a hand." They have an understanding that kindness is very important.

The greatest strength that I have as a teaching artist is conveying to the children how much I love them, by caring about what they say, and letting them know it. I convey it by looking them in the eye, by being honest with them, being straightforward with them, not letting them get away with anything not in their favor. The stern loving hand is my way. It's important to me—that they understand that when they have something to say with me, I want to hear it. I think that is my greatest gift. I feel like I'm channeling a child in me. And I'm grateful. What a gift!

What a life!

Chapter 13

THE MAGIC OF WRITING

Organic Creativity in Teaching Fiction Writing

Stephanie S. Tolan

"Schools are to Creativity as Zoos are to Wildness." That's the title of a talk I once gave teachers. Just as the very nature of zoos curbs much of the wildness of its inhabitants, the nature of schools curbs creativity.

I got a clear picture of this when doing a school visit many years ago with kindergarten students. All of my other school visits and poets-in-the-schools writing workshops had been with students from fourth grade through high school. I was used to having to get the kids "turned on" before asking them to venture into a discussion of writing and books or to try writing some poems or stories of their own. So I made the mistake of turning on that group of 25 or so kindergartners. Chaos and pandemonium ensued. I never got them back. By the end of the class period, I felt as if I'd been run over by a stampeding herd of wildebeests.

It had not been clear to me before then that the reason I had to turn on my usual target audience was that they had passed the age of a well-documented phenomenon known as the "fourth grade creativity slump."[140] Originally suspected to be caused by some developmental change related to the children's age, it turns out to be rare in homeschooled populations of the same age. The conclusion is clear: School itself blunts the natural creativity of children. In an article about *emergence theory* (the study of how new things come into being), Joanne Blum pointed out that "Creation flourishes in an atmosphere where ideas are shifting and open-ended—not where they are settled and

Stephanie S. Tolan, M.A., began writing at the age of 8, but had discovered her passion for stories and the magical power of imagination long before that. The author of more than 25 works of fiction for children and young adults and winner of the Newbery Honor for *Surviving the Applewhites*, Tolan has also published poetry and plays and taught for the Institute for Children's Literature. Wearing her "other hat" as a consultant on the educational and social-emotional-spiritual needs of gifted and talented children and adults, she coauthored *Guiding the Gifted Child* and has written a wide variety of articles and a blog (http://www.welcometothedeepend.com).

certain."[141] *Settled and certain* is an excellent descriptor of the majority of the curriculum in school. In addition, tests give students the sense that questions have two kinds of answers—the right one and all of the others. There is little room for shifting, open-ended ideas. In addition, of course, schools have settled on certain methods, organizational strategies, and rules. After 4 years, most kids have learned and more or less adapted to these constraints.

Robust Creators

Just as there are some zoo animals that remain considerably wilder (and more dangerous to their keepers) than others, there are some kids whose creativity is stronger than average and, therefore, less likely to be socialized out of them. These are the kids who persistently refuse to follow directions, insist on doing things their own way, and are willing to accept standing out from the crowd, however painful that may sometimes be, and however harmful it can be to their grade point average. Among the robust creators, there are others who essentially go underground, acting the part of compliant student during class hours and exhibiting their creativity only outside of school. In spite of the overall restrictions of a school environment, there may be a modest place for creativity in school, depending on the student's domain of interest.

Kids with a passion for reading and writing are among the lucky ones (although the current obsession with standardized testing and the new preference for nonfiction over fiction in the Common Core State Standards seems to be changing that) because literature remains a major part of the language arts curriculum, and imagination, *one of the most important components of creativity*, is not only allowed, but *encouraged* in literature. In most of the rest of the school environment (as in our whole culture), intellect is the primary focus of attention, as it is associated with *reality*. Imagination, on the other hand, is associated almost solely with *fantasy*, and as children get older, they are admonished to give it up and "get real."

My Own Story

Although I was one of those "robust creators" who went underground early, ironically enough it was in the fourth grade that I first found a place for myself. It was 1950, the year I turned 8 years old, when my teacher asked our class to write a story. Not a report—a *story.* It was the first creative writing assignment I'd ever had. Mind you, as a highly imaginative child, I tended to do nonstandard reports—my report on the agricultural products of Mexico, for example, had been written from the point of view of a pineapple. But this time I didn't have to worry about squeezing in a bunch of necessary facts. I was allowed to make the whole thing up, to create the characters, the setting—the plot! That story (which I still have, imperfectly spelled and copied over "in ink") turned out to be the beginning of the rest of my life.

Let me back track a moment. I was the youngest child in my family, born when my brother was 5 and my sister was 7. Our mother believed in reading to her children, so my time *in utero* was inevitably full of stories. And once I was out in the world, I spent many years listening to much longer, more complicated, and more exciting literature than she would have read to me alone. I can't remember a time when I didn't love (and have access to) rich and interesting stories.

I do remember the immense frustration of holding a book in my hands, staring at those little black marks, unable to work the magic of turning them into the words that would conjure whole worlds full of people and animals having what felt like real lives very different from my own. So, at about 4, with the help of comic books, I taught myself to read. Oddly enough, as exciting as this accomplishment was, I was disconcerted by the discovery that I could no longer *not* read. I would try squinting to blur the letters in the hope of getting back the sense of mystery that had existed in the print itself. Now that I was a reader, just looking at the words automatically filled my mind with the stories they told. It was liberating to be able to enter the world of the story on my own, but there was also a sense of loss. The black marks themselves could never again be magical and mysterious.

I had always spent a great deal of time in my imagination. Pretending was a major part of every day. I would be a pirate (one of my favorites, since that also led to the creation of treasure maps), a cowboy (with a pair of pearl-handled six shooters in fancy holsters), Robin Hood, a soldier, a knight, a spy, and—on rare occasions—a princess. When I started school, I invented characters to be and stories to tell on my way there and back (kids walked in those days), and at home, I turned our backyard apple tree and bushes into a forest or a jungle, the space under the spirea bushes serving variously as log cabin, thatched hut, teepee, or secret cave.

School's version of teaching us to read, which in those days involved Dick and Jane and a "red, red ball," bored me silly, but I could look forward to burrowing under my covers at night with a flashlight to venture out onto the banks of Plum Creek, or to join Jim Hawkins and Long John Silver on the way to Treasure Island. Gradually I realized that the enduring magic was the power of printed words to transport me to other worlds and other times, where people, for better—and sometimes for worse (like Bill Sykes in *Oliver Twist*)—came fully and completely alive in my mind.

Back to 1950. That first assignment to write a story gave me the astonishing revelation that I could make that magic myself. I could imagine a story of my own, capture it in words on a page that a reader could experience. I knew then and there that I wanted to be a writer when I grew up.

There followed, in my sixth-grade year, a teacher who was not fond of students who challenged her (I did) and whose standard punishment for troublemakers was to send them to a desk at the back of the room to do ditto sheet after ditto sheet of long division problems. Having read and loved the tale of Br'er Rabbit and the briar patch, I put it to use. All year, I pretended to *love* long division and hate writing so that when she sent *me* to the back of the room, my punishment was writing stories. "Do I have to?" I would whine as I trudged reluctantly to what was in truth my personal classroom refuge. I still have all of those stories as well.

By the end of that year, I was so committed to writing that during the summer I moved a cot, a desk chair, and a card table along with my parents' big old black Underwood typewriter onto the second floor sun porch of our house and declared it my "writing studio." There I wrote poems and stories and sent them off to *The Saturday Evening Post* and the children's magazine, *Jack and Jill*, both of which duly rejected them. Stung, I stopped submitting but kept on writing. I made up a whole book that summer, entitled *The Mystery of the Jeweled Dagger*. Because typing on that Underwood was a challenge, I didn't actually write it all down, but my seventh-grade English teacher allowed me to give an oral book report on it. When my classmates asked where they could find the book so they could read it themselves, my career plans were confirmed. Not only could I create the magic of story, now I had readers eager to read it.

More than six decades after that first story, I'm still writing. I've published plays, poetry, nonfiction, and 27 works of fiction for young readers. Some of my books have won awards, including the Newbery Honor for *Surviving the Applewhites*.[142] It was the space that language arts and English classes provided for my imagination that kept it alive and functioning in an environment that otherwise pinched it off by treating it as "kid stuff" to be outgrown as quickly as possible. Rather than treating imagination as fantasy that interferes with children's ability to concentrate on the real, it's vital to remember that *imagination is the source of future reality*. To support creativity in any domain, one of the most important things to do is make a safe place for exercising imagination in our classrooms.

The Crucial Role of Magic

It's no wonder that as a child I found mystery in the black marks on paper and magic in the ability of those black marks to create worlds in my mind that felt as real (and sometimes more so) than my actual life. We don't understand how that happens. Science is just beginning to explore human consciousness. Many, perhaps most scientists still consider consciousness an "epiphenomenon," a mere byproduct of the chemical and electrical interactions within the brain. What *is* intellect? Imagination? Intuition? What are dreams? The truth is, while we have named these aspects of mind and are able to use—or at least experience—them, we really do not understand them.

There's a famous cartoon that shows two men looking at a blackboard on which a long and complex mathematical formula is written. In the middle of the formula, there are the words "then a miracle occurs." One of the men is saying to the other, "I think you should be more explicit here in step two."

Magic, mystery, wonder, awe—these are components of creativity that the scientists wish to turn into a more explicit formula. I'm one of those people who doubt this will ever happen. I'm interested in reading what scientists say about creativity, but I invariably come away from such reading shaking my head. They haven't captured it, much less explained it. In most cases they haven't even come close.

Before I write a book, nothing about it exists. When the process is over, the miracle has occurred. The words on the page allow other people to share that world that grew in my imagination, as it comes to life in theirs. When people ask me (this is probably the single most common question writers are asked), "Where do you get your ideas?"—I tend, nowadays, to shrug my shoulders and say, "It's magic." I'm old enough now that I don't care if anyone scoffs at that answer.

Of my 27 books, few have begun in the same way. Sometimes a character comes into my mind, fully formed, demanding a story. Sometimes I have a dream so memorable and intriguing that it's easily recognizable as an incipient book. Sometimes a philosophical concept comes to me that I feel is worth exploring. Sometimes it begins with a setting. And occasionally I feel a need to deal with something that happened in my real life through fiction. But the process of growing a book from these initial seeds is deeply mysterious and usually extremely challenging. I suspect it is the challenge of it—the effort, the discipline, the occasional genuine agonies and struggle—that tend to mask the magic.

When I began my actual writing career, I was what my education and our culture had turned that imaginative 8-year-old into—a rational materialist. I knew, of course, that writing a book was creating something new that had never before existed in the world. But I thought it was essentially the same thing I did when writing a paper, a report, a thesis. It was my intellect at work, taking bits and pieces of information, experience, ideas I had heard or read, images I had seen, and more or less "stirring them together" to come up with something new. At most, I thought, the writing rearranged the pieces, the way a kaleidoscope does when you turn it, to make a new picture. I knew that sometimes there was a feeling that something unexplainable occurred during the process—something I called "the magic of writing"—but my rational self suspected that there was some logical explanation that was just not easy to see.

Books about creativity that spoke of "incubation" as part of the creative process allowed the magic to stay under the radar. Having a name for something gives us the comforting illusion of understanding. The first time I had a direct experience of the nonrational process powerfully enough to feel the term *magic* really did fit was while writing my second book, *The Last of Eden*.[143] I'd come to a brick wall in the creation of the plot and had no idea where the story should go next. I very clearly remember sitting at my typewriter and being overcome with an intense need for sleep. I wasn't in the habit of taking naps, because my writing time (while my 5-year-old son was in school) was short and I didn't intend to waste it sleeping. But I couldn't keep my eyes open, so I left the typewriter, lay down on the couch in my office, and drifted off. Less than half an hour later, I woke up, fully refreshed, but still stuck against that brick wall. I went to the typewriter, sat down, put my hands on the keys, and found myself writing this line of dialogue for my principal character: "Who are the Kincaids?"

I sat for a moment, looking at those words. I had no idea what the answer was, or where the name came from. Then my fingers went on typing, answering the question and giving the whole rest of the book its shape. None of what flowed from my fingers had bothered to move through my conscious mind beforehand. And none of the words they wrote over the next hour or so ever had to be changed in the many revisions the book went through. There was no question that what had happened felt like magic.

Let me share another experience from the multitude that have brought me the joy of that magic over the years. I was in the midst of writing *A Time to Fly Free,*[144] one of my books whose seed was a character—a child named Josh who was partly my son and partly myself, but different from both of us. Again, the story had come to a standstill because, while I knew Josh and what his conflict was, I hadn't a clue about the story that might resolve it. (Plot is my greatest writing challenge!) We were living in Norfolk, VA, at the time, and I had set the book in a fictional version of it that I called Tidewater. I had to fly to a speaking gig in a distant city, and during the flight I pulled the airline magazine from its pocket on the back of the seat in front of me. One of the articles was about the Suncoast Seabird Sanctuary in Sarasota, FL. As I read about the way the sanctuary had been created, I realized that it could readily be adapted to my story's setting and could lead to everything necessary for resolving Josh's conflict. I took the magazine with me when I left the plane.

When I packed to go back home the next day, I put the magazine in the suitcase, which went into the plane's overhead storage. Partway through the flight I decided I wanted to read the article again, but I was in the window seat and didn't want to bother my seatmate to get it. Instead, I reached into the pocket in front of me and got out the airline magazine. It had an unfamiliar cover, and the article I wanted was not in it. I asked my seatmate if I could borrow the magazine from his place. His copy was the same as the copy I had in my hand. So I rang for the flight attendant and explained the problem.

"I don't understand," she said. "The new issue is put out the first day of the month—that was more than a week ago, and every seat pocket in every plane is checked. I can't imagine how an old issue could have been left on a plane for so long. I've never heard of that happening before." *The magic at work,* I thought. Not only had that particular magazine been left on the plane I'd flown on the day before for a week after the new issue had come out, but it had been in *my* seat pocket, with the answer to my plot problem. One could call it synchronicity—a *meaningful* coincidence. But whatever one calls it, I still get goose bumps when I think of it.

It's important to take note of the fact that I was committed to writing that book before the synchronicity happened, and as I got on the plane, my mind was filled with the story I had created thus far. The following quotation from William H. Murray, a Scottish mountaineer and writer, describes this particular kind of magic in his 1951 book, *The Scottish Himalayan Expedition*:

> This may sound too simple, but is great in consequence. Until one is committed, there is hesitancy, the chance to draw back, always ineffectiveness. Concerning all acts of initiative (and creation), there is one elementary truth, the ignorance of which kills countless ideas

and splendid plans: that the moment one definitely commits oneself, then Providence moves too. All sorts of things occur to help one that would never otherwise have occurred. A whole stream of events issues from the decision, raising in one's favour all manner of unforeseen incidents and meetings and material assistance, which no man could have dreamt would have come his way. I learned a deep respect for one of Goethe's couplets:

> Whatever you can do or dream you can, begin it.
> Boldness has genius, power and magic in it![145]

Similar synchronicities have happened to me over and over again, and I have come to trust that they will.

The Place of Intuition

As a confirmed rational materialist (who had come to accept only that bit of magic about writing) I used to scoff at the idea that anyone could have what I called "psychic powers." In fact, I got an idea for a book in which one of the teenaged characters fancied herself a psychic, and I intended the debunking of her fantasy to be a part of the story. My experience is recounted in an article entitled "Imagination to Intuition, the Journey of a Rationalist into Realms of Magic and Spirit," first published in *The Journal of Advanced Development*.[146] The short version is that the research I did for that novel convinced me that there were aspects of mind that exist—are "real"—whether most of us believe in them or not. During my research visiting psychics to get background information, I kept being told by them that I, too, was highly psychic. I dismissed this, believing, as I often said, that I had not one psychic bone in my body. Finally, when I had been told by a professional psychic once again that I, too, was highly psychic, and I had once again denied it, she said, "I thought you said you're a writer."

"I am!" I replied. "Have been since I was 8."

"How do you think you do what you do?"

Remembering the magic, I couldn't answer.

I had known that I was far out on the intuitive continuum on the Myers-Briggs Type Indicator (MBTI) scale, but had not previously connected the word *intuitive* with *psychic*. I didn't realize that the terms are frequently used interchangeably. It was that conversation that gave me a different way to see the magic. To the rational, logical mind—intellect—intuitive knowing seems impossible. And yet it is part of the way our minds work. We are able to *know* without an external source of information, and what we know that way is verifiable. A friend of mine who writes historical fiction often composes whole scenes without checking the known facts, only to find when she does, that the scene fits what is known of the time. She calls it "hearing whispers from the past." Ever since that conversation about how I do what I do, I have not only engaged in a purposeful exploration of the nonrational aspects of consciousness, I have actively worked to learn how to use my intuition more effectively not just in writing, but in the rest of my life as well. The exploration has become a spiritual journey as well as a way to increase my own creativity.

I know of writers (one such is a friend) whose *whole* creative process is intuitive. Some describe the writing they do as "taking dictation," since their stories, characters, plot—all that goes into their creative work—flows through their fingers in that magical way I first experienced writing *The Last of Eden*. My own process is far more rational—a blend of thinking and intuition. As much as I'd like the writing to be so easy, I also revel in the process that lets me experience not just the "flow" moments, but the intellectual work that is the craft of writing. I enjoy the challenge of consciously integrating intellect, imagination, and intuition. I don't agree with the saying that writing is 1% inspiration and 99% perspiration. For me there's considerably more inspiration involved, but there is still a whole lot of sweat! The goose bump part that feels like magic comes along just often enough to keep the hard work from turning me into one of those writers (there are many such) who say they love "having written," but hate writing. There is nothing more exhilarating than having key parts of the story appear fully formed in one's mind seemingly out of nowhere. When reading the first few chapters of the second revision of my book, *Applewhites at Wit's End*,[147] made it clear to me that the story wasn't really working yet, I stormed out of the house with our two dogs to go for a walk and get away from my computer for a while. As I scuffed through the leaves on the trail through the woods to the boulders that were my destination, these words came unexpectedly into my mind: "It was a dark and stormy night when Randolph Applewhite arrived home from New York to announce the end of the world." That line was clearly the first line of the book and brought with it into my mind everything else I needed. I wrote the final revision in a few weeks. Trusting the magic is essential to my surviving the tough parts of my process.

Encouraging Creativity

So how do we go about bringing the magic into the classroom? Most students are *not* robust creators whose very nature will make it possible to keep their native creativity alive and working in an atmosphere that mostly shuts it down. And there are a great many creative endeavors and domains besides writing. Humanity needs all of the new and original ideas it can get as we face the many cultural and global problems that have arisen from our intense focus on intellect.

We can begin by finding ways to support imagination as much as possible. Fairy tales are only part of the rich heritage of literature we can share with kids. Read stories and books aloud. Use visualization exercises in class. A couple of splendid sources for these are *Spinning Inward* and *He Hit Me Back First!*[148] Relabel visualization exercises if necessary—call them "brain boosters."

Help students realize how interesting and magical imagination is—and how little we understand it. Think awe and wonder. Encourage them to push their own boundaries, try new things, experiment. Avoid giving them rules (creativity is all about breaking rules). Relabel those, too. You might call them "principles that might (and often do) work."

It isn't necessary for schools to try teaching children how to use their intuition, but it's important to let them know it exists and, however mysterious, is a natural part of how the mind works. Share your own creative impulses and interests with the students. Although writing is usually a fairly solitary activity, students can be gathered sometimes into "idea exploring groups" so that both introverts and extroverts have an opportunity to work in ways that are comfortable for them.

Turning a typical classroom into a greenhouse for creative exploration that supports every student's natural creativity is unlikely—there is not space within the schedule to do that. But it is important to understand what helps so as to offer that when you can and what hurts so as to avoid it as often as humanly possible.

Some Things That Stifle Creativity

Criticism (both positive and negative). This includes grades. When children are told that what they have created is wonderful (or are given an A or A+ on a writing project), they are all too likely to try to repeat their success. Instead of heading off in new directions, they tend to do a new version of the same thing. When they are told that what they have created is bad (and it's important to remember that for *some* kids anything less than an A is counted as failure), they may decide not to try again. If it is necessary to assign grades to creative work, it is essential to assign many projects and give a grade to only one or two, allowing the children to choose the ones that you agree are the most successful to get a grade.

Product orientation. Creation should be dealt with as a process, not focused solely on creating products. Experimentation can be encouraged, and the point should be made that every bit of creation, whether it works well or not, is valuable for the experience it provides.

An emphasis on revision. This is a part of product orientation. There is a huge emphasis on revision in most classrooms where children are asked to write. If I had been asked to revise the stories I wrote in my early years, I doubt that I'd be a writer today. Revision is necessary (and even fun) for professional writers. But it should not be regularly expected of children, whose focus is the adventure of seeing where the story goes. Revision should seldom be required earlier than middle school.

Busy-ness. When all of the children's time is taken up with some task that must be done, the internal quiet time essential to generating ideas is lost. Daydreaming is not harmful to mental processing, it is essential.[149] As Katherine Paterson, one of children's literature's leading lights, says of her own school years, "I was saved by the windows!" It isn't *always* necessary to call a child's attention back from looking out the window to whatever is going on in the classroom.

Too much sitting down and shutting up. One real (and perhaps surprising) spur to creativity is physical movement. Ideas come when walking in nature, when running or bicycling, or doing any physical activity that allows the mind to wander while the body works. Often the best physical activity for creative thinking is solitary, but the opportunity to toss ideas around with someone else while moving can also be valuable. If this can't be added to the school day, consider giving students credit for physical activity not involving organized games.

Fear. This comes in part from criticism (grading) or the idea that every creation must be appreciated by someone else. Creation involves the ability to take a risk, and all creators experience times when they aren't sure they'll be able to finish something they've started, or come up with another new idea. Share this fact with the kids, and maintain as much as possible a sense of play and exploration. Regularly remind students that creators need to be courageous.

Here's to Doing the Best We Can

I want to point something out before I end this chapter. School was mostly a difficult, frustrating, boring, and sometimes truly painful place for me from first grade up until high school. There were bright spots and a couple of teachers who stand out in my memory for being nice to me, in spite of the challenges I sometimes presented. But even the scourge of my life—that sixth-grade teacher who seemingly lost no chance to try to crush my spirit—ended up giving me something useful.

What kids need from the adults in their world is not perfection. It's a willingness to *see* them for the individuals they are and to at least try to make a place for them in a system that was not designed for differences. Here's a quote from Jacob Nordby to consider: "Blessed are the weird people—poets, misfits, writers, mystics, painters, troubadours—for they teach us to see the world through different eyes." [150] I would add "creators" to the list, whatever their domain. The fact that you are reading this book means that you are willing to see the world through different eyes. It may be one of the most important things you have to offer children.

Chapter 14

INVITING CREATIVE WRITING

Organic Creativity in Teaching Poetry Writing

Carl Leggo

The Pleasures of Writing

I have been in school for 55 years. I have spent my life in classrooms as a student, teacher, and professor. One of my recurring, even haunting, regrets is that I cannot remember experiences with creativity in school. Instead, because of many experiences I had as a student in school classrooms, I often call myself a wounded writer. So, all of my writing, and teaching writing, and writing about writing, emerge from complex autobiographical experiences that generally failed to support and nurture me as a writer. Nevertheless, or perhaps as a consequence, I am still always hopeful that I can foster creativity in writing and writers.

In March 1990, I was interviewed for a faculty position in the Department of Language and Literacy Education at the University of British Columbia. At the UBC interview, I cited *The Pleasure of the Text* by Roland Barthes. I recently returned to the book, in which Barthes writes: "The text you write must prove to me *that it desires me.*"[151] I regard Barthes' advice as still some of the best I know for writers (beginning and experienced). Barthes wants texts

Carl Leggo, Ph.D., is a poet and professor at the University of British Columbia. His books include: *Come-By-Chance*; *Teaching to Wonder: Responding to Poetry in the Secondary Classroom*; *Lifewriting as Literary Métissage and an Ethos for Our Times* (coauthored with Erika Hasebe-Ludt and Cynthia Chambers); *Creative Expression, Creative Education* (coedited with Robert Kelly); *Poetic Inquiry: Vibrant Voices in the Social Sciences* (coedited with Monica Prendergast and Pauline Sameshima); and *Sailing in a Concrete Boat: A Teacher's Journey*. Integral to his current creative and academic life, Carl Leggo is a happy grandfather to three darling granddaughters with the magical names Madeleine, Mirabelle, and Gwenoviere.

that do not bore or prattle. I am now a grandfather of a 4-year-old grand-daughter. Madeleine is in love with language, with the sounds and shapes of words, with the possibilities of the alphabet, with *the pleasure of the text*. So, I write this paper about inviting creative writing especially for Madeleine and other children, a paper filled with a grandfather's hope that children and their teachers will always revel in Barthes' *pleasure of the text*, and nurture and celebrate a vibrant and lively love for language and writing and calling out in their creative voices.

Seeing the Alphabet Again

Hanging over the desk in my office is a poster of the alphabet. I put the 26 letters of the alphabet over my desk in order to remind me that as a writer and a language educator, I work (and play) daily with the alphabet. These are the raw materials of my craft and art. Sometimes I forget to see the alphabet; sometimes I take the alphabet for granted. As an initial writing exercise I invite my students to write down the 26 letters of the alphabet. Then I ask them to circle their five favorite letters. Some students look surprised. Some say, "I've never thought about letters that way." After they have circled their five favorite letters, I ask them to write quickly five words that begin with each of the five favorite letters. Some students mumble that they wish they had not picked X. Next I invite them to look through their list of 25 words for poems. Many are delighted with the music of alliteration and the zaniness of connections that they discover among the seemingly disparate words. In this brief introductory writing exercise, the students begin to look at the alphabet with heightened consciousness, and they catch glimpses of a wild energy that pulses in the process and experience of word-making.

As a poet I live by the maxim that the world is words. As human beings, we are born into language, and as human beings we are borne up by language. We are awash in a sea of language. Like a whale that moves through the oceans with its environment pressing on its sides while it in turn presses its shape on its environment, we move through the ocean of language, universally pervasive, pressed and pressing. In our language use, we are constantly shaped and informed and defined, and we are constantly shaping and informing and defining. We are the words we speak and write and think and hear and read. We speak and write and think and hear and read ourselves into existence.

The challenge for educators is to celebrate the ubiquity, the multiplicity, the plurality, the wildness of language full of wonder. We weave words and in weaving words we weave our worlds. My concern is that in schools we often get in the way of word-weaving. We try to tame the wildness of language. We try to categorize and box and control the messiness of language. We try to contain the ocean in a pail. We try to chart the stars on poster paper. We try to squeeze an energetic foot into a pretty but nonfunctional glass slipper. We try to reduce language to basics, essentials, rules, conventions, and patterns.

In my teaching, I meet many wounded writers. I tell them that I too am a wounded writer. I tell them about my high school English teacher. One day she passed me back a writing assignment and said, "Carl, you will never be a writer." Then she added, "But you don't want to be a writer anyway." I respected that elderly woman with frosty hair like cotton candy. I would not tell her that all my life I had harbored only two ambitions. I either wanted to be an astronomer or a writer. When I realized that I would have to study science and math in order to become an astronomer (I thought astronomers reveled in the wonder of stars without end), I knew that I wanted to be a writer. But I could not tell my English teacher that I burned with fire to make words and play with words. Instead I believed her pronouncement that I would never be a writer, and for a whole decade, I wrote nothing except academic essays for university credit.

Following my English teacher's judgment, I limped through years of university studies and years of school teaching, always convinced that I was not a writer, and that I could not be a writer. Only in my late 20s with my personal life exploding around me did I begin to write out of my emotions and fears and turmoil, and only then, after a decade of hearing the echo of my English teacher's dictum, "You will never be a writer," did I find that I had words, words filled with questions and fire and affection, words like stones that invited and enabled me to cross the river, always rushing swiftly, and only then, after a decade of silence, did I hear my voices, voices filled with hope, spirit, and wonder, voices filled with an abiding desire for others, seeking a symphony of singing. I now tell other wounded writers that for more than three decades I have walked in the world as a poet who acknowledges his wounds, but also insists on celebrating the joys of word-making, the joys of journeying.

Teachers need to question with boldness their practices as writing teachers. As a teacher, I am committed to nurturing in others desire and confidence in word-making and word-weaving. I invite my students to write creatively and interrogatively and expressively. I encourage them to take risks, to experiment with diverse discourses, to challenge conventions, to seek truth. I have many fears. I am always concerned about inviting people to walk in the dark, hidden places of their hearts and memories, fearful that they might be lost, fearful that they might not be strong enough to make the journey. And I am always concerned about inviting people to question and contravene the rules, only to encourage them to confront and reject me.

Ideally, I want to nurture an experience of community where our differences of opinion and story and personality and desire can be celebrated. We write and share our writing with one another. We tell stories of our lives, and we reveal ourselves in intimate ways, and we grow stronger in our conviction about the power of words to write our lived stories and to transform our living stories and to create possibilities for more life-enhancing stories. With my students, I want to nurture a relationship that is mutually supportive, a complementary relationship, a relationship of writers who sing in our unique voices and who in our unique singing also seek ways to harmonize with one another. We are wordsmiths, weaving our ways and our words, on journeys that are separate and isolate, occasionally convening to sing together, recognizing how often our journeys are parallel, how often our journeys intersect, how often our journeys are redirected and mapped anew in our sharing, how often our journeys are fueled by the conviction that we are not alone. My hope is that my words will invite others to enter into dialogical relationships of word-making founded on risk-taking, trust, truth-seeking, courage, encouragement, nurture, desire, and unwavering commitment to the power of words for singing our worlds into creation.

Remembering Writing in School

When I was a student in school in the 1950s and 1960s, my experiences with writing were essentially the same from grade to grade. Most of my writing comprised written answers to questions, answers that were embedded in the prose of the textbooks and required a simple effort of excavation. Or I wrote notes, essentially wrote the words that the teacher wrote on the blackboard or dictated. Only seldom was I invited to write where the writing was not a simple exercise of copying. Only seldom was I invited to write a story or a poem or even a composition that required a thoughtful collection and selection and inscription of thoughts instead of blatant plagiarism. But even on those infrequent occasions when I was invited to write a story or a composition, the approach that I was required to take was largely counterproductive.

I remember that the teacher always presented the class with a list of potential topics. We chose one. I do not remember students, even once, suggesting topics. The composition that I wrote was written quickly because the assignment was typically completed in one class period of 40 minutes. This meant that there was usually time for only one draft. Errors were corrected with a rubber eraser. Because compositions always had to be written in ink, the composition could look like a scuffed rug by the end of the class period. If compositions were assigned for homework, there was at least the opportunity to write a clean, neat final copy. Writing was a very private affair. When I wrote a composition at home, I would occasionally ask a parent to read it, but not often. I did not have a sense that writers sought advice from others. I did not see writing as dialogical or communal. Instead I almost always perceived writing as a private affair between me and the teacher.

I wrote almost exclusively for the teacher, who waited expectantly for my composition with the red pencil in hand. I submitted the composition to the teacher, who read it, circled the mistakes, and wrote a grade as well as a word of commendation or complaint at the end: *Excellent work*; *Needs improvement*; *Very good work*; *Shows progress*. I learned in this experience that writing was a product that I produced for the teacher's consumption and evaluation. And I learned that writing in school was always practice writing, never real writing. The only purpose for writing was learning to write. Writing in school was akin to pushing a big rock up the hill, like Sisyphus, only to see it roll back down again and only to continue the effort time after time. Not once in school did I ever write to an audience other than the teacher, not even to my classmates, unless one counts the occasional surreptitious note. Writing was not integral to our lives; writing was an activity that we engaged in because we were required to and cajoled with promises that this kind of school writing would one day be beneficial in our lives outside school. The promises were false. I did not learn to be a writer in school. Instead I claim that writing in school impaired my progress by making writing boring, ineffectual, and artificial.

For many years as a student in school and university, I wrote with neurotic attention to the conventions of composition handbooks, endlessly afraid of the teacher's red pencil. I was zealously committed to themewriting—a prose that does not call attention to itself, a prose that is standardized and homogenized, a prose that is a copy of some hypothetical ideal model that students are expected to strive after. I was years and years overcoming the bad habits instilled in me by teachers who drilled me in grammar and writing exercises until I was convinced that I could only turn abruptly to the right and left or march straight ahead. My writing was the feeble mechanical offspring of intercourse with conventions and rules and the teacher's red pencil, of intercourse without desire. And as a teacher, I perpetuated the same bad habits for too long, until I began writing with an earnest wish to construct my world and to share my world with others. Then I learned that I had a voice—boisterous and playful, pertinent and germane—a voice filled with desire. And desire seeks its object. Writers who write with desire will write desirable writing.

Contravening Conventions

Conventions of writing are typically understood as restrictions or rules that dictate the way that writing ought to be done. But the word *convene* also means *to call together*. In a sense, writers call to one another, a chorus of voices, calling out, calling together. This notion of convention suggests that writers determine together the rules and standards and patterns that will constrain different kinds of writing, but this notion of convention also suggests that the rules and standards and patterns can be changed if enough people decide to change them. Therefore, the conventions of writing are flexible and fluid, not fixed and fast. I claim that conventions are meant to be invitations like signs on a hiking trail, not rules that trip us up like unseen obstacles.

What is the relationship between conventions (learning conventions, knowing conventions, using conventions) and composition (learning how to compose, knowing how to compose, actually composing)? For example, do I need to know the conventions before I can compose, or before I can contravene the conventions, or before I can legitimately claim that I know what I am doing in composing? I spent years learning the conventions. My teachers apparently believed that you learned to write by memorizing the rules of grammar and completing numerous exercises that were isolated and atomistic and compartmentalized—10 sentences with something wrong in them, except that one sentence was probably correct, a surefire way to complicate the whole drill. My task as the student was to find out what was wrong with the sentence and correct the error. In turn, it was hoped that my experience with detecting and correcting errors would lead to my writing without errors.

What I really learned was that writing was a kind of detective game, hunting for the culprit, hidden but insidious, in the language use. My mission was to expose errors, stamp out incorrectness, eradicate nonstandard use, support the strictures and structures stated by sages of grammar. I learned the rules of comma use. I learned not to begin a sentence with a conjunction. I surgically sutured comma splices. What I did not learn was that *real writers* like journalists and novelists and poets use commas in ways that contest the rules of standard use, and begin sentences with conjunctions, and dangle modifiers with colorful exuberance, and run on with comma splices as if the comma splice is a useful and legitimate way to link words and ideas. I learned that I was not a *real writer* and that to be a *real writer*, I had to learn rules first, and then eventually I could contravene the conventions, if I had any interest in writing left.

Do great chefs and cellists first learn the rules and then improvise and substitute and modify, their greatness exhibited in the modification, or do they exhibit their greatness because they interact with their craft in imaginative, innovative ways, even initially? This is a big question, and I suspect it can only be answered by asking people to tell their stories about how they learned their craft. In my case, I am adamant that I only learned to write when I began taking risks, when I began to interrogate the conventions (and I recognize that I am here suggesting that I now know the conventions) by writing with openness. If it works, I am glad, and if it does not work, I try something else. In this way, I am constantly pushing my craft. I am interacting with the raw materials, not to produce that which has been produced many times before, but to produce that which seems new (even though I know there is nothing new under the sun). In this process I learn what does not work and what does work, at least for now. I am always seeking to attend to my writing as an intuitive process that is full of mystery, a process that I do not consciously determine or control. Instead, I remain open to the writing that emerges, listening constantly and carefully to the heart's rhythms, to the possibilities of intuition. My writing and I are always in flux, always changing.

Writers learn to write by writing. We would not teach figure skaters to skate by teaching them in the locker room using a board and chalk. We would not teach people to drive a car by teaching all the rules and then giving them the keys and telling them to go for it. We would not train children for years about playground etiquette and then finally release them into the world of the playground.

Consider the rule that a declarative sentence ends with a period and an interrogative sentence ends with a question mark. That is a simple rule. Most students can memorize that rule quickly. Students will perhaps need to be taught that there is a sentence that is an indirect question ("I asked her if she had been awarded first prize."), but the rule is simple and straightforward. So, why do so many students apparently have difficulty with the rule? I think it is because they do not care about their writing. They know the rule, but it is like being told by their parents to make their beds—who really cares about bed-making and correct punctuation? The problem is not a lack of under-standing the rules; the problem is a lack of desire for the writing. If there is desire, writers will find the most appropriate ways to express themselves.

I learned the rules in school. I was a good kid who did what my teachers told me. I was so naïve, I would have believed anything my teachers told me. In fact, I was so naïve, I would have believed lies my teachers told me. In fact, my teachers did tell me a lot of lies, and I believed them for years. For years I wanted to write with desire and imagination and freedom, but for years I heard my teachers tell me to avoid split infinitives and prepositions at the end of sentences and faulty parallelism and incomplete sentences, and for years I have been constrained by fear of error and a neurotic concern about correct-ness, and for years I have been seeking to imitate models of effective prose, convinced that there is a template for the ideal expository essay and the ideal poem and the ideal narrative and the ideal business letter, and all I have got to do is find the template and all of my writing will be effective and exemplary.

Do I need to know the conventions before I contravene the conventions? I doubt it. I think that contravening conventions is done unconsciously and without conscience. Then eventually the contravener recognizes that she or he has created something that does not fit or conform, something that is original. The conventions of standard usage need to be learned in the context of composing composition. Instead of teaching students the myriad rules of comma usage, let students write and play with commas. Let the one rule be: "Use commas where they help you make sense in the sentence." Then as stu-dents write with desire and care, they will learn the rules in order to improve their writing, and they will learn to expand and challenge the rules in order to accomplish their rhetorical purposes. If there is no desire or caring, there will be no writing worth encouraging, no meeting to sing in chorus the pleasures of word-making.

The Seduction of Reduction

I am not sure that anyone can teach anyone else how to be a writer or how to teach writing. We each need to find our own ways as we engage in writing and teaching writing. And we each need to communicate with others about our experiences, what worked and what did not work. There are no easy formulae for writing. Each writing situation is different, and requires that the writer approach each situation on its own terms. Many writers and teachers and scholars have made efforts to categorize writing, and I have learned significant lessons from them, but I am always concerned that every effort to structure and order writing creates boundaries that exclude possibilities, boundaries that constrain writers instead of nurturing writers.

Diagrams and illustrations and tables and categorical labels for differentiating types of discourse are seductive because they are reductive. They tame the wildness of writing. In traditional rhetoric and in many composition textbooks used in classrooms, the modes of discourse are narration, description, exposition, and argumentation. I have taught my students in both university and schools the four modes of discourse. I readily acknowledge that there is value in this kind of effort to categorize the writing process and experience, as long as writers are not given the impression that all writing can be contained in four boxes, even capacious and flexible boxes. Writing is not always or necessarily a steady, step-by-step progression through identifiable stages like baking a double-fudge layer cake. Writing cannot be successfully accomplished like completing a paint-by-numbers kit. Writing teachers must not reduce writing to lists of concepts and skills that can be taught to all students in ways that can be evaluated for purposes of report cards and evaluation.

We need to promote and celebrate positive, productive experiences with language in our classes and our homes and our workplaces. We need experiences with language that invite risk-taking and innovation and play. In my experience, the writing that takes risks is the writing that gives the most satisfaction to both writers and readers.

Reveling in the Mystery of the Writing Process

As a writer in school, I almost always felt inadequate, not quite sure where to put commas, concerned that I did not have anything worth saying, fearful that I was not as humorous or witty or bold or eloquent as my classmates, convinced that I was inferior because I wrote slowly, ashamed that my drafts were messy and chaotic and confusing, a litter of letters sprawling over scraps of paper. I was sure everybody else wrote as if transcribing dictation from speakers inside their heads or hearts or souls or stomachs. I heard voices, too, but they were always too quiet or too loud or too contradictory, voices that drowned one another out, voices that I could never master, confusing voices that silenced my voice. And so I wrote little, and found scholastic success in memorizing facts and formulae and definitions and transcribing them faithfully in short-answer and fill-in-the-blank tests.

Only in recent years have I begun to revel in the process of writing. I do not know what I want to write until I can read what I have written. Therefore, I like to fill blank pages with blue-ink squiggles and screens with perfectly shaped pixels in order to discover meaning, in order to discover what I want to say. As I write and write, and read and reread what I have written, the writing speaks to me and reveals meaning. And it is a wonderfully rich and adventurous experience.

The writing process model emphasizes writing as a process, not writing as a product. The chaotic nature of the writing process is acknowledged. Writers do not begin with a clear understanding of what they will write. Instead they discover meaning during the process of writing. The writing process paradigm stresses the significance of writing as a meaning-making venture. Writers do not begin with a mentally constructed text that needs to be transcribed. Writers engage in an ongoing dialogue with their written words. Out of that dialogue, meaning is produced and constructed and revealed.

There are many different processes of writing. Perhaps everybody has a different writing process. What are the primary forces or dynamics that generate the writing process? Generally the writing process comprises five main stages: prewriting, drafting, revising, editing, and publishing. But I think the process needs to be understood in more complex ways. Therefore, I suggest that the writing process includes the following forces or dynamics: writing, reading, collecting, selecting, connecting, talking, thinking (convergently and divergently), doubting, guessing, reducing, paraphrasing, ordering, seeking, hypothesizing, wondering, deducing, inducing, constructing, deconstructing, reconstructing, reflecting, listening, viewing, representing, drawing (in, out, through), conjecturing, questioning, (day)dreaming, rehearsing in the sense of trying on and taking off, exploring, clarifying, revising, reviewing, and drafting.

The process is not linear, at least not for most writers; it is more like a spiral, a maze, a waterslide that twists, even the path of a balloon that is inflated and pinched but not tied and when released shoots through the air. The path is not predictable. There is something scary about understanding the writing process in this way, but in practice we use language in these ways all of the time. When we speak, we are using these same dynamics or forces. We use them without concentrating on them much of the time. Born into language, we have learned to use language with the automatic, seemingly natural ease we use to breathe air. I write, therefore, I am. To write is to be. Writing is not a big deal. The main reason that people grow up nonwriters is that they have been taught that they cannot be writers.

Words Surprise in Freewriting

Perhaps the single most important book that has influenced my writing is Peter Elbow's *Writing With Power*. I was in my early 30s when I read Elbow's book for the first time. His suggestions about freewriting changed my approaches to writing. Elbow recommended that a writer begin with freewriting: "To do a freewriting exercise, simply force yourself to write without stopping for 10 minutes."[152] I tried Elbow's suggestions about freewriting, and began to write freely for specified periods of time when my main goal was to keep the pencil moving on the page, and I discovered what Elbow claims:

> Freewriting makes writing easier by helping you with the root psychological or existential difficulty in writing: finding words in your head and putting them down on a blank piece of paper. So much writing time and energy is spent not writing: wondering, worrying, crossing out, having second, third, and fourth thoughts.[153]

Since reading Elbow's book, I now begin most of my poems and stories with a remembered image or word, which in turn generates a free-writing exercise. I like to get a block of words on the page or the screen. I then have something concrete to react to, to question, to listen to, to expand and compress, to shape and sculpt. When I have words on paper, there is the sense of a dialogue between me and the words. The words have their own voices. I read and reread the words. I speak the words in different vocal arrangements. I listen to the words, in both the silent and the oral readings. There is no clear direction provided by the words. They do not address me, "Well, Carl, we think that you ought to employ our cousin Zeb and put some zip into the fourth line." But there is a sense in which the words speak to me and I respond, a growing conviction that one word is more effective than another, a surer conviction that decisions about lineation and structure are not only arbitrary but meaningful, or at least meaningful in their arbitrariness.

Freewriting is a way of thinking on paper, a way of letting words surprise the writer. What often happens in freewriting is that the conscious mind loses some of its control, and suddenly memories that have been long forgotten call out, and connections between events that have been little understood emerge, and emotions that are often suppressed laugh and cry out. Above all, freewriting is a way of tapping into the energy of words and word-making. In all of my commitments to nurturing writing and writers, I am seeking to honor the dynamic possibilities of creative engagement with language, always hopeful that we can learn together to tell our stories in artful and heartful ways that are full of play and wisdom and joy. As a grandfather, I am always eager to nurture in writers, beginning and experienced, a love for language and a desire for communing and communicating. I draw to a kind of conclusion with a poem, written freely and offered hopefully.

THE TOWER OF BABBLE

what do I remember
of my teachers' words

I recall they spoke
many words

but I don't remember
any

we spoke the same English
we knew the same alphabet

did I understand
their words

probably not
so many words

tongue-worn texts
in deaf ears

mostly mumbo-jumbo
prattling gibberish

alien tongues
without sense

echoes only
long lost

I did not belong
in their classrooms

I found no places
for dwelling in their words

we stacked the words
a tower of babble

my teachers' words
not mine

borrowed words
that didn't fit

one day
a tower of rubble

now I begin again
at the end of the alphabet

where other letters
can be written

Chapter 15

ON IDEAS

Organic Creativity in Teaching Visual Arts

Charles Caldemeyer

The popular conception of art in contemporary American culture is that it is primarily decorative and is not supposed to furnish serious ideas or to challenge a viewer on an intellectual level. To this way of thinking, the acquisition of skill is the primary function of an art education, and accurate depiction is the highest goal. Any hierarchy of quality in art is strictly dependent on the taste of the viewer, and no particular education or experience is necessary to determine that taste. This sensibility asserts that art objects do not need to imply meaning, or if they mean something it should be interpretable by as wide an audience as possible. It has given rise to the enormous popularity of kitsch artists such as Thomas Kinkade, kitsch art "teachers," such as Bob Ross, and countless self-taught practitioners. It has also furnished the subject for commentary work by serious contemporary artists such as Komar and Melamid,[154] whose work critiques it, and it has provided the foil for shock artists, whose work seeks to insult it.

But in practice, contemporary art is about the exploration of ideas by visual means. Artists work to develop a visual language that juxtaposes formal and symbolic elements to create unique expressions. There is even a conception within at least an element of the contemporary art scene that skill is unimportant, or even a detriment—a relic of the meretricious academic art of the late 19th century. This approach seeks to define quality of work only in terms of visual or conceptual experimentation, and denotes a hierarchy

Charles Caldemeyer was born in Washington, DC, in 1953. While in his 20s, he taught himself to paint and began exhibiting his work in juried exhibitions. Returning to college, he received his B.A. from the University of South Florida in 1986 and M.F.A. from Washington University in St. Louis in 1990. Following graduation, he accepted a teaching position at Ashland University, where he remains as professor of art, teaching painting, drawing, and color theory. Caldemeyer's studio work has evolved in two major directions over the past 20 years. The Grids (see Figure 15.1) are oil-on-canvas abstractions with an emphasis on viewer inference of image from pattern and color. Structures (see Figure 15.2) implies narrative in a variety of media, including oil and encaustic painting along with various graphics techniques, integrating the representational and expressive strategies of European art with cartooning traditions. Both bodies of work have been exhibited widely in juried national solo and group exhibitions and have won numerous awards.

Figure 15.1. *Charles Caldemeyer,* The Inquiry, *Oil and wax on canvas, 72"*
x 48", From the Grids *series.*

that is virtually the opposite of the popular one. According to this view, anything in the mainstream of Western culture, such as a focus on pictorial skill
and craftsmanship, caters to the lowest elements of art appreciation, and is
to be eschewed. For examples of this attitude, one need only look at many
recent recipients of the Turner Prize,[155] along with some of the exhibitions
at the Brooklyn Museum and others. They see widespread communication
as a weakness, and deftness of execution as a symptom of disingenuousness.
Although the numbers of artists truly in this camp represent a small percentage of the overall total, they tend to control many of the most valued venues,
and they make the art that is most generally publicized. Therefore, they are
likely the examples that occur to the general public when the subject of contemporary art comes up.

From the fortresses of these mutually exclusive vantage points, both sides
disdain the other. The gulf between the popular assessment of a discipline
and its actual practices is as wide in art as in any area of academic endeavor,
and misunderstanding abounds. The art world has, in large part, successfully

Organic Creativity in the Arts

Figure 15.2. *Charles Caldemeyer,* Circus Life, *Encaustic, Oil, Watercolor, and Ink, 50" x 50", From the Structures series.*

divorced itself from the general public, and the public is only too happy to see them go. The issue of accessibility connects both of the extremes, with one believing that all persons should be able to easily understand and appreciate art in its decorative glory, and the other that any art that emphasizes widespread communication is suspect as not elite enough. Any references to the spiritual are to be of the formulaic, predigested variety in the art of popular culture, and they are nonexistent with the conceptual crowd, which regards them as artifacts of the superstitious world before the rise Marxism and Existentialism. In popular culture, there is the stereotype of the contemporary artist as snide loser; conversely, much of the contemporary art scene sees the general public as unemancipated troglodytes.

Obviously, these two positions are extreme, and there is a wide variety of art in between them that exudes strong craftsmanship and skillful execution, visual interest, historical awareness, formal competence and personal expression, and emanates from a sincere artistic intent. As an educator of artists, I often ask myself how best to communicate to students understanding of, and respect for, the wide range of beliefs that drive the creation of contemporary art, and how to lower the level of contempt for that which lies opposed to their interests and predilections. The studio experience should challenge students to venture out of their comfort zones without totally alienating them (temporary alienation, if coupled with support, may be a productive stage in the student's growth process; permanent alienation obviously is not). I also believe that my job involves the exposure of some of the aforementioned preconceptions, since many students are armed with them when they arrive on campus. In upper levels, especially, they can be relentless in their defense of premises that are demonstrably fallacious, and some of them do battle on this territory throughout much of their undergraduate years, much like Monty Python's Black Knight.

The technical aspects of painting, from developing skill at depiction to understanding its materials and processes, remain components of the art foundations sequence and Painting I classes. There have been some trends recently in academia to focus on developing conceptual abilities in these classes, but I believe it is important for the foundations sequence to remain largely free of them, for a variety of reasons. Such emphasis is usually the product of new professors, assigned to teach foundational classes, trying to make the course material more interesting to themselves, irrespective of student needs. But the foundations sequence remains the only area where students can practice their skills largely free of the necessity of tying them to a statement of artistic intent, and it is important that these skills be developed thoroughly in order for them to operate intuitively at the upper levels. Only in this way will students be prepared for the variety of directions their artistic interests might take them, as well as the rough seas that voyage will inevitably encounter. Although the rudiments of depiction are relatively straightforward and can be managed quickly by adroit students, its subtleties require years of practice, and most of the advocates for developing concept early are exactly artists who have acquainted themselves with the former, but have not mastered the latter, and who do not value the skills these classes are designed to teach. Also, the inclusion of a strong emphasis on concept in foundational classes sends a mixed message—that content is every bit as mechanical as skill—however, it is clear that it is a more elusive entity. Its development, along with the subtleties of artistic intent, should be largely left to the upper levels precisely to convince students of the sophistication and advanced nature of such endeavors.

The relegation of skill development to foundations classes has, however, encouraged the hierarchies that are operative in the two points of view mentioned at the beginning of this article. The popular front believes that skill development (usually termed "talent" to both elevate the student and to exonerate the viewer from the responsibility of having it), comes first because that is what art is, and that the communication of content demanded at the upper levels is just the product of professors who are too smart for their own good, or who have to fill up a curriculum. The conceptualists imply that if skill development is simply basal to idea development, then it cannot possibly be as important and should perhaps be omitted altogether. Both of these beliefs fit neatly into the stereotypes already in play in each group.

Of course, such attitudes are naïve and dishonest, and the result of a superficial understanding of the discipline. The fact that paintings are interpreted by viewers, and not seen simply as decoration, indicates that content is a major component of the artistic process and has been since its beginning. Content was the reason that humans developed painting in the first place—Magdalenian cave art, after all, was made for its symbolic powers, not just for its decorative appeal. The reason Plato (along with every totalitarian philosophy since) sought to strictly control the production of artists is precisely because of art's power to communicate, and in a language that is in many ways more powerful than verbal or written communication. And the fact that paintings will be interpreted no matter how much the artist protests that they are devoid of meaning indicates that we want more in our paintings than simple *tours de force* of artistic skill. Conversely, a strong artistic skill set is like a speaker's good vocabulary, enunciation, and timing. Regardless of medium, one's visual literacy is vital to visual communication, and one's statement must travel through this territory.

Students who arrive for their college art instruction convinced that their personal expression or devotion to the development of some concept exempts them from a rigorous study of skill and technique are usually relieved of those ideas by a strong art foundations sequence, with multiple instructors demonstrating otherwise to them on a daily basis. They may transfer to institutions that are less demanding, but they will never develop their full artistic potential, and they are of no further interest to us here. But students who arrive convinced that a well-developed skill set is all that is necessary to be an artist may thrive in a foundations sequence but struggle with upper level work. Their foundations experiences may have reinforced in them a sense of wonderfulness of self and made them accustomed to being at the head of the class, and they may react poorly to the demands that they now make art—that is, add the communicative aspects of their discipline to their already well-developed skill sets. Professors may find themselves looking for ways to both convince such students to fully develop their artistic intent and to get them to change their thinking processes so that ideas occur to them more readily. The most creative minds, of course, are those that are supple and flexible enough to find analogy in seemingly disparate things. But students have often built rigid mental constructs by which they identify themselves (in fact, our culture requires this), and asking them to make those more flexible may threaten their views of the world. It is normal for art professors to encourage students to reconfigure or eliminate elements of their everyday routines, and to attach new significance and context to aspects of their lives that they do perfunctorily, in order to break this cycle. We want to increase the student's awareness of the both the inner and outer events of their lives, to allow them to recontextualize those events into the basis for a symbolic language.

The Artistic Life: Making Connections

I believe that the most fundamental characteristic of an artistic life is the development of connections between life experiences and the processes of art-making. This is not easy and takes years, but beginning to see one's life in terms of one's art, on as many levels as possible, is crucial to making paintings resonate with meaning for the artist, and so to having interpretive value for viewers. It is important to ask students to connect their life events to painting events, and to establish correlations between the tenets of their inner world and the colors, textures, and brushstrokes of their work. In some ways, this is simply an extension of the observational processes of the natural world that we encourage in the foundations sequence—I recommend that my drawing students ask themselves, "How would I draw that?" when looking at the light and spaces of their everyday lives, and so come to understand, on some internal level, how to process the world around them into a picture. But encouraging a habitual and minute observation of the physical world for the purposes of depiction is a natural enough request for a professor to make; asking students to delve into elements of their psyche that they may not want to interrogate, or make public in their paintings, is quite another. Students are often very resistant.

It is through discovery of analogy that artists find their way into the world of symbol—when an element of our shared existence is found to be like an inner event it may serve as a representative for it. Our culture surrounds us with public symbols, such as crosses and eagles, which require no interpretation because they are universally understood, and so are to be avoided as artistic clichés. But we also have our personal symbols, and they are more intransigent, with esoteric meanings attached to aspects of our experience that may have no obvious relationship to the signified content. It is the finding of these elements, and tying them together, that is the first problem for a student in upper level studio work. The next is crafting this symbolic structure so that it is a visual language (i.e., capable of communication to others) yet not clichéd. These processes are the goal of each artist's inner ruminations.

The final assignment in my Painting I class reads:

> After consulting with your instructor and making some preliminary sketches, do a painting that makes an artistic statement that is yours and yours alone. Artistic intent, content, scale, and style all need to be considered and developed in concert with one another. A written statement of purpose must accompany this work.
>
> <u>Things to remember:</u>
> Please, remember the viewer.

I often see students staring off into space after I introduce this material—there is a sense of unease that the parameters of previous assignments (my "Things to remember" category is usually more extensive) are missing. The parameters of this assignment exist only in their personal worlds, and they are often at a loss. I try to get them to sketch, saying things such as, "Ideas are in pencils." The process of developing the thumbnail sketch as the entry into their inner visual worlds needs to be emphasized at this stage.

As we proceed, I may ask the student to think about how the elements of art are like other aspects of their lives. Every foundations sequence course provides one with a potential vocabulary. Color symbolism or color combinations can be particularly evocative. If this is one of their interests, we begin by discussing the work of Franz Marc and Wassily Kandinsky. I then encourage them to develop their own color symbolism. Design principles form another avenue where the elements of formal training may be converted into symbols. If the center of interest is in the center of the canvas, then it yields a sense of stasis, or maybe evokes a totalitarian situation; if, however, there are multiple areas of interest in more marginal places, then it might evoke a sense of movement, a journey, or a decentralized, egalitarian view. Similarly, if the illusion of light has a spotlight effect, then it may denote a star/supplicant relationship between the elements of the piece while a diffused light may indicate a murkier, less hierarchal situation. The way the paint is layered, its texture, the direction of the mark, and other elements of drawing and design all may readily be transposed into a foundational vehicle for a symbolic language. At more advanced stages, I ask students to just "follow their paint," meaning to let their intuition guide them from mark to mark, the previous step determining the next. This old abstract expressionist trick allows a student who is clearly on to something, but is not yet able to articulate it, the freedom to discover ways to express aspects of their lives. In all of these areas, the goal is to induce students to associate their paint with aspects of their inner worlds.

One problem we sometimes encounter is that students may not regard their personal life as important enough to develop into artwork. Although much contemporary work is devoted to expression of individual inner reality, most historical work deals with great societal themes. Unless they are closely following the contemporary art world, students are exposed to historical work first. If they are struggling to find artistic intent to guide their upper level decision-making processes, they may feel that they need to develop something similar to the grand works of Poussin or Delacroix, and the results are usually stilted, especially in the early stages. I often tell them that they don't have to try to teach me something with their work.

Students may also feel undermined if they make personal paintings that are greeted with skepticism, and since their initial efforts are likely to be less subtle than we would like our art to be, acceptance and encouragement in early critiques is vital to the continuation of the growth process, provided the effort to search for something deeper is present. It is important that students feel free to "go for it," and not second-guess themselves, at this stage. I often tell students that if they connect their most personal feelings to their canvases they will find an audience that is receptive and responsive, that will say, "I've found the same thing in myself." Artists such as van Gogh and Kollwitz are loved precisely because of their willingness to build connections between their psychology and their paint, to pour their innermost selves into their work.

One of my shortcomings as a teacher is that I tend to sometimes be too assertive, and I have to guard against this as I guide students through this process. Sometimes the elements of a student's inner expressions need to simmer quietly, and as my teaching has grown I have tried to develop sensitivity to these periods, and just leave the student alone during these times. Seeing this, however, some students have tried to make these times stretch out, and so delay the process as long as they can get away with it. This leads me to the story of Denise (a pseudonym).

Case Example of Denise

Denise was a very good student—a standout in drawing and design, able to understand and manipulate the illusions of space and light, and to adjust drawing transitions skillfully. She was intelligent and responsive in class, and she knew her art history well. She came from a middle-American background and her upbringing instilled in her the values of hard work, respect for authority, and appreciation of instruction that had served her well throughout the first 2 years of her college art experience. Her foundations review was a success, and all of the professors complimented her ability to render, compose, and to truly understand and apply foundational concepts. Her Painting I class was equally successful until we came to that dreaded last assignment. Along with "content," I use the more descriptive term, "artistic intent," and emphasize that this painting must have meaning to the artist and project meaning to the viewer. This meaning must be more sophisticated than, "Here is a portrait of my dog, whom I love."

Denise resisted from the beginning. Over and over, she asked, "Why does it have to mean something?" and she expressed a longing for the structure of previous assignments. Our conversations focused on all of the ways that art is visual communication, and I showed her images of artists whose work she might appreciate, but she found something to dislike in each of them. She just wasn't buying it, and she was putting up any defense in an attempt to escape the responsibility of making work that had meaning. My argument gained some traction when I put it in human development terms—that she was stuck in an artistic childhood that demanded prescription rather than the creative freedom of adulthood—but still she fought like the Black Knight. Her transition as a visual artist proved to be a long one, and it is worth noting its stages.

The final Painting I assignment was a disappointment, although she maintained the self-respect to finish the piece. Before that semester ended, we had some conversations about how she would adjust to Painting II, where students set their own problems. She was in our Bachelor of Fine Art (BFA) program, which is designed to prepare students for graduate school, and so she knew that I would insist that she develop a contemporary artistic intent. When she left that semester, I was unsure whether she would even come back to painting.

But she did, and she began Painting II with what I called her "fallback position" of landscape. D painted some fine landscapes—they had wonderful light and good detail, and there was usually some sense of mystery about them. But critiques revealed that this was a decorative haven that protected her from having to develop personal symbolism and a philosophy of painting as inquiry. Landscapes may communicate more than a picture of part of the planet, but at their most literal, landscape is a form of Western art that has long since been exhausted. There is no reason why the landscape cannot become the basis for developing a personal symbolism, and Denise's intelligence and ability to think associatively clearly showed she was capable of it, but the artist must supply the symbols to the forms and processes, and let them evolve. Denise's landscapes sometimes gave the illusion of that progress—they would seem to be arriving at a meaningful place, but our conversations would reveal, at length, that she was simply decorating. Through Painting II and Painting III we went around and around—I was alternately patient, encouraging, and insistent on more progress. She was quietly dedicated to resistance. I constantly prodded her with questions such as, "What does it mean when that kind of light is connected to those forms?" and other open-ended points for her to ponder, hoping she would begin to attach significance to the elements of the artistic process. Waiting for an epiphany, both of us were frustrated. Denise still believed that I was asking for more than was necessary; I thought she wasn't trying hard enough. (Entitled *Silica Road*, the small (20" x 30") oil-on-canvas landscape in Figure 15.3 gives a good idea of Denise's representational abilities. A BFA body of work could have been developed by expanding on the implications of pieces such as this, but she resisted all efforts to interpret them.)

The conduct of the professor is very important throughout a student's art education, of course, but particularly at this stage of the process, when the tender shoots of a student's ideas are struggling to establish themselves. The student is often still unconvinced about his or her direction and has misgivings as to its importance. Denise knew that she had an artistic statement within her, and she knew that I knew it. But she was also averse to it, because it undermined the view of art imbued in her in her youth, or it seemed too revelatory of a part of her she wanted to keep private, or because she just hadn't fashioned the vehicle for it yet. It was likely a combination of varying degrees of all three. I had to walk a line between empathy for her inner turmoil and insistence on progress toward meaning. When I saw her begin to become alienated from the process, I made every effort to dial it back a notch. But I also sometimes felt as if I was being played, that she was using my understanding to maintain the status quo and avoid putting the effort into developing her work. Finally, I decided that the only way to end this cycle was to prohibit her from doing any work that was simply decorative. I made

Figure 15.3. Silica Road *by Denise.*

a rule, for her and her alone—she could paint whatever she wanted, but I would not give her class credit for landscape paintings, or any other painting, that did not have an artistic intent deeper than decoration behind it.

The breakthrough that followed did not come in the painting studio, although I believe the discussion of content we had there, along with her art history sequence and a comparative religion class she took around this time, influenced Denise to ponder life processes. She writes,

> During that time I was going through a real low point in understanding my value and purpose. I had always feared death and I was tired of it haunting me. It didn't help that I was also studying ancient art in art history with Dr. S. Egyptian art and life was centered around the after-life—at that point in time I was unsure that there even was an after-life! Since you banned me from painting pretty things, like landscapes, where I think I avoided my fear, I decided to focus on my internal struggle and try to make the darkest thing in my life pretty.

From this beginning grew the visual metaphors that allowed Denise to develop her artistic intent. All of a sudden, flies began to appear in her work—lots of them. She did diagrams of flies, studies of dead flies, color-coded flies, and ultimately, a large canvas of a gigantic dead fly, a sophisticated painting

Figure 15.4. Fly Study Series, *oil on canvas boards, approximately 8" x 32".*

for an undergraduate. Her compositions cropped the subjects in unnatural ways, adding to the sense of unease and grotesquery. (Figures 15.4–15.7 contain some of her work during this period.) As her metaphors became more sophisticated, so did her paint application. She began experimenting with expressive brushwork, dripping paint textures, and medium-intensity color combinations that were strangely reassuring. Her thesis elucidated her fears about death and her spiritual reservations and helped her find the questions to which her paintings were an answer. Her exhibition contained her paintings as well as her ceramics, and one large bowl was filled with dead flies, which she had asked friends and faculty to collect for her. As Denise wrote in her thesis,

> I had never used my art for such a deep self-expression. Displaying my inner emotion in this way has made me feel vulnerable at times, but the positive reactions to my work during my exhibit and even throughout the process of making the work was very encouraging and liberating.

Denise's senior exhibition and thesis defense were very successful. Her committee was impressed by her work, as well as the existential questioning in both her painting and her writing. After graduation, she married and began a house remodeling project (including a studio) which is still in process, and painting has, unfortunately, become secondary in her life. But maybe that was to be expected. I believe that the struggle of opening the door to a symbolic world exhausted her on some level, and she took a step back into the comfortable parameters of the world she knew. But I also believe that she will paint seriously again, and maybe develop her work into a viable contemporary artistic investigation. She confirms this, writing,

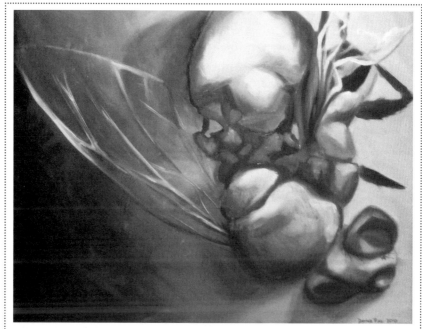

Figure 15.5. Fly Study II, *oil on canvas, approximately 20" x 30".*

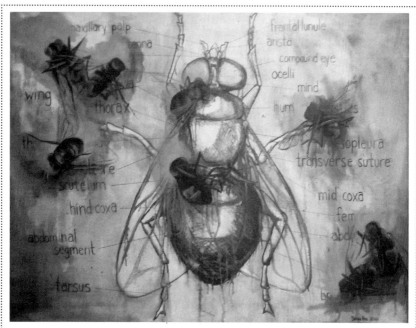

Figure 15.6. Rational Thinking, *oil on canvas, approximately 24" x 36".*

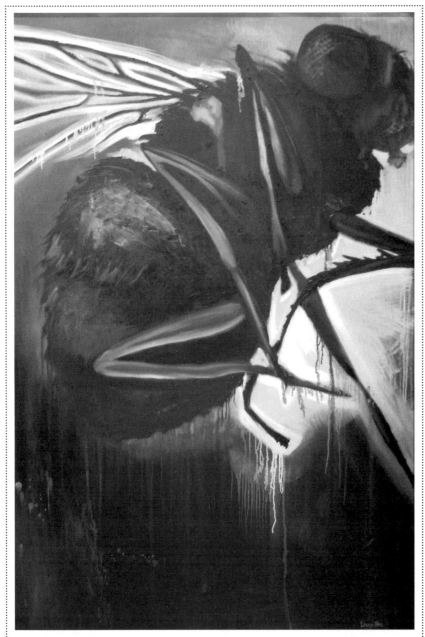

Figure 15.7. Acceptance, *oil on canvas, approximately 72" x 48".*

I still have a lot to uncover in those bugs of mine. I set them aside too early (life after graduation didn't help) but I do hope to revisit them very soon. I've since become a Christian and my bugs have a new meaning to me now. At first they were a symbol of the transformation of death, but now they are a symbol of the transformation in eternal life or salvation in Christ! I just thought it was neat that the meaning takes on polar opposite ideas.

Denise discovered something about herself through her painting that she could not have discovered by any other means, and she is still processing it. But the stress of that road has demanded some time for assimilation.

Conclusion

Ideas are gifts from the great unknown. It is important for artists to follow their ideas, because ideas that are dispensed but ignored will slowly drive one insane, or at least lead to compensatory neuroses and insecurities. Developing one's ideas allows an artist to understand and order his or her world, and to reconcile outer and inner experiences. Some aspects of this process are rational and prescriptive, and these techniques form the bulk of foundations training. But artists with well-developed skills sets usually set their sights on something greater, such as communication of the enigmatic, and must develop methods of solving problems intuitively.

The artistic process is only vibrant when it is one of discovery. Processes of life readily translate into painting processes, and the most creative artists are those who live to learn, and for whom life and art are translatable into one another. Development of strong intuitive skills is vital to successfully making this translation, but social training, with the conventional thought patterns it demands, is corrosive of this growth. Techniques we use to develop intuitive skills involve (a) elimination of routines, (b) the recontextualization of everyday events, and (c) the use of associative patterns to view life, as well as painting, experiences. It is also important that artists know how to set their own parameters when they investigate areas that become increasingly subjective or they will revert to conventionalized solutions. I often ask my students to follow their ideas within the spirit of the idea.

The process of finding strategies to make one's private self public may yield some uncomfortable critiques before the artist's visual language has been fully developed. Finding this language is not a straightforward process, and students may not feel inclined to make such personal transpositions. Thus, it is important to emphasize to students that art is both a form of unique personal expression and a form of visual communication. I like to tell students that good paintings stand halfway between the artist and the viewer, reflective of the artist's intent, yet equally interpretable by the viewer in their terms. Those interpretations may vary somewhat, but a well-done painting is its own life form, and can handle, and even thrive because of, the range of readings derived from it.

Part III

ORGANIC CREATIVITY IN THE TEACHER, THE CLASSROOM, AND THE SCHOOL

Figure III.1. *Inspiration of nature field trip for teachers of the talented: Singer/songwriter and contributor Jennifer Groman.*

Chapter 16

CARS ON BLOCKS AND ROADKILLS

Organic Creativity in Teaching in the G/T Resource Room

George W. Johnson

"George!" My fifth-grade teacher called out my name, probably because I looked like I was not paying attention. Perhaps I was thinking about something she had said earlier. Perhaps I was staring off into space. Perhaps I really *wasn't* paying attention; after all, she marked it on my report card every 6 weeks.

"George, please tell the class what the largest island continent in the world is."

It was 1957, and I had a surprise for her; not only had I been paying attention to her lectures on world geography, I had also thought of a startling revelation that would now make all geography books obsolete.

My moment of epiphany had come as I stared at the 10' by 6' map we had wallpapered on our living room wall. Now, I knew the answer to the question of the largest island continent was *supposed to be* Australia. I knew the seven continents, and I knew an island was a piece of land completely surrounded by water. "North America," I confidently replied, waiting for the "Oh, my God! He's right!" moment. But, it never came.

"Class, tell Georgie what the largest island continent is."

About half the class dutifully replied with, "Australia"; I'm sure if there were still conical dunce hats and stools in the corner, I would have been instantly placed there.

George Johnson, Ed.D., is the Director of Gifted Services for a small rural district in Southeastern Ohio who provides coordinator services for students Pre-K–12 and direct instructional services for grades 2–6. Johnson is also a Professional Fellow of Education for Ashland University specializing in talent development education classes. He has made presentations on the education of the gifted and talented at the local, state, national, and international levels. He has a passionate interest in history and in creativity, and he has written five books on antiques. A member of the Ohio University's Gifted Educators Hall of Fame and the Governing Board for the Ohio Association of Gifted Children, he has also served as an independent consultant for using gifted curriculum in regular classrooms.

She had no time or interest in listening to my logic that North America was much larger than Australia and surrounded on four sides by water—the Atlantic, Pacific, and Arctic Oceans and, what she had forgotten about, the Panama Canal. This was the discovery I was ready to share. Unfortunately, the question "Why" was never asked. Such was my first brush with creativity in the classroom.

Six years later, I was in what passed for the 1960s differentiated classes for the gifted and talented track, and I encountered a teacher who had a different perspective on education. For her junior English class, she threw out the textbooks, and we read, discussed, and debated real issues of the day. There was no rote memorization of lines of poetry, no writing of book reports that merely regurgitated the text, and no multiple-choice tests. She encouraged real thinking. With every answer she received she asked, "Why?" She challenged us to think, analyze, synthesize, and evaluate our thoughts and beliefs. Not only was creativity encouraged, it was required and rewarded. Many "all A" students did not like this class, but I loved it.

The most important element for encouraging or killing creativity in the classroom is the teacher. How can educators reward creativity if they cannot recognize it and do not value it because it is an inconvenience to teaching the standard answer?

Always Ask "Why?"

After 40 years in education, 30 in talented and gifted (G/T) education, teaching everyone from second graders to graduate students, I have found that the easiest and most consistent way to encourage creativity in the classroom is to ask the question "Why?" Even if the answer is the standard, *correct*, textbook answer, always ask "Why?" That question must be delivered in the same tone of voice as the original question. "Why" makes students think, synthesize, evaluate, articulate, and logically defend the answer they have given. Asking "Why" is also the easiest way to separate a truly creative answer from a nonsensical one.

The Paradox of Standardized Education and Creativity

Politicians, business people, and the media call for more creativity and innovation to keep the United States "on top." Often, creators are the stubborn survivors of a social and educational system that labeled them as nerds or geeks. Creativity is *not* nurtured in the current educational system. Teachers are not required to study creativity in a formal manner, even though they are required to emphasize it with the current emphasis on 21st-century skills.

A teacher next door to me posted two pictures outside her door and invited students to guess what they were. Now the standard, the *correct* answers, were that they were the Washington Monument and the White House. However, there were no identifying elements in the picture that *specifically* identified them as those two landmarks—I checked. I put into her answer folder these two answers:

- For the first picture: "This is a picture of the famous obelisk known as Cleopatra's Needle which is located in Central Park, New York City. It is one of three known by the same name, the other two being located in Paris and London."

- For the second picture I wrote: "This is a model of the White House created by the special effects team of Vogel, Smith, Pinney, and Viskocil, for the movie *Independence Day*. During one of the highlights of the movie, it was destroyed by 40 explosive charges and earned the team an Academy Award for Special Effects."

My peer educator responded: "Oh, it's just Dr. Johnson being weird again."

In the age of standardized education is there a place for creativity? The politicians and business people say yes—but you'd be hard pressed to find the same answer in the general classroom. Where do we find the time for creativity? Public school programs in art, music, and drama have disappeared at an alarming rate across the country in order to make more time to prepare for standardized tests. At the same time, many schools spend 4–5 hours a week preparing students for state graduation or achievement tests. Our programs that require and encourage creativity have disappeared because of a lack of time, lack of funds, and a lack of interest on the part of administrators and communities. These classes and their teachers do not fit into the concept of standardized education and "core subjects."

The Box

On one hand, we want people who can "think outside the box," a hackneyed phrase. The Box is normal behavior, normal actions, normal thoughts, normal standard answers, the expected answer, the regurgitated one-true-answer. The Box is made of the walls that confine us and that many children are afraid to even try to scale. The Box is the coffin from which creative people struggle to escape.

Creativity is the gray answer, the humorous smart aleck answer that is unexpected, perhaps unappreciated, but nevertheless correct. Creativity is the ephemeral answer. Creativity is what teachers get when they allow ambiguity. Standard answers conserve the past and pretend that we know all there is to know. Standard answers never develop new alternatives, never think futuristically, and never ask "What if?" Only within certain environments is creative thought rewarded and rarely is that environment the regular classroom. We must encourage creativity, learn to recognize it, value it, and reward it from the preschool classroom to the boardroom.

The element of creativity is part of several recognized definitions of giftedness. Renzulli defined giftedness as the intersection of above average ability, creativity, and task commitment. Sternberg said that the gifted person has creativity as well as executive ability and practical ability. The federal definition has creative thinking as a type of giftedness.[156]

Standardized Education and the Creative Child

Standardization is the antithesis of creativity. In standardized education, creativity is not rewarded; indeed, it is often punished. On multiple-choice tests there is no opportunity for students to be asked "Why?" and no opportunity to explain their reasoning. When students score low on standardized tests, it reflects on their teachers' evaluations. Thus, teachers have no interest in developing creative answers, only correct ones. Standardized education and its tests are killing creativity. Unfortunately, teachers of creative children must teach them how to game the system and not outthink themselves. Such tests don't allow educators to distinguish among the guesser, the thinker, and the creative. Most rubrics for grading standardized writing exercises do not give points for creative elements. I've had several G/T students whose creative writings did not match the state's standardized rubric and thus they failed the writing section of a graduation test.

Creative answers to exams abound on the Internet—so do the big red Xs beside them. Here are some examples.

♣ Question: Can you name the capital of Outer Mongolia? Answer: No. This was not the expected answer, but nevertheless must be counted as a correct one because of the way the question *was worded*. If you want a better answer, then ask a better question, don't penalize creativity.

♣ Question: The Hocking River flows in what state? Answer: Liquid

♣ Question: How can you drop a raw egg onto a concrete floor without it breaking? Answer: Anyway you want. Concrete floors are hard to break.

Creativity and the G/T Classroom

In recent years, programs for gifted and talented students have increasingly embraced acceleration or enrichment, and of the two, acceleration appears to be the more predominant model. Acceleration has the advantage of being well-structured with regard to state or national standards, and schools can often show significant growth on standardized tests in the students' strength area(s). However, acceleration seems to deal with only a facet of the child and not necessarily the whole person.

The enrichment model may be more oriented to the development of the whole child. This curriculum often focuses on thinking and problem-solving skills, project-based learning, overall above grade-level instruction, and creativity. For exceptionally bright children can't there be 6 hours out of their standards-driven week in which they can do something that is different? A place where the "why" question will always be asked and creativity will be honored? Creativity in the classroom takes place when the teacher, student, and curriculum interact with each other.

The Teacher

The single most important factor in the creative classroom is the teacher who has certain personal traits that foster creativity. Teachers must be able to appreciate and admire ideas and answers that are not standard, should not be overly judgmental, should be receptive to new ideas, should be holistic in their approach to education, and need to be willing to take a risk. They should be playful, sharing appropriate humor. Teachers of the creative should be well-educated, perhaps generalists. They must have some basic knowledge of the domain in which the child seeks to be creative. They must be willing to help students find outside opportunities, tutors, and mentors. Teachers must enjoy gifted and talented children and have an extended repertoire of instructional methods or techniques in order to meet the learning styles of a diverse group of students.

Piirto recommended that teachers set a creative tone in the classroom and value the creative work of others.[157] Elementary programs that focus on enrichment can do these things. Acceleration alone does not introduce the child to Mozart, Beethoven, Shakespeare, Einstein, da Vinci, or Picasso.

Teachers should let students see their own creativity. When students write a story, write one yourself; when they do an art project, do one too. Analyze how you create, research how others create, and apply this knowledge in your classroom, keeping in mind that the process is very individualistic—what works for others may not work for your students. Teachers must establish the creative environment.

The Environment for Creativity

There is no one environment that is conducive to creativity. Different people have different preferences for their physical environment—bright or dim lights, fluorescent or natural, warm or cool temperatures, music/sound or quiet; these are just some of the considerations. The more students there are in a room, the less likely all of their needs will be met for a creative environment. One of the hardest elements to implement in the classroom is the quiet and solitude that leads to the creative state often called "oceanic consciousness," or "flow,"[158] in which ideas, images, words, or sensations flow in a steady stream from the subconscious and the individual often loses all sense of time.

Class bells, public address announcements, noise in the hallways, and disruptions as students call out, "How do you spell . . .", "I need . . .", "I'm on page 3, where are you?" all interrupt flow. The group should be small, with plenty of space between individuals. Children should raise their hands or use some other silent signal to get the teacher's attention; the best solution is to use headphones that block out external distractions. Students should listen to music that can inspire them to create. Some may prefer white noise, and still others may need the absolute quiet that the headphones can provide.

Teachers should provide a classroom in which children can comfortably find their own space. A desk, a cubicle, a corner, carpet squares, and overstuffed chairs all help establish individual space. Students may also work under tables, standing, pacing, etc. Children will gravitate to the spot where they can be creative. They must have the freedom to choose, but must also take the responsibility to produce. Production comes from practice and the

Organic Creativity in the Teacher, the Classroom, and the School

self-discipline of working every day on the product. Eminently creative people are judged on what they *have* produced, not what they *are going* to produce.

Grouping. Grouping highly creative and marginally creative students in the same classroom and insisting they work together is not necessarily a good idea. Creativity is often a private, solitary practice, not best done in groups. However, collaboration with other highly creative individuals is a hallmark of creative development. Left on their own, children generally want to socialize, choosing to be with friends. I often assign partners randomly. Students then begin to see with whom they can and cannot work well. The size of the group matters—the smaller the better. Four or five is too many. Avoid always having gender grouping—boys with boys and girls with girls.

The psychological environment. The teacher also sets the tone of the classroom. An environment that encourages creativity is playful, relaxed, and not always constrained by a schedule. Students should be encouraged to take risks—small unimportant, inconsequential ones at first. But these establish the atmosphere of trust—trust in the teacher and in classmates—that questions, answers, thoughts, and ideas will not be put down, but appreciated for what they are. Belittling is a killer of creativity. As group trust builds, so will the instances of risk-taking.

Organic creativity encourages young students' innate sense of wonder and their need to find out "why." Naïveté is not so hard to develop when working with young children, because their innocence and longing to know has not yet been jaded by the real world or their less talented peers. The teacher need not be, and should not be, an encyclopedic dispenser of knowledge. Elementary G/T students need to learn that teachers do not have all of the answers and they need to learn how to independently research information.

The teacher establishes a class environment where students know that in order to stay in the program they must produce both in the regular classroom and in the G/T classroom. Students must develop the self-discipline to complete assignments, projects, and other activities. There should be activities in which clear, concrete, step-by-step directions are *not* given. Let some directions be purposefully ambiguous. Teachers themselves must not have a preconceived idea of what they expect. Any result or product that follows the purposefully vague directions must be acceptable.

Here is a simple activity that I use with young elementary students that embraces this concept. I call it the *Go to the Door Game*. I have two doors in my room, one that leads to the hallway and one that leads into a courtyard. I ask the students to line up single file across the room from the door to the courtyard, and I tell the first student in line, "Go to the door."

Inevitably, that student dutifully walks quietly to the door just exactly as teachers have instructed since preschool.

I ask, "Did Johnny go to the door?"

" Yes," comes the reply.

Then I say to the next student, "Suzy, go to the door." She too walks silently and straight to the back door. Again I ask, "Did Suzy go to the door?" As we proceed through all the students, I begin to get some strange looks as if saying, "This is kind of stupid."

Once all students have gone to the door, we come back, reverse the line and start over with the same directions—"Go to the door." The sideways glances increase. At the end of the second cycle, some students realize there is something going on and they begin to think, they begin to question, and the "Aha!" moment occurs—Larry *skips* to the door, going to it in a roundabout way.

He turns and looks for approval.

In a feigned, shocked voice (that even second graders understand), I ask, "Did Larry go to the door?" There is a pause. Some answer yes; others are more hesitant.

I ask, "Did I say he had to walk straight to the door?"

"No."

"Did Larry follow the directions and go to the door?"

"Yes!"

Now the floodgate of creativity opens.

What do I hope that students learn from the exercise? To think, question, and analyze. The directions were purposefully ambiguous—thus there were many possible solutions. I want students to learn that this classroom is going to be different, that multiple solutions to a problem may be acceptable, and this teacher has a sense of humor. Students learn that they can take a risk in this class; it's okay to be a little weird here. Creative solutions will be honored here.

I learn who the thinkers, questioners, and risk takers are. The elements of risk, group trust, naïveté, self-discipline, and a tolerance for ambiguity should be consciously fostered in the classroom environment and embedded into any curriculum aimed at developing creativity.

The Curriculum: The Elements of Creativity

Along with establishing the environment, the teacher sets the curriculum. Ideally, individuals who lack a strong background in talent development edu-

Organic Creativity in the Teacher, the Classroom, and the School

cation should never set the curriculum of a G/T classroom. The domain or curriculum in which the student is working must match his or her creative spark. A creative writer may not be creative in physics and may not excel in a pottery, music, or photography class.

The curriculum needs to be structured, even if that structure does not match the standardized classroom or is not readily evident to educators who do not have a background in talent development education. To avoid the appearance of a "fluffy" curriculum, it is important that educators know exactly the objectives they are trying to accomplish with creativity activities and why that objective is important to the overall development of a talented child.

The overall curriculum in the G/T classroom should appeal to the creative side of the student. Not all children identified as gifted and placed in a G/T classroom are creative; most are placed there solely on IQ or achievement scores. However, as noted by Renzulli, the element of creativity must be present for the person to be considered gifted and talented, and these children will embrace those activities.[159] A considerable literature—books and Internet sites on brainstorming, as well as convergent, divergent, and lateral thinking activities/exercises—exists. Such activities can nurture and improve creative thought; however, they are just that—activities. They are not creative products in themselves, only *tools* for developing or enhancing creativity, just like learning how to punctuate is only a tool for creative writing. Real creativity is in production and comes from inside the individual.

Piirto discussed seven elements that can be used for developing a curriculum for creativity: incubation, improvisation, inspiration, imagery, imagination, intuition, and insight.[160] All are important in the creative classroom, but some are easier to implement than others.

Incubation. Incubation is the time needed to think—to hear the quiet voice from inside that wells up from the subconscious. After 25 years of marriage, my wife has come to understand my need for incubation time. It may come while listening to music in a relaxed meditative state, or it may occur while performing some monotonous task.

"Honey, how's that project coming?" she'll ask.

"It's coming," I reply as I sit staring at some mindless television program. But the mind *is* working. The subconscious is looking for the structure, the skeleton on which to hang the ideas that have been developing. When that happens, most often in a flash, the dam breaks and the ideas flow into place.

Our classrooms do not give children the same opportunity. Classroom time is very limited; thus the time to incubate is also limited. The bell rings, a student leaves the classroom, and his or her mind is filled with the next classroom's demands. A student's afterschool life is often just as hectic, filled with sports, extracurricular activities, chores, social networking, and video games. It is an unusually well-disciplined child who sets aside time for incubation at home.

It is important to interact with students as they work on their creative projects. The teacher should watch them to get an intuitive feel for what is going on. When the ideas are pouring forth and students are furiously working to get them down is *not* the time to interrupt with, "How's it going?" But when a student is staring off into space and quiet, what's happening in his or her mind is less clear. The teacher should decide whether he or she is interrupting incubation or whether he or she can help clear a roadblock with a brief discussion.

"What are you thinking, Richie?"

"I can't figure out . . ."

"Well, have you thought about X or X?" The conversation should always give options, should not be judgmental, and the child must feel free to reject the teacher's ideas.

In the modern classroom, instruction is expected to be direct and dynamic. There is no time for playing around. That is not always the case with developing creativity, which is often associated with play. Picture this: The principal walks into your classroom, the lights are a little dimmer, music is playing, and children are scattered around the room in corners, under tables, staring into space, doodling, eyes closed. She wants to know what's happening.

"Creative incubation," comes your reply.

She shakes her head and leaves, stating, "Your evaluation will be ready on Friday."

Improvisation. When faced with a problem, we often have to improvise. We must ask ourselves, "How can I go around this problem? What can I do differently; what can I do instead? What else will work just as well or even better?" I work in Appalachian Ohio, and a standard joke is that hillbillies have six cars up on blocks in their yards. Although this is an exaggeration, there is a grain of truth. Out of necessity, many men are backyard mechanics. They cannibalize junk cars for parts, modifying them as needed to keep a family car running. Improvising is a fact of life among the poor. Our high school physiology class can't afford animal specimen kits, so students bring in roadkills for anatomy and skeletal reconstructions. Teachers often try to remove roadblocks for their students, but when teaching improvisation they may want to create some.

Organic Creativity in the Teacher, the Classroom, and the School

I do an activity with upper level elementary students in which they are to imagine that they are the survivor of a small plane crash in a remote wilderness. The decision is made that the best chance for survival is to hike out, and students are given a list of items they have scavenged from the wreck. They can carry only a limited number of items and none of these are survival gear. Students must improvise and find alternative uses for the items they choose. For example, an empty Gatorade bottle may seem like trash, but because there is no canteen, the survivor might want something to carry water in. Students need to decide whether a lighter is better than a pack of matches or what to do with $1,000 in $20 bills. Although many students will leave the money behind, some cannot bring themselves to leave it in the wilderness—"But it's money!" Still others will humorously suggest its use as toilet paper or a fire starter. A can of peaches seems to have endless possibilities in the creative mind. The peaches and syrup provide food and liquid, the empty can is used to boil/sterilize drinking water and used as a cooking pot. Rocks could be placed in it and string tied to it to scare off wandering animals in the night. It can be beaten on like a drum as a signaling device—the improvised ideas go on. There is no rubric of *correct* answers; students must imagine alternate uses for items, make decisions, and defend their choices. Creativity, improvisation, and higher level thinking skills all are developed in this activity.

Inspiration. Inspire students by surrounding them with the creative products of others, especially from the domain in which you hope to inspire creativity. If it's writing, have books, books on tape, or Kindles. Have easy access to a library and a mini-library in the room. In art, display a wide range of visual art in pictures and posters; exhibit quality student and instructor artwork. Have a graphic art library on your computer, and art books on the shelves. In science, have models of inventions, patent drawings, and magazines such as *Scientific American* and *Popular Mechanics*. For a more playful aspect, have drawings of Rube Goldberg machines, and encourage students to create their own. The game Mousetrap is a good place to start.

Whatever the domain, allow the students to immerse themselves in the work of peers, the work of their teacher(s), and the work of others, including, but not limited to, individuals eminent in the domain. Materials and supplies appropriate to the domain should be provided. Probably the most important item for any domain is a series of computers connected to the Internet. Today, the world is only a keystroke away. But cyberspace should not be a substitute for a hands-on, real-world experience.

Imagery and imagination. Imagery is the ability to imagine, to see things with the mind's eye. I tell students that the secret to writing a great story is getting the idea, the images, and the voices out of their heads and into the mind of the reader as accurately as possible. Everything that has become reality was first imagined by someone. Science-fiction gadgets from the TV series *Star Trek* were so well-imagined that they have become modern technologies—flip cell phones, tablets, voice interaction with computers, and voice-activated translators, to name only a few. Walt Disney had a team he called "imagineers" that built his visions of Disneyland and Disney World.

How can educators develop imagery? If you want creativity in the classroom, then time must be made for creativity in the classroom. This makes it important for G/T classrooms to be organized around a *block of time*—ideally a whole school day.

In a relaxed setting, allow students to close their eyes and use their mind's eye to see. There must be time to incubate, to allow the images to come forward. Try reading selections from appropriate literature with highly descriptive scenes. Play audio recordings of stories and allow the students to create/play the "movie" in their heads. Play music from different genres and allow it to create pictures or images. Afterward, have students draw the images they saw and discuss them.

An activity well-suited to developing imagery is to play old radio programs from the golden age of radio. In the era before television, people used their own imaginations to "see" the story. These programs are still readily available. Imagery often plays into the strengths of the visual/spatial learner. Have students map out a story, idea, or an invention in pictures. Have students describe in detail graphically, orally, or in writing some reasonably common item or sensation. Have students create a story based on an image, photo, or random item.

Teachers should stimulate students with visual images: posters, art, photos, etc. in the classroom. Sights and sounds are not the only ways to create imagery. Certain smells can bring back powerful memories or evoke vivid images. An old party game I've used is to put a highly tactile item, maybe something like crushed grapes, in a covered box. Allow students to feel the item and use their imagination to describe or determine what it is. There are many old-fashioned activities like this and the radio programs that will be novel to elementary children. There are also many books on guided imagery on the market. The activities just need to be organized into an objective/goal driven curriculum. In developing imagery, the teacher should bring into play as many senses as possible

Intuition and insight. Intuition is the ability to listen to the quiet voice inside, to trust one's feelings, and to be willing to act on a hunch. It is the visceral feelings, thoughts, or reactions that well up from the subconscious that may or may not have any logical basis. Intuition is sometimes referred to as instinct, gut reaction, or a funny feeling, and it is often dismissed as a lucky guess. Intuition and insight are the "Aha!" moments when inspiration comes or an idea becomes clear. This often comes as a result of thoughtful quiet solitude or incubation.[161] Insight often refers to grasping the gestalt or wholeness of a thing or idea—the ability to look past petty details or to synthesize the details into the big picture or true essence of the idea.

Once again, intuition is best developed in a quiet, relaxed environment that is not rushed by time constraints. It is a solitary activity designed to develop a trust in one's own intuition and in sharing it with others. Dream logs and thought logs are a good way of capturing the fleeting imagery and ideas that come from intuition. Games like Clue, Stratego, and Battleship can help develop intuition or at least a trust in it.

Here is an activity I have used to develop intuition. It requires a temporary suspension of disbelief, a type of naïveté that younger students are better at than sophisticated high school students. Take an artifact, something old with a history to it, and place it in the student's hand. Let him or her sit quietly until the item "speaks"—tells a story. Then have the student tell, write, or draw that story. The teachers should not necessarily tell the history of the object.

Historic reenactors giving first-person presentations can give younger children insights into people, activities, attitudes, and beliefs of a bygone era better than a textbook. They are often experts on their chosen time period, and can share artifacts as well as knowledge. However, junior high and high school students do not necessarily benefit from first-person presentations. It is harder for them to suspend their disbelief and so they spend too much of their time trying to trip up presenters.

The Student

First, we must remember that not every student in the G/T classroom is highly creative. Most are placed there because of high IQ or achievement scores. There are few programs designed solely for the creatively talented. Many published checklists present traits of the creative student, and such lists are used in some states as the lone means of identification. In my opinion, that is not the best way to identify creativity, as the checklists often ignore the important element of creative production. A better way would be to look at a portfolio of work. Be that as it may, the checklists may be useful in understanding the traits that need to be nurtured in the G/T classroom. These behaviors include a willingness to take risks; an openness to new experiences; a sense of humor and playfulness; a challenging or nonconformist attitude; flexible thinking (the ability to produce a wide range of clever or unusual solutions to problems); the ability to manipulate and modify ideas or objects; an ability to see the big picture in spite of the details that bog others down; a tolerance and even enjoyment of ambiguity; sensitivities and overexcitabilities; and a good imagination that can fantasize alternative ideas, scenes, or worlds.

The student must be interested in the domain or area being taught, but just as importantly, must be open to new experiences in other domains. Through this process, the teacher and student may be able to work together to discover areas of passionate interest and the learning styles that will enable the student to develop that interest.

Teachers, administrators, and parents are often overly concerned with a student's socialization and whether or not he or she is "normal." Fortunately, creative people are not normal—unfortunately, that seems to bother parents, educators, and even the creative individuals. There must be a time and place to not only allow the child to be "weird," but also to honor difference and idiosyncrasy. At the very least, that place must be the G/T resource room.

The Last Great Box

The last great box that teachers of the gifted and talented must *think outside of* is the box created by the four walls of their own classroom. How do you get out of that box? Open the door and walk out. Step outside and take your students with you. Take a risk—go on a field trip. Let the world become your classroom. Take students on trips to plays and musicals, as well as art, science, and natural history museums.

A wide background of experiences is important to be considered well educated. As a reenactor of the Middle Ages, I have shown rapier fighting to the class studying *Romeo and Juliet*, put seniors into historically accurate clothing and armor from the *Beowulf* saga, and put elementary students into clothing and armor from the 5th to 16th centuries. Such opportunities provide inspiration, insight, and imagery. After a field trip to Gettysburg, one of my students became a Civil War reenactor himself and then a career army officer.

We will never know what little things we do, or the offhanded comments we make, that will inspire or uninspire children. Students should participate in project-based learning where they can self-select projects or experiences and pursue areas of interest. Those interests may only be temporary; a casual exploration may be all that is needed to satisfy the student. But other times those experiences will become the thorn that drives them to so much more. Experiences sit in the soul and incubate, sometimes for years. One former student, now working on his Ph.D., told me his inspiration was the little chemistry set I had in the room and a field trip to a science center.

Intuition and insight are also based on a wide range of experiences that the person is able to subconsciously rearrange into the gestalt. The more experiences, the stronger improvisation, inspiration, imagery, imagination, intuition, and insight will become.

Travel broadens the mind. I have taught music history in the Rock and Roll Hall of Fame, taught *Beowulf* and Egyptian history in the British Museum, taught structural integrity at the Eiffel Tower, taught art history at the Louvre, taught about fresco painting at the Sistine Chapel, and taught the development of medieval armor at the Cleveland Museum of Art. I've taught about Goya at the Prado, about volcanism in the ruins of Pompeii, and about pterodactyls at the top of Mt. Pilatus in Switzerland. Each year for 30 years, I have taken rural Appalachian elementary children (as young as second grade) to New York City, Chicago, Detroit, Cleveland, Mammoth Cave, Gettysburg, Williamsburg, and Washington, DC, and high school students to Europe. Our school is 70% economically disadvantaged. If it is important enough, it can be accomplished. Yes, there's a risk; there needs to be group trust among the teacher, administrators, and parents. But your students will see with new eyes the wonders of the world firsthand.

Conclusion

Developing creativity in the G/T elementary classroom is indeed a lot of work. Any job in education, done right, is a lot of work. But it is worth it.

Share the creativity of others and model it yourself. Consciously foster an environment of trust for risk-taking, for ambiguity, for the childlike wonderment of naïveté, and demand self-discipline. Create a defensible curriculum that incorporates projects, products, thinking skills, incubation, improvisation, inspiration, imagery, imagination, intuition, and insight.

Provide a wide range of experiences for students and always, always ask, "Why?"

Chapter 17

TOWARD A MORE HOLISTIC APPROACH TO TEACHING

Organic Creativity in Teaching Educational Psychology

Diane Montgomery

Education is not the piling on of learning, information, data, facts, skills, or abilities—that's training or instruction—but is rather a making visible what is hidden as a seed.—Thomas Moore[162]

Growing up on a farm in Northern Minnesota, the oldest of four daughters, third generation Finnish-American, I went to public schools and colleges, leading to the study of education. I wanted to be a teacher or a keypunch operator. Good thing that I chose teaching! Many reading this will have to look up what keypunching was in the early days of computers. Here, I plan to weave my experiences into the life I have created to become a Regents Professor deeply committed to teaching and research. This creation has been dependent upon listening to the story of each person coming to me, learning to trust my own intuition, and becoming conscious of the gifts of opportunity and reflective understanding. Creating this consciousness for intuitive learning means shining a light on the soul or psyche and becoming aware

Diane Montgomery, Ph.D., is Regents Professor of Educational Psychology at Oklahoma State University in the College of Education, where she coordinates graduate programs in gifted education and talent development. She has held positions on several editorial boards and boards of directors of national professional organizations, including The Association for the Gifted, a division of the Council for Exceptional Children, and American Council on Rural Special Education. Her research interests include transpersonal development, creativity, and Q methodology.

of the seeds that I plant and those that have been planted for me by others, trusting that the experiences bring growth and maturity.

As a university professor, I hope to narrow the gaps among theory, research, and practice in the classroom, in schools—indeed, in the ways that people interact with each other. This chapter demonstrates some of the theories or principles that have guided the way I teach, learn, conduct, and interpret research, all in hopes of making myself present to others. I discovered my true process of creativity from many wise people, from reading, and from just living. I have been teaching for 40 years. I have been an educational psychologist and special educator, and my keypunch career has morphed into the advising of more than 60 dissertations and theses for brilliant students who have honored me by choosing me to lead them. They seemed to approve of the way I teach. Some may mimic pieces of my style or practice. I teach the psychology of consciousness and an awareness of self, no matter what course, topic, or age of student I teach.

Authentic teaching and learning is more than what is learned and assessed in school; rather, education extends to how we mature, grow in all areas, and develop throughout a lifetime. Moore said, "One of the great problems of our time is that many are schooled but few are educated."[163] He instructs a life journey with greater consciousness resulting from learning how the past instructs the future and the learning we carry, often deeply hidden, within our soul.[164] So, our job as teachers and psychologists is to assist our students to acquire the depth necessary in the learning and also to bring to awareness the greater potential that each learner has for a full and joyful life, giving not only their craft, but themselves to others.

Consciousness

Although consciousness has been variously defined and studied as a science and a mystery, the definition that resonates with me is from Schlitz, Vieten, and Amorok: "Consciousness is the quality of mind that includes your own internal reality."[165] This idea encompasses the psyche (conscious and unconscious), in addition to a keen awareness of self and knowledge of the waking world that can be used to better understand our mind, our own unconscious processes, and the more transpersonal experiences that can serve us rather than confuse us. I use consciousness work in my teaching practice to increase awareness, and some strategies will be reviewed here.[166] Think of this process as learning to increase what is unknown (or unconscious) to transform into what is known (becoming aware or conscious). Although it is obvious that learning increases what is known, we often rely only on factual knowledge, science, logic, and concrete skills, and ignore other types of information, believing less technical sources are less important.[167] This creative educational journey includes learning through emotion, intuition, inspiration, or imagination and is of great importance to excel in a domain, learn about a life calling, or discover how to contribute to the greater good, employing universal values, and keeping an open heart in addition to an open mind.

I have adapted what I learned from Christopher Reynolds (see Chapter 7 in this volume) one summer when we team-taught a few lessons in psychology in the Ashland University Intensives courses for gifted and talented adolescents. He simplifies the conscious and unconscious understanding to four levels. We learn about psychology and ourselves in the universe in this way: the waking world (what is available to our senses and knowledge); the personal unconsciousness (what we carry as wounds, forgotten memories, or experiences, the personal psychodynamics of Sigmund Freud); the collective unconsciousness (the archetypal, deeply transpersonal, beliefs across wisdom traditions, and complexes of Carl Jung); and the spirit world (those transpersonal and spiritual experiences, events, or beliefs unexplained by science or logic).

I believe that living deeply takes on a special meaning for us when we pay attention to the subtle, synchronistic clues that are revealed by our life circumstances that teach an intuitive knowing, and we awake to our own creative spirit. As I connect to this mystery, teaching is more than what I do; it becomes who I am as I embrace needs and respond to each person I meet.

The Framework

When I worked at the medical school in Oklahoma, Dr. Dean McGinty (a faculty family physician) and I collaborated on a research project to explain education, teaching, and learning. Every class that I teach begins with an explanation of what we discovered in those discussions and use of the research. The physician's goal was to inform family medicine residents how to teach patients about disease and wellness. Additionally, our goal was to inform faculty physicians about the ways that residents learn how to provide good care. After reviewing literature, conducting multiple observations of

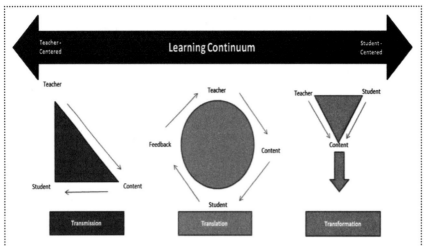

Figure 17.1. *The Framework for Understanding Educational Encounters. Created by Diane Montgomery and Dean McGinty. All Rights Reserved.*

classrooms, and integrating our experiences, we designed the Framework for Understanding Educational Encounters (See Figure 17.1).

The Framework for Understanding Educational Encounters

To summarize our work that resulted in the framework, we conceptualized three explanatory models along the continuum of learning according to who takes, assumes, or provides the most responsibility for learning. On the left side, we designated the end of the continuum as mostly teacher-directed learning and the opposite or right side of the continuum was fully learner-directed discovery.

The Transmission Model

The teacher-directed model was observed the most in our research. We named it the Transmission Model, because the goal appeared to be a concentration on performing the act of Informing as a priority in instruction. Instructors commonly provided the same knowledge and skills to any group of learners who arrived in the classroom, felt responsible for transmitting the knowledge assumed to be learned in the larger scope and sequence, often used lecture (including PowerPoint presentations and notes of the information that must be taught), and assessed students with tests consisting of right and wrong answers. This is a classic, traditional model of direct instruction with much research to substantiate its effectiveness in teaching knowledge to pass tests. It has been my goal to avoid this model of instruction, because I believe students have the most experience with demonstrating success in this model. Short-term gains in information outweigh long-term change, transformation of understanding, and personal interactions. Consciousness work is thought to be too time-consuming or unrelated to the necessary learner outcomes.

Walking into a stuffy classroom of about two dozen sweaty third graders, we notice all of them working on the same worksheet. The questions each answers with dark circles around the correct response are variations of the examples on the whiteboard. The dynamics of this observation were duplicated when we walked into the second-year medical student class in the biological sciences. Out of a huge class of hundreds of students, only 25 percent were attending the lecture in that large hall about the massive readings assigned for that section. The students had formed small groups of four. Each group member took a turn to be the one who would attend the lecture and take notes on what was going to be on the test. They then shared notes in the study group. The following teacher-directed instructional strategies focus on covering the content regardless of who steps into the class.

- ♣ Choosing the textbook that all students will use for the year's curriculum on social studies.
- ♣ Reviewing the content of the end of instruction tests with all students in the class.
- ♣ Teaching a favorite unit in which all activities, although interesting, are identical in what the learner experiences and all products look alike.

Translation Model

We named the model in the middle of teacher and learner responsibility the Translation Model or the Knowing priority, in that there was now a concern by the instructor for the knowledge and skills gained by the learner. We used a circle to denote the iterative process of preassessment of needs with the context of the domain, making a plan to implement instructional strategies appropriate to the learners in the class, and using feedback and revision in the assessment process. In many cases, we observed how other learner characteristics were assessed and played a major role in the development and delivery of instructional strategies.

When working with teachers of the talented, I use the Myers-Briggs Type Indicator (MBTI) to demonstrate the psychological preferences in the way we take in information and make decisions, the psychological understanding of Jungian theory. Although in this model the instructor is making many of the decisions, the needs and nature of the learner(s) are used as input in addition to the content that needs to be learned. In this case, the characteristics of the learner act as a foundation for building remedial, review, accelerative, or other advanced learning strategies. I learned this model as a classic foundation or the guiding principle for curriculum development when I studied in New Mexico for my master's degree in special education. There are two guidelines that resonate with me as I serve as a model for developmentally appropriate teaching practices: (a) I will not teach what is already learned, and (b) I cannot teach what learners are not ready developmentally to learn.

These are some instructional strategies in which the teacher is making decisions, but in these, she is basing the goals on the information she gathered from the specific learner. For example:

- The high school science teacher returns the preassessment test for the 6-week unit. Students get a study group assignment; the teacher adjusts the lessons based on the variety of skills presented in the class.
- When talking about lack of progress on a project, the sixth grader says, "I wanted to try to watch my uncle work with his horse first." In response, the teacher says, "Maybe you would get more information from interviewing the mentor I have chosen for you," or "Here is a list of books you could get to help you in your project."
- The teacher explains how she learned about the special interests, learning style, content in the science class, and other input to direct and negotiate the learning for students.

These teachers are translating the information they formally and informally gather to assure that progress in learning new information, skills, or awareness occurs for each student who comes to the class.

The Transformational Model

The third model along the continuum we named the Transformational Model with a Deciding priority. We found the literature full of suggestions for the value of constructed knowledge (social constructivism). We read about the need to offer respect and equivalent value for learners. Yet it was difficult for us to find this model in practice. Once, I observed a teacher of the talented negotiating an independent study project; she had the characteristics of the model for coplanning and coevaluating with the student. However, upon further reflection on this observation, I detected that the interaction, which we thought would be synergetic between the teacher and the learner, was in reality an argument, with the teacher providing continuous reasons to the learner why there was one right avenue—the plan of the teacher.

The plan from the learner's point of view was less effective, and the teacher was unwilling to allow the learner to discover other paths to success. I've learned how important it is to state advice, but allow room for learning by experiences or mistakes, a learning process that resembles a mastery learning goal over the entity or performance goal.[168] This means being willing to find out more, make mistakes, and take risks rather than perform, show how smart or capable one is, or get the grade one wants.

The Montessori classroom allows learner freedom that can lead to transformational learning. Once when I was a principal of a small, private school for children with high potential, I was eating lunch with a 5-year-old boy in the Montessori class. He explained to me why dividing fractions required turning the numbers upside down. When asked how he figures this relationship about the fractions, he said he could see it in the center where he worked in the morning in his classroom.

In another example, a dissertation student comes with an idea, a career path, and questions about inquiry. Professors create a path of awareness and understanding with her. These teaching models have unknown problems and unknown responses leading to creative transformations for both the teacher and the students.

The importance of the framework is apparent as we use it to become conscious of our own goals and motivation. Some teachers want to cover material (transmission); others want to make sure learners achieve outcomes (translation); others want to honor the directions chosen by the learner to construct a new insight or way of knowing (transformation). The key for me has been to consistently evaluate the goal with my behavior and intention in the teaching and learning action. This means if I ask a group of students to be vulnerable and to take risks, I must be willing to do the same. A colleague I had in class more than a decade ago told me that my graduate course was the most different—and often difficult—he had experienced. He couldn't tell who the instructor was when he entered the room, as I was sitting in a student's desk, I brought food for the class, and when I spoke, I called myself the facilitator of learning for the semester. He reminded me that I revealed an embarrassing story about when I was once traveling old mining roads far north of Minnesota, drinking too much liquid, needing to use a bathroom, and only wearing a one-piece jumpsuit. The reader can imagine the embarrassing end of the story.

Intuition

Think of this scene: I am standing in front of a lecture hall with 80 talented teenagers on raised tiers in front of me. I am giving them a master class in psychology. I ask them to rise, face their neighbors in pairs, and stare into each other's eyes. They giggle, embarrassed, uncomfortable. Then they do it because they are "good kids," with high IQs, at a special summer honors institute where I have taught the Psychology of Consciousness for more than 10 summers. We faculty, who have come back year after year, call it our summer camp. We have made lifelong friends of each other, as the students come and go.

My purpose in this master class is to introduce all participants in the institute to what my own class of 10 students has been studying. Here is a poem Jane Piirto published about what we studied in this class:[169]

The Art and Science of Psychology
Eyes Closed

All week we've meditated
So we took our group picture
With our eyes closed
But we've learned so much
They don't teach psychology at our high schools
We are 9 girls
Only 1 boy
But I held my own, didn't I?
Yes, James you did.
Here's our summary web
All this in one week!
Freud, Jung, Dabrowski, Kohlberg, Erikson
Intuition, Sensing, Feeling, Thinking
Judging, Introversion, Extraversion, Perceiving

> We built a labyrinth
> We all cried, even the adults
> Sketching, Clay, Fingerpaint
> Archetypes, dreams, consciousness
> Mandalas, Dance, Poems, Journals

The students find comfort with one another and imagine stories that they share to assist each other in dealing with the issue each has written on paper. The vulnerability of these young adolescents and the willingness to make intuitive connections for each other is colored by the social acceptance of the story. For example, one tells of a song that was running through her head as she concentrated on the other student. The song intuitively informed the other student of ways to resolve his issue, start facing challenge, and risk saying the words that were deeply hidden. I have used this same strategy with graduate students, often with over half of the class full of emotion, even tears, for breaking through to insight, gratitude for the experience, and an openness that comes with relief or joy.

When I teach a doctoral seminar on the development of emotion and cognition, I place high value and importance on intuition as a mechanism to unite what sentiment and logic reveal to us. Graduate students who have studied these developmental areas separately often are relieved that their implicit theories are valuable to their practice in education or psychology—receiving the academic permission to trust intuition, insight, and imagination in practice. Gladwell[170] provided concrete examples of trusting intuition in the information we obtain in a very thin slice of data. For example, you may have impressions of someone when you first meet him or her in person or on video and later find out that you were correct in what you assumed. The information in the first 5 minutes is often validated over much longer periods of time. Yet becoming aware of what is prejudice and what is another way of knowing emerges from our practices of reflection, empathy, and compassion.

The Holistic Educational Model

It began with my work as a consultant to several of the Indian tribes. I grew up in the middle of reservation lands in Minnesota and worked with tribes in New Mexico as a young teacher of the talented. Now, as you probably know, Oklahoma has the most tribes of any state because of the Trail of Tears, Andrew Jackson's final solution to the problem of the Cherokees. In order to do my job better, I began to study the ways of the tribes, and of American Indian spirituality. I myself am a cradle Lutheran, with an abiding involvement in my own ethnicity and its Reformation roots. But what I learned from working with American Indian colleagues and children is the wisdom of distinctly different, but honored traditional ways of tribes (not all revealed to me, the outsider). Yet, at the same time, the literature, conversations, and insight from others show some of the similarities among tribes for the medicine wheel[171] as a metaphor for holism. As I combined these wisdoms, Jungian psychology, and transpersonal values, the Holistic Educational Model (See Figure 17.2) evolved.

The medicine wheel was the inspiration for the Holistic Educational Model. The medicine wheel focuses on the four geographical directions (east, south, west, and north) or areas of development—physical, social/emotional, spiritual, and intellectual. Four is considered a whole number, and there are numerous schemas for extending teaching and learning to at least four ways or methods. My focus then has become to use all four domains, developmental areas, questions, or methods for conscious and holistic planning for learning. The holistic model includes (a) the mind, (b) the body, (c) the spirit, and (d) the heart.

I'm not the only psychologist or teacher who thinks this way.[172] Sternberg mixed practical, analytical, and creative intelligences with the wisdom to know which is most important to serve others. Piirto embedded creativity into learning through the three areas of thinking, working with others, and implementing innovations by using intuition. Tying back into consciousness, Goswani explained the quantum level of creativity that supports the Holistic Educational Model in this description:

> The possibilities of consciousness are quantum in nature and are four-fold: material (which we sense); vital energy (which we feel, primarily through the chakras and secondarily through the brain); mental meaning (which we think); and supramental discriminating contexts such as physical laws, contexts of meaning and feeling such as ethics and love and aesthetics (which we intuit).[173]

The parenthetical explanations of the quantum explanation mirror the four quadrants of the holistic model: thinking, feeling, doing, and creating, as used in my work.[174]

Organic Creativity in the Teacher, the Classroom, and the School

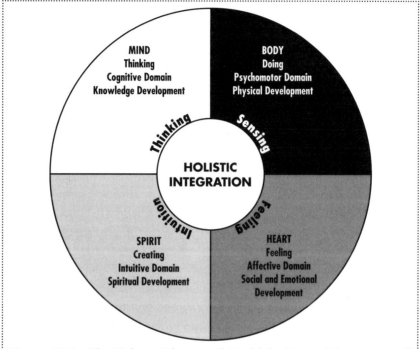

Figure 17.2. *The Holistic Educational Model by Diane Montgomery. All rights reserved.*

Another way to integrate the medicine wheel is to connect it to Jungian concepts of personality with two processes that each run along a continuum between two functions (See Figure 17.2). The perceiving process, the form and function of information taken in by individuals, ranges from sensing to intuitive. The sensing function is taking information in concrete forms using the senses, relying on previous experience, or having physical evidence for knowing. The intuitive function as discussed here and elsewhere is more abstract, trusting in the possibilities and taking information in more abstract forms. The second process is judgment, which ranges from making decisions using the logical thinking function to making decisions using a more senti-mental and value-laden feeling function. Humans have all four functions in these two processes; however, personality is defined by the strength of pref-erences with the processes. The MBTI has been used by researchers to define the learning preferences of those studying in many fields. But we advocate teaching and learning in all four functions, which resembles the holism por-trayed in the American Indian medicine wheel. Briefly, this means to plan curriculum to accommodate the total developmental needs of learners—cognitively, socially and emotionally, physically, and creatively.

Consciousness Building—Becoming Aware

There must be thousands of ways to assist holistic development and to increase awareness of one's learning, role in life, and future goals. Most of all, an increased awareness of one's own consciousness is needed. Jung declared and practiced on the shores of Lake Zurich his belief that the arts were one mechanism for making the unconscious more conscious.[175] I have incorporated the arts into my practice as a teacher of psychology. For example, playing with clay revealed a deeply rooted angst for one student in a class on the arts and science of psychology. Seeing that she had placed a large lump of clay on the back of a fragile insect, other students asked her what was her metaphorical burden. Only tears revealed the depth of a story she partly revealed to us. Play with arts media is worth every second invested, even though some say that students need more time on academic tasks. I have learned through working with all ages how sometimes knowledge on the conscious, waking level is not in tune, congruent, or consistent with the burdens, cares, or passions carried on deeper levels of self. Here are some brief descriptions of ideas to get you started.

Creativity Is More Than the Arts

Project CREATES,[176] a multiyear privately funded grant project, was one way that I learned how creativity is more than the arts. Although we infused the arts into learning across the curriculum, we investigated the connections between learning outcomes in the arts and other academic content areas. Artists, arts educators, teaching artists, and elementary teachers were inspired when we were able to get time for them to plan lessons, coteach in ways that transformed them and their students, and reflect on the lessons that motivated students for continued learning. We discussed and learned about brain-based learning and teaching. Without passing judgment on technique, ability, skill, or aesthetic, I aim to allow a childlike playfulness when working with various arts media. The key is to encourage the artist to perceive what was created with a deeper level of awareness, to think about the metaphor of the shapes, the meaning of the colors, the representation of the figures. I am cautious in offering suggestions to the artist, and remind the group members they do not have the psychological credentials to make diagnoses, but can offer ideas, suggestions, or impressions. Here are some exercises where intuition is trusted and ideas are tested, keeping all thoughts tentative.

Movement. Movement is a way to experience the mind and body connecting, opening the pathway to the heart, bringing in vulnerability for authentic interactions with one another. I have used structured creative movement, planned movements in yoga, or open-ended improvisation as ways to unblock thinking, thereby accessing creative spirit or energy. Yoga poses offer stability and physical flexibility; theatrical improvisation provides a sense of elaboration, humor, or quick-witted thought.

Mandala. Using large circles of paper, I ask students to make designs that come to them when they think about their lives. This process reveals symbols, stories, and meanings that may have been hidden to the conscious mind. Using a variety of arts media, the students' created work can relate to the psychological constructs for the class or the proposed projects for the semester. The students talk about what they see without passing judgment or trying to go too deep psychologically. These unconditional practices provide safety when stories about identity, families, and education are told. Try it by yourself first. What did you discover?

Meditation. Dawn peeks at the edge of the fog in the twilight, and 10 adults scattered throughout the tangled underbrush of the woods wait in silence for the sunrise. Our Shambhala teacher bows to the light and leads our way back to the organic breakfast, cleaning our own dishes in continued silence. The bell rings to signal our way back to sitting. We called it the Lake House. We have since downsized, but it lives in memory as a beautiful space. Perched high above the lake, looking through a vale of mature trees, facing the sunrise, it had many levels, waterfalls in the swimming pool, and an atmosphere my students loved. I am standing on the landing of the stairs to one of many levels, tinkling a bell. My students sit zazen in this profoundly quiet space, with only birdsong to be heard. They agreed to spend the weekend in retreat here. Here is not a villa in the mountains of India north of Pune, but Tulsa, OK. My students work in many professions, from aerospace to arts administration to medicine to teaching. I have done this retreat in various locations for different groups of students for more than 15 years. It started when I was a student in a colleague's class (Joe Pearl) on altered states of consciousness, where I learned to meditate, keeping a journal of my experience.

Mindfulness is a broad term often cited in the literature to demonstrate the effectiveness of meditative practices on physical health or psychological well-being. In the Buddhist sense, seeking meditation for personal gain slows the process and gives unnecessary emphasis to self-improvement over discovery. When continuing the practice, a shift from self-centeredness to serving others pours into a life.

Walking the Labyrinth. Two women and one man are poring over the diagram of the seven-circuit labyrinth with rolls of masking tape in hand. The room is large, furniture pushed to the walls. We just finished saying blessings of poetry or meaningful quotes to all four directions, choosing east to be the direction to face as we enter the circular path. The space is considered sacred, and we move around each other in our stockings. Others begin to come to class, helping in the construction, laughing when lines don't meet. I give short instructions for walking meditation: Keep right if you meet someone coming out when you walk in, sit on the chair in the middle to think about nothing or keep open to what comes to mind. I turn on the spa music, and after 30 minutes we talk in low tones, and students reveal images, feelings, and insights. Some may express discomfort, some indicate a willingness to try again without getting the giggles; however, generally, many express a transforming silence to serenity.

Memory Work. I worked with a group of women using the feminist research method of memory work.[177] After 5 years of meeting for 2 hours three to four times each month, I learned how I am a scientist and how we need to make students more aware of the unconscious processes that shape their thinking. Our work resulted in two books,[178] one an edited volume. We would generate, analyze, and describe our earliest memories using these words as triggers to remember and write in third person: earth, air, fire, water, and tree. This is my earliest memory for water:

> It was long before Diane went to school, maybe she was four. She was in the basement of the Lost Lake home when Grandma still lived there. It was Saturday night family sauna night. Every sense is involved as the water sizzles into steam on the hot rocks and envelops naked skin. Grandma has long, saggy breasts, the pails filled with cool water were left in the sauna (getting hot), children used only cold water, the water was piped up from the lake and smelled like swimming time. The Lost Lake Sauna was a very hot one, and Diane never got to go to the top shelf where the steam was the hottest.

This memory research project expanded to our classrooms as we planned to assist our students to better interrupt their own processes of socialization to view a personal and collective deeper meaning. Depending on the topic of the course, I used various triggers to encourage written memories. In addition to trying *fear* and *fire,* I've tried school-related terms with undergraduate preservice teachers, such as *chalk, recess, lunch tables,* or *principal.* Students write third-person accounts of early memories, come to the group to read them aloud, and make observations of what is said and not said in the narratives, revealing a world of knowing now available to think about. The practice of memory work brings an awareness of those social influences previously unknown. "How much does a fish know about the water in which it swims?" is a metaphoric question for memory work as a means to increase awareness.

Concluding Thoughts

Maturity in teaching has meant for me an awareness of my role to plant seeds of knowledge, skills, psychological concepts, or understanding and then to trust that growth will follow. Maybe this came from my farming background, or maybe I learned early in my career that the rewards of teaching are not found in financial resources, status in the community, or even immediate gratitude from students. Rather, the reward of teaching is to get the opportunity to witness the holistic development of students who become leaders, wise teachers, authentic psychologists, and compassionate human beings who care for one another in their lives—in work, relationships, and play. I grow in my understanding of the psychology of learning, not from the research journals as much as from the former students who tend their crops, harvest the fruits of many seeds planted over the years and create a meaningful life for themselves and others, perhaps using some seeds from their psychology courses. My students have created new schools based on holistic education, use the framework in their pedagogy, infuse the arts in therapy, and practice creative techniques in their practices. Some practice or write about these ideas, tending and harvesting the seeds as their own. This is a nourishing reward for me.

Without demanding or presenting one right way, the purpose of this chapter has been to offer suggestions, ignite ideas, and demonstrate my own path for increasing awareness of the creative process of teaching and learning, its practice, and products. As I enact the practice to learn more about myself, I learn to be more open-hearted to the many who cross my path, better able to solve problems creatively with both heart and mind, and facilitate a healthy reliance on intuitive knowledge.

Chapter 18

VISCERAL CREATIVITY

Organic Creativity in Teaching Arts/Dance Education

Celeste Snowber

The body is the canvas for creativity. We paint with our hands, dance with our feet, sing with our breath, and sculpt with our palms. Our very beings are creative——we are made with the glorious impossible——ears that hear, flesh that remembers, pulse that regulates, and hair that protects. As the visceral imagination is opened up, the intuition is given muscles, and we can teach on our feet, and be informed by what has great capacity to guide us. Intuition resides in the sinews of the flesh where tissue can be transformed to wonder. Creation and creatures echo the ultimate creativity, and the gift of the senses brings beauty that is both bearable and unbearable. Beauty has the capacity to be dissonant and consonant, and creativity is found in our bones and cells, which bear witness to this reality.

Creativity is our birthright, and the first verb one makes as a human being is the movement within the womb. Who knows where that will go, within the womb, or when one is born, but birth alone becomes an invitation for continual improvisation. Yet it only takes a few years into being schooled for creativity to stop becoming as natural as breathing. As small children, we are in touch with the heartbeat of our body's language. We express with our arms and legs, bellies and shoulders and exclaim with all of our physicality. It is normal to skip and to tell stories, to swing our limbs and shake, or to cry when upset. When I was a child, perhaps 4 or 5 years old, I was on the Boston subway with my mother. It was the time period when all of the trains

 Celeste Snowber, Ph.D., is a dancer, writer, and educator who is an associate professor in the Faculty of Education at Simon Fraser University. She has written numerous essays and poetry in various journals and chapters in books in the areas of the arts and is author of *Embodied Prayer* and coauthor of *Landscapes in Aesthetic Education*. Celeste continues to create/perform site-specific work in connection to the natural world and is a mother of three adult sons, all a tribe of artists. She lives outside Vancouver, BC, Canada, and her website can be found at http://www.celestesnowber.com.

were connected, and you could travel from one to the other in one long line. I have a very strong memory of being on the train, getting up from where my mother was sitting, and dancing throughout the train, looking at people, smiling, almost falling into their laps, and my little body being filled with absolute unfiltered joy. I moved through each train, going through the doorways to another and letting my arms and legs spontaneously twirl with abandon. As we departed the train, I recall the conductor sternly scolding my mother to never let her daughter do that again! My child's heart thought it was normal to dance outside, to follow the joy within, until I learned it was scandalous and it stopped. Of course now as an adult, many years later, I do this all of the time and call it performance, but my body knew its call to create long ago.

All of life is an infinite exploration, and it is the fullness of the senses—tactile, kinesthetic, visual, auditory—which becomes the brushes to explore existence. Creative existence *is* living, until one learns better, or actually worse. Many of us as educators went into teaching in the beginning because of the possibilities to explore creativity or, ultimately, the place of wonder. Wandering into wonder was the task and the call. Wandering out of wonder becomes the place where children find themselves, as they grow into adults, forgetting the gifts of sensuous knowledge, given from the beginning of birth. Of course, many of you reading this book will have a different sensibility, but it doesn't take brain science to notice the lack of attention on creativity and the emphasis on what is instrumental and economically advantageous, compared to a creative life.

Physicality

Whether you are working with children, teens, or adults in or out of the school system or postsecondary institutions, unless you open up the place for yourself and make the connections between an embodied way of knowing and creativity, it is difficult to open it up for others. Parker Palmer, a well-known educator, says, "We teach who we are," and so it is vitally important that we can celebrate life and teaching as full embodied human beings.[179] As I work with my student teachers, I often tell them that as soon as they walk through the classroom, the students know how the teacher holds the space, just by the teacher's nonverbal language. I have found it of utmost importance to bring what I call "body pedagogy" to the practice of teaching, where we feel at home with our bodies and allow the place to access intuition on the fly.[180]

As a movement educator, dancer, and poet, and one committed to the area of embodiment for many decades, I am passionate about bringing the body, somatic knowledge, embodied knowing to the creative process. One can call it many things, but I see this chapter as a place to inspire—to put breath back into what was familiar and resonant from when we were children. I have said many times that too often humanity talks of "having bodies" rather than "being bodies." We are all too aware of the size of our stomach or hips, shape of the nose, texture or color of skin, or length of the feet; the body becomes what is "seen" by the outer image. Any trip to the grocery store will dictate the body's image as important when looking at the tabloids at the checkout counter. Oh, I would just love to see an irregular body, sharing the excitement of curves, and their connection to red peppers, rather than slimmed down, made up, fake bodies, selling sexuality! Reminders are constant, dictating that unless one has perfection, one is flawed. No doubt, eventually one separates from the body that is constantly demanding perfection. It is exhausting keeping up, so we keep down. We keep down the beauty and wisdom of what is possible. The grammar of the gut becomes extinct. Passion becomes dulled, and, most of all, the deep intuition connected to the inner body is dumbed down and our creativity is on the endangered species list.

This chapter is about calling back the body to the membranes of creativity, to the actual soil of what needs to be a foundation for creativity to bloom and bust out from within us and into the lives of others. And creativity goes into all aspects of our lives: living, being, writing, teaching, researching, loving, conversing, growing vegetables, or raising children. I was raised in a creative home, where I was taught at an early age that color was part of cooking, and dance and looking at stars were part of being alive. Recently, I was given a letter my mother wrote to my aunt, and it gave much wisdom. Her words still ring true.

> Creativity cannot be just painting pictures, molding clay, writing music—of course this is part of it. Just think when people can communicate with others, or they can bring love to another, or they can be clear and bright and true and constant, and they do their everyday work with love or they meet life and STAND UP to it, knowing "all they can do is stand": like St. Paul says. To me this is creating—energy—action![181]

The body is like a free GPS system within our beings—a place of inward direction and discernment. In this day and age, no one can afford to not pay attention, and the fabulous component is that it is free. I believe the body is also the GPS system for unleashing unlimited creativity. There is no shortage of two essential ingredients in life. One is love, and the other is creativity—both have an infinite source. They coincide, for we create out of love in deep attention, whether that is combining chemical elements in a lab; combining colors, sounds, and gestures; or combining ways of leadership. Creativity is not limited, of course, to the arts, but it is the fabric of what it means to be human. To make something out of nothing, to make something out of something. The artist works with the materiality of form, whether it is movement, sound, syllable, or image, in order to create and recreate. The creative work has a life of its own, and the invitation is to listen and serve where it is going.

Life can be filled with drudgery. Unfortunately, there are too many times one has to do the laundry, mark papers, make a meal, change a tire, or pay a bill. And, yet, all of these endeavors can be done with creativity—well, perhaps not paying a bill. I would propose what is most important is not just "being creative," but living creatively and fostering the conditions that support the roots of creativity to spring and become fully formed.

Four Principles Toward Embodied Creativity

In connection with reclaiming the body as a place of knowledge and wisdom, I propose four principles in connection to embodied ways of being and knowing and releasing creativity. These are necessary in order to live an embodied creative life, one that has the capacity to sing in the midst of hardship, to invent in difficulty, or to soar on the wings of lived experience. These are *play*, *passion*, *physicality*, and *practice*. I have already been speaking of physicality and, I admit, I am on a roll with the letter p, but somehow I love the interconnections of these areas, which have become true principles (another p word) for my own life and the lives of my students as I have nourished, cultivated, and let creativity be the heart of a life well lived.

Context

The principles I will speak of can be connected to any education context, and to life itself for that matter, since life is an ongoing process of learning, growing, forming, and transforming. However, I will share the specific context in which I work so when I give examples in my own creative life, research, and teaching practice, it will situate both the theorizing and practice of these ideas. I have taught for more than two decades in a postsecondary institution where I work with undergraduate students, student teachers, and graduate students pursing master's degrees and doctorates within a faculty of education. I teach across disciplines, although primarily within arts education, but also teach in cohorts connected to philosophy of education, health education, and ecological education. In all of my classes, I incorporate movement, dance, and the practices of writing from the body. I work with the premise that our teaching, living, writing, creating, being, and knowing are not separate, but interlinked in a delightful, messy, exquisite array of connections, and it is our bodyselves that are truly the place of integration. My students and I have big lives, children to raise, meetings to go to, and deadlines, which are not lifelines. So I have learned to live in the cracks of life, and ultimately see the beauty break in surprising and delicious ways. I raised three amazing sons as a single parent, in the midst of teaching full-time in a university, and even getting tenure, so it was crucial that I developed small practices that would nourish me, in order to be continually ignited by what I would call a visceral creativity. This brings me to the principle of practice.

Practice

The practices that have nourished and sustained my creativity over the years consisted of a daily walk with my black Lab around the Port Moody Inlet outside Vancouver, British Columbia, where the sea hugs a long, winding path. On my walks, I journal-write. This is the place for me to empty and release the "monkey mind" and deeply attend and listen. I am in the presence of bald eagles, seals, blue herons, coastal giants of Western red cedar, and always the seagulls. This is a place where I feel I belong, on the border between sea and land. Out of these walks emerged a whole body of poetry and, eventually, I extended my response to creation to making dances and reading poetry as I danced. I opened this up for others to accompany me on a contemplative walk, and I share these site-specific performances and have now incorporated them into all of my undergraduate and graduate classes. Site-specific work has become a huge part of the way I engage with the creative process—to create from the place where we physically are.

I am fascinated by a pedagogy of place, and how place shapes who we are and who we are becoming. It often astounds me that there is always a shortage of space where I teach at the university, and classes struggle to find classrooms, yet there are magnificent grounds, hallways, staircases, or spaces in between underutilized. So I have taken up the practice of bringing my classes outside the confines of the classroom and integrating the arts as a place of inquiry in every space imaginable. We make up haikus and read them in the hallways. Student teachers write their philosophies of teaching, create expressive movement to them, and go in a public area of the university and perform them. I lead a movement warm-up outside on the grass, and dance creation occurs in the midst of trees, grass, and the edges of concrete buildings.

A big part of creativity is about listening, and as a dancer, writer, and educator, my task is to listen to the language and nuances of movement, words, and the subtleties of the gestural and tonal language of my students. Our research is a place of listening to our own lives, knowledge, and longings. I have therefore focused for years on methods of research that include the personal as integral to forms of qualitative research, as arts-based inquiry, autobiographical inquiry, poetic inquiry, lifewriting, performative inquiry, and embodied forms of inquiry. As a dancer/poet/scholar/educator, my dedication in scholarship has resulted in theorizing insights that honor and recognize the connection between the artistic process, inquiry, and scholarship.

But what allows us as human beings to get into a kind of flow? Csikszentmihalyi said,

> The metaphor of "flow" is one that many people have used to describe the sense of effortless action they feel in moments that stand out as the best in their lives. Athletes refer to it as "being in the zone," religious mystics as being in "ecstasy," artists and musicians as "aesthetic rapture."[182]

It is this flow in creativity that we can leave the "monkey mind" and go into a place where inspiration dwells. Where breath dwells. The root word of inspiration goes back to breath, to breathe into, yet many of us are breathing from the neck up, racing around, or with our necks protruded forward with an iPhone or gadget attached. Seldom are our sternums raised to the sky. The sky is longing to come into our lives, letting us feel the breath of creation, where we can be stopped by the pulse of the natural world.

As I sit at my computer, I look out and see a crow go by. They fly with ease, and there is something about that ease I am longing for. My life has been guided by small times of solitude, when I can dwell in my body and get out of my head and descend into the territory where I am in my heart, emotions, and intuitions and can be open to what is possible. I am drawn to

Organic Creativity in the Teacher, the Classroom, and the School

these practices, whether it is swimming, yoga, writing, or walking, because I am an expert worrier—thus the inspiration for a performance piece on "The Spirituality of Worry," in which I actually teach the audience to worry, in case they don't have this expertise! I way too easily get into my head and try to manage everything, living in a paradigm of pushing the river instead of flowing with the river. But key to these practices is a time to descend into a bodily awareness.

So I have not only instituted embodied practices in my own life, but I have also invited my students to integrate them in their lives. Every class I teach, my students are required to take a practice of solitude and to try to find the connections between physicality and writing. It is a small thing, yet very big. Seldom are we required to take solitude. I'm convinced as educators that we need more emptying than filling, more letting go than taking on, and ultimately we need to be invited into letting be. I'm not after long hours of contemplation, but for students to have the permission to take perhaps three times a week, 20 minutes each time, to go into some kind of rhythm, which allows a different flow. It is a slowing down, where a bodily mindfulness can be cultivated. There is a lot of literature, research, and practice around reflection, yet less is being done where there is the practice of an embodied reflection.

Something happens when we are in the flow of our lives, when every cell, fiber, and tissue is singing from the inside out. This is what children long for at recess. It is necessary for adults to have recess as well. Time and time again, I find students tell me how life-changing it has been for their teaching practice, writing, creativity, and art making to give themselves permission to drop down into the recesses of sweet solitude. It is difficult at first, but it can become a practice, and here they honor and hear their own beautiful voices. I think of the poet Rilke's wonderful words, which I have carried within me for many years, "Being-silent. Who keeps innerly silent, touches the roots of speech."[183]

Practices that root us to our embodied knowing have the capacity to stop us in our tracks—bringing our sensual knowledge to the forefront, allowing us to be halted and pay attention to the surprises in our lives. Yesterday, while writing this chapter, I had an unexpected visitor of fog. Here I am writing a chapter on creativity, but it was the announcement of creation that called me to sink into my chair, to breathe deeply and to linger in the landscape outside my office window. I had to stop writing and take notice. Here is an excerpt from my observations:

The fog is bent on winning today; enveloped in a sea of cream gray, it is all I can see out my office window, and it beckons me to stillness. Ushered into the silence of mist, on this Monday afternoon where there are many deadlines, I am invited to stop and be enveloped in its presence, where I cannot see what I normally see. To be invited into not seeing, not knowing. There is the unknown waiting. The fog descends, and everything in the landscape is altered. The weather is performing fog. I am accompanied by mist, color, and the knowledge that I am small, and what is beyond is much larger, always waiting.

Creativity waits at our gate, breaks into the cracks, in the openings, where one thinks it will not be, and says, "listen," "see," "behold." I am here. I am in the absences. I am in the presences. I await, to accompany you on this spectacular, paradoxical journey and are here to co-create with you. The mist is everywhere; one cannot escape it. It is playing outside, inviting me to look past my own organization, my own plan, and I need to see things differently. But my bodily presence feels it, even through the small crack in the window. I am changed, and I am waiting, and I will surrender to its mystery.

Thomas Merton, the Christian mystic, said that "hurry ruins saints and artists"; with an intentional slowing down, even an afternoon reverie, one settles the body in a different place.[184] We need time to saunter into the light, to let our thoughts arise from a different place. I leave the tyranny of *chronos* time, the time that has all of the moments ordered, to dip into *kairos* time, where there is an infinite quality in the finite. This union between the finite and infinite is where creativity dwells, and it asks me to sit. But it lingers into different ways of being, where the body can sink into the chair, couch, floor, where gravity will pull one into levity. As my body collapses into a place of deeper relaxation, my thoughts drift, and I somehow am open to insight, the imagination, and the poetic, which becomes both prophetic and astounding. Winterson put it well: "For the artist, any artist, poet, painter, musician, time, in plenty, and an abundance of ideas are the necessary basics of creativity. By dreaming and idleness and then by intense self-discipline does the artist live."[185]

Physicality: Writing From the Body

For years I have integrated practices with both myself and my students that explore writing and the body. I entered the art of writing as a dancer and was determined to find a way for words to skip, twirl, dance, and have a resounding connection to the breath and body. Language originates through orality, where it resounds in the belly and breath, throat and tongue, and syllables and sentences form through our mouths. Writing too often has become separated from the physicality of the body, yet there is a way to return to grammar of the gut. For years, I have created a methodology around writing and the body, as well as had my students integrate bodily practices and the art of writing. In turn, they have incorporated a bodily writing with their students from K–12, and it continues to be a place of unleashing creativity, where words have opportunity to dance.

The language of the body is fundamental to human expression—a language of physicality, which has the capacity to connect to the inner life. It is not uncommon in my classes to do a whole movement warm-up, which consists of dance, creative movement, and improvisation and then to directly write out of this physical experience. I then time the writings. The limitation of only a short write, in conjunction with getting the blood moving and the ligaments limber, allows for the cells to burst into words on a page, which have a totally different resonance. It is such a joy to be told by students that writing now has become something they truly love, rather than something to dread; in fact, writing has become as natural as breathing. Many times during any class I teach, I often get students to take a deep sigh, standing up and inhaling and exhaling air through their whole bodies. Interrupting class with elongated breaths and short writes has become a way of life in my classes. We need to unwrite to learn to write, where creativity can take root. The interconnection between language, breath, motion, and gesture becomes a living studio to manifest the deep flow of creativity. We are the living studio. Next comes the principle of play.

Play

The saying by Descartes many years ago should be changed to "I play, therefore I am." The act of playing, which is truly the work of childhood, has been relegated to certain ages and, as adults, we don't play much unless it involves drinking or lots of money. Yet, play is a way of humans entering time, a way of allowing the spontaneous and improvisational to occur. In other words, play is the work of creativity or of the spiritual practice of creativity. However, there are not too many places one can just go to play as an adult, or even after middle school, without money being involved. I would suggest there is a call for humans to live playfully and to rediscover the art of improvisation. As a dancer, I know the importance of the relationship between improvisation and moving and creation.

I often take my whole undergraduate class to the playground, where we get on the swings, to be reconnected to the movements of what it was like as a child. The movement of play on the playground can bring forth the kinesthetic memory of what it was like to experience the acts of skipping, hopping, throwing, stomping, or hanging. My students write and reflect on these visceral activities, for the ingredients of play, creativity, improvisation, and risk elicit the language of the body, soul, and heart. Recapturing play and the risk-taking of play allows us as humans to be in the moment and to be open to spontaneity. Adults have forgotten how to play, and the body at play is a way of going on an all-inclusive vacation and never leaving home. Why is it we can't raise our hands in joy in the middle of a meeting, or skip home, or dance during a break at work? Whatever happened to the physicality of joy? Why are we restricted to only exclaiming with our bodies at a certain age? Twirling and dancing, which was once so organic to us as children, has gotten replaced in adulthood with conventional ways of moving. When was the last time any of us rolled down a hillside, played hide and seek in the woods, or had a snowball fight?

Movement reaches us emotionally and physically at our foundations, provoking the deepest emotions and releasing the creative river in our lives. The class we most often remember most clearly from our childhood is gym. Many times, there are negative experiences associated with gym, yet recess is where our bodies truly leapt! Movement, whether it is creative, spontaneous, on the playground, or through the daily practice of walking has the capacity to be the muscle of the imagination and the entrance to the visceral imagination. It is within the process of finding movement and improvisation that dance can become a site for embodied inquiry. Here the mover literally thinks with the body, allowing the improvisational process to be a discovery of what we do not know. The body knows where our mind may not be able to lead us. The dancer and performer have long known that the creative process is one of questioning and sifting, forming and unforming, making and remaking, and always a place of discovery. In my classes and in the many workshops I give at conferences and in local venues, we dance our questions together and uncover together a place for openings. When students ask questions through their bellies or shoulders, hips or backs, different questions arise. How do we hold in our guts the children we teach? What do our shoulders tell us about the responsibilities we hold? Literally dancing our questions opens up different ways of perceiving and seeing our lifeworld.

Play, movement, dance, and the body connect each of us to worlds that are often dormant, and we are able to reconnect with the primal imagination. Play is the spiritual practice, the notes we need to rehearse to lose inhibitions of self-consciousness and remember our bodies back to themselves. I would invite you as a reader to find where you can enter practices of play as a sacred place, a place apart to nourish your creativity. Perhaps you may not see a direct relationship at first, but I am inviting you into living a creative life, one which overflows into all you do. We cannot know the river unless we are physically in it; play is the river of creativity, where one can learn to flow with it, instead of pushing it. The principle of passion is next.

Passion

I often tell my students that the most important thing they can do for their lives is to really show up. Each of us has a unique perspective, stories, and lived experiences, which form individuality. What would it look like if one were totally present to his or her passion? To listen to our passions is to fall into our lives more deeply. To fall into our own lives requires releasing to the weather within, whether that is disappointment, grief, joy, trust, shame, or exhilaration. The terrain of the emotions is weather, and part of our invitation is to be fully human. Here are the paints for the canvas, the gestures of the dance, the sounds for listening to our creative lives.

My own attention to exploring grief through writing and dance creation has allowed me to see the passage of grieving as a possibility of inquiry for graduate students. I had a student who was experiencing a great deal of grief, and all she wanted to do for her project was work in her garden. I encouraged her to make that the practice where she fed her creative soul. By attending to growing the flowers in this little city garden, much fruit was born: paintings, poetry, and a space for the entire class to share their final projects in a place set apart for beauty, which was hospitable for depths of their research into embodiment. Out of the passion for what we are drawn to in the moment grows the organic development of imagination to be born.

When one is being creative, one is often in synchronicity with where the river is flowing. I ask undergraduate students what they are majoring in and what is their passion, and seldom is there a connection. I believe passion resides in the cells of the body, the embodied knowledge and body wisdom, waiting for attention. It is my task as an educator to pedagogically provide hospitable and safe spaces for students to access what is within them. I often invite students into experiential ways of learning through the senses, as a way to uncover what really matters and where they find life. I often bring ripe strawberries to class and ask each student to write an "Ode to a Strawberry," inspired by the poet Pablo Neruda, who wrote such luscious odes. I read Neruda's "Ode to a Tomato,"[186] and give the students strawberries to examine, observe, and write about. Over and over again, students who would never consider themselves poetic or even creative write the most beautiful and immediate odes, surprising themselves and each other with the connections between delicious writing and sensual knowledge.

What accompanies this writing is joy; joy is a guide to how passion is lived out in our lives. Creativity becomes the place of inquiry, as do embodied ways of knowing, to access the place where joy is found. To live a passionate life is to be wide awake, and to be so crisply aware of the rises and falls of the intuitive that one can go with the impulse. How does this get acted out in the creative process, or even in the act and art of teaching?

A consideration is that we might not go toward the lesson plan but go without a plan, to trust in expertise and experience and to see what happens. I may come in with a lesson plan, but I may find out that day that there was a huge tragedy, and the only way the class could bear this is to write poems around grief, or create movements about what it means to have loss. I am interested in the emergent curriculum; therefore, as I am attentive to my students' issues, I need to be willing to shift where I thought we would go. One must be so open, so fluent in the language of the creative in its many textures that it is right at your fingertips and your footsteps. I am more interested in what I don't know than what I know. Vulnerability is required for the journey, to allow the place to be broken open, for the creative process is seldom neat and is an invitation to both wonder and difficulty, but it is a process, which resides in the text of our bodies and souls. Following the footsteps of what gives one passion allows a passage for creativity to move. The body's embrace is an invitation to be fully awake to all that arises within and without, and here is found, no matter what subject is being taught, a curriculum of creativity.

This chapter is only a beginning in seeing the relationship of reclaiming the body as a place to nourish creativity as a way of life. In the daily practice of nourishing our own creative bodyspirits, we are practicing the scales for a life rooted in what can flow as naturally as the air we breathe. Attending to our own embodied knowledge is a daily practice, and one of the writing practices I engage in myself and incorporate with my students is to write Bodypsalms (http://www.bodypsalms.com). These are basically letters to ourselves, to pay attention to the ways one can attend to our own embodied wisdom. I offer you a Bodypsalm for Visceral Creativity—a poetic call to cultivate the inclusion of the body within the creative flow into all aspects of our lives.

Bodypsalm for Visceral Creativity

Take me along the journey
bring me with your fingers and feet
hips and pelvis
and let me announce my ways
within your tissues and cells

The flow of creativity
asks for you to be wide open
raw to every syllable
of life's terrain—
in grief, disappointment, joy, and laughter

Fall into the discovery
of the *physicality* of your own life
trust each passage as
a new color—vibrant hues
in the folds of *passion*

Play till you are tired
Practice
the rare beauty
of making up stories and dances
conversations and plans
rewrite the curriculum
of your heart
and glance into the wonder
of wandering into each day

Have no judgment
around what you create or do
but relish in the art of being awake
and let your body take you
to a new place.

Chapter 19

THE MIRROR: CREATIVITY AS SEEING AND BEING SEEN

Autoethnography of a Teacher

Jennifer L. Groman

There are two ways of spreading light: to be the candle or the mirror that reflects it.—Edith Wharton

Who would ever think that so much went on in the soul of a young girl?—Anne Frank

Look! My first gray hair! This job is aging me.—Jennifer (age 33)

My first diary was a small orange bound book, the kind with the tiny lock and key. I sat in the crook of an oak tree behind the garage writing my odd little childhood dreams and hopes in it. I wished that my stuffed animals could talk, and I wrote about cute Robert who sat in front of me in math class. I still have one decaying photo album with photos and scrawls of a young girl, although water damage claimed all of the other childhood diaries and journals, a fact for which I am sometimes grateful, sometimes sad.

 Jennifer Groman, M.Ed., is a teacher, singer, and songwriter. As a teacher, she has worked with students from 2 years old to the graduate level, in general education, talent development education, creativity studies and songwriting, reading, and math intervention. She is a Professional Fellow for Ashland University. She has worked at the state level as a talent development coordinator and teacher trainer and at the local level in arts administration. As a singer, she has performed music from big band jazz to rock to bluegrass to indie, and performs locally as a singer/songwriter with four self-produced albums of her own music. She is currently working on a dual doctorate/masters in curriculum and instruction and transpersonal psychology at the University of Akron and Sofia University, respectively. She lives in Wooster, OH, with a dog named Benny and a cat named Jett.

I took an organic creativity course as part of my endorsement in talent development education. Keeping a journal was a requirement so as to practice Jane Piirto's Core Attitude of self-discipline in creative people. My journal—Piirto calls it a Thoughtlog[187]—became a place to respond to the creative in my life. I again made writing a daily practice. My creative growth is in these depths, ideas that moved and changed me, and the creative expression that explored me while I explored it and the intuition revealed in my creative work. I have been asked to trace my transformation as a teacher, creator, and thinker by revisiting my Thoughtlogs. As I revisit the Jennifer who is tucked in those pages, she speaks to me vividly, like the old friend she is, and I can see the subtle little shifts, false starts, and places of growth.

I believe that organic creativity as a life practice transforms and deepens our understanding of ourselves and those around us. The creative products we generate as we work in this way act as a mirror, reflecting our transforming identity back to us and out to the world. The work is intuitive. The work changes us. It grows us.

Over time, I have learned to braid my creative work with my teaching—it has shifted how I teach as well as what I teach. This chapter chronicles my journey of change as a teacher. In intellectual terms, it is an autoethnographical integration of personal and professional creative work as it frames and develops my teaching practice. Just between you and me, I'll tell personal stories directly from my journals to show how my philosophy of teaching has grown alongside this work. I include examples from my daily writing, drawing, meditation, and song lyrics to show how organic creativity activates this change. Journaling illustrates not only Piirto's Core Attitude of self-discipline, but also the idea of incubation (one of the "Seven I's") and the need for solitude (one of the General Practices). In this style of working, there is a powerful focus on ways of seeing and being seen that not only enlighten us to our own strengths as teachers but also allow us deep vision into the capacities of our students that goes well beyond what our standardized curriculum paradigm can offer.

I tell these stories for the same reason I sing my songs: I think that maybe, just maybe, you might find a mirror in them that reflects your own creativity and process back to you.

4/14/02
I don't want to be just another teacher who sang once.

Organic Creativity in the Teacher, the Classroom, and the School

My business card reads: Jennifer Groman, "Singer/Songwriter/Teacher." This is how I define myself now, and it has taken me years to come to. Before all of this work in what we call "organic creativity," I was a teacher who sang on the side. My teaching experience is as varied as my musical experience. I taught in Ohio, Florida, and Scotland, all ages, all areas. I worked at a day care in Georgia, checking the diapers of nine 18-month-olds every hour, writing down the exact color, shade, and consistency of what I found there for each loving parent (I hope I don't sound bitter. Do I sound bitter?). When I settled in Ohio, I found a job teaching talented and gifted students at a small rural town, many miles worth of teaching experiences later.

I've sung pop, jazz, rock and roll, folk, and bluegrass. I sang nursery rhymes to those babies in Georgia (it took my mind off my other duties). In returning to Ohio, I also returned to singing jazz in a local big band. I dabbled in songwriting during my high school years; I composed three or four songs of saccharine teenage love and sadness over some break-up or another, but gave it up after harsh criticism. For years, I sang other writers' words, with my music life divided from my teaching life.

> *Philosophy of teaching, 1996: To open up a world of exciting and unique teaching situations and to help children find joy in discovery and learning, all the while emphasizing that each child is unique as well as promoting respect for self and others. I strive to cultivate inquisitive and creative students.*

This is my original teaching philosophy, from my very first, deeply naïve, earnestly hopeful (and very short) resume. That first run-on sentence still makes me laugh. My undergraduate professors must have limited us to two sentences, so I decided to get the most out of mine.

This is my current philosophy, from my recent, slightly skeptical, still hopeful (and much longer) resume:

> *Philosophy of teaching, 2012: Singer/Songwriter/Educator. "There are two ways of spreading light: to be the candle or the mirror that reflects it." Edith Wharton.*
>
> *As a teacher I am a mirror, and as such I use my time with others to show them who they are and who they can become. My Purpose is to encourage others to develop their minds, their gifts and their self-efficacy, to help them on their way to reflecting their full potential back into the*

world. I use the arts and creativity as a catalyst for positive growth, enjoy-
ment, and a unifying presence in my classroom.

How did I go from helping children "find joy in discovery and learn-ing" to helping them reflect "full potential back into the world?" I traveled through my journals—Thoughtlogs—to find out.

3/6/96
I CAME IN WITH A LEAP
I came in with a leap—
laughing
Now I can't wait to leave
crying.
But those behind desks don't cry—
do you?
Those behind desks fight back—
don't you?
I can't reach you with smiles
frowns will do
I can't reach you with knowledge
fear will do.
I regret this pathway—it hurts
my feet, too.
My hands shake—breaking the spirit
won't change things.
Your hatred still heats me
Your cold hearts still freeze me
I haven't an ear
nor enough words to say
Teach me.

Can you guess? I was substitute teaching in a middle school. After 9 years of traveling and teaching, I was still so very inexperienced. It's not a great poem, but writing it helped. It gave me an insight into being taught by my students in a deeper way, as if I were saying, "teach me how to know you." A short month later I found my first gray hair, taped it to a piece of black paper and fixed it into my journal, stating: *This job is aging me.*

Soon afterward I started coursework in Talent Development Education at Ashland University. This next entry was from my Creativity for Teachers of the Talented Thoughtlog, after an exercise in drawing the creative process.

7/17/97
My picture shows how hard the creative process is—you work and struggle, eat worms, stretch your wings, pump 'em up and then jump! Sometimes you make it, sometimes you fall flat and have to climb up and try again. The joy—the 'red'—is in the moment when your wings hit the air—the risk is there to divebomb into the bushes, but the feeling of the flight is definitely worth a few bent feathers.

This image eventually inspired me to write my first song in 15 years, "Away Again," for my final creativity project for the course.

During my creativity work I rediscovered a concept from my high school years called the "Sacred La." To elaborate, here is an excerpt from the liner notes of my first solo CD, released in 2000.

In high school, I was given the responsibility of tuning the orchestra by playing an "A" on my bassoon. My high school orchestra director would point to me and say, "Miss Groman, please present us with the Sacred La." An "A" ("La" on the solfege scale), would sing out from my bassoon and the orchestra would tune to that one note. Then the stringed instruments could use their "A" to tune the rest of the strings on their instrument. When I graduated the director gave me a tuning fork with a little tag that said "Sacred La" so I would always have one with me.

It wasn't until some 15 years later that the deeper meaning of the Sacred La was revealed. Each of us has one Truth that, once found, can tune the rest of our being. This metaphor echoes Hillman's Acorn, the Greek's Daimon, and Piirto's Thorn. It has become the purpose of my music, to seek the Truth in my life and put my part of the musical conversation in motion. Globally, if we could all find one common Truth, be it peace, kindness, or awareness of the greater good, we could tune the strings of all humanity. This Truth can heal and it can bind together that which has been broken. I have begun similar work now, using art to communicate and teach at a deeper level.

Slowly I realized the power of this kind of creativity. It gave me a language with which to realize my Calling—my Sacred La—as a teacher. It gave me a way to connect my Calling to my budding creativity. I began to elaborate on the meaning of the Sacred La in further entries.

7/11/98
I feel I can be a better teacher if I can help my students find this in themselves. I feel I can be a better teacher if I can keep this center. What is my Sacred La? How can I build a curriculum for younger students to help them to begin to look for their Sacred La?

7/22/98
Maybe that is part of my Sacred La—and why I felt so driven to continue teaching at this school despite all the different pulls to go in another direction. Maybe next year I need to use this creativity grant to explore activities to help students use their creativity to its fullest.
    The LPDC (Local Professional Development Committee) could also be a good way to do this. Teachers have sometimes lost the drive to be mindful at what they do—maybe they feel lost in the paperwork or in the lesson planning. It would be a good thing if I could somehow find a way to help others find their Sacred La— teachers who might need the rejuvenation.

7/23/98
Jennifer, you need to understand that, from now on, you have chosen the more difficult path. It is a conscious choice. And although I may get discouraged because of the pay, the hours, the lack of respect, this is my course. This is my calling and this is what I am—for better, for worse. Ha! For richer or poorer!
    This profession is about reaching people. For me it's not about Proficiencies or grades it's about reaching lives. If I'm not going to have children of my own, I owe it to these children to care about where they're going and how they're getting there. The teachers, too. My anthem will be, "act as though what you do makes a difference."
    Because it does.

These ideas began to light me up inside. I started growing my own creative work and giving students more opportunities for deeper, organic creativity. I brought working artists into my classroom to share, I started the process for making a CD with the big band, I took a Discipline-Based Arts Education (DBAE) class with the art teacher.

> *9/3/98*
> *I've planned a 7/8th grade creativity course, based on* The Artist's Way[188] *and the two other creativity courses I've taken. It's a definite risk that could blow up in my face, but I'll try it once.*

I learned to play the guitar and started writing songs again.

> *7/16/99*
> *JOIN THE DANCE*
> *Come and join in the dance, be a part of the joy.*
> *Come and join in the dance, grab a girl, grab a boy.*
> *Come and join in the dance, for the now, for the past.*
> *Who knows how long it will last?*[189]

> *1/17/01*
> *In* Women Who Run With The Wolves, *I think Estes talks about the Sacred La.*[190] *How the stories we tell resonate in us and make our whole being sing—like the strings on a guitar, the Sacred La in the orchestra. She also said that the story can also resonate in those around you. I think for some people I know their La is so intense that it ripples out and makes the people around them vibrate, too. These are the teacher/healers and I think to teach creativity well this is what we really need to be.*
>
> *When I am focused on the task of seeing and working through the heart, the most wonderful things happen. The kids stick around after class to share their stories and in some cases their dreams.*

I found that life as a teacher of the talented and gifted is very difficult. Heartbreaking, even. Now when I hear stories of the breaking hearts of teachers around me and the questions my young teachers-to-be ask about the difficulties of the profession, I think back to these days. Today I think my creative work made the road a bit more difficult: I saw the slow, steady movement toward standardization with the No Child Left Behind Act and the standards-based legislation and at the same time was aware that teaching could be different—deeper and more soulful. I also think that my creative work saved me in many ways: I had an outlet for expression when I was frustrated, sorrowful, and ready to give up. I had a connection to like-minded individuals who bolstered me.

7/4/01

Sometimes I think it's hopeless, this search for a more creative life. Ridiculous. A stupid, silly thing to do, really. I push life into myself, fire up my energy and my potential, and the world in which I've placed myself just wants more. The ground is drenched with blood, sweat and tears and yet it pulls it all in and asks—begs, demands—more and more. Always wanting more. And those demands and the energy to fulfill them just saps me dry.

7/9/01

The way is not in the sky, it is in the heart. the Buddha

7/12/01

HARDLY HERE AT ALL

I feel I'm hardly here at all.
The weight of something pulling me but what I cannot see
the mirror clouds the image of what I am to be.
I feel I'm hardly here at all.
Try to see what keeps me tied to earth, my captor seems so strong,
when I finally see that I'm the one who's holding on.
I see what's happened since the start, the jailer's not out there, he's in my heart,
I wish that I could let it go, I pray for the strength to make it so.

7/14/01

Is this art joy or a chore?

How does one let go of an idea or thought that has been holding you back from taking the healing? I always want what I can't have. I want what makes this easier. I don't want the aloneness. What exactly is making me so damn angry? A sense of not controlling the truck that is barreling by. Annoyed by issues I don't want to be bothered with. Sheer, utter exhaustion and mental shutdown so that I can't think or feel.

This is a pivotal time.

I feel I'm hardly here at all means that all that I am is reaction. Duty. Anger. Hurt. But these things don't really have a face—they are imagined.

I want them gone. I want music to be joyful—life to be joyful. I want the dance.

7/19/01
So—what is my message? What is my bigger purpose—my deeper meaning? I want to wake kids up. I want to wake adults up. I want my school to be alive and kicking. I want my world to be joyful. I want to communicate with music. I want to put myself in song and give myself away.
And with my kids I want to see the art in them.

I created an afterschool group called Poetic License and started two pull-out creativity classes—one of identified gifted students and one of at-risk students identified by the counselor.

9/17/01
I am afraid of being discovered. Found out. If I sing and share my songs, my lyrics, my heart, anyone who wants will be able to tear them down. And the teachers at school, well, I don't know if I can trust them with this.

9/18/01
My first recording session last night with Jeremy and Christopher. My emotions right now are wild and free and so hopeful. Conditions in the world have not changed but I have aligned myself a little more with my cosmic purpose. I have altered my outlook, I am set on my path and I cannot stop now. I cannot make this CD, check it off my psyche's to do list and move on. I feel as though this is a bigger thing. Yesterday I intuited that things were about to change, to shift for me. And they most definitely have.

9/19/01
I feel very Jennifer. As if I've become. Become me. Sharing it with people, especially people I care about is—feels like a death-defying high wire act. Thrilling/sickening.
Carl's reaction to seeing himself in "The Dreamer" song went beyond words. Maybe it's time to wear my medicine bag on the outside of my clothes. Show the world exactly who it is they are dealing with.

10/6/01
Response to (sculpture) Nocturne Navigator[191], *Columbus Museum of Art*
NOCTURNE NAVIGATOR
I am waiting
and ready
for whatever may come.
I shall throw back my head
and let the joy flow out,
fill the space with light
and song.
I will lift up the world
and balance it on my song
to spin, to twirl
to dance to harmonize
with all of the vast unknown.
A pinprick of sound
that can change the course of man.

10/29/01
I'm writing these songs to hope, to wish the positivity into being. Dream my life's future.

> *A singing teacher.*

> *How do you get out of a never ending circle of negativity around me? Dance. Sing my way out! How do I know what my soul wants? Dance. Sing my way in.*

1/13/02
My at-risk Creativity students are drawing satanic symbols on their note-books and hurting themselves. I feel so out of my element—not sure I can help them in the way they need . . . knowing that they need a sense of who they are, is different than knowing what to say and do to get them there . . . do I truly believe in the power of this work enough to get knee deep in it? To go out there and meet those kids where they are, filthy and frightening as it may be? I have to believe that my heart knows the way—my hands and feet know the way. My journey isn't much different from theirs, is it?

> *There is a delicate balance to this work. Revealing too much puts me in their way, revealing too little separates me from their lives. These*

children have something that they need to give to the community. Their gift is their affliction, their inability to bring their gift to the community is OUR affliction.

2/25/02

SING YOUR WAY HOME

Sing your way home

Sing little girl, sing, sing your way back,

It might take some time to find the courage you lack.

Keep your eye on that guiding star, you're never alone,

don't forget you're a child of mine, and sing your way home.

12/4/02

I had one of those landmark moments today. I played "Daddy's Shoes" for my 7/8 grade classes to talk about using metaphor, images to convey meaning. It was an introduction to Plato's "Allegory of the Cave." They have to read into the deeper meanings. When I finished playing it I looked up to see Angie consumed in tears. I was stopped, silenced, honored. I thanked her and told her that was the best compliment she could give me.

The classes that got through the Allegory of the Cave worked well, good discussion. Those boys I usually lose during discussions actually came alive, made meaningful, well-reasoned arguments and comments. Did the song help?

I started teaching Creativity for Teachers of the Talented, as an adjunct professor in the very same program and the very same graduate course that woke me up those years ago.

1/28/03

Today I am thinking that I need to step out of the way in my creativity class. I feel like I do too much force-feeding when I should allow them to see and do and experience it themselves. The most important thing, I think, is to let the art do its job—that's what I mean by stepping aside. The art activities are specifically geared to bring out a piece of them. I should let it.

I know the effect of too harsh of a criticism on my own creativity. I made me stop writing songs in high school. It just wasn't fun anymore.

I wonder how many of the teachers in my graduate class have a story like that from their youth? Something that made them close up shop and go home? Something that made them think that their only creativity is when they put together lesson plans?

3/11/03

Today it feels like what I don't know is a lot. My life is beginning to turn away from traditional teaching to a more personal, deeper type. I, once in a while, see a light in these students. I see a push to think on their own. A love of discussion, thinking, and learning. But I don't know that public school will be satisfied with what I'm doing for very long. My balance is tipping more in favor of a life where, I don't know, where I can use my music and art a little more.

MY HANDS, MY VOICE, MY BODY
My hands, my voice, my body
The days in which I live
A clumsy art to offer
But all I have to give.

10/24/03

I'm struggling with a classroom problem. 6th grade girls writing notes about a student, foul language, derogatory names and comments, a 6th grade boy with scratches on his neck from another student. It's very emotional. We did art yesterday—creating the monster and the victim. I'm trying to work through how I'll discuss it to drive the point home. It hurts me how, time after time we read about guns, knives in schools, and think that we'll never have to deal with that while the behaviors that precede these things run rampant. This is a broken place in our school community, a broken place in our existence and I want to heal it. I want to change it. My course of action today is that I want them to visualize the thoughts and feelings of the bully and victim, give them faces. I want them to know who is most likely the victim and what tools the monster uses, why talented and gifted kids are on both sides. Then I want to give them tools to stop the behavior—to become heroes. Heroes have courage and stand up for people. They are good decent individuals who don't brag, belittle or bully. Between their monster and their victim I want them to put a hero—themselves.

This is where Art intercedes.

Organic Creativity in the Teacher, the Classroom, and the School

Written on the back of the art featuring the monster and the victim: *Bully*—"I sometimes feel like I am the strongest and best person, but other times I feel left out and lonely. I want people to know I exist and it seems like the only way to get their attention is to make them cry." *Victim*—"I'm nice, I try hard, find the good things about something. I try my hardest, but someone always tells me that it's wrong, or it should be better."

Meanwhile, the school leaves me feeling left out and exhausted. The grade-level teams don't want to talk to me about talented and gifted accommodations. They say they don't need me. I have made friends with the art teacher, Jack, who has an impossible schedule, and I can see that he is struggling to keep it together. He plays guitar, too, and we do some writing together. I make more of an effort to listen to him.

3/10/04
I go out of my way for Jack—that empty, fearful look in his eyes scares the other teachers—they know just how quickly the tide could turn and they would look like that, feel like that. I don't fear it, actually, because I am it. I've had—maybe sometimes I still have—that deadeye look. I don't fear what I know myself to be. I became that way—why? How? I wonder. Walking through school hallways alone. Too many confrontations about stuff I strongly believe in. Being forgotten or not included. Seeing the deep, dark secrets in our schools: they don't care, and the few who do are exhausted.

The district decided to close the arts magnet school, so I left at the end of my second year.

6/2/04
I will miss Jack. I regret for him because I worry he will be forgotten and pushed aside. I feel like I really helped him, really helped myself in the process. Camaraderie certainly comforts.

6/5/04
I think that sometimes, when we feel unappreciated, it helps just to be seen. To have someone see your pain, hardships and acknowledge it. Jack needed a lot more than I could give him, but I think that having it feel like someone cared, every day, helped. It is detrimental to put people in a job and forget them, leave them to flounder when it gets tough. Depression breeds more depression because people avoid the depressed

person. No one wants to be depressed by proxy, it's like we're afraid it's catching.

For the next 4 years, I took a foray into arts administration, and my life changed immensely. I did some work temporarily with the Ohio Department of Education, more with adults than children, doing professional development on the education of the gifted and talented as well as on the arts. When the state job wound down, I began thinking about what was next for me, for my teaching and for my art.

I was also teaching college education courses, graduate and undergraduate, at two local universities. I integrated art into the courses: mandalas into the graduate educational psychology course to allow for deep reflection, and sculptures into my undergraduate courses to help them determine what matters to them in teaching. I didn't ask permission, I just fit it in and made sure the activities were strongly justified with research. It occurred to me that I like teaching adults, and teachers need to be taught by teachers, not by theoreticians. If anyone knows the joys and hardships of the profession, that person would definitely be me.

9/13/08
Today I spent the day working on my doctoral school application. I'm scared—unsure about this. The time, the effort, the major change to my life this will make. I won't finish school and be ready to find a job until I'm past 50. A new career at 50.

For my doctoral assistantship, I taught Introduction to Education. I was amazed at the student sculptures on "What matters in teaching," as these undergraduate sophomores contemplated their futures. One of these was called Pearl (see Figure 19.1).

These sculptures and the initiating discussion became students' educational philosophies, the main goal of the course. We also created "teacher identity boxes" using collage to integrate words and images of what students valued, their emerging philosophy, and the knowledge they gained from the course.

In the place of a final examination, students created installation art. The pieces gave students a sense of their own critical voice because they made a strong statement about current paradigms and their own beliefs. Figure 19.2 shares an installation that speaks to the existing standardization paradigm in education today.

Organic Creativity in the Teacher, the Classroom, and the School

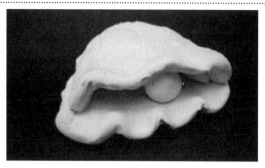

Figure 19.1. *Pearl.*

Figure 19.2. *Education installation art.*

In 2008, I took a workshop in drawing mandalas. Mandalas have a long history as meditative tools in many spiritual traditions. Jung used them in his psychotherapy work. I draw mandalas often to help me process events in my life, gain insight into problems, and just have a little bit of fun.

7/16/12
MANDALA
Mandala: This work becomes me.
They couldn't know,
writing their stories, that
I exist right there
on the printed page.
I speak in margined notes
to my beloved author friends
years and miles away.
And, in drawing my delight,
if I listen closely
even the pencil knows what to do!
This work becomes me.

11/1/12

I spoke this evening at Joan's epistemology class, I talked about organic creativity and the arts as an epistemology. I shared some mandalas, they made sculptures and we discussed them. I used the Eisner article, "Art and Knowing"[192] and two other articles. I do love Eisner. I always notice that graduate students are slightly less willing to open to these ideas than undergrads. They have lived with a positivist paradigm for so long they've lost touch with the wildness of their raw ideas and the intricacies of their own learning. It's OK that it is a stretch. I really just wanted to give them another viewpoint.

10/28/12

Mandala: My Eupsychian world[193] Many times I feel as though I work in a field that mistrusts the heart and degrades the soul. It makes me sad sometimes, those are days I want to give up and go back to waitressing or be a lounge singer. It makes me indignant on other days; those are days I have a chip on my shoulder, feeling alone and ignored. More often it looks like a challenge, those are the days I keep studying, reading, writing, working, so that whatever I do will be for the Greater Humanity of this field.

In my transpersonal reading this week Ruumet[194] uses the word Eupsychian—and it clicked for me that this is what education is supposed to be for me, growth promoting, encouraging self-actualization, but it doesn't often hit the mark. It made me ask, What does a Eupsychian edu-

cational world look like? Feel like? For me . . . and for my students . . . and for their students . . . ?

I didn't over analyze, I just drew. It's a start.

Philosophy of teaching, 2012: As a teacher I am a mirror, and as such I use my time with others to show them who they are and who they can become. My Purpose is to encourage others to develop their mind, their gifts and their self-efficacy, to help them on their way to reflecting their full potential back into the world. I use the arts and creativity as a catalyst for positive growth, enjoyment and a unifying presence in my classroom.

My growth as a teacher and as a creative are intertwined, so much so that now it's difficult to discern one from the other. And why should I? I can no longer divide myself into Teacher, Singer, Songwriter, Mirror. I am all of these things.

As my chapter comes to an end, I wonder: Has this work acted as a mirror? Has it shown you pieces of your own sweet calling? Has it given you a little insight into your own soul?

On the day students work on their first piece of artwork, which is always a bit intimidating, I take my guitar and start with a little risk-taking of my own. I share a song called, "I'll Be There" and a slideshow of former students' simple, elegant sculptures, including my own, called "Mirror."

I'LL BE THERE
Take a look at yourself in my mirror
Awaken yourself if you dare
And if you carry a tune in your heart from tonight
The song gives me wings
I'll be there.

Chapter 20

THE MISSING LINK

Teaching the Creative Problem Solving Process

Cyndi Burnett

Background: Beginning With Myself

The right phrase, at the right time, can change one's life. I experienced this firsthand, while sitting in my first doctoral class, The Contemplative Practitioner, at the University of Toronto. Guest professor Dr. David Hunt sat in front of the class and shared his various experiences as an applied psychologist and researcher. I can vividly recall his gentle recommendation, "When you think about the research you want to pursue, stop looking for theories on which to base your work. Instead, begin with yourself. Your personal and practical knowledge will create the foundation, and the richness of discovery will start with what you already know."

For me, this was an epiphany moment because my education (or training) had generally emphasized that what others knew was more important than what I knew. At that moment, I made the decision to focus my research on my own experiences. That decision compelled me to uncover the missing elements in the cognitive, rational, and semantic approaches to Creative Problem Solving, something I had been studying and teaching for years, but which rarely provided me comfort. However, before I go any further, let me begin with myself.

Cyndi Burnett, Ed.D., is an assistant professor and the Director of Distance Education Programs at the International Center for Studies in Creativity at Buffalo State. Since joining the faculty in 2001, she has taught, lead, and facilitated in the education, arts, and business sectors locally, nationally, and internationally. Dr. Burnett holds a bachelor's degree in theatre and dance, a master's degree in creative studies, and an Ed.D in curriculum, teaching and learning from the University of Toronto. Her research interests include the following: holistic approaches to Creative Problem Solving, the creative processes of artists, and the use of creative models and techniques in children.

My Life as an Artist

As a young child, I was restless and emotional. My mother caught on quickly and subsequently enrolled me in dance classes—one place where she knew I wouldn't have to sit still. Each Thursday evening, I entered into a state of bliss as I conquered new ways to move my body and express my emotions. I found a world of play in performing. My dance shoes were conduits for my imagination. I would perform for anyone who would watch and would imagine a make-believe audience of friends and family as I danced around the house. Often, I would go out to the bus stop a half hour early and dance for people as they drove by. When it was raining at the bus stop, I would perform my own version of *Singing in the Rain*. And, although I had four older brothers and sisters, my imaginative family was the Von Trapp Family Singers from *The Sound of Music*, who, at any given moment in time, would bust into song and dance with me.

I was an artistically talented child, full of emotion and with whom it was difficult to reason. Logic was not particularly valuable to me because I typically followed what my gut told me to do. When confronted with problems, I would choose what felt right, rather than what logically made sense on paper. It was my intuition that led me to an early career as a professional actress, despite the logical naysayers who told me it could not be done. In my heart, anything was possible. And, with my intense passion for the stage, coupled with hard work and dedication, I entered into Actors' Equity by landing a first National Broadway tour on my first day in New York City. To the outside world, my future career was now mapped out.

Unfortunately, my dream of being an actress did not match the reality. Most of my time touring the country was spent sleeping on a tour bus. Arriving at a new city meant a brief burst of activity, as the show was delivered, followed by a return to the hypnotic hum of wheels on tarmac. I felt my creativity being squashed by the humdrum routine of performing the same show over and over. For me, the stage had lost its magic. After touring 89 cities, I decided to take a break and head home to Buffalo, NY. At the airport I picked up a copy of *Time* magazine to pass the time on the flight. On the cover was a photograph of the two boys who were responsible for the Columbine massacre. The story had a profound effect on me. Tears streamed down my face. I found their actions utterly incomprehensible, and yet I knew they were neither the first, nor—as time has shown—the last to express their madness in this way. By the time I landed, my intuition had, once again, turned my life in a new direction. I decided to leave the theatre because I felt the intense desire to find more meaning in my life. Unfortunately, even though my goal was clear, the means were quite opaque. And, because I lived in my emotions, I found myself moving into a state of depression. I was caught between knowing what I wanted, and finding myself unable to chart a path forward. My emotions allowed me to be aware of the dissonance in my life, but they offered no support in developing a strategy for resolution. I was left feeling alone and despondent.

My state persisted for several months. Eventually, during a lunch with a friend, I admitted, "I don't know what I want to do anymore!" Fortunately, she didn't offer me the usual sympathetic platitudes. Instead, she said "Stop asking what you want do with your life. What do you want to learn about?" Learning as a route to self-discovery! Obvious, in hindsight, but until that point, I had been expecting inspiration to provide a fully formed path. My friend's suggestion seemed to be offering a detour, but I was intrigued. What was even more interesting was that I knew the answer. Without hesitation, I responded, "Creativity." THAT was it! I was ecstatic.

My life-long passion for the stage had evaporated because I had unwittingly exchanged creativity for simple reproduction. Now I had the chance to revoke the bargain. But, where could I learn about creativity? Was it even something that could be taught? For me, like many of my friends, creativity was something one did. There was no mechanism; ideas just magically appeared. Granted, this was usually after some painful episode of "artist's block," but the point was that creativity just happened. So, the thought that I might be able to learn to overcome those blocks, and even help others to do the same, was enticing.

Two days later, through a series of serendipitous events, I was sitting in my first graduate course at the only place in the world (at the time) where someone could study a scientific and deliberate approach to creativity—the International Center for Studies in Creativity (ICSC) at Buffalo State, in my hometown, Buffalo, NY.

The Introduction to Creative Problem Solving

Entering the scientific world of creativity at ICSC induced two conflicting states of mind: bliss and confusion. Bliss in knowing that creativity was a field that one could actually study, and confusion because my classmates and professors were so different from me. They were amazing people, but they were teachers, business consultants, marketing directors, and engineers.

I couldn't understand where all of the artists were hiding. Wasn't creativity, fundamentally, an artistic endeavor?

My first graduate class introduced me to the Creative Problem Solving (CPS) process—a deliberate, cognitive, rational, semantic problem-solving methodology with a 50-year history of development and research.[195] At the core of the process was the idea of a dynamic balance between divergent and convergent thinking.[196] CPS aims to carefully manage this balance through each of the defined stages of its methodology. Although the terminology was new to me, I did recognize this dichotomy in my own life, so learning about it, in this abstract manner, didn't feel entirely alien to me. It was also fascinating to see the processes broken into constituent and logical parts. For example, divergent thinking was often viewed through the lens of Guilford's factors—fluency, flexibility, problem sensitivity, and originality.[197] Guilford suggested that these skills assisted in acquiring quantity, diverse categories, and novel ideas. In contrast, convergent thinking skills consisted of envisioning, evaluating, screening, sorting, prioritizing, supporting, developing, and evaluating.[198]

Equally enlightening was my introduction to a host of deliberate tools that could be used at each of the various stages of the process. These CPS tools included brainstorming, highlighting, ladder of abstraction, evaluation matrix, and forced connections, to name a few.[199]

Learning CPS empowered me because its methodical, scientific approach gave me a sense of control. It seemed as though I could tackle any problem and develop a creative solution. I took to the approach with great enthusiasm. Almost overnight, my bedroom walls became covered in sticky notes and sticky dots, the basic materials for practicing divergent and convergent thinking tools. I also felt more grounded using this systematic approach, because it was so different from the rapid, emotional problem-solving process I had previously relied on.

As I began to open myself up to learn about the scientific perspectives on creativity, and the CPS process, I found that, unintentionally, I was quieting the emotional, intuitive, and artistic voice inside of me. She just didn't fit in. Although I knew that my new self wasn't quite me, I was happy to be lifting myself out of a dark state, and into a newfound light.

Organic Creativity in the Teacher, the Classroom, and the School

Intuition: The Missing Link

Over the course of my studies, the faculty recognized my enthusiasm for the topic. Upon graduation, I was asked to join the Creative Studies department as a lecturer. I was excited to be teaching the subject I loved, but, at the same time, I felt as if there was something missing, particularly when it came to teaching the CPS process. Many of my students connected with the process, but, to me, it often felt as if their solutions were superficial. I desperately wanted to achieve the level of emotional connection that I had experienced as a theatre student. Creativity, in the studio, was often painful, but ultimately emotionally fulfilling. Additionally, in an effort to stay aligned with the Center's cognitive orientation, I felt as if my teaching was also operating at a superficial level. Clearly, something was not right.

What I didn't notice, at the time, was that I was living a dual existence. During the day, I would teach—cognitively oriented—CPS courses, while at night, I would work as a teaching artist and choreographer. To the casual observer, the roles would seem completely congruent, because they were both focused on the creative process. But, for me, they were worlds apart. Despite this gulf, I simply did not notice the contradiction. When I would choreograph a performance, I wouldn't bring out my notepads and sticky dots or do an evaluation matrix. Instead, I would put on the music and let my body move in the direction that felt right. And, despite the split in beliefs and perspectives, I found great passion and joy in both areas of creativity.

After several years of teaching in higher education, I decided to pursue a terminal degree to secure a tenured position. My challenge was that I didn't know exactly what I wanted to study. On a whim, I decided to attend the Holistic Education Conference at the Ontario Institute for Studies in Education (OISE) at the University of Toronto. The conference was fantastic. It had attracted an audience of thoughtful, interesting educators who looked at the world in holistic terms. They offered a perspective on education in which analysis and intuition were equally important. Lightbulbs went off in my head. May I say, "Aha!"? I suddenly realized that intuition was wholly missing from the CPS process, and that I had been deliberately silencing one of the most important aspects of my natural, organic, and creative process! I immediately knew this was where I needed to focus my research.

I began to use my classes as a laboratory to explore what holistic Creative Problem Solving might look, sound, feel, and even smell like in action. Suitably emboldened, I began to experiment with any intuitive tools and techniques I could find. However, I quickly became aware that these effects were hit or miss because I didn't have a clear understanding of what tools to use, when to use them, or why the tools worked for some and not others. I felt my research question gradually narrowing.

What Is the Role of Intuition in CPS?

After some contemplation, I realized that my first challenge was to establish whether I was alone. Were there others in the field who recognized the importance of intuition and its absence from the Creative Problem Solving methodology? I decided to develop a questionnaire directed at the International Center for Studies in Creativity alumni. My assumption was that these would be people who both understood creativity and probably used the tools and techniques in their work. The results were striking. Out of 100 participants, 99 agreed that there was a role for intuition in CPS. The hundredth person stated, "not sure . . . this is something worth investigating."[200] However, despite this ringing endorsement, only 50 participants said they made it a practice to foster the use of intuition or used deliberate intuitive tools and techniques in their CPS sessions.

I felt befuddled by these results. Why was there such a significant gap? How could almost all of the participants state that there was a role, but only half be fostering it in their CPS sessions? I spent a year grazing the data, and discussing the topic with friends and colleagues. Eventually, I concluded that the most obvious explanation was also the most realistic. Many of the participants simply didn't know how to integrate intuition into their CPS sessions. However, this shortage of support hadn't hindered everyone. Fifty percent of the survey participants *did* foster intuition, which meant that my next challenge was to distinguish how they did this.

Returning to my data set, I sifted the responses, and gradually realized that three major intuitive themes existed. I have come to categorize them as: ubiquitous, passive, and active intuition.

Ubiquitous Intuition

Much of the literature on intuition describes people's experiences in the form of "and then I had this miraculous insight." In fact, some of my respondents talked about intuition in similar terms. Not surprisingly, this has tended to mythologize the experience, and also present it as a distinct step in the process. In my mind, it was almost as if intuition were a character in a play, arriving just at the point that the protagonists had given up hope, solving the problem, receiving all the credit, and then leaving. The protagonists, while very grateful, would also be irritated that intuition hadn't been around to help with all of the boring grunt work!

However, as I trawled through the responses, I realized that some of my respondents weren't describing intuition in that way at all. They saw it as cognition's equal, but distinct, partner—not a step in a process, but rather an element that was present throughout the entire endeavor. As one respondent stated, "I feel that intuition is the breath and CPS is the body. One needs unhindered deep circular breaths to energize the body into action. By giving people permission to 'trust their gut' and use all information available to them."[201]

These responses gave me two great insights. First, I realized that in our haste to reach a solution, we often do not allow people the time and space to examine their emotions and gut feelings when working through challenges. It's almost as if every time the intuition "character" is about to speak, we skip their lines and move on. Second, many of the respondents who were actively employing intuition in their work had recognized that it was ubiquitous, in the same way as logic. In other words, they expected intuition to play an important role in the process and were not surprised when it appeared.

Passive Intuition

Expecting intuition to appear is an important state of mind, but it appears to leave the emergence of insights entirely to chance. Could more be done to encourage the actor to speak? One theme that many respondents identified was tapping into the power of incubation. People reported becoming aware of their insights when engaged in unrelated activities such as walking, gardening, meditation, or just making a drink. The insights arrived unbidden, and revealed themselves when their minds were slightly distracted, but not so engaged in another task, as to mask their arrival.

A key point in people's reports was that this was more than just accidental incubation. People who recognized the importance of intuition consciously designed their problem-solving sessions to allow for incubation. My colleague, Janice Francisco, and I described this deliberate strategy as passive intuition, and defined it as "creating the space for intuitive insights to make themselves known through the use of incubation and excursions."[202] As is so often the case, the importance of this approach had already been identified. In fact, as long ago as 1926, Wallas included the idea in his four-stage model (preparation, incubation, illumination, verification), and explicitly advocated that time and space should be allocated for incubation, in order to support the generation of subsequent illumination, which would be described as insight.[203]

However, despite its reported value, there is a problem with passive intuition. The problem is that, in our very action-oriented culture, people can find it difficult to make a distinction between passive intuition and just wasting time. It's not that they dispute the importance of intuition. The logic is irrefutable, but people can experience significant emotional angst when asked to not do anything.

Notwithstanding this barrier, I have shifted my classes from the constant dynamism and liveliness that typically defines a CPS session, to a balance between the dynamic and reflective nature of solving problems. And, given the extensive research on the benefits of incubation, we, as educators, need to find ways to legitimize this inaction as an action, to teach our students the importance of taking time away from a problem and not rushing to a solution.[204]

Here are some of the ways that my colleagues and I have used incubation when solving problems with students:

- ♣ When students become stuck on what to do next, ask them to take an incubation break.
- ♣ Ask students to do short bursts of exercise in between divergence and convergence.
- ♣ Put the problem away until the next day.
- ♣ Go for a quiet walk outside of the building.
- ♣ Don't try to do too much in one session. Instead, give students time to reflect and think about their processes.

Each of these ideas is obvious, but I have been amazed at the effect they have had on students when they are applied systematically. Of course, before you adopt any of my suggestions, I strongly encourage you to follow the words of David Hunt, and "begin with yourself." Build in time for incubation to your routine, and decide if it helps you.

Active Intuition

Passive intuition is a powerful approach. But, for a proportion of my respondents, waiting for the muse to speak was not enough. They identified a range of techniques that they employed to deliberately engage their intuition in the overall process. Perhaps not surprisingly, we named this general approach "active intuition" and defined it as "recruiting intuitive capabilities through the use of deliberate tools and techniques that honor gut feelings and blink-of-an-eye insight."[205] In addition, active intuition encompasses trying to deliberately tap into the unconscious through reflection, mindfulness, and "visionizing."[206]

There are a number of tools and techniques that we, as educators, can use to help our students actively engage their intuition. The tools I have successfully applied include the following: visualization and imagery, artistic tools, the use of analogies, centering tools such as meditation and labyrinths, and the deliberate focus on an intuitive response (i.e., what does your gut say?). I also developed a data-gathering tool called Facts, Feelings, and Hunches (and unanswered questions) to help overcome the "tunnel vision" challenge I sometimes encountered with my students. I describe the tool below.

What Are Facts, Feelings and Hunches?

Facts, Feelings and Hunches (and unanswered questions)[207] is a data collection tool that helps people look at all aspects of the challenge (see Figure 18.1). When I use this tool with my students, we write a challenge in the center of the circle. Next, we work around the circle to answer all of the facts regarding the question, followed by the feelings and emotions, and then the intuitive hunches. Finally, we explore all of the unanswered questions relating to the challenge. These three pieces fit together to form a complete circle and to help to build a comprehensive picture regarding the challenge at hand.

From Process to Person

When I embarked on my research, I was trying to find a way to give intuition a role within the CPS *process*. It was an attempt to bring the process into, what I felt, was a more balanced place, and to provide a way for artistic types to engage with CPS. However, as I continued to explore the data, I was struck by the fact that many participants described intuition from the perspective of the *person* involved in the CPS process, rather than as an element within the actual process. For example, one respondent said, "Yes there is a role for this, much like the role of natural ability for leaders. I think it can be taught, learned, as well as something some people are born with. Being

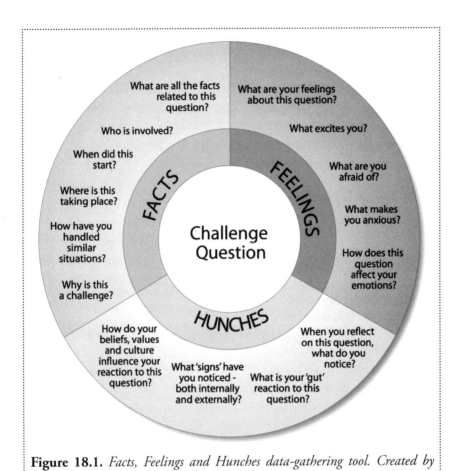

Figure 18.1. *Facts, Feelings and Hunches data-gathering tool. Created by Cyndi Burnett. All rights reserved.*

intuitive is a gift and a skill."[208] At one level, one could simply say that this is what any good educator would do, but I think that would be dismissing the comments too easily. I believe what the respondents were saying was that intuition is a skill that exists outside of any process, and can be applied as one chooses. Furthermore, bringing intuition into the CPS process means not only integrating it into the process itself, but also more importantly, into the people involved in the process. This was a significant shift in my perspective of the problem.

As if to reinforce my insight, I came across the following quote written by one of the originators of CPS, Sid Parnes:

I contemplate a fourth generation of deliberate creativity development processes by the turn of the century. My vision of it is the blending of the third generation (spontaneous imagery supported within the solid CPS structure) applied together with self-healing technology toward the goal of high-level wellness—not merely physical wellness, but psychological, sociological, political, and spiritual wellness as well—moving toward what Maslow meant by the self-actualizing person.[209]

One might think of this as a creative problem-solving mechanism for achieving human happiness, rather than just focused upon finding new names for cookies. For me, it was another example of stumbling across the right phrase at the right time. It provided the bridge that ultimately linked my views of the artistic and scientific perspectives on creativity.

Intuitive and Affective Skills

Improving the human condition is clearly a lofty, and worthwhile, goal. And, at the same time, I feel that academics must also stay grounded in the day-to-day reality of the communities we serve. Or, to put it another way, how might these insights affect the way an educator engages with her class on a cold, damp Monday morning? Fortunately, theory and practice are both advancing in this area.

A few years before my realization, my colleagues, Gerard Puccio, Mary Murdock, and Marie Mance[210] developed a new version of CPS—the Creative Problem Solving Thinking Skills Model (TSM). This model focused much more on the thinking skills required throughout the process rather than the process itself. The thinking skills they described included visionary thinking, strategic thinking, ideational thinking, evaluative thinking, contextual thinking, and tactical thinking. Essentially, they argued that once you learn these skills, and know when to use them, then they become a natural part of any creative problem solving process. Additionally, the TSM described a number of affective skills. These have been defined as "ways in which we deal with attitudinal and emotional aspects of learning, including feelings, appreciation, enthusiasm, motivation, attitudes and values."[211] These affective skills included dreaming, sensing gaps, playfulness, avoiding premature closure, sensitivity to environment, tolerance for risk, curiosity, openness to novelty, tolerance for complexity, and tolerance for ambiguity.

When I compared the affective skills list with the descriptions of intuition in my data, I noticed a significant overlap. Basically, my respondents were saying that the intuitive person exhibited all of the affective skills identified in the TSM. However, there was one intuitive skill that was not described in the TSM, and that was mindfulness.

Mindfulness

Mindfulness is a term that is generally associated with being in the present moment, and deliberately slowing down. A more formal definition was suggested in an excellent article titled, "Mindfulness: A Proposed Definition." The authors, 11 doctors, collaborated to develop a universal definition of this word.[212] What they created was a two-component definition:

1. Mindfulness begins by bringing awareness to current experience—observing and attending to the changing field of thoughts, feelings and sensations from moment to moment—by regulating the focus of attention

2. The second component involves adopting a particular orientation toward one's experiences in the present moment, an orientation that is characterized by curiosity, openness and acceptance[213]

Reading their definition, I was immediately struck by how their language elegantly linked the two worlds of intuition and cognitive CPS. Without the management of one's awareness, it would be very difficult to hear the quiet voices of intuition that many of my participants had described. Equally, the orientation toward curiosity, openness, and acceptance seemed to be essential if one were going to avoid the trap of intuition acting as the tacit censor of one's thoughts. The concept of mindfulness therefore seemed to be a critical enabling factor to bring intuition into deliberate creativity, and thereby produce a holistic CPS. But how might one become more mindful?

Well, a substantial body of literature exists on this topic. Jon Kabat-Zinn has been a major contributor to the field, and according to Kabat-Zinn, mindfulness requires us "to pause in our experience long enough to let the present moment sink in; long enough to actually feel the present moment, to see it in its fullness, to hold it in awareness and thereby come to know and understand it better."[214]

In practical terms, as educators, I believe we need to deliberately build time into our classes so that our students can be mindful about what they are learning. This doesn't have to be complex, or time consuming. For example, if your students were learning about apples, ask them to spend 5 minutes exploring what an apple looks like, feels like, and tastes like, while looking for new things that they might not have noticed about apples before. These small steps will help to make mindful contemplation a part of their thinking skills.

Conclusion

I started my journey as an artist who engaged with her creativity exclusively through an emotional channel. My love of creativity led me to study it formally and opened my eyes to a scientific approach to the topic. Although to start with these two schools appeared to be in opposition, I have come to see them as essential pillars that support the development of a truly holistic approach toward problem solving. Logic and intuition are not at odds with each other, but simply different aspects of a whole person.

Some decisions are led with our hearts, some with our heads, and some with our inner selves, but fundamentally, I believe that we are intended to live integrated lives, in which all aspects of ourselves are combined in concert. I have seen the profound and meaningful impact of integrating ubiquitous, active, and passive intuition into the CPS process, especially when it is accompanied by the nurturing and development of intuitive and affective skills. Our goal, as educators, is ultimately to help our students be better equipped with the fundamental skills they need to deal with the complex and multifaceted problems they will experience throughout life.

It is my hope that by helping my students to move beyond the purely cognitive approaches to life, it will allow them to unravel the complexities of the challenges they face, creating deeper meaning with themselves and the world around them.

Chapter 21

THAT "UH-OH" FEELING

Organic Creativity in School Counseling

Maria Balotta

Introduction

I often reflect on my experiences as a school counselor. Deeply committed to my chosen task, I remain of the belief that I am doing what I was born to do. I am exactly where I need to be. I learned long ago that there are no irrelevant jobs in education. We each make a difference. The question is, what type of difference do we aim to make and do we hit the mark?

School counseling, formerly known as guidance counseling, became my chosen path even before I knew its name. It was a school counselor who helped me name my career of choice. This was not in a formal counseling session. Indeed, effective school counseling interactions can take place anywhere within the confines of the school building and beyond.[215] She was a young counselor on a bus trip just making conversation with a teenager. I, the teenager: She, the sage. She just asked me about my career aspirations—a simple question in an informal setting. And I said, "I want to be a school counselor, like you."

As I look back at that night, I wonder what made Eva ask about my career dreams. Did her intuition guide her, me, or both of us to that pivotal exchange? Four years ago, I saw Eva and approached her, expressing my grat-

School counselor and motivational speaker **Maria Balotta, Ed.D.**, taught second language learners in Puerto Rico until 1989 when she relocated to Cleveland, OH. In 1997, she began working as a school counselor. Maria was the only school counselor from Ohio to serve on the National School Counseling Standards Committee for the National Board for Professional Teaching Standards. She has a doctorate from Ashland University where she received the award for outstanding graduate student in 2011. Dr. Balotta is the school counselor at Facing History New Tech, an innovative high school in the Cleveland Metropolitan School District, and the only one of its kind in the U.S.

itude for that inspiring interaction of many years ago. I was at the end of the dissertation process. She was at the onset of hers. She said I was an inspiration; for a moment, the encouraged became the encourager and the inspired became an inspiration.

The Population I Serve

I am a school counselor in an urban setting in Cleveland, OH. I was one of the teachers recruited from Puerto Rico in the decades of the 1980s and 1990s.[216] I came to Cleveland and taught English language learners (ELLs). In 1997, I was hired as the "bilingual counselor" for a school serving a large percentage of Latino students who were ELLs. The counselor holding the position before had resigned. I was a certified school counselor and was offered the job. I declined. I would not abandon my first-grade class in the middle of the year.

The director warned that if I waited until the summer, I would then have to interview and, with my lack of counseling experience, I might lose the job to a seasoned counselor. He expected multiple candidates to apply. I said, "If this job is mine, no one will beat me to it." My response felt right. My intuition told me that I was making the right decision. I felt content and at peace.

The summer arrived, and I was granted an interview at the middle school. The new principal was looking for energetic and creative people. The school had a terrible reputation in the district and needed a quick turnaround. Despite a couple of people on the interview team who did not like my lack of counseling experience, they hired me. The time was right. My initiation into school counseling happened in a large urban middle school serving students as diverse as the array of issues that plagued them.

From the inception of my career as a school counselor, it is an understatement to say that following my intuition has led me to be in the right place at the right time. Sometimes lives have been spared because I have stopped to listen to the inner voice that points me to the not-so-obvious signs that my senses may miss.

Attending to the Voice of Intuition in Student-Counselor Interactions

My school district sits in a city designated as one of the poorest in our country. For this reason, all of our students receive free breakfast and lunch. The students I have served through the years have brought a wealth of talent and a variety of experiences to our interactions. Extreme cases can be disheartening and sometimes inspiring.

I have learned that despite rocky beginnings and environments devoid of nurturing and support, students can find their resilient selves and overcome the limitations placed on them by less than desirable family and/or community environments.[217] The Sun of School (on Piirto's Pyramid of Talent Development) has a compensatory effect for individuals for whom the Sun of Home and the Sun of Community and Culture fail to shine brightly.[218] I believe that shutting my ears to the voice of intuition is too costly a proposition for the students I purport to serve. Countless times throughout my career I have averted tragedy just by heeding its voice. What follows here are several case examples of gifted and talented students with whom my intuition helped me intervene. I serve all students, but given the focus of this book, I will discuss those whose intellectual talents pointed them to college. In most ways, all of my students of ethnic and language diversity face similar challenges.[219]

Luzmarie

Luzmarie, a bright Latina student, came to us from a middle school where she had attended classes for the gifted and talented. Her mother had transferred her out of there because she was being bullied. This parent had allegedly tried to get the school to address her bullying allegations to no avail. Luzmarie came to us in a state of apprehension. Her emotions, masked by a flat affect at worst and a controlled anger at best, stood in the way of her ability to connect with adults and peers. Teachers wondered how they could make a connection with a student who, while intelligent, refused their efforts to build rapport with her. They observed that she always traveled the halls alone.

I sought Luzmarie out, taking advantage of every chance to engage in positive contact with her. The first time she smiled back at me, I experienced intense joy. Little by little, Luzmarie began to communicate more in class and let her teachers see what she was able to do. Her academic improvement made her the recipient of compliments from teachers. Now a contributing member to the learning process, Luzmarie had finally made a successful transition. Suddenly, she took a turn for the worst. Her sullen and dark disposition returned. One morning as I headed to a classroom on business, I saw Luzmarie in the hallway. Her hair looked like someone had taken a pair of scissors and gone about cutting it with complete abandon. She wore red sweatpants and a dingy white hooded sweatshirt. She headed directly toward me but walked right past me in the direction opposite to where her class was at that time. I called to her and turned to follow her.

Luzmarie's demeanor seemed calculated and cold. In an instant, I felt a chilly stream rise up my spine. Something was terribly wrong. I asked Luz what was bothering her. Head hung low, she nodded and whispered, "Nothing." I said, "Okay, so neither one of us believes that, right?" A directive counselor, more often than not I will make a request rather than ask a question. I said, "Walk with me to my office and there you can tell me what's going on and how I can help without putting your business out there where someone could hear us." She complied. We entered into my office and she sat down. I told her how I did not want to pry and that I could not make her tell me what was going on, but that I was getting an "uh-oh" feeling. I said, "I feel like something is really wrong, but I cannot put my finger on it. Help me understand."

Silence in school counseling settings is largely underrated. We are frequently expected to provide brief counseling and make referrals. With caseloads upward of the size recommended by experts[220], there is no time available for long sessions with students. Of course, many times the agenda behind that is that the counselor is then free to engage in noncounseling administrative tasks that have little to do with the three domains of a comprehensive school counseling program.

I told Luz that I did not believe in coincidences and that I knew deep inside there was a reason why I had run into her. I said,

> No matter how bad what you're feeling seems, it's not the end of the world. It's okay to ask for help. Remember, you can tell me anything and I don't have to tell anyone unless you're being harmed in some way, planning to harm yourself, another person, or another person's property. If that is the case, then I have to tell, but I promise I won't leave you alone.

Luz raised her head and looked straight at me as if examining my thoughts. She told me how some girls had started persecuting her during lunch and trying to fight her after school. She did not want to fight. There were three of them, and she was only one. Allegedly, one of the girls threatening to jump her was related to one of her bullies at the other school. She felt afraid, and with reason. They had looked for her on the way home from school the night before, but she had hidden in her English teacher's classroom. They left when they couldn't find her. Luz walked home that afternoon in terror. I could see hopelessness in her eyes. That is when I said, "Wow! I am so sorry to hear that. No one should have to come to and go from school feeling that way. I can see how someone may be so upset that they might decide to defend themselves. Luz, is that how you feel?"

Her hand quickly moved to her waist as if I had just reminded her of something there. I said,

> Is there something there? If there is, please give it to me. I cannot promise not to tell. I have to follow the rules of my job and I have to keep you and others safe, but I will insist that they take into consideration that you have been honest and cooperative in giving up whatever it is you are hiding. You're so smart—a bright light in a world that can seem so dark at times. Don't let these girls make you a victim by doing something that will take away the future you can have.

Luz lifted her sweatshirt and turned out her pant waist to reveal a bright red switchblade, its jagged edge five inches long. I remained calm and asked for divine protection. I extended my hand and she placed it there. I took the weapon, placed it in my drawer, came around, and with my hand on her shoulder told her how proud she should be of herself. I called the principal and told her what had happened as per district protocol. Luz did get expelled for the rest of the year, but the bullies were dealt with by the administration.

The last time I saw Luz and her mother, they were cleaning out her locker. The parent was not happy with the outcome of the expulsion hearing at the district headquarters, but was glad that Luzmarie had not followed through with her intent of pursuing these girls and hurting them before they could hurt her. Luz was able to start fresh the next year and then later successfully move to high school. That she had voluntarily relinquished the knife had worked in her favor. I lost touch with Luz after those events.

When I think of this case and others, I often wonder how many lives could be saved and disasters thwarted just by really looking at our students and by tuning into and following the voice within. Intuition is a gift that we human beings possess. Some may call it instinct, but instinct to me is more primal and much less refined. Our instincts, I believe, can put us in danger while intuition, if heeded, can serve as a life preserver; sometimes our own and sometimes another's.

Elias

Fall. This season that is known more for reaping than for sowing and as the absence of hope reborn, is indeed a season of beginnings. Aren't they all? It was in the fall of some years ago that I met Elias. Elias looked like a character taken out of a modern day situation comedy. His features told more of his Middle Eastern heritage than of his Latino roots. Elias had been born stuck in between two cultures whose traditions and deep-rooted religious precepts stood diametrically opposed to the identity that he had discovered inside.

Happy-go-lucky but a quiet sort, Elias spent his time buried in books. Students and teachers alike held Elias in high regard. There was no doubt that this young man had the capacity to become anything he wanted to. Still, there was this calm unrest that I sensed within him, and I wondered what his dark green eyes were hiding. During the countless times we exchanged words, our brief conversations always ended on a positive note. A handsome young fellow, Elias was clean cut and fashionably attired. Although no obvious visual cues informed my perception, I wondered if he was struggling with his sexual identity, afraid of what it would mean to come out to his parents and others.

Elias dreamed of becoming a world-known architect. He was academically talented in math and science and did very well in all other subjects. His test scores were outstanding. The years progressed and before Elias knew it, the spring of his eighth-grade year arrived. He would be finishing middle school having secured a place in the honor roll and with many choices for high school. Things were looking great for him, or so it would seem.

It was a chilly spring day. On days like this, nature cannot hide the signs creeping up from the ground and springing from tree branches everywhere as if someone has let out a beautiful secret. One can smell, see, and feel the changes, and the promise of warmer weather hangs in sight but is barely reachable. On that day, my colleague and I had decided to leave the building for lunch. We opted for a quick sandwich from a popular fast food place. We drove back to school and sat in the parking lot eating and talking, all the while admiring the beautiful day.

Upon our return to the building, we each headed to our respective offices and our agendas for the afternoon. As my friend Michelle arrived in her office, a teacher brought Elias in and told Michelle that Elias had told her that he wanted to die. She brought him to my office first, and in my absence, decided to take him to see my colleague and friend Michelle. Michelle called me before escorting him to my office.

I wish that I could say that upon laying eyes on Elias I heard voices speak wisdom in my ear, but I did not. No life-altering words of wisdom entered the realm of my consciousness. I only felt a jolt of impending danger hit me and my mind uttered, "Uh-oh." The danger I sensed was not personal. A bright flame, I felt, could be snuffed if this situation was mishandled.

I interviewed Elias and followed the district protocol for student crises. I spent every minute with Elias while the principal made her calls. I asked about family history of suicidal ideation, whether or not he had a plan, and all the customary questions that go with making a judgment about a person's intention of as well as access to carrying out a plan to commit suicide. Still, I sensed that a piece of information was missing. What was the force behind his intent? What had triggered this?

It occurred to me that his perception of a perfect world might give me some indication of what he thought was missing. In my experience, suicidal ideation seems to always be related to something that the individual feels he or she is lacking. Perceived lacks of freedom, love, or acceptance are three top reasons behind the suicidal intent of students I have worked with. As a teen, I myself experienced suicidal thoughts and remember the desolation and hopelessness that comes with being in the darkest of places that I believe anyone can experience. I asked the question and it elicited the response that I needed to inform my approach in helping Elias.

Elias said, "In a perfect world, my parents would accept me just as I am." I explored the meaning of his statement. I asked what about him that he thought his parents did not accept. He said, "Who I am inside. I can't help what I am. I've tried so hard!" As he uttered those words, he sobbed and bowed his head. I asked, "What else is there?" Elias whispered, "I'm gay." Silence filled my office as he heard himself tell an adult for the first time ever this secret that seemed to torment him. He looked me in the eyes as if trying to discern whether or not I was shocked and whether or not I was accepting. Perhaps he was testing what it would feel like to tell an authority figure, or maybe it had nothing to do with my role and everything to do with being able to say it out loud in an institution where conventional practice views homosexuality as taboo.

I smiled and told him that there was nothing wrong with him. "Being gay does not make you a lesser person," I said. "Thank you for trusting me with your truth." I asked him what other clues, aside from his family's cultural traditions, led him to believe that his parents would not be accepting of him. He spoke of his father's joking about homosexuals and how he had said that if he ever found out that a son of his was gay, he would beat the gay[221] out of him and then disown him. His sons were to be and act like machos.[222] I assured Elias that if he wanted to tell his parents and needed my support, I would be there for him and I would face them with him. I also promised him that I would not tell them unless he wanted me to. He opted not to have them know.

When his parents came in, we had a discussion about Elias' feelings regarding wanting to kill himself. I could sense from the conversation with the parents that they were not ready to hear their son tell them about his sexual identity. Elias was right in his assessment of the situation. It was not the appropriate time to broach the subject with the parents. We talked about their son needing support and help and how he needed to be seen by health care professionals in the context of a clinical setting. At first, the young man's father refused to take him to the hospital. My colleague and I used every argument that we could think of to convince the father that his son needed urgent care. The mother was present, but she had taken the role of silent partner, deferring to her husband's decision. From a cultural perspective, her behavior did not shock me.

The father was a strong-willed male, and we were all women. I knew this presented a challenge. Our principal was a Latina and very frail. Her assistant was a Caucasian woman treading with excess caution so she would be perceived as culturally sensitive, which rendered her as empowered as a person walking barefoot on broken glass. They seemed intimidated by this man with his dark mustache and rugged features, his skin burned with the wind of age.

It occurred to me that if reason would not save the day, then certainly meeting the parent's dominant energy with a language that he could understand might do it. The language of authority might work. It had to—even if he was not accustomed to women taking a dominant stance. I personally did not have any authority over this parent, but decided that as agents of the district, we had some leverage. I said, "Sir, I need you to either take Elias to the hospital or sign a statement that you are refusing to take him there." He refused. I looked at the investigative officer/security officer and then right into the father's eyes and said, "Unless you sign a promissory statement that you are leaving from here directly to the emergency room with your son, I cannot release him to you and will have to call on the Department for Children and Family Services for assistance."

There was nothing else I could say. It was now close to 7 in the evening and we were at a stalemate. The man looked at me, and I held his gaze. He looked at his wife, then his son, and then back at me and said, "Fine, where do I sign?" I typed up a note that stated that the parent was agreeing to take Elias directly to the emergency room and that he would then bring proof to us the next day. We completed the crisis plan with the father's cooperation, and he followed through with his promise. That night, Elias's life was saved.

Almost 5 years later, I walked into a school building in a suburb not too far from our district. From somewhere in the hallway, I heard a voice call my name. I turned around to see an older, more sophisticated version of Elias. He hugged me and asked about school. He said, "Thanks Ms. You saved my life." He was now a high school senior ready to graduate. Having been admitted to the out-of-state university of his dreams, Elias was ready to take on the world. His parents had moved out of the city and were doing much better generally speaking. Elias had come out to his mother, and while his father was not ready to openly admit it, he had stopped making the comments and threats that had driven his son to believe at one time that he would be better off dead.

I believe that resilience is possible even in the presence of depression. In my days as a school counselor, I have dealt with suicidal ideation more times than I care to count, but I gladly accept the challenge because I know from experience that the pain is real, deep, and survivable.

Ninoshka

Not all cases are the same. Generalizations, in my opinion, can inflict unnecessary pain on a student who is already hurting. Sometimes the only information one has leaves many interrogatives and a minefield of emotions to address while trying not to send the student into a deeper sense of despair. Such was the case of Ninoshka.

On a morning of a day for which I had a full agenda, one of the teachers walked Ninoshka to my office. The girl had broken down in tears in the middle of her class. She was upset, claiming that her mother called her names like "bitch." She claimed that she found herself fantasizing about killing everyone in the house and then running away and killing herself in some secluded place where by the time she was found, she would already be dead. Her plan included staging the scene so that the authorities would think that the murderer had kidnapped her.

I informed the principal, and she called the crisis help center at the central office. She also called the parent. The trigger for the student's suicidal attempt came from home. She did not feel loved. I suspected that the mother would not be very cooperative if she felt like she was being blamed as the cause of her daughter's suicidal and homicidal thoughts. I knew that we needed her mother to work with us to get the student to the hospital. Ninoshka's counselor from another agency joined us.

Ninoshka's mom had given birth to her when she was 16 years of age. By the time Ninoshka came to us, her mother had six children and she was 32 years old. Stressed and frustrated, Ninoshka's mom had the appearance of a teenager whose body showed the wear and tear of a chronological number far greater than her age. Mother and daughter were replicas of each other down to the hairstyles and tattoos. Their encounter in my office was very volatile.

Accusations began flying in every direction; Ninoshka's mother, "What the hell are you depressed about? I can't give you everything you want. What do you want me to do?" Ninoshka responded, "Stop calling me a bitch! It hurts when you say stuff like that!" Turning to the agency counselor, she said, "I don't want her to talk to me." With this, the mother inched her bottom closer to the edge of the chair and threatened to hit her.

I stopped them, asserting that my office was a safe place, a place of healing, and that in this space, no one yells at anybody and nobody hits anyone. The argument stopped, and it occurred to me that they were both crying out for healing. The mother told us that we could take Ninoshka to "the crazy house" if that was what she wanted. She said she would sign whatever and stormed out of the office in tears. I followed her, not sure of what I was going to say, but my intuition compelled me. "Mom," I said as I caught up with her in the stairwell, "Don't leave. I know that your heart is breaking, that you feel overwhelmed and frustrated. I would too if I were in your shoes. Your daughter is crying out for help, and this does not make you a bad mom."

"But the mental ward is an awful place. I don't want her to go there," she said, words interchanged with soulful sobs.

I persuaded the mother to come back to the office. I switched places with the agency counselor and returned to speak with my student again. We talked about how changing the messages that we send ourselves is so much more important than what anyone says about us. Ninoshka insisted that her mother used the words on purpose. I needed an analogy that she could relate to. I thought about how in my experience students and others who are speakers of a second language tend to use their vernacular when emotions are riding high. Words we need in a hurry seem to be more readily accessible to us in our native language. It occurred to me that the mother's choice of words was more a manifestation of the vocabulary she owned rather than her feelings toward her daughter.

I believe that when we are upset or really excited and want to express it, expediency takes a front seat to eloquence. I needed to express this idea in words that my student could understand. What would be a good analogy for this kind of idea? Ninoshka continued to tell me how her mother always used derogatory words toward her. An image of a bucket and a mop flashed in my mind and I said,

> Your mom is feeling overwhelmed, frustrated, and worried and is trying to express it in a hurry. When we experience such intense feelings, we tend to grab the first words that come to mind to express ourselves. It's like cleaning up a mess. Let's say I had planned to come in here and mop my office floor. What might I bring?

She said, "A mop." "Yes, and a bucket, clean water, some cleanser, and such. But let's say that we are sitting here talking and a container that has been sitting on my desk tipped over and its contents spilled all over. What do you think would happen?" She said, "You would grab whatever you had at hand to stop the spill and dry the mess." Yes! That was the conclusion that I needed her to reach. I explained to Ninoshka that every time they argued, her mom could only access the words that she owned, which in this case was the vocabulary that she was using to try to get her point across. Ninoshka looked at me with the understanding that seemed to be that of an old soul, and she got it.

Once the parent understood that she was not being attacked, she agreed to be escorted to the emergency room with her daughter. Although Ninoshka still felt angry at her mother, she agreed not to say anything disrespectful to her. We reminded her of phrases that she could use to communicate with her mother and suggested she tell the person at the hospital how she felt and continue to ask for the help that she was so desperately seeking.

Ninoshka went to a local hospital where she remained for a week. She came out with a counseling plan that included communication work with both mother and daughter. This episode became the opportunity for Ninoshka to experience unconditional positive regard for the first time. Before coming to our school, she had felt ugly and unworthy, at best she felt invisible. This crisis marked a new beginning for Ninoshka. She will graduate this year and plans to attend college to major in design. I am no longer her counselor, but know that when Ninoshka looks in the mirror on graduation day, she will see someone who is beautiful, smart, and worthy of living her dream. Even if she is not the top student in her class, she will feel like she is on top of the world.

Sophia

Sophia legitimately earned the title of valedictorian of her class, but forces would come together in attempts to rob her of the distinction. My intuition and creative management of the case protected her right.

When Sophia began school, she could not speak English. Her parents were hardworking people for whom the dream of seeing their daughter graduate college drove every effort to provide her with the best education they could afford. Being of modest financial means, the best they could do was to send her to school and provide all of their support.

Sophia began to learn English, and by the end of first grade, she was already at the top of her class. When it came time to go to high school, Sophia's parents moved to ensure that she was assigned to what they deemed the best comprehensive high school in the district. That was where I met Sophia.

Sophia was brilliant, the type of student that teachers would clone if they could. Every time I saw her transcript as I updated my students' academic maps, I smiled. By 10th grade, she attended a Post Secondary Options Program at a local college. She maintained excellent grades. Sophia applied for a summer internship at one of the top universities in the state and was admitted. She completed the program, receiving accolades and an invitation to return.

In the winter of her senior year, I began receiving the usual notices from the different foundations and groups that traditionally honor high school valedictorians. One of them requires that you submit the name by early spring so that the student's name is engraved and added to an infinity plaque for that year. I reported to the principal that I was submitting Sophia's name. She told me to wait because calculations were in progress, and we did not have evidence yet to support that Sophia was the valedictorian for sure.

I felt my heart race. Something was very wrong. I could not shake that "uh-oh" feeling. I ran to my office and printed out a ranking report for the senior class. I looked at the top-ranking four students and printed out their individual transcripts and schedules. I saved the documents. Mathematically, there was no possible way that any one of the other three could achieve a grade point average greater than Sophia's, so I sent in the form declaring her the valedictorian. I kept my eye on the records and began to see discrepancies in the grades and course codes. For obvious reasons, I cannot give more details here, but let me just say that I had to advocate for Sophia to the point where an investigation was conducted to show that she was the only class valedictorian.

We adults are sometimes adept at twisting the truth. That year, as far as the world could see, the position of valedictorian was shared. As far as the official recognition for valedictorian and all of the honors that it carries, Sophia received the distinction she rightfully earned. She also received a full scholarship from a top university. Not too long ago, as I dug through my boxes after moving to a new school, I found the folder with all of the evidence that the central office had asked for from me and copies of all of the electronic messages that I had sent trying to gain clarification on the issue from my boss. In an old calendar, I found the graduation picture that Sophia gave me that year. "Thanks for everything" was written on the back—her simple message meant a great deal to me. She had experienced how the truth coupled with deliberate action is a powerful tool.

Once again, my intuition had steered me in the right direction. Sophia and her parents had worked a lifetime, knowing that unless she worked hard, they lacked the means to send their daughter to college. I know that she would have been awarded the scholarship anyway, had she not been valedictorian, but it was the principle of the thing. That year, Sophia graduated top of the class at her high school and simultaneously earned a 2-year college degree. As she stood behind the podium and delivered her speech to the graduating class, I saw a woman empowered taking her place on that stage and ready to take on the world. During her first year of college, Sophia came to visit. I never saw her again, but an advisor from the university she attended told me that she was doing very well. Sophia had decided to study law.

The Gift That Keeps Giving

I feel blessed to have discovered the voice within. This thing that we call *intuition* leads me to carve new paths when at times the road seems to have reached its end. Not all of the stories are about students whose lives have been in danger or students denied their earned rewards. The incubation period for creative solutions is frequently seconds long, but as I look back at my journey as a school counselor, I cannot think of any story where intuition did not play a significant role.

Recently, I was invited to the Eagle Scout award ceremony for a former student. When his mother stood at the podium to talk about her son, she thanked several family members and others. She identified me as the educator having made the biggest difference in his life. I held back tears as this parent expressed such gratitude. He will be graduating both from high school and with a 2-year college degree this year. Through the years, I have had many conversations with this student. I have celebrated his achievements and lamented his heartbreaks and losses. There have been times when only the voice within could lead me in this work. The willingness to act on it kept me authentic in our interactions. His mother said she hopes that he finds someone in college who inspires him as much.

Recently, I received a communication from a student that his dream university denied him admission. Perhaps if intuition had played a role in the decision-making process of the admissions committee, they would have admitted him. If they only knew the resilience and the perseverance of this young man, but rules are rules, right? My advice to him was to go inward and find out what his gut feeling tells him about where he needs to go. Stopping is not an option. I told him, "They can rob you of your dream college, but they can't steal your dreams." He chose another university.

I am thankful that many years ago I encountered her—intuition. I am fortunate that my work allows me to use this organic gift to build paths and help others. I know my place. I have a purpose. I am blessed to be a part of a greater picture that is organic creation doing what it does best.

Chapter 22

IMAGINING SCHOOL COMMUNITIES

Organic Creativity in Elementary School Adminstration

Rebecca McElfresh

On a balmy spring afternoon, we gathered together in the sunken living room of one of our faculty members. Surrounded by the subtle earth tones of her southwestern décor, we sifted through magazine images and word phrases, looking for those that caused us to respond intuitively, from the gut, trying not to use purposeful thought to select one image over another. Once we had gathered a pile of images, we worked to arrange them on a large sheet of blank paper. We agreed, once again, to respond intuitively to this process as well.

Our purpose that afternoon was to examine what had happened to us during the course of a very difficult year. I became principal of this elementary school due to the vacancy created by the death of the previous principal. She was a community icon, well-loved and well-respected by teachers, parents, and administrators. Her death came after a long life, but her diagnosis of cancer became troubling several months after her death. One month after my arrival, two teachers were diagnosed with cancer. In both cases, the prognosis was poor, and both women would not recover. Neither was close to achieving

Rebecca McElfresh, Ph.D., has served students in two Ohio public school, Pre-K–grade 12 settings as a teacher, coordinator of talent development education programming, elementary school principal, and human resources director. Additionally, she has instructed preservice and in-service teachers at Ashland University, Ursuline College, and the University of Akron in Ohio where she received the Outstanding Teacher/Scholar award. She also served as a visiting instructor at the Massachusetts College of Liberal Arts in the summer Leadership Academy designed to prepare school leaders. Rebecca earned her Ph.D. at Kent State University where she studied the role of the arts in the process of social change. Now retired from full-time teaching, she is enjoying a newly opened space for her own creative work.

the average life expectancy for women with access to good health care in the United States.

Over the course of the next year, four additional staff members were diagnosed with breast cancer, a different form of cancer than the other three. As you might imagine, this information became most unsettling to the staff. Were we working within a toxic environment? How would we know? How would we proceed to find out without disturbing the children? In addition to our concern about safety, we were deeply grieving. We had experienced too much loss in such a short space of time.

As the building principal, I felt responsible to find ways to assist staff members in several ways. We proceeded quickly to find one of the nation's experts in sick building syndrome and followed this physician's advice with regard to testing the environment. For weeks, workers crawled through the attic spaces, placed air sampling machines in the hallways and classrooms, tested the soil surrounding the building, and sampled the water. As we waited for the results, our emotions were on edge. On the one hand, we hoped that nothing would be found to be the cause of our illnesses. On the other hand, we wished to have answers that would help us to avoid further diagnoses of cancer. In the end, the expert determined that there were no environmental factors creating these diseases and that our data represented a "cancer cluster," not uncommon for a building full of women of our average age. Although I had thought this information might be calming, it was, in fact, disturbing to some who were not able to return to thinking they were safe in the building.

I knew I had to reach more deeply within me to find the courage to help. I knew we needed to deal with our grief, but when I examined the list of community resources available to us, I could not find what I thought might help us. I could not imagine that the usual clinical review of the stages of grief would result in any real help. Instead, I relied on my intuitive understanding of the power of creativity, and in particular, my own experiences with visual art as medicine through my own midlife grief process.

You might be wondering how I found myself in a position where the risk to take on such work within a school community might be the wise choice. Lest you think it was simply a magical infusion of momentary grace, or a significant lucky break, I will build a picture of the path by which a school community might find itself able to engage in this work. I suggest here that three factors make this work possible. First, I suggest strong curriculum development, not only in the areas of visual art, music, drama, and movement, but in the cross-curricular connections that so readily allow for the integration of all art forms. Second, regular and planned schoolwide emphasis on the arts promotes the opportunity to learn experientially and to "release the imagination" necessary to promote intuitive work[223]. Finally, guided practice with intuitive work through the arts allows staff members to explore this way of thinking and working within a safe space. All of these factors help to create teachers who feel safe moving forward in their work with students, helping them to explore these same ways of working and of knowing.

The activities and processes described in this chapter represent two school communities where I served as the building principal. One was in an inner-ring suburban community with many schoolwide, Title I supported programs. In other words, each of these buildings had a poverty rate at or above 40%. The second school was within a high wealth district about 35 miles from the first school.

Curriculum Development

School leaders have the opportunity to shape much about the curriculum of the local school, even in the midst of the heavy standardization of our time. It is important to allow for a more broadly conceived notion of curriculum than the subject area content taught in school classrooms. Others, particularly those aligned with the movement known as "Curriculum Reconceptualization"[224] suggest the curriculum refers to the word "path" and has implications for our development that extend beyond the particularities of subject matter understanding. Reconceptualists argue that decisions about curriculum should ask questions such as, "What makes a meaningful life?" and "What questions really matter for us to consider in schools?"[225] When school leaders view curriculum in this way, they are able to find many opportunities for deepening the understanding of teachers and students.

Helping teachers develop units of study that integrate subject matter, including the arts, provides the opportunity to address the significant life questions I have described above. This can take place while assuring that required standards are met. With imagination and a lot of work, teachers can create opportunities that do both. Often when this integration is done, teachers of the arts are asked to emphasize academic content in their classrooms. When properly done, teachers of the arts are also able to have their content standards reinforced in other subject matter content. Teachers of the arts should not be expected to be merely an extension of the regular classroom. They have significant content to teach as well. It should be noted that curriculum work takes time. School leaders will want to creatively provide that time for teachers through release time so that fresh bodies and minds are given to this important task.

School leaders can also do much to support the curriculum within the disciplines of the arts. Foremost, it is important to understand that the arts are valuable content areas in their own right. Scheduling, budget allocations, and staffing decisions should be made with this in mind. Although some would suggest that arts integration can be accomplished without significant exposure to the arts as separate disciplines (theatre, visual art, dance, music), I would argue that they should best be addressed by concurrent study of the arts and other subject area disciplines. In other words, our ability to express ourselves in any language is dependent upon our level of skill at the time we seek to express ourselves. This does not mean that we should limit our expression until we have developed sophisticated skills. We would never argue this point when discussing oral or written language expression. We allow students to express themselves at their own level of development while, at the same time, we work to further develop their skills. Therefore, we should do all that we can to help teachers of the arts have the materials and time they need to effectively teach students skills in their content area, while at the same time helping students to regularly express their ideas through these forms. School leaders must become creative budgetary planners and/or creative fundraisers so that elementary music teachers have Orff instruments, rhythm instruments, sheet music, and risers for performance opportunities. Visual art teachers must have a wide variety of equipment, a room set aside for the teaching of art, and a wide variety of consumable materials. When building budgets are limited, raise funds.

Finally, school leaders will find themselves more closely attending to the development of an arts-integrated curriculum, as well as opportunities for strong disciplinary learning within the arts, when they attend to the integration of the arts in their own personal lives as both an observer of the arts and a participant. I strongly urge regular attendance at local choral and orchestra performances, theatre events, and regular visits to art museums. Additionally, I encourage school leaders to explore an art form experientially. Sing in a church choir, try out for a community theatre production, take an art course through community adult education. Then, when you have explored several options, choose a discipline and continue to develop your skills.

As a youngster, I grew up in a home surrounded by art and music. My father, a musician, and my mother, an artist, taught me that the arts provided meaningful ways to spend my time. They taught me that these pursuits required disciplined study[226] and they taught me that I needed the arts to most fully express myself and to understand the expressions of others. Although I did not study any art form to the degree that I could choose it as a profession, I continue to develop my skills in visual art and music. While serving as a school principal, I sang in a small ensemble and I studied painting and ceramics. My free time included many visits to art museums and concerts, and I looked for opportunities to invite staff members to join me in these pursuits. Through these activities, I was able to continually ask myself an essential curriculum question, "What makes a life meaningful?"

Regular and Planned Schoolwide Emphasis on the Arts

School leaders also have the opportunity to provide regular, schoolwide events focused on the arts. These events set a tone that celebrates artistic expression and provides role models for students who may be considering careers in the arts. It also normalizes experiences with the arts, making them an accepted part of life in schools. These experiences can be provided in a variety of ways.

In one school community, the faculty and I applied to be a partner school to the Cleveland Orchestra, one of the world's finest professional orchestras. Through this program, our school was assigned three mentors from the orchestra who visited classrooms regularly, providing instruction in content such as the physics of sound, music theory, and literature. Once per year, we were the benefactors of a community concert held in our school. Additionally, teachers were given release time to work with teachers from all three partner schools to develop arts-integrated curriculum based on state content standards. Financial support for this relationship was provided through competitive grants written by both the orchestra and our school.

In this same school, a long-standing tradition of the annual student art show supported our work with arts integration. Each spring, all students entered at least two pieces of art into the show. Parents, administrators, and community members were invited to attend. Professional display boards were used and student work was signed and labeled. Some teachers framed students' pieces, further honoring their work.

On one sunny evening in May, our school community celebrated our vision-building process by combining our annual student art show with a program of music provided by our orchestra partner as well as music performed by our students and group singing led by our faculty. We choose a particular piece of music to represent our vision. One teacher choreographed movement for this piece and students and faculty carried streamers and banners as they moved to the rhythm of this piece. Following the program in the gym, students and their parents toured the building throughout which student artwork was displayed. In one area of the building, we displayed art created by family units. Finally, we celebrated with food and gathered in the cafeteria to enjoy homemade cookies in the shape of children's hands.

In the other school community, we developed a tradition of hiring an artist-in-residence each year. One year, we hired a ceramic artist. She worked with each classroom and all of our 550 students created a ceramic tile. We created a dozen tile panels and then hired someone to install the panels throughout the building. Each panel had a theme that supported our districtwide emphasis on healthy emotional living. In celebration of this work, we invited parents to an evening open house where students guided their families throughout the displays. We placed comment books beneath each display so that parents and students could express what meaning they had made of the art. We were able to have parents and their children think and talk together about healthy emotions through their experience with the art.

Another year, we hired a poet who worked with students in large group assemblies and in smaller classroom groups. During this residency, the poet helped each classroom to create a book of poetry. One parent, familiar with desktop editing, volunteered to prepare each classroom book for publication. We used an on-demand publisher and provided each student with a copy of her or his classroom book. Additional copies were available for sale, and we discovered that our parents wanted many copies. Our students were amazed to find their creative writing in a real book! In the end, our profit from these sales significantly supported the cost of the residency.

Our PTO organized an annual fundraising event in which student artwork was printed on a variety of objects. Each student in the building submitted a piece of art, guided by the art teacher, and parents were given the opportunity to purchase these items. One of the items available for sale was a T-shirt imprinted with student art. We discovered that the children were happy to wear their created images to school, and we found these shirts to be a constant reminder of the creativity of our students. Additionally, we found this to be a most successful way to finance our artist-in-residence programs.

Field trips can also be used to support regular experiences with the arts. We were fortunate to be located near an outstanding orchestra, three outstanding music conservatories, and a major museum of fine art, as well as an institute of art. Cleveland's University Circle area is rich with cultural institutions, and they are within an easy drive for many schools. Young students can easily visit older students to attend choral and instrumental programs during the school day. They can also travel to other schools to view art exhibits and theatre productions.

Although obvious and very simple, it is most important to continually display student artwork throughout the building. Principals can support this by attending to display space in hallways and classrooms. Principals and teachers can support the creation of student designed and painted murals on the walls.

Music can become a regular part of each day by incorporating it into morning routines. The public address system can be utilized to provide "moments for music." Teachers can play appropriate selections of music as students engage in independent work. Students studying instrumental music can perform for others during designated times. School choirs, orchestras, and bands should be performing for students on a regular basis.

Young students experience theatrical performance as a natural part of literacy development. A planned and regular routine of sharing performances across classrooms supports students developing understanding of theatre and its role in human expression. Puppetry combines both visual and dramatic arts, and students enjoy the opportunity to create in these varied ways.

The possibilities for regular and planned experiences with the arts are many and varied. What matters is that they are tailored for the students within the context of the community in which they reside. Communities differ in terms of the cultural resources they offer. Explore and discover these resources within your own community. Work with your faculty to purposefully plan regular experiences with the arts. Be careful not to limit your thinking based on cost. Reach out to parent and community groups to assist you and consider the possibility of raising your own funds for these purposes. And remember that although you are developing students through these experiences, you are also contributing to the development of the teachers who serve them.

Guided Practice With Organic Creativity

Supported by a foundation of regular excursions into the imagination,[227] teachers, students, and administrators can be guided into experiences with organic creativity. I suggest that these experiences must be guided at first because I have found that years of standardized practice lead both students and teachers to be limited in their capacity to take risks and to move into any activity that is open-ended in its possible outcomes. Students frequently ask, "What should this look like when I'm done?" Teachers often ask, "What do you want me to do?" Experiences with organic creativity open us to different ways of working in which we must, in a sense, begin to recognize and depend on our intuitive sensibilities. Therefore, initial guidance provides enough scaffolding for the organic nature of the work to unfold.

During the course of the year following our award of the orchestra partnership, I worked with the faculty to envision what our relationship with the orchestra might be like. Organizational development literature would have guided us through a typical process for the development of mission and vision statements, with subsequent setting of goals and the means by which we would measure them. Although effective for the task, I envisioned deeper work and I knew that this process would take time and energy.

We began by studying together and by asking essential curriculum questions such as "What makes for a meaningful life?", "What is important for us to know in order to have a meaningful life?", and "What role does the development of our imaginations play in our ability to create the future we envision?" We also studied the ideas of John Dewey and Maxine Greene, and we decided to embrace the arts as a way of knowing and determining our vision for the future. We hired an artist-in-residence to work with us in the area of visual art.

On one particular afternoon, we worked together in the cafeteria after the students went home for the day. Our facilitator gave each participant a piece of clay and we were asked to close our eyes for the remainder of the time we had clay in our hands. First, she asked us to simply experience the clay, to move it around in our hands, to notice how it felt and how it moved as we pushed and pulled it. Then, she asked us to shape it in some way, still without the benefit of our vision. In other words, she asked us to work with our inner vision. She asked us to consider how we would like to shape our teaching. She reminded us that we should respond to the first ideas that come to us through our hands. She also comforted us by explaining that our understanding of these creations may not come before they are created. Their meaning might be revealed afterward as we considered the metaphoric meaning of the objects or image created in our hands. As we finished our work with clay, our facilitator began to ask us to share our thoughts about what we had done. One by one, and with timidity in the beginning, we shared our creations with one another. Each was able to determine what meaning he or she might assign to his or her created object. In subsequent weeks, we asked our students to consider the same questions through their own art creations. Our facilitator worked with them and created materials to send home so that families could work together to create art that would enhance their discussions about their vision of schooling.

When I worked with students as a disciplinarian, as each school principal must, I often asked them to create visual images to help them express the emotions that lay beneath their behavioral choices. I found that such discussions changed discipline situations from punitive to growth-focused meetings. I kept a small sand tray on my desk so that students could comfort themselves by creating images in the sand. I noticed that the number of children bringing me pieces of their art to hang on my walls began to increase. I smiled and accepted each gift as it was offered and promptly found a place to display it. They had no idea the degree to which their gifts were, for me, strong confirmation of our allowance for organic ways of being through the arts.

So you can imagine why, when faced with the tragedies I described at the beginning of this chapter, I felt strong guidance from within to approach our healing through such organic explorations with visual art. I trusted my intuitive sensibilities and made an appointment with the superintendent to explain my plan for helping us to process the enormous amount of loss in our lives. With his support, we hired a consultant and spent one Saturday together at the Cleveland Museum of Art. We looked deeply into grief and loss through the visual images we found in that setting. At each stop, we would talk to each other about what we saw, what we felt, and what meaning we made of the images before us. We left with a different kind of understanding of the meaning of our grief as it arose organically from our shared visceral responses to the art.

I am also reminded of our collective response to the events of September 11, 2001. It seemed natural to us to respond organically through the creation of art. Students created art, teachers created art, poems, and song. We gathered together in a large group assembly, surrounded by our art, and listened to poetry and music. We had found confidence in this way of working, and we were able to turn to it at a time when we knew little else to do.

Conclusion

I have described ways of working with organic creativity in school settings from my perspective as the building leader. I hope you are encouraged by my stories and that you feel free to borrow some of these ideas. More important, I hope that you take whatever steps are necessary for you to sur-round yourself with the arts such that organic work becomes a natural way to respond to life within schools.

Piirto[228] noted Five Core Attitudes found in creative individuals: self-discipline, naïveté, risk-taking, tolerance for ambiguity, and group trust. We can wonder whether these attitudes are necessary for participation or whether these are attitudes that develop as a result of engagement with the arts. Although we may speculate, I suggest we consider that creativity is develop-able, even in adults, and that organically arising creative experiences support such development.

Curious about the transformation that occurs in such situations, I have studied the nature of personal and social transformation through experiences with the arts.[229] I concluded through my research that our bodies, minds, and spirits can be engaged and transformed through experiences with the arts. Interaction with the arts provides embodied ways of knowing and requires from us a physical presence with all sensing systems active. Within our minds, we develop identity and voice from the expression of our innermost ideas and feelings. We can create locations for our memories through works of art and we are able to engage in dialogue with others about it, offering us the opportunity to build community. On a spiritual plane, we are able to work emergently, allowing ourselves to be led as we work, listening to the "voices" of the clay or the paint, responding and interacting in the moment. We might find individual or collective guidance as we did in our school community as we looked for our vision of the future. Finally, we find sustenance and nur-turing in these organic ways of working so that we might better cope with grief and loss.

So although we tend to think of school as a place where we learn subject area content, we can envision something more. Our schools can be places where we seek to understand our inner lives, as well as the inner workings of others. We might find community and together envision and build a better future. As you work within your school community, consider my stories. Let them travel with you as you ask the essential questions. Your path, your cur-riculum, is yet to be determined.

FINAL THOUGHTS

Jane Piirto

The writers in this volume first responded to a query from me, and then wrote about their own experiences as teachers who teach their subject matter creatively. The terms *organic creativity* and *intuition* in the title were not previously defined but the definitions arose holistically and qualitatively in each essay. Here are some commonalities that could be take-aways from this compendium:

1. Students matter. Knowing the students matters. (Dubin, Balotta, Johnson, Groman, Reynolds)
2. The current climate of multiple-choice assessment, single-target standards, and pressure to have students score high or be fired leaves teachers with little chance to be their intrinsic creative and authentic selves as professionals. (Groman, McElfresh, Peppercorn, Davis, McKenzie, Kettler and Sanguras)
3. The teacher should teach improvisationally—that is, the lesson can be changed when the situation changes. (Reynolds, Davis, McKenzie, Nicoll, Kettler and Sanguras)
4. The teacher should feel free to stray from the lesson plan and use his or her intuition to determine the direction of the classroom situation and the lesson. (Reynolds, Davis, McKenzie, Nicoll, Daniels, Taber, MacDowell and Michael, Snowber, Oreck, Groman, McElfresh, Leggo, Tolan, Dubin, Peppercorn, Kettler and Sanguras)
5. The teacher should seek to develop a climate of feedback in the classroom where the students trust each other. (Reynolds, Nicoll, Dubin, Davis, Peppercorn, Stephenson, MacDowell and Michael)
6. Students should be encouraged to learn from failure and vulnerability. (Dubin, Davis, McKenzie, Oreck, Leggo, Snowber, Tolan)
7. Creative humor teaches and engages students. (Peppercorn, Snowber, Dubin)
8. "Trusting the gut" often leads to a successful intervention by a trained counselor with students having situational difficulties. (Balotta, McElfresh)

9. Techniques such as meditating, slowing down, paying attention, and mindfulness should be part of a teacher's repertoire. (Burnett, Montgomery, Snowber, Tolan)

10. Field trips increase the likelihood of students' engagement and remembering. (Reynolds, Johnson, McElfresh, Snowber)

11. The classroom is a mutual learning environment, not an environment for the teacher alone. (Burnett, Reynolds, Johnson, MacDowell and Michael, Nicoll, Davis, Montgomery, Snowber, Tolan)

12. Self-knowledge tools such as mandalas, walking the labyrinth, reflections, nature walks, and the like help give students insight. (Montgomery, Groman, Burnett, Reynolds)

13. Music, theatre, art, dance, and performance are not extras, but vitals. (Oreck, Nicoll, McKenzie, Davis, Stephenson, McElfresh, Montgomery, Caldemeyer)

14. Talent is omnipresent, but there is a "certain something" beyond talent that is indefinable, that experts and audiences know when they see it. (Oreck, McKenzie, Caldemeyer)

15. "Know thyself" is a goal for teaching and living creatively. (Reynolds, Groman, Johnson, Caldemeyer, Nicoll, Oreck, Balotta, Leggo, Tolan, Burnett, Stephenson, Montgomery, McElfresh, Davis, Kettler and Sanguras)

16. Students should be encouraged to improvise, theorize, elaborate, discuss, explore, create, conjecture, ask why, and not to just focus on "the right answer." (Daniels, Johnson, Reynolds, Stephenson, Oreck, McKenzie, MacDowell and Michael, Nicoll, Leggo, Tolan, Burnett, Davis, Snowber, Kettler and Sanguras, Peppercorn)

ENDNOTES

1   Frontispiece Poem used with permission by Susan Katz (see Katz, 1988). Katz is also author of children's books, most recently *O Theodore: Guinea Pig Poems* and *The President's Stuck in the Bathtub* (Houghton Mifflin). Her e-mail is susankatz@yahoo.com.

Preface

2   "Thinking hats" are part of the Lateral Thinking method of Edward de Bono. See de Bono, 1970.

3   My website contains a list of my literary publications and copies of many poems, essays, journal articles, and short stories. See http://www.ashland.edu/~jpiirto.

4   Brainstorming is a technique advocated in the Creative Problem Solving process; generating of alternative solutions is also. SCAMPER is a mnemonic device for generating alternative solutions: Substitute, Combine, Adapt, Modify, Put to another use, Eliminate, Reverse. It was first advocated by Eberle, 1971.

5   Gorel was quoted in Erikson, 1988, p. 144.

6   Charlie Musselman, *Tavis Smiley Show*, Public Broadcasting Service, Feb. 21, 2013.

7   See Harrison, 1991, p. 128.

8   See Ghiselin, 1952, Intro.

9   To theorize the Core Attitudes, Seven I's, and General Practices:

    1.   I read and reread several hundred biographies, memoirs, autobiographies, and interviews of creators in visual arts (including sculpture and architecture), creative writing (including poetry, fiction, creative nonfiction, drama), music (both classical and popular), science, mathematics, invention, athletics, dance, and drama (both theatre and film);

    2.   I conducted a literature review of psychological studies of creators that utilized psychometric and biographical data such as:

        a.   Institute for Personality Assessment and Research Studies (e.g., Barron, MacKinnon, Gough, etc.);

        b.   Chicago studies (e.g., Wallach, Kogan, Csikszentmihalyi, etc.); and

        c.   British studies (e.g., Cattell, Eysenck, etc.);

3. I coded for personal accounts of the creative process from these creators; and

4. These were gathered into several themes. Three overarching themes were elicited:
   a. Five Core Attitudes for creativity,
   b. Seven I's in the creative process, and
   c. General Practices for Creativity.

Listed below are subcategories for each theme:

1. Five Core Attitudes for creativity:
   a. Self-discipline
   b. Group trust
   c. An attitude of openness to experience (naïveté in seeing the old as if it is new)
   d. Risk-taking
   e. Tolerance for ambiguity

2. Seven I's in the Creative Process:
   a. Inspiration
      i. inspiration from love
      ii. inspiration from nature
      iii. inspiration from transcendent experience
      iv. inspiration through substances
      v. inspiration by others' creativity
      vi. inspiration from dreams
      vii. inspiration of travel
      viii. inspiration of tragedy, sorrow, illness, war
      ix. inspiration from being thwarted

   b. Imagery
   c. Imagination
   d. Intuition
   e. Incubation
   f. Insight
   g. Improvisation

3. General Practices for Creativity
   a. The need for solitude
   b. The creativity ritual
   c. The practice of meditation
   d. Exercise, especially walking
   e. The quest for silence
   f. Creativity as the process of a life

This qualitative research into actual biographical material has yielded a framework for the creative process that elaborates on and goes beyond the research into problem solving and problem finding. See also Piirto, 1992, 1998, 2002, 2004, 2005a, 2005b, 2007a, 2007b, 2009a, 2010, 2011.

10   See Piirto, 2011.

11   See Sahlberg, 2011.

12   See Bache, 2008, pp. 22–23.

13   See Dalton, 2010, p. 3.

Chapter 1

14   See Stevens, 1951.

15   See Florida, 2002.

16   See National Governors Association for Best Practices, & Council of Chief State School Officers, 2010.

17   Lawrence, 1926/2007.

18   See Oates, 1967/1999. See Carver, 1997. See O'Brien, 1990b.

19   See Albee, 1962.

20   See Haft, Witt, Thomas, & Weir, 1989.

21   See Piaget, 1971. See Kaufman & Beghetto, 2009. See Sawyer et al., 2003.

22   See Melville, 1924/1962.

23   See Gardner, 1942.

24   See O'Brien, 1978, 1990c.

25   See Egan, 2005, p. viii.

26   See Meyer, 2005. See Collins, 2008. See Lu, 2011.

27   See Tan, 2007.

28   See Getzels, 1975. Tolerance for ambiguity was a term coined at the Institute for Personality Assessment and Research (IPAR) research project in the 1960s at the University of California, Berkeley. See MacKinnon, 1978. Piirto has tolerance for ambiguity as one of her Five Core Attitudes for creativity. See Piirto 2004, 2011.

29   See Stockton, 1882.

30   See Piirto, 1998, 2004, 2011.

31   See Green, 2005.

32   See DiCamillo, 2000.

33   See O'Brien, 1990a.

34   As Sternberg and Lubart (1995) argued, it takes courage to pose a new idea and risk being a minority of one. Torrance (1995) went so far as say that courage is the most essential quality required to be creative.

35   See Lowry, 1993.

36   See White, 1952.

37   See Anonymous, 1971.

38   See Getzels & Csikszentmihalyi, 1976. This is the seminal study of visual artists that introduced problem finding as a primary way that creators operate.

39   See Alexie, 2007.

40   See Camus, 1946/1989.

41   See Heiligman, 2009.

42   See Hemphill, 2007.

43   See Longinus, 250 A.D./1890.

44   See Kant, 1764/2003.

45   See Wordsworth, 1798, lines 37–41.

Chapter 2

46   See Piirto, 2004, 2011.

47   See Piirto, 2004, Chapter 4.

48   See Piirto, 2004, p. 108.

Chapter 3

49   Victor Miller (writer), personal communication in a workshop about how teaching is like theatre at the Westtown Seminar, June 2000.

50   Retrieved from http://www.brainyquote.com/quotes/quotes/s/stevejobs416 925.html

51   Retrieved from http://www.steveshapiro.com/2008/02/07/do-we-get-less-creative-as-we-age

52   Retrieved from http://thinkexist.com/quotation/here-s-to-the-crazy-ones-the-misfits-the-rebels/761372.html

53   See Haft et al., 1989.

54   See Hughes, Jacobson, & Hughes, 1986.

55   See my book, Peppercorn, 2011.

56   Retrieved from http://www.quotesdaddy.com/author/Larry+Brown/9

57   See DeVito, Shamberg, Sher, & LaGravenese, 2007.

58   I used to play taped messages from King Pepper, but in recent years the students have only met him on Halloween when I put on a crown, white beard, and cape and magically transform into the monarch.

59   See McBride, 1999. See Aversa, 2011.

60   His talk at the "Save Our Schools" march in the summer of 2011 can be found by going to this website: http://www.youtube.com/watch?v=HqOub-heGQc

61   See Peppercorn, 2011.

62   See "Ken Robinson says," 2006. Retrieved from http://www.ted.com/talks/ken_robinson_says_schools_kill_creativity.html

63   See Yeganeh, 2011. Retrieved from http://www.anglohigher.com/key_announce/key_announce_detail/11

64   See "Ken Robinson says," 2006.

Chapter 4

65   See Perry, 1970.

66   See, for example, Polanyi, 1962/1969.

67   See Popper, 1989.

Chapter 5

68   Cited in Christian & Belloni, 2001, p. xvii.

69   See Hake, 1998.

70   See Meltzer & Thornton, 2012, p. 478.

71   See Piirto, 2004, p. 265.

72   See Simonton, 1999.

73   See Adams, 1986, p. 100.

74   See Piirto, 2009b.

75   See Gribbin, 1984, p. vii.

76   Described in Knight, 2004.

Chapter 6

77   See Campbell, 1968.

78   Like many artists and thinkers, I have written a manifesto. See Reynolds, 2001. I, along with Piirto, have also published some of the only articles on depth psychology and the gifted and talented. See Reynolds & Piirto, 2005, 2007, 2009.

79   See Somé, 1998.

80   Brewster Ghiselin (1952) coined the term "oceanic consciousness" for the sense of trance-like wellbeing that one feels while creating. Mihalyi Csikszentmihalyi called it "flow," indicating that same timeless feeling. See Csikszentmihalyi, 1990.

81   See Tarnas, 2006.

82   See Wilhelm, 1950.

83   See MacIntyre, 2007.

84   See Danchev, 2012.

85   See Bache, 2008.

86   See Jung, 1984.

87   See Grasse, 1996.

88   See Campbell & Moyers, 1988.

89   I am also a long-time singer-songwriter with 12 albums. See my website: http://www.urrealist.com or iTunes. They are *A Suburban Negredo*; *Ex Uno Plura: Out of One Come Many*; *Aquarium of the Amphibian*; *Released from the Past*; *Uno Mentalis: The Mind of the Land*; *Creation: The Pyramid and the Suns: Urfeo in the Urground*; *The New Heavens and the New Earth*; *The Age of Magnification: Lamp of the Archer*.

Chapter 7

90   Dance included specialists in modern, West African, ballet, creative movement, Flamenco, and jazz. Music included vocal, percussion, classical, Caribbean/West African, Orff, and Kodaly. Theater included improvisation, storytelling, classical, and other text-based theatre.

91   See Renzulli, 1978.

92   See Oreck, 2004, 2005. See Oreck, Owen, & Baum, 2003.

93   See Maslow, 1971.

94   See Csikszentmihalyi, 1997.

95   See Vygotsky, 1971, p. 256.

96   See Dewey, 1934.

97   See Clark, 1993.

98   See Ohio Department of Education, 2004.

99   The most powerful statistical result came from the factor analysis, which looked at the relationship between the separate art forms and a larger construct called artistic talent. The three performing arts formed a single con-

struct with the virtually perfect statistical correlation of 1. Adding visual art lowered the fit equation to .93, but is still a strong correlation.

100   More than 65% of identified students scored below grade level in reading and/or math and fully 25% of students were in the lowest reading or math quartiles and considered at risk for school failure. The profile of students selected for advanced instruction generally mirrored the school populations as a whole including representatives from special education and self-contained bilingual classrooms.

101   See Oreck, 2004.

102   See Oreck, Baum, & McCartney, 2001, pp. 58–59.

103   See Baum, Owen, & Oreck, 1997.

104   Personal communication, April 16, 1993.

105   See ArtsConnection, 1997.

106   See Oreck et al., 2001, p. 31.

107   Ibid., p. 68.

108   Ibid., p. 76.

109   Ibid., p. 96.

110   Ibid., p. 25.

111   Ibid., p. 104.

Chapter 8

112   See Miller, 1964, p. 25.

113   See Sarason, 1999.

114   See Schaefer-Simmern, 1948.

115   See Oreck & Nicoll, 2010.

116   See Starko, 1995, p. 129.

117   See Bohm, 1996, p. 27.

118   See Shahn, 1957, p. 19.

119   See Stenhouse, 1985, p. 16.

120   See Oreck & Nicoll, 2010, p. 119.

Chapter 9

121   See de Mille, 1991, p. 264.

122   See Linklater, 1992, p. 4.

123   From Shakespeare, *Hamlet*, Act 3, scene 2.

Chapter 10

124   See Moyers, 1982.

125   See Lambert & Newman, 1963–1989.

126   See Rose & Sherman, 1955.

127   See Moyers, 1982.

Chapter 11

128   See Overbye, 2003.

129   "Do" = 1, "re" = 2 and so on. So "Mary Had a Little Lamb" would begin 3-2-1-2-3-3-3, for example.

130   Incidentally, the prototype residency that began the Kid Pan Alley project in 2000 was featured in my dissertation research. See Stephenson, 2001. Also see http://kidpanalley.org

131   See Csikszentmihalyi, 1997, p. 2.

132   See Stephenson, 2001, p. 123.

133   This song is copyright 2000 by S. D. Stephenson with gifted students at Ridgedale Elementary School, Morgantown, WV.

134   See Stephenson, 2001, p. 123.

135   Ibid., p. 128.

136   One beautifully written and illustrated book of American folk songs, stories, and poetry is Cohn, 1993. Numerous valuable websites exist as well, such as the University of Pittsburgh Library System's "Voices Across Time: American History Through Music" which can be found at http://www.library.pitt.edu/voicesacrosstime.

137   See Warner, 1991. See also the American Orff-Schulwerk Association website, http://aosa.org.

138   Self-discipline is one of the core attitudes for creativity, according to Piirto, 2004, 2011.

139   See Stephenson, 1998.

Chapter 13

140   See Torrance, 1967.

141   See Blum, 2013, p. 11.

142   See Tolan, 2002.

143   See Tolan, 1980.

144 See Tolan, 1983b.

145 Attributed to Goethe by William Hutchinson Murray in his book, *The Scottish Himalayan Expedition*, this has been shown to be a misattribution at "German Myth 12: The Famous 'Goethe' Quotation" from Answer.com and "Popular Quotes: Commitment" from Goethe Society of North America.

146 See my article, Tolan, 2006b. For my books, see Tolan, 1978; 1980; 1981a; 1981b; 1983a; 1983b; 1986; 1987a; 1987b; 1988; 1990; 1992a; 1992b; 1992c; 1993; 1994; 1996a; 1996b; 1998; 1999; 2001; 2002; 2004; 2006a; 2009; 2012.

147 See Tolan, 2012.

148 See Murdock, 1987, and Fugitt, 2001.

149 See Paul, 2012. Retrieved from http://blogs.kqed.org/mindshift/2012/06/why-daydreaming-isnt-a-waste-of-time/

150 This quote is so omnipresent that it must be considered common knowledge.

Chapter 14

151 See Barthes, 1975, p. 7.

152 See Elbow, 1998, p. 13.

153 Ibid., p. 14.

Chapter 15

154 Russian conceptual artists Vitaly Komar and Alex Melamid's "Most Wanted Paintings" and "Least Wanted Paintings," created from 1994–1997, examine popular conceptions of art via polling, then making paintings based on the results of the poll. More information on their work may be found at http://www.komarandmelamid.org.

155 A prestigious art award in the United Kingdom.

Chapter 16

156 See Renzulli, 1978. See Sternberg, 1985. See the federal reports, *National Excellence* (U.S. Department of Education, 1993) and the Marland Report (Marland, 1972).

157 See Piirto, 2004. Piirto has 13 suggestions for parents and teachers in Chapter 4 of this book.

158 "Oceanic consciousness" was Ghiselin's term; "Flow" was the term coined by Csikszentmihalyi. See Ghiselin, 1952. See Csikszentmihalyi, 1997.

159   See Renzulli, 1978 above.

160   See Piirto, 2011.

161   Students at Ashland University's high school honors institutes overwhelmingly—75% (N=650)—preferred Intuition to Sensing on the Myers-Briggs Type Indicator (See Piirto, 2004). However, 25% preferred Sensing—and so teaching to intuition must include these students.

Chapter 17

162   See Moore, 1996, p. 3.

163   Ibid.

164   Reynolds and Piirto wrote three articles explicating the principles of depth psychology and their relationship to teaching and learning with the gifted and talented. See Reynolds & Piirto, 2005, 2007, 2009.

165   See Schlitz, Vieten, & Amorok, 2007, p. 7.

166   See my recent chapter, Montgomery, 2012.

167   I find Tobin Hart's work inspiring here. See, for example, his 2001 book.

168   See Carol Dweck's work, particularly her popular book published in 2006.

169   See Piirto, 2009b.

170   See Gladwell, 2007.

171   Kenneth Meadows has a few books on the medicine wheel, which have been used in constructing therapeutic interventions for children and youth. I especially recommend his 1997 book.

172   For example, see Sternberg, 2003, and Piirto, 2011.

173   See Goswami, 2009, p. 134.

174   See my recent publication with a doctoral research and teaching team: Montgomery, Strunk, Steele, & Bridges, 2012.

175   See his astonishing *The Red Book*, recently revealed and published, in which he weaves artistic symbolism and personal symbolism: Jung, 2009.

176   We reviewed our process and the findings in this document: Montgomery, Otto, & Hull, 2007.

177   The two books that informed our process are these: Crawford, Kippax, Onyx, Gault, & Benton, 1992, and Haug, 1983/1987.

178   These are obscure works now: Hyle, Kaufman, Ewing, & Montgomery, 2008; Kaufman, Ewing, Montgomery, Hyle, & Self, 2003.

Chapter 18

179   See Palmer, 1998.

180   See Snowber, 2005. Over the years I have written many chapters, articles, poems, and books that explicate my thoughts on embodiment, dance, and teaching. My latest is Snowber, 2012. Also see Snowber, 2011.

181   Written by Grace Snowber, 1974.

182   See Csikszentmihalyi, 1997, p. 29.

183   See Rilke, 1984, p. 71.

184   See Merton, 1961, p. 98.

185   See Winterson, 1995, p. 198.

186   See Neruda, 1971, p. 318.

Chapter 19

187   See Piirto, 2004, 2011.

188   See Cameron, 1992.

189   The five songs in this essay can be found at https://soundcloud.com/jennifer-groman/sets/organic-creativity-teaching-to

190   See Pinkola-Estes, 1995.

191   *Nocturne Navigator* by Allison Saar is housed at the Columbus Museum of Art.

192   See Eisner, 2008.

193   *Eupsychian*, a word coined by Maslow, means having or moving toward a superior mind or soul.

194   See Ruumet, 1997.

Chapter 20

195   See Miller, Vehar, & Firestien, 2001.

196   J. P. Guilford coined these terms in his theory of the Structure of Intellect. See Guilford, 1967.

197   See Guilford, 1975.

198   See Puccio, Murdock, & Mance, 2006.

199   See Miller et al., 2001.

200   See Burnett, 2007.

201   See my dissertation: Burnett, 2010.

202   See Francisco & Burnett, 2008, p. 244.

203   See Wallas, 1926.

204   See Sio & Ormerod, 2009, p. 95.

205   See Francisco & Burnett, 2008, p. 246.

206   See Parnes, 1992.

207   See Burnett, 2007.

208   See Burnett, 2010, p. 112.

209   See Parnes, 1992, p.152.

210   See Puccio et al., 2006.

211   See Butler, 2002, p. 3

212   See Bishop et al., 2004.

213   Ibid, p. 9.

214   See Kabat-Zinn, 2005, p. xiii. See Piirto, 2011. Piirto includes Naïveté, or Openness to Experience as one of her Core Attitudes for Creativity.

Chapter 21

215   See National Board for Professional Teaching Standards, 2002.

216   See "Schools raid Puerto Rico for teachers," 1999.

217   See my dissertation: Balotta, 2011.

218   See Piirto's Pyramid of Talent Development, as described in this book's Preface.

219   All names are pseudonyms.

220   See the American School Counselor Association website for current recommendations at http://www.schoolcounselor.org

221   The word actually used here was an expletive for *gay*.

222   *Macho* is a Spanish word indicative of male virility and prowess. For more, see Stevens, 1973.

Chapter 22

223   This is a term used by both Dewey (1934) and Greene (1995).

224   See Pinar, Reynolds, Slattery, & Taubman, 1995. See Henderson & Gornik, 2007.

225   See Noddings, 2007.

226   One of Piirto's core attitudes for creativity is self-discipline. See Piirto 2004, 2011.

227   See Greene, 1995, cited above. Imagination is one of the Seven I's Piirto (2004, 2011) describes.

228   See Piirto, 2004, 2011.

229   See my dissertation, McElfresh, 2008.

REFERENCES

Adams, J. L. (1986). *The care and feeding of ideas: A guide to encouraging creativity.* Reading, MA: Addison-Wesley.

Albee, E. (1962). *Who's afraid of Virginia Woolf?* New York, NY: Atheneum.

Alexie, S. (2007). *The absolutely true diary of a part-time Indian.* New York, NY: Little, Brown.

Anonymous. (1971). *Go ask Alice.* New York, NY: Simon & Schuster.

ArtsConnection. (1997). *New horizons. Report to the Jacob Javits gifted and talented students education program, United States Department of Education, Office of Education Research and Improvement.* New York, NY: Author.

Aversa, D. (2011). *Exercise and brain health.* Retrieved from http://www.dhinfo. org/2011/02/exercise-and-brain-health

Bache, C. M. (2008). *The living classroom: Teaching and collective consciousness.* Binghampton, NY: SUNY Press.

Balotta, M. (2011). *Como el cantar del coquí: Educators of the Puerto Rican diaspora in the U.S. describe what resilience means to them* (Unpublished doctoral dissertation). Ashland University, Ashland, OH.

Barthes, R. (1975). *The pleasure of the text.* (R. Miller, Trans.). New York, NY: The Noonday Press.

Baum, S., Owen, S., & Oreck, B. (1997). Transferring individual self-regulation processes from arts to academics. *Arts Education Policy Review, 98*(4), 32–39.

Bishop, S. R., Lau, M., Shapiro, S., Carlson, L., Anderson, N. D., Carmody, J., Segal, Z. V., . . . Devins, G. (2004). Mindfulness: A proposed operational definition. *Clinical Psychology: Science and Practice, 11,* 230–241.

Blum, J. (2013). Way leads on to way. *Science of Mind,* 18–25.

Bohm, D. (1996). *On dialogue.* New York, NY: Routledge.

Burnett, C. (2007). *Facts, feelings and hunches.* Unpublished manuscript, Ontario Institute for Studies in Education, University of Toronto, Canada.

Burnett, C. (2010). *Holistic approaches to Creative Problem Solving* (Unpublished doctoral dissertation). Ontario Institute for Studies in Education, University of Toronto.

Butler, B. (2002). *Learning domains or Bloom's taxonomy adapted for public garden educational programs.* Presented at the AABGA professional development workshop, Toronto, ON.

Cameron, J. (1992). *The artist's way.* Los Angeles, CA: Jeremy Tarcher.

Campbell, J. (1968). *The masks of god, Vol. 4: Creative mythology.* New York, NY: Penguin.

Campbell, J., & Moyers, B. (1988). *Joseph Campbell: The power of myth with Bill Moyers.* New York, NY: Doubleday.

Camus, A. (1989). *The stranger* (M. Ward, Trans.). New York, NY: Vintage International. (Original work published 1946)

Carver, R. (1997). Where I'm calling from. In R. Carver, *New and selected stories* (pp. 227–242). New York, NY: Atlantic Monthly Books.

Christian, W., & Belloni, M. (2001). *Physlets: Teaching physics with interactive curricular material.* Upper Saddle River, NJ: Prentice Hall.

Clark, G. (1993). Judging children's drawings as measure of art abilities. *Studies in Art Education, 34*(2), 72–81.

Cohn, A. L. (1993). *From sea to shining sea: A treasury of American folklore and folk songs.* New York, NY: Scholastic.

Collins, S. (2008). *The hunger games.* New York, NY: Scholastic.

Crawford, J., Kippax, S., Onyx, J., Gault, U., & Benton, P. (1992). *Emotion and gender: Constructing meaning from memory.* London, England: Sage.

Csikszentmihalyi, M. (1990). *Flow: The psychology of optimal experience.* New York, NY: HarperCollins.

Csikszentmihalyi, M. (1997). *Creativity: Flow and the psychology of discovery and invention.* New York, NY: HarperCollins.

Dalton, M. (2010). *The Hollywood curriculum: Teachers in the movies.* New York, NY: Peter Lang.

Danchev, A. (2012). *Cézanne: A life.* New York, NY: Random House.

de Bono, E. (1970). *Lateral thinking.* New York, NY: HarperColophon.

de Mille, A. (1991). *Martha: The life and work of Martha Graham.* New York, NY: Vintage Books.

DeVito, D., Shamberg, M., & Sher, S. (Producers), & LaGravenese, R. (Director). (2007). *Freedom writers* [Motion Picture]. United States: Paramount Pictures.

Dewey, J. (1934). *Art as experience.* New York, NY: MacMillan.

DiCamillo, K. (2000). *Because of Winn-Dixie.* Cambridge, MA: Candlewick Press.

Dweck, C. (2006). *Mindset: The new psychology of success.* New York, NY: Ballantine Books.

Eberle, B. (1971). *SCAMPER: Games for imagination development.* Buffalo, NY: D.O.K. Publishers.

Egan, K. (2005). *An imaginative approach to teaching.* San Francisco, CA: Jossey-Bass.

Eisner, E. (2008). Art and knowing. In J. G. Knowles & A. L. Cole (Eds.), *Handbook of the arts in qualitative research* (pp. 1–24). Thousand Oaks, CA: Sage Publications.

Elbow, P. (1998). *Writing with power: Techniques for mastering the writing process.* New York, NY: Oxford University Press.

Erikson, J. M. (1988). *Wisdom and the senses: The way of creativity.* New York, NY: W.W. Norton.

Florida, R. (2002). *The rise of the creative class and how it's transforming work, leisure, community and everyday life.* New York, NY: Basic Books.

Francisco, J., & Burnett, C. (2008). Deliberate intuition: Giving intuitive insights their rightful place in the Creative Problem Solving Thinking Skills Model. In G. Puccio, C. Burnett, J. Cabra, J. Fox, S. Keller-Matthews, M. Murdock, & J. Yudess (Eds.), *Proceedings of the 2nd Creativity and Innovation Management (CIM) Community Conference* (pp. 238–253). Buffalo, NY: Buffalo State University, International Center for Studies in Creativity.

Fugitt, E. D. (2001). *He hit me back first!* Torrance, CA: Jalmar Press.

Gardner, M. (1942). The dinner party. *The Saturday Review of Literature, 25*(5), 15–16.

Getzels, J. (1975). Creativity: Prospects and issues. In I. A. Taylor & J. W. Getzels (Eds.), *Perspectives in creativity* (pp. 20–45). Hawthorne, NY: Aldine de Gruyter.

Getzels, J., & Csikszentmihalyi, M. (1976). *The creative vision: A longitudinal study of problem finding in art.* New York, NY: Wiley.

Ghiselin, B. (1952). *The creative process.* New York, NY: Bantam Books.

Gladwell, M. (2007). *Blink: The power of thinking without thinking.* New York, NY: Little, Brown.

Goswami, A. (2009). Quantum creativity in business. In D. Ambrose & T. Cross (Eds.), *Morality, ethics, and gifted minds* (pp. 133–146). New York, NY: Springer.

Grasse, R. (1996). *The waking dream: Unlocking the symbolic language of our lives.* Wheaton, NY: Theosophical Publishing House.

Green, J. (2005). *Looking for Alaska.* New York, NY: Dutton.

Greene, M. (1995). *Releasing the imagination.* San Francisco, CA: Jossey-Bass.

Gribbin, J. (1984). *In search of Schrodinger's cat: Quantum physics and reality.* New York, NY: Bantam Books.

Guilford, J. P. (1967). *The nature of human intelligence.* New York, NY: McGraw-Hill.

Guilford, J. P. (1975). Varieties of creative giftedness, their measurement and development. *Gifted Child Quarterly, 19,* 107–121.

Haft, S., Witt, P. J., & Thomas, T. (Producers), & Weir, P. (Director). (1989). *Dead poets society* [Motion Picture]. United States: Buena Vista Pictures Distribution.

Hake, R. (1998). Interactive-engagement verses traditional methods: A six-thousand student survey of Mechanics Test Data for introductory physics courses. *American Journal of Physics, 66,* 64. doi:10.119/1.18809

Harrison, J. (1991). Everyday life. In K. Johnson & C. Paulenich (Eds.), *Beneath a single moon: Buddhism in contemporary American poetry* (pp. 124–132). Boston, MA: Shambhala.

Hart, T. (2001). *From information to transformation: Education for the evolution of consciousness.* New York, NY: Peter Lang.

Haug, F. (1987). *Female sexualization: A collective work of memory.* (E. Carter, Trans.). London, UK: Verso. (Original work published 1983)

Heiligman, D. (2009). *Charles and Emma: The Darwins' leap of faith.* New York, NY: Henry Holt & Company.

Hemphill, S. (2007). *Your own, Sylvia: A verse portrait of Sylvia Plath.* New York, NY: Alfred Knopf.

Henderson, J., & Gornik, R. (2007). *Transformative curriculum leadership* (3rd ed.). Upper Saddle River, N.J: Prentice Hall.

Hughes, J., & Jacobson, T. (Producers), & Hughes, J. (Director). (1986). *Ferris Bueller's day off* [Motion Picture]. United States: Paramount Pictures.

Hyle, A., Kaufman, J. S., Ewing, M., & Montgomery, D. (Eds.). (2008). *Dissecting the mundane: International perspectives on memory-work.* Lanham, MD: University Press of America.

Jung, C. G. (1984). *Dream analysis 1: Notes of the seminar given 1928–30.* London, England: Routledge.

Jung, C. G. (2009). *The red book.* New York, NY: W. W. Norton.

Kabat-Zinn, J. (2005). *Wherever you go, there you are.* New York, NY: Hyperion.

Kant, I. (2003). *Observations on the feeling of the beautiful and sublime* (J. T. Goldthwait, Trans.). Berkeley: University of California Press. (Original work published 1764)

Katz, S. I. R. (1988). Playing candleland. *Sing, Heavenly Muse: Women's Poetry and Prose, 96.*

Kaufman, J. C., & Beghetto, R. A. (2009). Beyond big and little: The four c model of creativity. *Review of General Psychology, 13,* 1–12.

Kaufman, J. S., Ewing, M. S., Montgomery, D., Hyle, A. E., & Self, P. A. (2003). *From girls in their elements to women in science: Rethinking socialization through memory-work.* New York, NY: Peter Lang.

Ken Robinson says schools kill creativity. (2006). Retrieved from http://www.ted.com/talks/lang/eng/ken_robinson_says_schools_kill_creativity.html

Knight, R. D. (2004.) *Five easy lessons: Strategies for successful physics teaching.* San Francisco, CA: Addison Wesley.

Lambert, V. (Producer), & Newman, S. (Writer). (1963–1989). *Dr. Who* [Television Series]. London, England: BBC.

Lawrence, D. H. (2007). *The rocking horse winner.* Logan, IA: Perfection Learning. (Original work published 1926)

Linklater, K. (1992). *Freeing Shakespeare's voice.* New York, NY: Theatre Communications Group.

Longinus. (1890). *On the sublime* (H. L. Havell, Trans.). London, England: Macmillan. (Original work published circa 250 A.D.)

Lowry, L. (1993). *The giver.* Boston, MA: Houghton Mifflin.

Lu, M. (2011). *Legend.* New York, NY: Penguin.

MacKinnon, D. (1978). *In search of human effectiveness: Identifying and developing creativity.* Buffalo, NY: Creative Education Foundation Press.

Marland, S. P., Jr. (1972). *Education of the gifted and talented: Report to the Congress of the United States by the U.S. Commissioner of Education and background *papers submitted to the U.S. Office of Education,* 2 vols. Washington, DC: U.S. Government Printing Office. (Government Documents, Y4.L 11/2: G36)

Maslow, A. H. (1971). *The farther reaches of human nature.* New York, NY: Penguin.

McBride, R., Jr. (1999). *Using art and art controversy to teach history.* Retrieved from http://www.pbs.org/wgbh/cultureshock/teachers/article1.html

McElfresh, R. (2008). *Imaginations of democracy: The lived experiences of teacher artists engaged in social change* (Unpublished doctoral dissertation). Kent State University, Kent, OH.

MacIntyre, A. (2007). *After virtue: A study in moral theory.* South Bend, IN: Notre Dame University Press.

Meadows, K. (1997). *The medicine way: How to live the teachings of the Native American medicine wheel.* Rockport, MA: Element Books.

Meltzer, D. E., & Thornton, R. K. (2012). Active-learning instruction in physics. *American Journal of Physics, 80,* 478–492.

Melville, H. (1962). *Billy Budd.* Chicago, IL: University of Chicago Press. (Original work published 1924)

Merton, T. (1961). *New seeds of contemplation.* New York, NY: Directions.

Meyer, S. (2005). *Twilight.* New York, NY: Little, Brown.

Miller, B., Vehar, J., & Firestien, R. (2001). *Creativity unbound: An introduction to creative process.* Evanston, IL: Thinc Communications.

Miller, H. (1964). *Henry Miller on writing.* New York, NY: New Directions Paperbook.

Montgomery, D. (2012). Facing dogmatic influences with consciousness work. In D. Ambrose, R. J. Sternberg, & B. Sriraman (Eds.), *Confronting dogmatism in gifted education* (pp. 141–152). New York, NY: Routledge.

Montgomery, D., Otto, S., & Hull, D. (2007). *Summative research report for Project CREATES: Learning through the arts.* Stillwater, OK: New Forums Press.

Montgomery, D., Strunk, K., Steele, M., & Bridges, S. (2012). Jungian typology as holistic teaching strategy in higher education. *Encounter: Education for Meaning and Social Justice, 25*(4), 63–72.

Moore, T. (1996). *The education of the heart.* New York, NY: Harper Collins.

Moyers, B. (1982). The adventures of a radical hillbilly. Interview with Myles Horton. *Appalachian Journal, 9*(4). Retrieved from http://www.jstor.org/discover/10.230 7/40932454?uid=3739864&uid=2129&uid=2&uid=70&uid=4&uid=373925 6&sid=21101821864103

Murdock, M. (1987). *Spinning inward.* Boston, MA: Shambhala.

National Board for Professional Teaching Standards. (2002). School counseling standards. Arlington, VA: Author. Retrieved from http://www.nbpts.org/sites/ default/files/documents/certificates/nbpts-certificate-ecya-sc-standards.pdf

National Governors Association for Best Practices, & Council of Chief State School Officers. (2010). *Common core state standards for English language arts.* Washington, DC: Author.

Neruda, P. (1971). *Selected poems*. New York, NY: Houghton Mifflin.

Noddings, N. (2007). *Critical lessons: What our schools should teach*. New York, NY: Cambridge University Press.

Oates, J. C. (1999). Where are you going, where have you been? In J. Updike & K. Kenison (Eds.), *The best American short stories of the century* (pp. 450–465). Boston, MA: Houghton Mifflin. (Original work published 1967)

O'Brien, T. (1978). *Going after Cacciato*. New York, NY: Delacorte Press.

O'Brien, T. (1990a). Church. In T. O'Brien, *The things they carried* (pp. 131–136). Boston, MA: Houghton Mifflin.

O'Brien, T. (1990b). Sweetheart of the Song Tra Bong. In T. O'Brien, *The things they carried* (pp. 99–126). Boston, MA: Houghton Mifflin.

O'Brien, T. (1990c). *The things they carried*. Boston, MA: Houghton Mifflin.

Ohio Department of Education. (2004). *Project START ID: Statewide arts talent identification and development project*. Columbus: Author.

Oreck, B. (2004). Assessment of potential theatre arts talent in young people: The development of a new research-based assessment process. *Youth Theater Journal, 18,* 146–163.

Oreck, B. (2005). A powerful conversation: Teachers and artists collaborate in performance-based assessment. *Teaching Artist Journal, 3,* 220–227.

Oreck, B. A., Baum, S. M., & McCartney, H. (2001). *Artistic talent development for urban youth: The promise and the challenge*. Storrs: University of Connecticut, The National Research Center on the Gifted and Talented.

Oreck, B., & Nicoll, J. (2010). Dance dialogues: Creating and teaching in the zone of proximal development. In M. C. Connery, V. P. John-Steiner, & A. Marjanovic-Shane (Eds.), *Vygotsky and creativity: A cultural-historical approach to play, meaning making, and the arts* (pp. 107–124). New York, NY: Peter Lang.

Oreck, B., Owen, S., & Baum, S. (2003). Validity, reliability and equity issues in an observational talent assessment process in the performing arts. *Journal for the Education of the Gifted, 27,* 62–94

Overbye, D. (2003, Sept. 16). Music of the heavens turns out to sound a lot like a B flat. *The New York Times*. Retrieved from http://www.nytimes.com/2003/09/16/science/music-of-the-heavens-turns-out-to-sound-a-lot-like-a-b-flat.html

Palmer, P. (1998). *The courage to teach: Exploring the inner landscape of the teacher's life*. New York, NY: Jossey-Bass.

Parnes, S. J. (Ed.). (1992). *Source book for creative problem solving: A fifty year digest of proven innovation processes*. Buffalo, NY: Creative Education Foundation Press.

Paul, A. M. (2012). *Why daydreaming isn't a waste of time*. Retrieved from http://blogs.kqed.org/mindshift/2012/06/why-daydreaming-isnt-a-waste-of-time

Peppercorn, D. (2011). *Creative adventures in social studies: Engaging activities & essential questions to inspire students*. Lanham, MD: Rowman & Littlefield.

Perry, W. G. (1970). *Forms of intellectual and ethical development in the college years: A scheme.* New York, NY: Holt, Rinehart & Winston.

Piaget, J. (1971). *Psychology and epistemology: Towards a theory of knowledge* (A. Rosin, Trans.). New York, NY: The Viking Press.

Piirto, J. (1992). *Understanding those who create.* Scottsdale, AZ: Great Potential Press.

Piirto, J. (1998). *Understanding those who create* (2nd ed.). Scottsdale, AZ: Great Potential Press.

Piirto, J. (2002). *"My teeming brain": Understanding creative writers.* Cresskill, NJ: Hampton Press.

Piirto, J. (2004). *Understanding creativity.* Scottsdale, AZ: Great Potential Press.

Piirto, J. (2005a). The creative process in poets. In J. C. Kaufman & J. Baer (Eds.), *Creativity in domains: Faces of the muse* (pp. 1–21). Mahwah, NJ: Lawrence Erlbaum.

Piirto, J. (2005b). Rethinking the creativity curriculum. *Gifted Education Communicator, 36*(2), 12–19.

Piirto, J. (2007a). *Talented children and adults: Their development and education* (3rd ed.). Waco, TX: Prufrock Press.

Piirto, J. (2007b). Creativity. In J. L. Kincheloe & R. A. Horn (Eds.), *The Praeger handbook of education and psychology* (pp. 310–320). Santa Barbara, CA: Greenwood Press.

Piirto, J. (2009a). The creative process as creators practice it: A view of creativity with emphasis on what creators really do. In B. Cramond (Ed.), *Perspectives in gifted education: Creativity* (pp. 42–67). Denver, CO: University of Denver, Institute for the Development of Gifted Education.

Piirto, J. (2009b). "All children" includes the talented: A poetic inquiry. Special issue of *Educational Insights, 13*(3). Retrieved from http://www.ccfi.educ.ubc.ca/publication/insights/v13n03/articles/piirto/index.html

Piirto, J. (2010). The five Core Attitudes and Seven I's for enhancing creativity in the classroom. In J. Kaufman and R. Beghetto (Eds.), *Nurturing creativity in the classroom* (pp. 142–171). New York, NY: Cambridge University Press.

Piirto, J. (2011). *Creativity for 21st century skills: How to embed creativity into the curriculum.* Rotterdam, The Netherlands: Sense Publishers.

Pinar, W. F., Reynolds, W. M., Slattery, P., & Taubman, P. M. (1995). *Understanding curriculum: An introduction to the study of historical and contemporary curriculum discourses.* New York, NY: Peter Lang.

Pinkola-Estes, C. (1995). *Women who run with the wolves: Myths and stories about the wild woman archetype.* New York, NY: Random House.

Polanyi, M. (1962/1969). The unaccountable element in science. In M. Greene (Ed.), *Knowing and being: Essays by Michael Polanyi* (pp. 105–120). Chicago, IL: University of Chicago Press.

Popper, K. R. (1989). *Conjectures and refutations: The growth of scientific knowledge* (5th ed.). London, England: Routledge.

Puccio, G. J., Murdock, M., & Mance, M. (2006). *Creative leadership: Skills that drive change.* Thousand Oaks, CA: Sage.

Renzulli, J. S. (1978). What makes giftedness? Reexamining a definition. *Phi Delta Kappan, 60,* 180–184, 261.

Reynolds, F. C. (2001). *Intercede: the urrealist manifesto.* Retrieved from http://www.urrealist.com

Reynolds, F. C., & Piirto, J. (2005). Depth psychology and giftedness: Bringing soul to the field of talent development education. *Roeper Review, 17,* 164–171.

Reynolds, F. C., & Piirto, J. (2007). Honoring and suffering the Thorn: Marking, naming, initiating, and eldering: Depth psychology, II. *Roeper Review, 29,* 48–53.

Reynolds, F. C., & Piirto, J. (2009). Depth psychology and integrity. In T. Cross & D. Ambrose (Eds.). *Morality, ethics, and gifted minds* (pp. 195–206). New York, NY: Springer Science.

Rilke, R. M. (1984). *Letters to a young poet* (S. Mitchell, trans.). New York, NY: Vintage.

Rose, R., & Sherman, S. (1955). *Twelve angry men: A play in three acts.* Chicago, IL: Dramatic.

Ruumet, H. (1997). Pathways of the soul: A Helical model of psychospiritual development. *Present: The Journal of Spiritual Directors International, 3*(3), 6–24.

Sahlberg, P. (2011). *Finnish lessons.* New York, NY: Teachers College Press.

Sarason, S. (1999). *Teaching as a performing art.* New York, NY: Teachers College Press.

Sawyer, R. K., John-Steiner, V., Moran, S., Sternberg, R., Feldman, D. H., Csikszentmihalyi, M., & Nakamura, J. (2003). *Creativity and development.* New York, NY: Oxford University Press.

Schaefer-Simmern, H. (1948). *The unfolding of artistic activity.* Berkeley: University of California Press.

Schlitz, M. M., Vieten, C., & Amorok, T. (2007). *Living deeply: The art and science of transformation in everyday life.* Oakland, CA: New Harbinger and Noetic Books.

Shahn, B. (1957). *The shape of content.* Cambridge, MA: Harvard University Press.

Simonton, D. K. (1999). *Origins of genius: Darwinian perspectives on creativity.* New York, NY: Oxford University Press.

Sio, U. N., & Ormerod, T. C. (2009). Does incubation enhance problem solving? A meta-analytic review. *Psychological Bulletin, 135,* 94–120.

Snowber, C. (2005). The eros of teaching. In J. Miller, S. Karsten, D. Denton, D. Orr, & I. C. Kates (Eds.), *Holistic learning: Breaking new ground* (pp. 215–222). Albany, NY: SUNY Press.

Snowber, C. (2011). Let the body out: A love letter to the academy from the body. In E. Malewski & N. Jaramillo (Eds.), *Epistemologies of ignorance in education* (pp. 185–196). Charlotte, NC: Information Age Publishing.

Snowber, C. (2012). Dancing as a way of knowing. In R. Lawrence (Ed.), *Bodies of knowledge: Embodied learning in adult education* (pp. 53–60). San Francisco, CA: Jossey Bass.

Somé, M. (1998). *The healing wisdom of Africa.* New York, NY: Tarcher/Putnam.

Starko, A. (1995). *Creativity in the classroom: Schools of curious delight.* White Plains, NY: Longman.

States raid Puerto Rico for teachers. (1999). *Curriculum Review, 38*(6), 3.

Stenhouse, L. (1985). *Research as a basis for teaching.* London, England: Heinemann.

Stephenson, S. D. (1998). Song of the Earth. On *So Much More to Tell You* [CD]. Frostburg, MD: Harmony Grove Studios.

Stephenson, S. D. (2001). *Portraits of the songwriting process in elementary classrooms* (Unpublished doctoral dissertation). Morgantown, West Virginia University.

Sternberg, R. J. (1985). *Beyond IQ: A triarchic theory of human intelligence.* New York, NY: Cambridge University Press.

Sternberg, R. J. (2003). *Wisdom, intelligence, and creativity synthesized.* New York, NY: Cambridge University Press.

Sternberg, R., & Lubart, T. (1995). *Defying the crowd: Cultivating creativity in a culture of conformity.* New York, NY: Free Press.

Stevens, E. P. (1973). Machismo and marianismo. *Society, 10,* 57–62.

Stevens, W. (1951). The house was quiet and the world was calm. In W. Stevens, *The auroras of autumn* (p. 35). New York, NY: Alfred Knopf.

Stockton, F. R. (1882). The lady or the tiger? *The Century, 25*(1), 83–86.

Tan, S. (2007). *The arrival.* New York, NY: Scholastic.

Tarnas, R. (2006). *Cosmos and psyche: Intimations of a new world view.* New York, NY: Viking Press.

Tolan, S. S. (1978). *Grandpa and me.* New York, NY: Scribners.

Tolan, S. S. (1980). *The last of Eden.* New York, NY: F. Warne.

Tolan, S. S. (1981a). *The liberation of Tansy Warner.* New York, NY: Scribners.

Tolan, S. S. (1981b). *No safe harbors.* New York, NY: Scribners.

Tolan, S. S. (1983a). *The great Skinner strike.* New York, NY: Atheneum Books.

Tolan, S. S. (1983b). *A time to fly free.* New York, NY: Atheneum Books.

Tolan, S. S. (1986). *Pride of the peacock.* New York, NY: Atheneum Books.

Tolan, S. S. (1987a). *The great Skinner getaway.* New York, NY: Atheneum Books.

Tolan, S. S. (1987b). *The great Skinner homestead.* New York, NY: Atheneum Books.

Tolan, S. S. (1988). *A good courage.* New York, NY: Scholastic.

Tolan, S. S. (1990). *Plague year.* New York, NY: William Morrow.

Tolan, S. S. (1992a). *The witch of Maple Park.* New York, NY: William Morrow.

Tolan, S. S. (1992b). *Sophie and the sidewalk man.* New York, NY: William Morrow.

Tolan, S. S. (1992c). *Marcy Hooper and the greatest treasure in the world.* New York, NY: William Morrow.

Tolan, S. S. (1993). *Save Halloween.* New York, NY: William Morrow.

Tolan, S. S. (1994). *Who's there?* New York, NY: HarperCollins.

Tolan, S. S. (1996a). *Welcome to the Ark.* New York, NY: William Morrow.

Tolan, S. S. (1996b). *The great Skinner enterprise.* New York, NY: HarperCollins.

Tolan, S. S. (1998). *The face in the mirror.* New York, NY: HarperCollins.

Tolan, S. S. (1999). *Ordinary miracles.* New York, NY: HarperTeen.

Tolan, S. S. (2001). *Flight of the raven.* New York, NY: HarperTeen.

Tolan, S. S. (2002). *Surviving the Applewhites.* New York, NY: HarperCollins.

Tolan, S. S. (2004). *Bartholomew's blessing.* New York, NY: HarperCollins.

Tolan, S. S. (2006a). *Listen!* New York, NY: HarperCollins.

Tolan, S. S. (2006b). Imagination to intuition: The journey of a rationalist into realms of magic and spirit. *Advanced Development, 10,* 45–57.

Tolan, S. S. (2009). *Wishworks, Inc.* New York, NY: Arthur A. Levine.

Tolan, S. S. (2012). *Applewhites at wit's end.* New York, NY: HarperCollins.

Torrance, E. P. (1967). *Understanding the fourth-grade creativity slump: Final report.* Minneapolis: University of Minnesota.

Torrance, E. P. (1995). *Why fly? A philosophy of creativity.* Norwood, NJ: Ablex.

U.S. Department of Education, Office of Educational Research. (1993). *National excellence: A case for developing America's talent.* Washington, DC: U.S. Government Printing Office.

Vygotsky, L. S. (1971). *The psychology of art.* Cambridge, MA: MIT Press.

Wallas, G. (1926). *The art of thought.* New York, NY: Harcourt.

Warner, B. (1991). *Orff-Schulwerk: Applications for the classroom.* Upper Saddle River, NJ: Prentice-Hall.

White, E. B. (1952). *Charlotte's web.* New York, NY: Harper & Row.

Wilhelm, R. (1950). *The I-Ching or book of changes.* (C. F. Baynes, Trans.). New York, NY: Bollingen.

Winterson, J. (1995). *Art objects: Essays on ecstasy and effrontery.* London, England: Jonathan Cape.

Wordsworth, W. (1798). *Lines written a few miles above Tintern Abby.* Retrieved from http://www.bartleby.com/145/ww138.html

Yeganeh, H. (2011). *The McDonaldization of society* (Review of *The McDonaldization of Society* by George Ritzer, 2007). Retrieved from http://www.anglohigher.com/key_announce/key_announce_detail/11

ABOUT THE EDITOR

Jane Piirto, Ph.D., is Trustees' Distinguished Professor at Ashland University in Ohio and the author of 16 books, both literary and scholarly. An award-winning poet and novelist, she is also an award-winning scholar who is the recipient of fellowships from the Ohio Arts Council, a Lifetime Achievement Award from the Mensa Education and Research Association, an honorary doctorate in humane letters, and the Distinguished Scholar Award from the National Association for Gifted Children.

INDEX